BEST Solution
Guaranteed •••

NCERT EXEMPLAR

Problems - Solutions

Chemistry 11th

Author
Pankaj Mittal

ARIHANT PRAKASHAN (Series), MEERUT

卐 Administrative & Production Offices

Regd. Office

'Ramchhaya' 4577/15, Agarwal Road, Darya Ganj, New Delhi -110002
Tele: 011- 47630600, 43518550

卐 Head Office

Kalindi, TP Nagar, Meerut (UP) - 250002
Tel: 0121-7156203, 7156204

卐 Sales & Support Offices

Agra, Ahmedabad, Bengaluru, Bareilly, Chennai, Delhi, Guwahati, Hyderabad, Jaipur, Jhansi, Kolkata, Lucknow, Nagpur & Pune.

卐 **PRICE** ₹275.00

卐 **PO No.** : TXT-59-T071671-6-26

Published by Arihant Publications (India) Ltd.

For further information about the books published by Arihant, log on to www.arihantbooks.com or e-mail at info@arihantbooks.com

Follow us on   

PREFACE

NCERT Exemplar Problems, published by the NCERT, are designed to provide students with a diverse range of quality questions in formats such as Multiple Choice Questions, Multiple Choice Questions (More Than One Options), Short Answer Type Questions, Matching The Coloumns, Assertion and Reason and Long Answer Type Questions, catering to varying levels of difficulty.

These problems are essential for success in school and board exams, as well as competitive exams like engineering and medical entrances. Regular practice with these problems prepares students to tackle challenging questions effectively.

This book, **NCERT Exemplar Problems-Solutions Chemistry 11th**, offers precise and detailed solutions to all the questions in the NCERT Exemplar Chemistry textbook. Each solution is complemented by explanatory notes and authentic explanations, enabling students to deepen their conceptual understanding and enhance their analytical skills.

Key features

- **Thinking Process** Provides simple steps to approach and solve the question, clearing up any confusion.
- **Concept Insight** Explains the main ideas and concepts needed to answer the questions correctly.
- **Mistake Alert!** Points out common mistakes students might make and helps them avoid these errors.
- **Notes** Highlights important points and useful tips to make learning easier.

I hope this book proves to be a valuable resource, aiding students in their academic journey and leading them to great success.

Author

CONTENTS

***Note(*)** These Chapters have been deleted from latest NCERT.*

Chapter 01

Some Basic Concepts of Chemistry

Multiple Choice Questions (MCQs)

Q.1 Two students performed the same experiment separately and each one of them recorded two readings of mass which are given below. Correct reading of mass is 3.0 g. On the basis of given data, mark the correct option out of the following statements

Students	Readings	
	(i)	(ii)
A	3.01	2.99
B	3.05	2.95

(a) Results of both the students are neither accurate nor precise.
(b) Results of student *A* are both precise and accurate.
(c) Results of student *B* are neither precise nor accurate.
(d) Results of student *B* are both **precise** and accurate.

Thinking Process Look at the reading of students *A* and *B* given in the question while keeping in mind the concept of precision and accuracy *i.e.*,

(i) Closeness of reading is **precision,** and

(ii) If mean of reading is exactly same as the correct value then it is known as **accuracy.**

Ans. ***(b)*** Average readings of student, $A = \frac{3.01 + 2.99}{2} = 3.00$

Average readings of student, $B = \frac{3.05 + 2.95}{2} = 3.00$

Correct reading = 3.00

For both the students, average value is close to the correct value. Hence, readings of both are accurate.

Actual readings of student '*A*' are more precise because both readings are close to correct reading (3.00) and has difference of 0.02 only. While readings of student '*B*' has difference of 0.1 to each other, hence less precise.

Q.2 A measured temperature on Fahrenheit scale is 200°F. What will this reading be on celsius scale?

(a) 40 °C (b) 94 °C (c) 93.3 °C (d) 30 °C

- **Concept Insight** The three common scales to measure temperature are °C (degree celsius), °F (degree fahrenheit) and K (kelvin). The K is the SI unit.

Ans. ***(c)*** The temperatures on two scales are related to each other by the following relationship.

$$°F = \frac{9}{5} t°C + 32$$

Putting the values in above equation

$$200 - 32 = \frac{9}{5} t°C$$

$$\Rightarrow \quad \frac{9}{5} t°C = 168$$

$$\Rightarrow \quad t°C = \frac{168 \times 5}{9} = 93.3° C$$

Q.3 What will be the molarity of a solution, which contains 5.85 g of NaCl(*s*) per 500 mL?

(a) 4 mol L^{-1} (b) 20 mol L^{-1} (c) 0.2 mol L^{-1} (d) 2 mol L^{-1}

Ans. ***(c)*** Molecular weight (NaCl) = 23 + 35.5 = 58.5 g/mol

$$\text{Molarity} = \frac{\text{weight} \times 1000}{\text{molecular weight} \times \text{volume (mL)}}$$

$$= \frac{5.85 \times 1000}{58.5 \times 500} = 0.2 \text{ mol L}^{-1}$$

Mistake Alert ! *Students may get confused in using formula of molarity or molality.*

Q.4 If 500 mL of a 5M solution is diluted to 1500 mL, what will be the molarity of the solution obtained?

(a) 1.5 M (b) 1.66 M (c) 0.017 M (d) 1.59 M

Thinking Process If solution is diluted, Molarity of resultant solution (M_2) can be calculated by

$$\underset{\text{Before dilution}}{M_1 V_1} = \underset{\text{After dilution}}{M_2 V_2}$$

Ans. ***(b)*** Given that, $M_1 = 5$ M

$V_1 = 500$ mL

$V_2 = 1500$ mL

$M_2 = M$

For dilution, a general formula is

$$\underset{\text{(Before dilution)}}{M_1 V_1} = \underset{\text{(After dilution)}}{M_2 V_2}$$

$$5 \times 500 = M_2 \times 1500$$

$$M_2 = \frac{5}{3} = 1.66\text{M}$$

Q.5 The number of atoms present in one mole of an element is equal to Avogadro number. Which of the following element contains the greatest number of atoms?

(a) 4g He (b) 46g Na (c) 0.40g Ca (d) 12g He

Thinking Process Mass of a substance is converted into moles and then moles of substance is changed to number of atoms as

$$\text{Number of atoms} = \text{Number of moles} \times N_A$$

More the number of moles, more will be number of particles.

Ans. ***(d)*** Moles of 4 g He $= \frac{4}{4} = 1\,\text{mol}$

$$46\text{ g Na} = \frac{46}{23} = 2\,\text{mol}$$

$$0.40\text{ g Ca} = \frac{0.40}{40} = 0.1\,\text{mol}$$

$$12\text{ g He} = \frac{12}{4} = 3\,\text{mol}$$

Hence, 12 g He contains greatest number of atoms as it possesses maximum number of moles.

Q.6 If the concentration of glucose ($C_6H_{12}O_6$) in blood is 0.9 g L^{-1}, what will be the molarity of glucose in blood?

(a) 5 M (b) 50 M (c) 0.005 M (d) 0.5 M

Ans. ***(c)*** 0.9 g L^{-1} means 0.9 g glucose in 1 L solution.

Molecular weight (glucose) $=(12\times6)+12+(16\times6)=180$ g/mol

$$\text{Molarity} = \frac{\text{Weight}}{\text{Molecular weight} \times \text{volume (L)}}$$

$$= \frac{0.9}{180\times1} = 0.005\,\text{mol/L}$$

$$= 0.005\,\text{M}$$

Q.7 What will be the molality of the solution containing 18.25 g of HCl gas in 500 g of water?

(a) 0.1 m (b) 1 M
(c) 0.5 m (d) 1 m

Ans. ***(d)*** Molality is defined as the number of moles of solute present in 1 kg of solvent. It is denoted by *m*.

Thus, $$\text{Molality } (m) = \frac{\text{Moles of solute}}{\text{Mass of solvent (in kg)}} = \frac{w_B \times 1000}{M_B \times w_A} \quad \ldots\text{(i)}$$

Given that, Mass of solvent (H_2O), $w_A = 500$ g

Weight of HCl, $w_B = 18.25$ g

Molecular weight of HCl, $M_B = 1\times1 + 1\times35.5 = 36.5$g

$$\text{Molality } (m) = \frac{18.25\times1000}{36.5\times500} = 1\,\text{m} \quad \text{[from Eq. (i)]}$$

Mistake Alert! *Students may confuse the mass of the solvent with the mass of solution.*

Q.8 One mole of any substance contains 6.022×10^{23} atoms/molecules. Number of molecules of H_2SO_4 present in 100 mL of 0.02M H_2SO_4 solution is ....

(a) 12.044×10^{20} molecules
(b) 6.022×10^{23} molecules
(c) 1×10^{23} molecules
(d) 12.044×10^{23} molecules

Ans. ***(a)*** One mole of any substance contains 6.022×10^{23} atoms/molecules.

$$\text{Molarity} = \frac{\text{Number of moles}}{\text{Volume (in L)}}$$

$$\therefore \quad \text{Number of moles} = \text{Molarity} \times \text{Volume (in L)}$$
$$= 0.02 \times 0.1$$
$$= 2 \times 10^{-3} \text{ mol}$$

$$\text{Number of molecules} = \text{number of moles} \times N_A$$
$$= 2 \times 10^{-3} \times 6.022 \times 10^{23}$$
$$= 12.044 \times 10^{20} \text{ molecules}$$

Q.9 What is the mass percent of carbon in carbon dioxide?

(a) 0.034%
(b) 27.27%
(c) 3.4%
(d) 28.7%

Ans. ***(b)*** Molecular mass of $CO_2 = 1 \times 12 + 2 \times 16 = 44\text{g}$

$\because$ 44 g of CO_2 contain C = 12 g atoms of carbon

$$\therefore \quad 100 \text{ g } CO_2 \text{ contain} = \frac{12}{44} \times 100 = 27.27\%$$

Hence, the mass per cent of carbon in CO_2 is 27.27%.

Q.10 The empirical formula and molecular mass of a compound are CH_2O and 180 g respectively. What will be the molecular formula of the compound?

(a) $C_9H_{18}O_9$
(b) CH_2O
(c) $C_6H_{12}O_6$
(d) $C_2H_4O_2$

● Concept Insight

(i) Find the number of moles by dividing molecular mass with empirical formula mass.

(ii) To calculate the molecular formula of the compound, multiply the number of moles with empirical formula.

Ans. ***(c)*** Empirical formula mass = CH_2O

$$= 12 + 2 \times 1 + 16 = 30$$

$$\text{Molecular mass} = 180$$

$$n = \frac{\text{Molecular mass}}{\text{Empirical formula mass}}$$
$$= \frac{180}{30} = 6$$

$$\therefore \quad \text{Molecular formula} = n \times \text{empirical formula}$$
$$= 6 \times CH_2O$$
$$= C_6H_{12}O_6$$

Q.11 If the density of a solution is 3.12 g mL^{-1}, the mass of 1.5 mL solution in significant figures is ....

(a) 4.7g
(b) 4680×10^{-3}g
(c) 4.680 g
(d) 46.80 g

Ans. **(a)** Given that, density of solution = 3.12 g mL^{-1}

Volume of solution = 1.5 mL

For a solution, Mass = volume × density

$$= 1.5 \text{ mL} \times 3.12 \text{ g mL}^{-1} = 4.68 \text{ g}$$

The digit 1.5 has only two significant figures, so the answer must also be limited to two significant figures. So, it is rounded off to reduce the number of significant figures. Hence, the answer is reported as 4.7g.

Q.12 Which of the following statements about a compound is incorrect?

(a) A molecule of a compound has atoms of different elements.
(b) A compound cannot be separated into its constituent elements by physical methods of separation.
(c) A compound retains the physical properties of its constituent elements.
(d) The ratio of atoms of different elements in a compound is fixed.

Ans. **(c)** A compound is a pure substance containing two or more elements combined together in a fixed proportion by mass.

Further, the properties of a compound are quite different from the properties of constituent elements. *e.g.*, water is a compound containing hydrogen and oxygen combined together in a fixed proportion. But the properties of water are completely different from its constituents, hydrogen and oxygen.

Q.13 Which of the following statements is correct about the reaction given below?

$$4Fe(s) + 3O_2(g) \longrightarrow 2Fe_2O_3(s)$$

(a) Total mass of iron and oxygen in reactants = total mass of iron and oxygen in product therefore it follows law of conservation of mass.
(b) Total mass of reactants = total mass of product, therefore, law of multiple proportions is followed.
(c) Amount of Fe_2O_3 can be increased by taking any one of the reactants (iron or oxygen) in excess.
(d) Amount of Fe_2O_3 produced will decrease if the amount of any one of the reactants (iron or oxygen) is taken in excess.

Thinking Process This problem is based upon the law of conservation of mass as well as limiting reagent.

(i) Law of conservation of mass states that total mass of reactants is equal to total mass of products.

(ii) Limiting reagent represents the reactant which reacts completely in the reaction.

Ans. **(a)** According to the law of conservation of mass,

$$\text{Total mass of reactants} = \text{Total mass of products}$$

$$(4 \times 56) + (3 \times 32) = (4 \times 56) + (6 \times 16)$$

$$224 + 96 = 224 + 96$$

$$320 = 320$$

Q.14 Which of the following reactions is not correct according to the law of conservation of mass?

(a) $2Mg(s) + O_2(g) \longrightarrow 2MgO(s)$
(b) $C_3H_8(g) + O_2(g) \longrightarrow CO_2(g) + H_2O(g)$
(c) $P_4(s) + 5O_2(g) \longrightarrow P_4O_{10}(s)$
(d) $CH_4(g) + 2O_2(g) \longrightarrow CO_2(g) + 2H_2O(g)$

Ans. ***(b)*** In this equation,

$$\underset{44g}{C_3H_8(g)} + \underset{32g}{O_2(g)} \longrightarrow \underset{44\,g}{CO_2(g)} + \underset{18\,g}{H_2O(g)}$$

Mass of reactants (76 g) ≠ mass of products (62 g)

Hence, law of conservation of mass is not followed.

Q.15 Which of the following statements indicates that law of multiple proportion is being followed?

(a) Sample of carbon dioxide taken from any source will always have carbon and oxygen in the ratio 1 : 2.
(b) Carbon forms two oxides namely CO_2 and CO, where masses of oxygen which combine with fixed mass of carbon are in the simple ratio 2 : 1.
(c) When magnesium burns in oxygen, the amount of magnesium taken for the reaction is equal to the amount of magnesium in magnesium oxide formed.
(d) At constant temperature and pressure 200 mL of hydrogen will combine with 100 mL oxygen to produce 200 mL of water vapour.

Thinking Process According to law of multiple proportions, "if two elements can combine to form more than one compound, the masses of one element that combines with a fixed mass of other element are in the ratio of small whole number".

Ans. ***(b)*** The element carbon, combines with oxygen to form two compounds, namely, carbon dioxide and carbon monoxide. In CO_2, 12 parts by mass of carbon combine with 32 parts by mass of oxygen while in CO, 12 parts by mass of carbon combine with 16 parts by mass of oxygen.

Therefore, the masses of oxygen combine with a fixed mass of carbon (12 parts) in CO_2 and CO are 32 and 16 respectively. These masses of oxygen bear a simple ratio of 32 : 16 or 2 : 1 to each other.

This is an example of **law of multiple proportion.**

Multiple Choice Questions (More Than One Options)

Q.16 One mole of oxygen gas at STP is equal to........

(a) 6.022×10^{23} molecules of oxygen
(b) 6.022×10^{23} atoms of oxygen
(c) 16 g of oxygen
(d) 32 g of oxygen

Ans. ***(a, d)*** 1 mole of O_2 gas at STP = 6.022×10^{23} molecules (Avogadro number) of

$$O_2 = 32\,g \text{ of } O_2.$$

Hence, 1 mole of oxygen gas is equal to molecular weight of oxygen as well as Avogadro number.

Q.17 Sulphuric acid reacts with sodium hydroxide as follows

$$H_2SO_4 + 2NaOH \longrightarrow Na_2SO_4 + 2H_2O$$

When 1L of 0.1M sulphuric acid solution is allowed to react with 1L of 0.1M sodium hydroxide solution, the amount of sodium sulphate formed and its molarity in the solution obtained is

(a) 0.1 mol L^{-1} (b) 7.10 g (c) 0.025 mol L^{-1} (d) 3.55 g

Ans. ***(b, c)*** For the reaction, $H_2SO_4 + 2NaOH \longrightarrow Na_2SO_4 + 2H_2O$

1L of 0.1 M H_2SO_4 contains = 0.1 mole of H_2SO_4

1L of 0.1 M NaOH contains = 0.1 mole of NaOH

According to the reaction, 1 mole of H_2SO_4 reacts with 2 moles of NaOH. Hence, 0.1 mole of NaOH will react with 0.05 mole of H_2SO_4 (and 0.05 mole of H_2SO_4 will be left unreacted), *i.e.,* NaOH is the limiting reactant.

Since, 2 moles of NaOH produce 1 mole of Na_2SO_4. Hence, 0.1 mole of NaOH will produce 0.05 mole of Na_2SO_4.

$$\text{Mass of } Na_2SO_4 = \text{moles} \times \text{molar mass}$$
$$= 0.05 \times (46 + 32 + 64)\text{ g} = 7.10\text{ g}$$

Volume of solution after mixing = 2 L

Since, only 0.05 mole of H_2SO_4 is left behind and NaOH is completely used in the reaction. Therefore, molarity of the given solution is calculated from moles of H_2SO_4.

H_2SO_4 left unreacted in the solution = 0.05 mole

$$\therefore \quad \text{Molarity of the solution} = \frac{0.05}{2} = 0.025 \text{ mol L}^{-1}$$

Alternate Method

$$\text{Molarity} = \frac{w_B}{M_B \times V_2}$$

Mass of H_2SO_4 in 1 L of 0.1 M solution = $0.1 \times 98 \times 1 = 9.8$ g

Mass of NaOH in given solution = $0.1 \times 40 \times 1 = 4$ g

$$\underset{98\text{ g}}{H_2SO_4} + \underset{(2\times 40)\text{ g}}{2NaOH} \longrightarrow Na_2SO_4 + 2H_2O$$

98 g H_2SO_4 react completely with = (2×40) g NaOH

9.8 g H_2SO_4 react completely with = 8.0 g

Given mass of NaOH = 4 g

∴ **NaOH is limiting reagent.**

Now 80g NaOH produce = 142 g Na_2SO_4

So, 4g NaOH produce = $\frac{4 \times 142}{80} = 7.1$ g Na_2SO_4

∴ Option (b) is correct.

$$\text{Molarity of } Na_2SO_4 = \frac{7.1\text{ g}}{142\text{ g mol}^{-1} \times 2\text{L}} = 0.025 \text{ mol L}^{-1}$$

∴ option (c) is also correct.

Q.18 Which of the following pairs have the same number of atoms?

(a) 16 g of $O_2(g)$ and 4 g of $H_2(g)$ (b) 16 g of O_2 and 44 g of CO_2
(c) 28 g of N_2 and 32 g of O_2 (d) 12 g of C(s) and 23 g of Na(s)

Thinking Process The concept in this question can be explained by using the formula :

$$\text{Number of atoms} = \frac{\text{mass}}{\text{molar mass}} \times \text{Avogadro number } (N_A) \times \text{atomicity.}$$

Ans. *(c, d)* Number of atoms in 28 g of $N_2 = \frac{28}{28} \times N_A \times 2 = 2\,N_A$

(where, N_A = Avogadro number)

Number of atoms in 32 g of $O_2 = \frac{32}{32} \times N_A \times 2 = 2N_A$

Therefore option (c) is correct.

12 g of C(s) contains atoms $= \frac{12}{12} \times N_A \times 1 = N_A$

Number of atoms in 23 g of Na(s) $= \frac{23}{23} \times N_A \times 1 = N_A$

∴ Option (d) is also correct.

Q.19 Which of the following solutions have the same concentration?

(a) 20 g of NaOH in 200 mL of solution. (b) 0.5 mol of KCl in 200 mL of solution.
(c) 40 g of NaOH in 100 mL of solution. (d) 20 g of KOH in 200 mL of solution.

Ans. *(a, b)*

$$\text{Molarity } (M) = \frac{\text{weight of NaOH} \times 1000}{\text{Molecular weight of NaOH} \times V(\text{mL})}$$

(a) $M = \frac{20 \times 1000}{40 \times 200} = 2.5\,\text{M}$ (b) $M = \frac{0.5 \times 1000}{200} = 2.5\,\text{M}$

(c) $M = \frac{40 \times 1000}{40 \times 100} = 10\,\text{M}$ (d) $M = \frac{20 \times 1000}{56 \times 200} = 1.785\,\text{M}$

Thus, 20 g NaOH in 200 mL of solution and 0.5 mol of KCl in 200 mL have the same concentration.

Q.20 16 g of oxygen has same number of molecules as in

(a) 16 g of CO (b) 28 g of N_2 (c) 14 g of N_2 (d) 1.0 g of H_2

Ans. *(c, d)* The number of molecules can be calculated as follows

$$\text{Number of molecules} = \frac{\text{Mass}}{\text{Molar mass}} \times \text{Avogadro number } (N_A)$$

Number of molecules, in 16 g of oxygen $= \frac{16}{32} \times N_A = \frac{N_A}{2}$

In 16 g of CO $= \frac{16}{28} \times N_A = \frac{N_A}{1.75}$

In 28 g of $N_2 = \frac{28}{28} \times N_A = N_A$

In 14 g of $N_2 = \frac{14}{28} \times N_A = \frac{N_A}{2}$

In 1 g of $H_2 = \frac{1}{2} \times N_A = \frac{N_A}{2}$

So, 16 g of O_2 = 14 g of N_2 = 1.0 g of H_2

Q.21 Which of the following terms are unitless?

(a) Molality (b) Molarity (c) Mole fraction (d) Mass percent

Ans. ***(c, d)*** Both mole fraction and mass percent are unitless as both are ratios of moles and mass respectively.

$$\text{Mole fraction} = \frac{\text{Number of moles of solute}}{\text{Number of moles of solution}} = \frac{\text{moles}}{\text{moles}}$$

$$= \frac{\text{Number of moles of solvent}}{\text{Number of moles of solution}} = \frac{\text{moles}}{\text{moles}}$$

$$\text{Mass per cent} = \frac{\text{Mass of solute in gram}}{\text{Mass of solution in gram}} \times 100$$

Q.22 One of the statements of Dalton's atomic theory is given below. "Compounds are formed when atoms of different elements combine in a fixed ratio"

Which of the following laws is not related to this statement?

(a) Law of conservation of mass (b) Law of definite proportions
(c) Law of multiple proportions (d) Avogadro law

Ans. ***(a, d)*** Law of conservation of mass confirms that there is no loss or gain of mass during a reaction. Avogadro law states that equal volumes of different gases contain the same number of molecules under similar conditions of temperature and pressure.

Short Answer Type Questions

Q.23 What will be the mass of one atom of C-12 in grams?

Ans. 1 mole of C-12 atoms = 12 g = 6.022×10^{23} atoms

$\Rightarrow 6.022 \times 10^{23}$ atoms of C-12 have mass = 12 g

$\therefore$ 1 atom of C-12 will have mass $= \dfrac{12}{6.022 \times 10^{23}}\ \text{g} = 1.992693 \times 10^{-23}\ \text{g} \approx 1.99 \times 10^{-23}\ \text{g}$

$\therefore$ The mass of a carbon-12 atom is 1.992693×10^{-23} g.

Q.24 How many significant figures should be present in the answer of the following calculations?

$$\frac{2.5 \times 1.25 \times 3.5}{2.01}$$

Thinking Process

(i) To answer the given question, least precise term decides the significant figures.

(ii) To round up a number, leave the last digit as such, if the digit next to it is less than 5 and increase it by 1, if the next digit is greater than 5.

Ans. Least precise term 2.5 or 3.5 has two significant figures.

Hence, the answer should have two significant figures

$$\frac{2.5 \times 1.25 \times 3.5}{2.01} \approx 5.4415 = 5.4$$

Mistake Alert ! *Student may incorrectly round off the answer which can lead to error in the final result.*

Q.25 What is the symbol for SI unit of mole? How is the mole defined?

Ans. Symbol for SI unit of mole is mol.

One mole is defined as the amount of a substance that contains as many particles or entities as there are atoms in exactly 12 g (0.012 kg) of the ^{12}C- isotope.

Q.26 What is the difference between molality and molarity?

Ans. Molality It is defined as the number of moles of solute dissolved in 1 kg of solvent. It is independent of temperature.

Molarity It is defined as the number of moles of solute dissolved in 1L of solution. It depends upon temperature (because, volume of solution $\propto$ temperature).

Q.27 Calculate the mass percent of calcium, phosphorus and oxygen in calcium phosphate $Ca_3(PO_4)_2$.

Thinking Process Calculate the mass percent of atom, using the formula

Mass percent of an element

$$= \frac{\text{Atomic mass of the element present in the compound}}{\text{Molar mass of the compound}} \times 100$$

Ans. Mass percent of calcium $= \dfrac{3 \times (\text{atomic mass of calcium})}{\text{molecular mass of } Ca_3(PO_4)_2} \times 100$

$$= \frac{3 \times 40 \text{ u}}{310 \text{ u}} \times 100 = 38.71\%$$

Mass percent of phosphorus $= \dfrac{2 \times (\text{atomic mass of phosphorus})}{\text{molecular mass of } Ca_3(PO_4)_2} \times 100$

$$= \frac{2 \times 31 \text{ u}}{310 \text{ u}} \times 100 = 20\%$$

Mass percent of oxygen $= \dfrac{8 \times (\text{atomic mass of oxygen})}{\text{molecular mass of } Ca_3(PO_4)_2} \times 100$

$$= \frac{8 \times 16 \text{ u}}{310 \text{ u}} \times 100 = 41.29\%$$

Q.28 45.4 L of dinitrogen reacted with 22.7 L of dioxygen and 45.4 L of nitrous oxide was formed. The reaction is given below :

$$2N_2(g) + O_2(g) \longrightarrow 2N_2O(g)$$

Which law is being obeyed in this experiment? Write the statement of the law?

Ans. For the reaction,

$$\underset{2\text{ V}}{2N_2(g)} + \underset{1\text{ V}}{O_2(g)} \longrightarrow \underset{2\text{ V}}{2N_2O(g)}$$

$$\frac{45.4}{22.7} = 2 \quad \frac{22.7}{22.7} = 1 \quad \frac{45.4}{22.7} = 2$$

Hence, the ratio between the volumes of the reactants and the product in the given question is simple *i.e.*, 2 : 1 : 2. Thus, Gay-Lussac's law of gaseous volumes is being obeyed. According to this law, "when gases combine or are produced in a chemical reaction, they do so in a simple ratio by volume provided all gases are at same temperature and pressure".

Q.29 If two elements can combine to form more than one compound, the masses of one element that combine with a fixed mass of the other element, are in whole number ratio.

(a) Is this statement true?

(b) If yes, according to which law?

(c) Give one example related to this law.

Ans. (a) Yes, the given statement is true.

(b) This statement is true according to the law of multiple proportions.,

(c) Hydrogen and oxygen react to produce two compounds water and hydrogen peroxide as follows.

$$\underset{2\,g}{H_2} + \underset{16\,g}{\frac{1}{2}O_2} \longrightarrow \underset{18\,g}{H_2O}$$

$$\underset{2\,g}{H_2} + \underset{32\,g}{O_2} \longrightarrow \underset{34\,g}{H_2O_2}$$

Here, masses of oxygen, (*i.e.*, 16 g in H_2O and 32 g in H_2O_2) which combine with fixed mass of hydrogen (2 g) are in the simple ratio *i.e.*, 16 : 32 or 1 : 2.

Q.30 Calculate the average atomic mass of hydrogen using the following data

Isotope	% Natural abundance	Molar mass
^{1}H	99.985	1
^{2}H	0.015	2

- **Concept Insight** Many naturally occurring elements exist as more than one isotope. When we take into account the existence of these isotopes and their relative abundance (percent occurrence), average atomic mass of the element can be calculated.

Ans. Average atomic mass $= \dfrac{[(\text{Natural abundance } ^{1}H \times \text{molar mass of } ^{1}H) + (\text{Natural abundance of } ^{2}H \times \text{molar mass of } ^{2}H)]}{100}$

$$= \frac{(99.985 \times 1) + (0.015 \times 2)}{100} = \frac{99.985 + 0.030}{100} = \frac{100.015}{100}$$

$$= 1.00015\ u$$

Q.31 Hydrogen gas is prepared in the laboratory by reacting dilute HCl with granulated zinc. Following reaction takes place.

$$Zn + 2HCl \longrightarrow ZnCl_2 + H_2$$

Calculate the volume of hydrogen gas liberated at STP when 32.65 g of zinc reacts with HCl. 1 mol of a gas occupies 22.7 L volume at STP; atomic mass of Zn = 65.3u

Ans. For given equation,

$$\underset{65.3\,g}{Zn} + 2HCl \longrightarrow ZnCl_2 + \underset{1\,mol\,=\,22.7\,L\text{ at STP}}{H_2}$$

65.3 g Zn reacts with HCl to produce = 22.7 L of H_2 at STP

$\therefore$ 32.65 g Zn reacts with HCl to produce $= \dfrac{22.7 \times 32.65}{65.3} = 11.35$ L of H_2 at STP.

Q.32 The density of 3 molal solution of NaOH is 1.110 g mL^{-1}. Calculate the molarity of the solution.

Thinking Process Determine the mass of solution from the given molality of the solution followed by volume of solution relating mass and density to each other, *i.e.*,

$$\text{Volume} = \frac{\text{Mass}}{\text{Density}}$$

Then, calculate the molarity of solution as

$$\text{Molarity} = \frac{\text{Number of moles}}{\text{Volume in litres}}$$

Ans. 3 molal solution of NaOH means 3 moles of NaOH are dissolved in 1 kg solvent.

$$\text{Molecular mass} = 23 + 16 + 1 = 40 \text{ g/mol}$$

$$\text{Mass of NaOH} = \text{Moles} \times \text{Molecular mass}$$

$$= 3 \times 40 = 120 \text{ g}$$

$\therefore$ Mass of solution = 1000 g solvent + 120 g NaOH (solute) = 1120 g solution

$$\text{Volume of solution} = \frac{\text{Mass of solution}}{\text{Density of solution}}$$

$$V = \frac{1120 \text{ g}}{1.110 \text{ g mL}^{-1}} = 1009 \text{ mL}$$

$$\text{Molarity} = \frac{\text{Moles of solute} \times 1000}{\text{Volume of solution (mL)}}$$

$$= \frac{3 \times 1000}{1009} = 2.973 \text{ M} \approx 3\text{M}$$

Q.33 Volume of a solution changes with change in temperature, then will the molality of the solution be affected by temperature? Give reason for your answer.

Ans. No, molality of solution does not change with temperature since mass remains unaffected with temperature.

Q.34 If 4 g of NaOH dissolves in 36 g of H_2O, calculate the mole fraction of each component in the solution. Also, determine the molarity of solution (specific gravity of solution is 1 g mL^{-1}).

Thinking Process

(i) To proceed the calculation, first calculate the number of moles of NaOH and H_2O.

(ii) Then, find mole fraction of NaOH and H_2O by using the formula,

$$\chi_{NaOH} = \frac{n_{NaOH}}{n_{NaOH} + n_{H_2O}} \qquad \left(\text{or } \chi_{H_2O} = \frac{n_{H_2O}}{n_{NaOH} + n_{H_2O}}\right)$$

(iii) Then, calculate molarity $= \frac{W \times 1000}{m \times V}$, so in order to calculate molarity, we require volume of solution which is, $V = \frac{m}{\text{specific gravity}}$.

Ans. Number of moles of NaOH,

$$n_{NaOH} = \frac{4}{40} = 0.1 \text{ mol} \quad \left\{\because \text{Number of moles } (n) = \frac{\text{Mass (g)}}{\text{Molar mass (g mol}^{-1})}\right\}$$

Similarly, $n_{H_2O} = \frac{36}{18} = 2$ mol

Mole fraction of NaOH,

$$\chi_{NaOH} = \frac{\text{Number of moles of NaOH}}{\text{Number of moles of NaOH + Number of moles of } H_2O}$$

$$\chi_{NaOH} = \frac{0.1}{0.1 + 2} = 0.0476$$

Similarly, $\chi_{H_2O} = 1 - \chi_{NaOH} = 1 - 0.0476 = 0.9524$

Mass of solution = mass of solute + mass of solvent

= 4 + 36 = 40 g

$$\text{Volume of solution} = \frac{\text{Mass of solution}}{\text{specific gravity}}$$

$$= \frac{40 \text{ g}}{1 \text{ g mL}^{-1}} = 40 \text{ mL}$$

$$\text{Molarity} = \frac{\text{Moles of solute} \times 1000}{\text{Volume of solution (mL)}}$$

$$= \frac{0.1 \times 1000}{40} = 2.5 \text{ M}$$

Q.35 The reactant which is entirely consumed in reaction is known as limiting reagent. In the reaction $2A + 4B \rightarrow 3C + 4D$, when 5 moles of A react with 6 moles of B, then

(a) which is the limiting reagent?

(b) calculate the amount of C formed?

Ans. Given, $2A + 4B \longrightarrow 3C + 4D$

According to the given reaction, 2 moles of A react with 4 moles of B.

Hence, 5 moles of A will react with 10 moles of $B \left(\frac{5 \times 4}{2} = 10 \text{ moles}\right)$

(a) It indicates that reactant B is limiting reagent as it will be consumed first in the reaction because we have only 6 moles of B.

(b) Limiting reagent decide the amount of product produced.

According to the reaction,

4 moles of B produces 3 moles of C.

$\therefore$ 6 moles of B will produce $\frac{3 \times 6}{4} = 4.5$ moles of C.

Mistake Alert ! *Limiting reagent limits the amount of product formed because it is present in lesser amount and gets consumed first.*

Matching The Columns

Q.36 Match the following.

A.	88 g of CO_2	1.	0.25 mol
B.	6.022×10^{23} molecules of H_2O	2.	2 mol
C.	5.6 L of O_2 at STP	3.	1 mol
D.	96 g of O_2	4.	6.022×10^{23} molecules
E.	1 mole of any gas	5.	3 mol

Ans. A. → (2) B. → (3) C. → (1) D. → (5) E. → (4)

A. Number of moles of CO_2 molecule $= \dfrac{\text{Weight in gram of } CO_2}{\text{Molecular weight of } CO_2} = \dfrac{88}{44} = 2\,\text{mol}$

B. 1 mole of a substance $= N_A$ molecules $= 6.022 \times 10^{23}$ molecules

$= $ Avogadro number

$= 6.022 \times 10^{23}$ molecules of $H_2O = 1\,\text{mol}$

C. 22.4 L of O_2 at STP = 1 mol

5.6 L of O_2 at STP $= \dfrac{5.6}{22.4}$ mol = 0.25 mol

D. Number of moles of 96 g of $O_2 = \dfrac{96}{32}$ mol = 3 mol

E. 1 mole of any gas = Avogadro number = 6.022×10^{23} molecules

Q.37 Match the following physical quantities with units.

	Physical quantity		Unit
A.	Molarity	1.	$g\ mL^{-1}$
B.	Mole fraction	2.	mol
C.	Mole	3.	Pascal
D.	Molality	4.	Unitless
E.	Pressure	5.	$mol\ L^{-1}$
F.	Luminous intensity	6.	Candela
G.	Density	7.	$mol\ kg^{-1}$
H.	Mass	8.	Nm^{-1}
		9.	kg

Ans. A. → (5) **B.** → (4) **C.** → (2) **D.** → (7) **E.** → (3) **F.** → (6) **G.** → (1) **H.** → (9)

A. Molarity = concentration in $mol\ L^{-1}$

Molarity $= \dfrac{\text{Number of moles}}{\text{Volume in litres}}$

B. Mole fraction = Unitless

C. Mole $= \dfrac{\text{Mass (g)}}{\text{Molar mass (g mol}^{-1})} = \text{mol}$

D. Molality = concentration in mol per kg of solvent

Molality $= \dfrac{\text{Number of moles}}{\text{Mass of solvent (kg)}}$

E. The SI unit for pressure is the pascal (Pa), equal to one newton per square metre (N/m^2 or kg. m^{-1} s^{-2}). This special name for the unit was added in 1971; before that, pressure in SI was expressed simply as N/m^2.

F. Unit of luminous intensity = candela.

The candela is the luminous intensity, in a given direction, of a source that emits monochromatic radiation of frequency 540×10^{12} hertz and that has a radiant intensity in that direction of 1/ 683 watt per steradian.

G. Density $= \frac{\text{mass}}{\text{volume}} = \text{g mL}^{-1}$

H. Unit of mass = kilogram

The kilogram is the unit of mass; it is equal to the mass of the international prototype of the kilogram.

Assertion and Reason

In the following questions a statement of Assertion (A) *followed by a statement of Reason* (R) *is given. Choose the correct option out of the choices given below in each question.*

Q.38 **Assertion** (A) The empirical mass of ethene is half of its molecular mass.

Reason (R) The empirical formula represents the simplest whole number ratio of various atoms present in a compound.

(a) Both A and R are true and R is the correct explanation of A.
(b) A is true but R is false.
(c) A is false but R is true.
(d) Both A and R are false.

Ans. ***(a)*** Both Assertion and Reason are true and Reason is the correct explanation of Assertion.

The molecular formula of ethene is C_2H_4 and its empirical formula is CH_2.

$\therefore$ Molecular mass of ethene $(C_2H_4) = 28$

Empirical mass of ethene $(CH_2) = 14$

Thus, Empirical mass $= \frac{1}{2} \times$ molecular mass

or Molecular formula = Empirical formula × 2

Q.39 **Assertion** (A) One atomic mass unit is defined as one twelfth of the mass of one carbon-12 atom.

Reason (R) Carbon-12 isotope is the most abundant isotope of carbon and has been chosen as standard.

(a) Both A and R are true and R is the correct explanation of A.
(b) Both A and R true but R is not the correct explanation of A.
(c) A is true but R is false.
(d) Both A and R are false.

Ans. ***(b)*** Both Assertion and Reason are true but Reason is not the correct explanation of Assertion.

One atomic mass unit is defined as one twelfth of the mass of one carbon atom because comparison of atomic masses of various elements with the mass of carbon comes out to be close to a whole number value.

Q.40 **Assertion** (A) Significant figures for 0.200 is 3 whereas for 200 it is 1.

Reason (R) Zero at the end or right of a number are significant provided they are not on the right side of the decimal point.

(a) Both A and R are true and R is correct explanation of A.
(b) Both A and R are true but R is not the correct explanation of A.
(c) A is true but R is false.
(d) Both A and R are false.

Ans. ***(c)*** Assertion is true but Reason is false.

0.200 contains 3 while 200 contains only one significant figure because zero at the end or right of a number are significant only if they are on the right side of the decimal point.

Q.41 **Assertion** (A) Combustion of 16 g of methane gives 18 g of water.

Reason (R) In the combustion of methane, water is one of the products.

(a) Both A and R are true but R is not the correct explanation of A.
(b) A is true but R is false.
(c) A is false but R is true.
(d) Both A and R are false.

Ans. ***(c)*** Assertion is false but Reason is true.

Combustion of 16 g of methane gives 36 g of water.

$$\underset{\substack{1\text{mol} \\ = 16\text{ g}}}{CH_4} + 2O_2 \longrightarrow CO_2 + \underset{\substack{2\text{ mol} \\ = 36\text{ g}}}{2H_2O}$$

Long Answer Type Questions

Q.42 A vessel contains 1.6 g of dioxygen at STP (273.15 K, 1 atm pressure). The gas is now transferred to another vessel at constant temperature, where pressure becomes half of the original pressure. Calculate

(a) volume of the new vessel.
(b) number of molecules of dioxygen.

Ans. (a) $p_1 = 1\,\text{atm},\ p_2 = \frac{1}{2} = 0.5\,\text{atm},\ T_1 = 273.15,\ V_2 = ?,\ V_1 = ?$

32 g dioxygen occupies = 22.4 L volume at STP

$\therefore$ 1.6 g dioxygen will occupy $= \frac{22.4\,\text{L} \times 1.6\,\text{g}}{32\,\text{g}} = 1.12\,\text{L}$

$$V_1 = 1.12\,\text{L}$$

From Boyle's law (as temperature is constant),

$$p_1V_1 = p_2V_2$$

$$V_2 = \frac{p_1V_1}{p_2} = \frac{1\,\text{atm} \times 1.12\,\text{L}}{0.5\,\text{atm}} = 2.24\,\text{L}$$

(b) Number of moles of dioxygen $= \dfrac{\text{Mass of dioxygen}}{\text{Molar mass of dioxygen}}$

$$n_{O_2} = \frac{1.6}{32} = 0.05 \text{ mol}$$

1 mol of dioxygen contains $= 6.022 \times 10^{23}$ molecules of dioxygen

$\therefore$ 0.05 mol of dioxygen $= 6.022 \times 10^{23} \times 0.05$ molecule of O_2

$= 0.3011 \times 10^{23}$ molecules $= 3.011 \times 10^{22}$ molecules

Q.43 Calcium carbonate reacts with aqueous HCl to give $CaCl_2$ and CO_2 according to the reaction given below :

$$CaCO_3(s) + 2HCl(aq) \longrightarrow CaCl_2(aq) + CO_2(g) + H_2O(l)$$

What mass of $CaCl_2$ will be formed when 250 mL of 0.76 M HCl reacts with 1000 g of $CaCO_3$? Name the limiting reagent. Calculate the number of moles of $CaCl_2$ formed in the reaction.

- **Concept Insight** The limiting reagent is the reactant that is completely used up in a reaction and thus, it determines when the reaction stops.

Ans. Molar mass of $CaCO_3 = 40 + 12 + 3 \times 16 = 100 \text{ g mol}^{-1}$

Moles of $CaCO_3$ in 1000 g, $n_{CaCO_3} = \dfrac{\text{Mass (g)}}{\text{Molar mass}}$

$$n_{CaCO_3} = \frac{1000 \text{ g}}{100 \text{ g mol}^{-1}} = 10 \text{ mol}$$

$$\text{Molarity} = \frac{\text{Moles of solute (HCl)} \times 1000}{\text{Volume of solution}}$$

(It is given that moles of HCl in 250 mL of 0.76 M HCl $= n_{HCl}$)

$$0.76 = \frac{n_{HCl} \times 1000}{250}$$

$$n_{HCl} = \frac{0.76 \times 250}{1000} = 0.19 \text{ mol.}$$

$$\underset{1 \text{ mol}}{CaCO_3(s)} + \underset{2 \text{ mol}}{2HCl(aq)} \longrightarrow CaCl_2(aq) + CO_2(g) + H_2O(l)$$

According to the equation,

1 mole of $CaCO_3$ reacts with 2 moles HCl.

$\therefore$ 10 moles of $CaCO_3$ will react with $\dfrac{10 \times 2}{1} = 20$ moles HCl.

But we have only 0.19 moles HCl, so HCl is limiting reagent and it limits the yield of $CaCl_2$.

Since, 2 moles of HCl produces 1 mole of $CaCl_2$.

0.19 mole of HCl will produce $\dfrac{1 \times 0.19}{2} = 0.095 \text{ mol } CaCl_2$

Q.44 Define the law of multiple proportions. Explain it with two examples. How does this law point to the existence of atoms?

Ans. *'Law of multiple proportions' states that,* "When two elements combine to form two or more chemical compounds, then the masses of one of the elements which combine with a fixed mass of the other, bear a simple ratio to one another".

e.g., hydrogen combines with oxygen to form two compounds, namely, water and hydrogen peroxide.

$$\underset{\text{(Hydrogen : 2 g)}}{H_2} + \underset{\text{(Oxygen : 16 g)}}{\frac{1}{2}O_2} \longrightarrow \underset{\text{(Water : 18 g)}}{H_2O}$$

$$\underset{\text{(Hydrogen : 2g)}}{H_2} + \underset{\text{(Oxygen : 32 g)}}{O_2} \longrightarrow \underset{\text{(Hydrogen peroxide : 34 g)}}{H_2O_2}$$

Reaction with chemical formulas should be present

Here, the masses of oxygen (*i.e.*, 16 g and 32 g) which combine with a fixed mass of hydrogen (2 g) bear a simple ratio, *i.e.*, 16 : 32 or 1 : 2. Similarly, carbon combines with oxygen to form two compounds, carbon dioxide and carbon monoxide

$$\underset{12\text{ g}}{\text{(Carbon) C}} + \underset{32\text{ g}}{\text{(Oxygen) }O_2} \longrightarrow \underset{44\text{ g}}{\text{(Carbon dioxide) }CO_2}$$

$$\underset{12\text{ g}}{\text{(Carbon) C}} + \underset{16\text{ g}}{\text{(Oxygen) }\frac{1}{2}O_2} \longrightarrow \underset{28\text{ g}}{\text{(Carbon monoxide) CO}}$$

Reaction with chemical formulas should be present

Here, the mass of oxygen (*i.e.* 32 g and 16 g) which combine with a fixed mass of carbon (12 g) bear a simple ratio, i.e. 32 : 16 or 2 : 1. As we know that, when compounds mixed in different proportions, then they form different compounds. In the above examples, when hydrogen is mixed with different proportion of oxygen, then they form water or hydrogen peroxide. Similarly, when carbon is mixed with different proportion of oxygen, then they form carbon dioxide or carbon monoxide. It shows that there are constituents which combine in a definite proportion. These constituents may be atoms. Thus, the law of multiple proportions shows the existence of atoms which combine to form molecules.

Q.45 A box contains some identical red coloured balls, labelled as *A*, each weighing 2 g. Another box contains identical blue coloured balls, labelled as *B*, each weighing 5 g. Consider the combinations AB, AB_2, A_2B and A_2B_3 and show that law of multiple proportions is applicable.

Thinking Process In this question, it is seen that the masses of *B* which combine with the fixed mass of *A* in different combinations are related to each other by simple whole numbers.

Ans.

Combination	Mass of *A* (g)	Mass of *B* (g)
AB	2	5
AB_2	2	10
A_2B	4	5
A_2B_3	4	15

Mass of *B* which is combined with fixed mass of *A* (say 1 g) will be 2.5 g $\left(\frac{5}{2}\text{g}\right)$, 5 g $\left(\frac{10}{2}\text{g}\right)$, 1.25 g $\left(\frac{5}{4}\text{g}\right)$ and 3.75 g $\left(\frac{15}{4}\text{g}\right)$. They are in the ratio 2 : 4 : 1 : 3 which is a simple whole number ratio. Hence, the law of multiple proportions is applicable.

Chapter

02 Structure of Atom

Multiple Choice Questions (MCQs)

Q.1 Which of the following conclusions could not be derived from Rutherford's α-particle scattering experiment?

(a) Most of the space in the atom is empty.

(b) The radius of the atom is about 10^{-10} m while that of nucleus is 10^{-15} m.

(c) Electrons move in a circular path of fixed energy called orbits.

(d) Electrons and the nucleus are held together by electrostatic forces of attraction.

Ans. ***(c)*** Concept of electrons moving in a circular path of fixed energy was put forward by Bohr and not derived from Rutherford's scattering experiment.

Q.2 Which of the following options does not represent ground state electronic configuration of an atom?

(a) $1s^2 2s^2 2p^6 3s^2 3p^6 3d^8 4s^2$

(b) $1s^2 2s^2 2p^6 3s^2 3p^6 3d^9 4s^2$

(c) $1s^2 2s^2 2p^6 3s^2 3p^6 3d^{10} 4s^1$

(d) $1s^2 2s^2 2p^6 3s^2 3p^6 3d^5 4s^1$

Ans. ***(b)*** $1s^2 2s^2 2p^6 3s^2 3p^6 3d^9 4s^2$ does not represent the ground state electronic configuration of any atom. This configuration corresponds to atomic number 29, i.e., Copper (Cu). However, this is not the actual ground state configuration of Cu. According to the observed electronic structure and extra stability associated with fully filled and half-filled subshells, the correct configuration of Cu is $1s^2 2s^2 2p^6 3s^2 3p^6 3d^{10} 4s^1$.

Here, one electron from the 4s orbital shifts to $3d$, making the $3d$ subshell completely filled ($3d^{10}$) and $4s$ half-fill ($4s^1$).

Q.3 The probability density plots of $1s$ and $2s$ orbitals are given in figure.

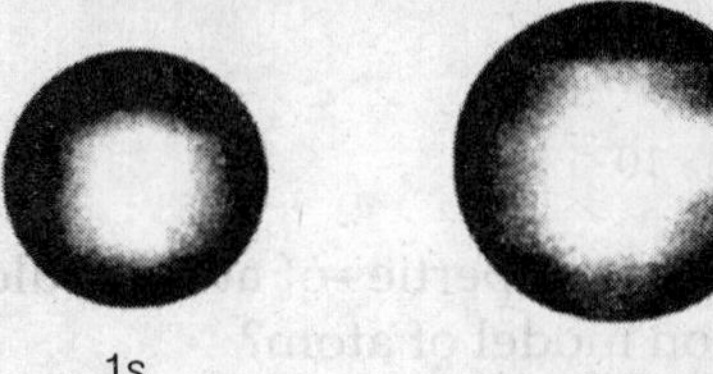

The density of dots in a region represents the probability density of finding electrons in the region.

On the basis of above diagram which of the following statements is incorrect?

(a) 1s and 2s orbitals are spherical in shape.
(b) The probability of finding the electron is maximum near the nucleus.
(c) The probability of finding the electron at a given distance is equal in all directions.
(d) The probability density of electrons for 2s orbital decreases uniformly as distance from the nucleus increases.

Thinking Process

(i) To solve the problem, keep in mind that s-orbital has a spherical shape.

(ii) Probability density representing the probability of finding an electron at a point within an atom is proportional to the square of the orbital wave function, *i.e.*, $|\Psi|^2$ at that point.

Ans. ***(d)*** The probability density of electrons in 2s orbital first increases then decreases and after that it begins to increases again as distance increases from nucleus.

Q.4 Which of the following statement is not correct about the characteristics of cathode rays?

(a) They start from the cathode and move towards the anode.
(b) They travel in straight line in the absence of an external electrical or magnetic field.
(c) Characteristics of cathode rays do not depend upon the material of electrodes in cathode ray tube.
(d) Characteristics of cathode rays depend upon the nature of gas present in the cathode ray tube.

Ans. ***(d)*** Cathode rays consist of negatively charged material particles called electrons. It was discovered by William Crookes. The characteristics of cathode rays do not depend upon the material of electrodes and the nature of the gas present in the cathode ray tube.

Q.5 Which of the following statements about the electron is incorrect?

(a) It is a negatively charged particle.
(b) The mass of electron is equal to the mass of neutron.
(c) It is a basic constituent of all atoms.
(d) It is a constituent of cathode rays.

Ans. ***(b)*** The mass of electron is very small or negligible as compared to the mass of the neutron.

Mass of electron $= 9.1 \times 10^{-31}$ kg

Mass of neutron $= 1.67 \times 10^{-27}$ kg

Q.6 Which of the following properties of atom could be explained correctly by Thomson model of atom?

(a) Overall neutrality of atom
(b) Spectra of hydrogen atom
(c) Position of electrons, protons and neutrons in atom
(d) Stability of atom

Ans. *(a)* J.J. Thomson, in 1898, proposed plum pudding (watermelon) model of atom. An important feature of this model is that the mass of the atom is assumed to be uniformly distributed over the atom. This model was able to explain the overall neutrality of the atom.

Q.7 Two atoms are said to be isobars if

(a) they have same atomic number but different mass number.
(b) they have same number of electrons but different number of neutrons.
(c) they have same number of neutrons but different number of electrons.
(d) sum of the number of protons and neutrons is same but the number of protons is different.

Ans. *(d)* Isobars have the same mass number (*i.e.*, sum of protons and neutrons) but different atomic number (*i.e.*, number of protons). *e.g.*, $_{18}Ar^{40}$ and $_{19}K^{40}$ are isobars.

$_{18}Ar^{40}$	$_{19}K^{40}$
Atomic number = 18	Atomic number = 19
Mass number = 40	Mass number = 40

Q.8 The number of radial nodes for $3p$ orbital is....... .

(a) 3 (b) 4 (c) 2 (d) 1

Ans. *(d)* For a hydrogen atom wave function,

Number of radial nodes $= n - l - 1$

$= 3 - 1 - 1 = 1$ [For $3p$-orbital, $n = 3$ and $l = 1$]

Q.9 Number of angular nodes for $4d$ orbital is ....

(a) 4 (b) 3 (c) 2 (d) 1

Ans. *(c)* **Number of angular nodes** $= l$

For 4th orbital, $n = 4$ and $l = 2$ for d-orbital.

$\therefore$ Number of angular nodes = 2

Q.10 Which of the following is responsible to rule out the existence of definite paths or trajectories of electrons?

(a) Pauli's exclusion principle
(b) Heisenberg's uncertainty principle
(c) Hund's rule of maximum multiplicity
(d) Aufbau principle

- **Concept Insight** Werner Heisenberg, stated uncertainty principle which states that it is impossible to determine simultaneously, the exact position and exact momentum of an electron.

$$\text{Mathematically, } \Delta x \times \Delta p \geq \frac{h}{4\pi}$$

Ans. *(b)* An important implication of the Heisenberg's uncertainty principle is that it rules out existence of definite paths or trajectories of electrons and other similar particles because position of electron cannot be fixed.

Q.11 Total number of orbitals associated with third shell will be ....

(a) 2 (b) 4
(c) 9 (d) 3

Ans. ***(c)*** Total number of orbitals associated with n^{th} shell = n^2

$\therefore$ Total number of orbitals associated with third shell = $(3)^2 = 9$

Alternate Method

For $n = 3$

l	0	1	2
m	0	+1, 0, −1	+2, +1, 0, −1, −2

$\therefore$ Total number of orbitals = 1 + 3 + 5 = 9

Q.12 Orbital angular momentum depends on ....

(a) l (b) n and l
(c) n and m (d) m and s

Ans. ***(a)*** Orbital angular momentum, $mvr = \frac{h}{2\pi}\sqrt{l(l+1)}$.

Hence, it depends only on 'l' (azimuthal quantum number). l can have values ranging from 0 to $(n-1)$.

Q.13 Chlorine exists in two isotopic forms. Cl-37 and Cl-35 but its atomic mass is 35.5. This indicates the ratio of Cl-37 and Cl-35 is approximately

(a) 1 : 2 (b) 1 : 1 (c) 1 : 3 (d) 3 : 1

Ans. ***(c)*** Chlorine exists as a mixture of two isotopes : Cl-35 and Cl-37, in the ratio Cl-37 : Cl-35 = 1 : 3. This means for every 1 atom of Cl-37, there are 3 atoms of Cl-35. Due to this, the atomic mass of chlorine is not a whole number but a weighted average of the isotopic masses, calculated as

$$\therefore \text{ Average atomic mass of Cl} = \frac{3 \times 35 + 1 \times 37}{4} = 35.5 \text{ amu}$$

Thus, the atomic mass of chlorine is fractional (35.5 u) due to the presence of its two isotopes in the ratio 1 : 3.

Q.14 The pair of ions having same electronic configuration is ....

(a) Cr^{3+}, Fe^{3+} (b) Fe^{3+}, Mn^{2+} (c) Fe^{3+}, Co^{3+} (d) Sc^{3+}, Cr^{3+}

Ans. ***(b)***

$_{24}Cr = [Ar]3d^5 4s^1$ $_{24}Cr^{3+} = [Ar]3d^3$
$_{26}Fe = [Ar]3d^6 4s^2$ $_{26}Fe^{3+} = [Ar]3d^5$
$_{25}Mn = [Ar]3d^5 4s^2$ $_{25}Mn^{2+} = [Ar]3d^5$
$_{27}Co = [Ar]3d^7 4s^2$ $_{27}Co^{3+} = [Ar]3d^6$
$_{21}Sc = [Ar]3d^1 4s^2$ $_{21}Sc^{3+} = [Ar]$

Thus, Fe^{3+} and Mn^{2+} have the same electronic configuration.

Mistake Alert! *Students may get confused while writing the electronic configurations of the atoms/ions.*

Q.15 For the electrons of oxygen atom, which of the following statements is correct?

(a) Z_{eff} for an electron in a 2s orbital is the same as Z_{eff} for an electron in a 2p orbital.
(b) An electron in the 2s orbital has the same energy as an electron in the 2p orbital.
(c) Z_{eff} for an electron in 1s orbital is the same as Z_{eff} for an electron in a 2s orbital.
(d) The two electrons present in the 2s orbital have spin quantum numbers m_s but of opposite sign.

Ans. ***(d)*** (a) Electrons in 2s and 2p orbitals have different screen effect. Hence, their Z_{eff} is different. **Z_{eff} of 2s orbital > Z_{eff} of 2p orbital.**

Therefore, option (a) is not correct.

(b) Energy of 2s orbital < energy of 2p orbital.
Hence, option (b) is not correct.

(c) Z_{eff} of 1s orbital $\neq$ Z_{eff} of 2s orbital
Hence, option (c) is incorrect.

(d) For the two electrons of 2s orbital, the value of spin quantum numbers, m_s is $+\frac{1}{2}$ and $-\frac{1}{2}$.

Hence, option (d) is correct.

Q.16 If travelling at same speeds, which of the following matter waves have the shortest wavelength?

(a) Electron
(b) Alpha particle (He^{2+})
(c) Neutron
(d) Proton

- **Concept Insight** From de-Broglie equation,

$$\text{wavelength, } \lambda = \frac{h}{mv}$$

Ans. ***(b)*** For same speed of different particles, *i.e.*, electron, proton, neutron and α-particle,

$$\boxed{\lambda \propto \frac{1}{m}} \qquad \text{[As } h \text{ is constant]}$$

Greater the mass of matter waves, lesser is wavelength and *vice-versa*. In these matter waves, alpha particle (He^{2+}) has higher mass, therefore, it has shortest wavelength.

Multiple Choice Questions (More Than One Options)

Q.17 Identify the pairs which are not of isotopes?

(a) ${}^{12}_{6}X, {}^{13}_{6}Y$
(b) ${}^{35}_{17}X, {}^{37}_{17}Y$
(c) ${}^{14}_{6}X, {}^{14}_{7}Y$
(d) ${}^{8}_{4}X, {}^{8}_{5}Y$

- **Concept Insight**

(i) Isotopes are the elements that have same atomic number (Z), but different mass number (A).

(ii) The digit written as subscript represents the atomic number (Z) and that as superscript represents the mass number (A) of the element *i.e.*, ${}^{A}_{Z}X$.

Ans. *(c, d)* (a) $^{12}_{6}X$ and $^{13}_{6}Y$ have same atomic number but different mass number. Thus, these pairs are isotopes to each other.

(b) $^{35}_{17}X$ and $^{37}_{17}Y$ have same atomic number, but different mass number. Thus, these pairs are isotopes to each other.

(c) $^{14}_{6}X$ and $^{14}_{7}Y$ have different atomic number but same mass number. Thus, these pairs are **isobars** to each other.

(d) $^{8}_{4}X$ and $^{8}_{5}Y$ have different atomic number but same mass number. Thus, these pairs are **isobars** to each other.

Q.18 Out of the following pairs of electrons, identify the pairs of electrons present in degenerate orbitals.

(a) (i) $n = 3, l = 2, m_l = -2, m_s = -\frac{1}{2}$ (ii) $n = 3, l = 2, m_l = -1, m_s = -\frac{1}{2}$

(b) (i) $n = 3, l = 1, m_l = 1, m_s = +\frac{1}{2}$ (ii) $n = 3, l = 2, m_l = 1, m_s = +\frac{1}{2}$

(c) (i) $n = 4, l = 1, m_l = 1, m_s = +\frac{1}{2}$ (ii) $n = 3, l = 2, m_l = 1, m_s = +\frac{1}{2}$

(d) (i) $n = 3, l = 2, m_l = +2, m_s = -\frac{1}{2}$ (ii) $n = 3, l = 2, m_l = +2, m_s = +\frac{1}{2}$

Ans. *(a, d)* Degenerate orbitals are orbitals which have equal energy and same n and l values.

(a) (i) $3d_{xy}$ (ii) $3d_{yz}$

(b) (i) $3p_x$ (ii) $3d_{xy}$

(c) (i) $4s$ (ii) $3d_{xy}$

(d) (i) $3d_{x^2-y^2}$ (ii) $3d_{x^2-y^2}$

Thus, $3d_{xy}$ and $3d_{yz}$; $3d_{x^2-y^2}$ and $3d_{x^2-y^2}$ represent pair of degenerate orbitals.

$\therefore$ (a) and (d) are correct option.

Q.19 Which of the following sets of quantum numbers are correct?

	n	l	m
(a)	1	1	+2
(b)	2	1	+1
(c)	3	2	-2
(d)	3	4	-2

Thinking process 'l' cannot have same or higher value than 'n'.

Ans. *(b, c)* If $n = 1, l \neq 1 (\because l < n)$

Hence, (a) is incorrect.

If $n = 2, l = 0, 1$, For $l = 1, m = -1, 0, +1$.

Hence, (b) is correct.

If $n = 3, l = 0, 1, 2$

For $l = 2, m = -2, -1, 0, +1, +2$.

Hence, (c) is correct.

If $n = 3, l \neq 4 (\because l < n)$.

Hence, (d) is incorrect.

Q.20 In which of the following pairs, the ions are isoelectronic?

(a) Na^+, Mg^{2+} (b) Al^{3+}, O^- (c) Na^+, O^{2-} (d) N^{3-}, Cl^-

Thinking Process To solve this problem, it should be kept in mind that isoelectronic are those species which have same number of electrons.

Ans. *(a, c)* For, $Na^+ = 11 - 1 = 10\,e^-$

$Mg^{2+} = 12 - 2 = 10\,e^-$

Thus, they have same number of electrons.

For, $Al^{3+} = 13 - 3 = 10\,e^-, O^- = 8 + 1 = 9\,e^-$.

They do not have same number of electrons.

For, $Na^+ = 10\,e^-, O^{2-} = 8 + 2 = 10\,e^-$

They have same number of electrons.

For, $N^{3-} = 7 + 3 = 10\,e^-, Cl^- = 17 + 1 = 18\,e^-$.

They do not have same number of electrons.

Thus, Na^+ is isoelectronic with Mg^{2+} and O^{2-}.

Q.21 Which of the following statements concerning the quantum numbers are correct?

(a) Angular quantum number determines the three dimensional shape of the orbital.

(b) The principal quantum number determines the orientation and energy of the orbital.

(c) Magnetic quantum number determines the size of the orbital.

(d) Spin quantum number of an electron determines the orientation of the spin of electron relative to the chosen axis.

Ans. *(a, d)* (a) Azimuthal quantum number '*l*' is also known as orbital angular momentum or subsidiary quantum number. It determines three dimensional shape of the orbital.

(b) The principal quantum number determines the size of the orbital.

(c) Magnetic quantum number determines the orientation of the electron cloud in a subshell.

(d) An electron spins around its own axis, much in a similar way as earth spins around its own axis while revolving around the sun. In other words, an electron has, besides charge and mass, intrinsic spin angular quantum number.

Short Answer Type Questions

Q.22 Arrange *s*, *p* and *d* subshells of a shell in the increasing order of effective nuclear charge (Z_{eff}) experienced by the electron present in them.

Ans. *s*-orbital is spherical in shape, it shields the electrons from the nucleus more effectively than *p*- orbital which in turn shields more effectively than *d*-orbital. Therefore, the effective nuclear charge (Z_{eff}) experienced by electrons present in them is $d < p < s$.

Q.23 Show the distribution of electrons in oxygen atom (atomic number 8) using orbital diagram.

Ans. This distribution of electrons in oxygen atoms is as follows

$_8O = 1s^2 \quad 2s^2 \quad 2p^4$

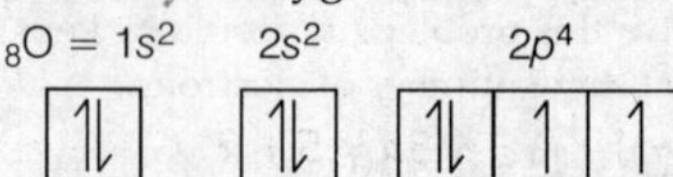

From the orbital diagram, it is seen that there are two unpaired electrons.

Q.24 Nickel atom can lose two electrons to form Ni^{2+} ion. The atomic number of nickel is 28. From which orbital will nickel lose two electrons?

Ans. $_{28}Ni = 1s^2\ 2s^2\ 2p^6\ 3s^2\ 3p^6\ 3d^8\ 4s^2$; Nickel (Ni) will lose 2 electrons from $4s$ (outermost shell) to form Ni^{2+} ion.

Hence, electronic configuration of $_{28}Ni^{2+} = 1s^2\ 2s^2\ 2p^6\ 3s^2\ 3p^6\ 3d^8\ 4s^0$

Q.25 Which of the following orbitals are degenerate?

$$3d_{xy}, 4d_{xy}, 3d_{z^2}, 3d_{yz}, 4d_{yz}, 4d_{z^2}$$

Ans. The orbitals which belongs to same subshell and same shell are called degenerate orbitals. ($3d_{xy}$, $3d_{z^2}$, $3d_{yz}$) and ($4d_{xy}$, $4d_{yz}$, $4d_{z^2}$) are the two sets of degenerate orbitals.

Q.26 Calculate the total number of angular nodes and radial nodes present in $3p$ orbital.

Thinking Process To calculate the total number of angular nodes and radial nodes of principal quantum number n, the following formula is used :

(i) Radial nodes (or spherical nodes) $= n - l - 1$

(ii) Angular nodes (or non-spherical nodes) $= l$

(iii) Total nodes $= n - 1$

Ans. For $3p$-orbital, principal quantum number, $n = 3$ and azimuthal quantum number, $l = 1$.

Number of angular nodes $= l = 1$

Number of radial nodes $= n - l - 1 = 3 - 1 - 1 = 1$

Q.27 The arrangement of orbitals on the basis of energy is based upon their $(n + l)$ value. Lower the value of $(n + l)$, lower is the energy. For orbitals having same values of $(n + l)$, the orbital with lower value of n will have lower energy.

I. Based upon the above information, arrange the following orbitals in the increasing order of energy.

(a) $1s, 2s, 3s, 2p$ (b) $4s, 3s, 3p, 4d$

(c) $5p, 4d, 5d, 4f, 6s$ (d) $5f, 6d, 7s, 7p$

II. Based upon the above information. Solve the questions given below.

(a) Which of the following orbitals has the lowest energy?

$$4d, 4f, 5s, 5p$$

(b) Which of the following orbitals has the highest energy?

$$5p, 5d, 5f, 6s, 6p$$

Ans. **I.** (a) $(n+l)$ values of $1s = 1 + 0 = 1$, $2s = 2 + 0 = 2$, $3s = 3 + 0 = 3$, $2p = 2 + 1 = 3$

Hence, increasing order of their energy is $1s < 2s < 2p < 3s$.

(b) $4s = 4 + 0 = 4$, $3s = 3 + 0 = 3$, $3p = 3 + 1 = 4$, $4d = 4 + 2 = 6$

Hence, $3s < 3p < 4s < 4d$

(c) $5p = 5 + 1 = 6$, $4d = 4 + 2 = 6$, $5d = 5 + 2 = 7$, $4f = 4 + 3 = 7$, $6s = 6 + 0 = 6$

Hence, $4d < 5p < 6s < 4f < 5d$

(d) $5f = 5 + 3 = 8$, $6d = 6 + 2 = 8$, $7s = 7 + 0 = 7$, $7p = 7 + 1 = 8$.

Hence, $7s < 5f < 6d < 7p$

II. (a) $(n+l)$ values of $4d = 4 + 2 = 6$, $4f = 4 + 3 = 7$, $5s = 5 + 0 = 5$, $5p = 5 + 1 = 6$

Hence, 5s has the lowest energy.

(b) $5p = 5 + 1 = 6$, $5d = 5 + 2 = 7$, $5f = 5 + 3 = 8$, $6s = 6 + 0 = 6$, $6p = 6 + 1 = 7$

Hence, $5f$ has highest energy.

Q.28 Which of the following will not show deflection from the path on passing through an electric field?

Proton, cathode rays, electron, neutron.

Ans. Neutron being neutral will not show deflection from the path on passing through an electric field.

Proton, cathode rays and electron being the charged particles will show deflection from the path on passing through an electric field.

Q.29 An atom having atomic mass number 13 has 7 neutrons. What is the atomic number of the atom?

Thinking Process

(i) Atomic mass (A) = Number of neutron (n) + Number of proton (p)

(ii) Atomic number = No. of proton= No. of electron

Ans. An atom having atomic mass number 13 and number of neutrons 7.

i.e., $A = 13, n = 7$

As we know that, $A = n + p$

$\therefore$ $p = A - n = 13 - 7 = 6$

Hence, $Z = p = 6$

Mistake Alert! *Students may make a mistake of incorrectly relating mass number (protons + neutrons) and atomic number (protons) while identifying elements.*

Q.30 Wavelengths of different radiations are given below.

$\lambda(A)$= 300 nm, $\lambda(B)$= 300 μm, $\lambda(C)$= 3 nm, $\lambda(D)$ = 30 Å

Arrange these radiations in the increasing order of their energies.

- **Concept Insight** Energy can be related to wavelength by following equation,

$$E = \frac{hc}{\lambda} \quad \text{[where } \lambda = \text{wavelength]}$$

Ans. $\lambda(A) = 300\text{ nm} = 300 \times 10^{-9}\text{ m}$, $\lambda(B) = 300\ \mu\text{m} = 300 \times 10^{-6}\ \mu\text{m}$
$\lambda(C) = 3\text{ nm} = 3 \times 10^{-9}\text{ m}$, $\lambda(D) = 30\text{Å} = 30 \times 10^{-10}\text{ m} = 3 \times 10^{-9}\text{ m}$

Energy, $E = \dfrac{hc}{\lambda}$

Therefore, $E \propto \dfrac{1}{\lambda}$

Increasing order of energy is $B < A < C = D$

Q.31 **The electronic configuration of valence shell of Cu is $3d^{10}4s^1$ and not $3d^9 4s^2$. How is this configuration explained?**

Ans. Electronic configurations that have exactly half-filled or fully filled orbitals are more stable due to symmetrical distribution of electrons and maximum exchange energy. In $3d^{10}4s^1$, *d*-orbitals are completely filled and *s*-orbital is half-filled. Hence, it is more stable configuration.

Q.32 **The Balmer series in the hydrogen spectrum corresponds to the transition from $n_1 = 2$ to $n_2 = 3, 4, \ldots$. This series lies in the visible region. Calculate the wave number of line associated with the transition in Balmer series when the electron moves to $n = 4$ orbit. ($R_H = 109677\text{ cm}^{-1}$)**

Ans. From Rydberg formula,

Wave number, $\bar{v} = R_H\left[\dfrac{1}{n_i^2} - \dfrac{1}{n_f^2}\right]\text{cm}^{-1}$

$\bar{v} = 109677\left[\dfrac{1}{n_i^2} - \dfrac{1}{n_f^2}\right]\text{cm}^{-1}$ [$\because R_H = 109677$]

Given, $n_i = 2$ and $n_f = 4$ (Transition in Balmer series)

$\bar{v} = 109677\left[\dfrac{1}{2^2} - \dfrac{1}{4^2}\right]\text{cm}^{-1}$

$\Rightarrow$ $\bar{v} = 109677\left[\dfrac{1}{4} - \dfrac{1}{16}\right]\text{cm}^{-1}$

$\Rightarrow$ $\bar{v} = 109677 \times \left[\dfrac{4-1}{16}\right]\text{cm}^{-1}$

$\Rightarrow$ $\bar{v} = 20564.44\text{ cm}^{-1}$

Q.33 **According to de-Broglie, matter should exhibit dual behaviour, that is both particle and wave like properties. However, a cricket ball of mass 100 g does not move like a wave when it is thrown by a bowler at a speed of 100 km/h. Calculate the wavelength of the ball and explain why it does not show wave nature.**

Ans. Given, $m = 100\text{ g} = 0.1\text{ kg}$

$v = 100\text{ km/h} = \dfrac{100 \times 1000}{60 \times 60} = \dfrac{1000}{36}\text{ ms}^{-1}$

From de-Broglie equation, wavelength, $\lambda = \frac{h}{mv}$

$$\lambda = \frac{6.626 \times 10^{-34}\ \text{kg m}^2\ \text{s}^{-1}}{0.1\ \text{kg} \times \frac{1000}{36}\ \text{ms}^{-1}} = 238.5 \times 10^{-36}\ \text{m}$$

As the wavelength is very small, so wave nature cannot be detected.

Q.34 What is the experimental evidence in support of the idea that electronic energies in an atom are quantized?

Ans. The line spectrum of any element has lines corresponding to definite wavelengths. Lines are obtained as a result of electronic transitions between the energy levels. Hence, the electrons in these levels have fixed energy, *i.e.*, quantised values.

Q.35 Out of electron and proton which one will have, a higher velocity to produce matter waves of the same wavelength? Explain it.

Ans. From de-Broglie equation, wavelength, $\lambda = \frac{h}{mv}$

For same wavelength for two different particles, *i.e.*, electron and proton, $m_1v_1 = m_2v_2$ (h is constant). Lesser the mass of the particle, greater will be the velocity. Hence, electron will have higher velocity, as it has lesser mass.

Q.36 A hypothetical electromagnetic wave is shown in figure. Find out the wavelength of the radiation.

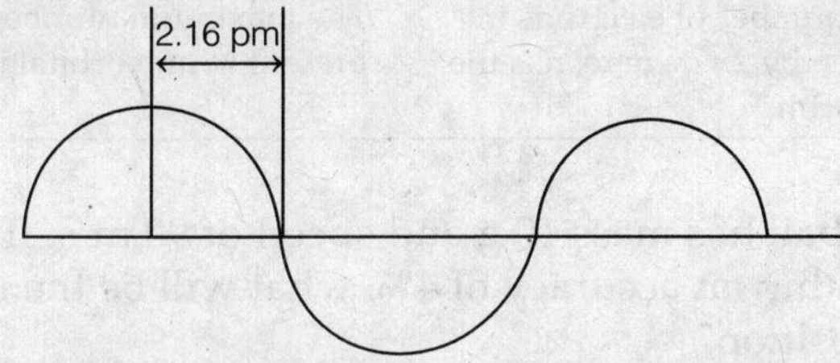

Ans. Wavelength is the distance between two successive peaks or two successive crests of a wave.

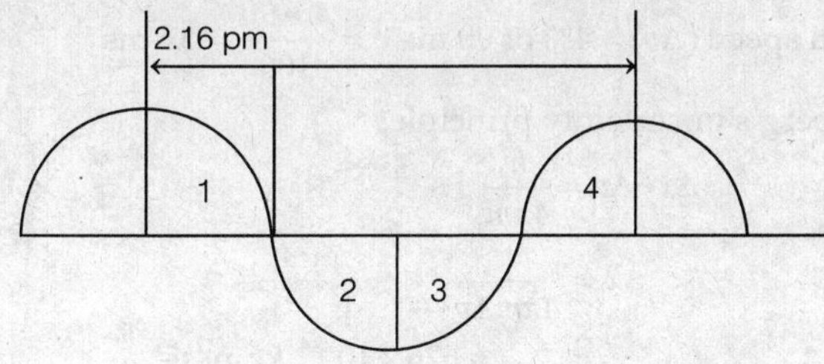

Therefore, $\lambda = 4 \times 2.16\ \text{pm} = 8.64\ \text{pm}$

$= 8.64 \times 10^{-12}\ \text{m}$ $[\because 1\ \text{pm} = 10^{-12}\text{m}]$

Q.37 Chlorophyll present in green leaves of plants absorbs light at 4.620×10^{14} Hz. Calculate the wavelength of radiation in nanometer. Which part of the electromagnetic spectrum does it belong to?

Ans. Given, frequency $(v) = 4.620 \times 10^{14}$ Hz or $4.620 \times 10^{14}\ s^{-1}$

$$\text{Wavelength } (\lambda) = \frac{c}{v} = \frac{3 \times 10^8\ ms^{-1}}{4.620 \times 10^{14} s^{-1}}$$

$$= 0.6494 \times 10^{-6} m$$

$$= 649.4\ nm \qquad [\because 1\ nm = 10^{-9} m]$$

Thus, it belongs to visible region of spectrum, because it falls within the range of 400–700 nm, which is detectable by the human eye.

Q.38 What is the difference between the terms orbit and orbital?

Ans. Difference between the terms orbit and orbital are as below.

Orbit	Orbital
An orbit is a well defined and definite circular or elliptical path around the nucleus in which the electrons revolve.	An orbital is the three dimensional space around the nucleus within which the probability of finding an electron is maximum (upto 90-95%).
All orbits are circular and disc like.	Different orbitals have different shapes.
The concept of an orbit is not in accordance with the wave character of electrons and uncertainty principle.	The concept of an orbital is in accordance with the wave character of electrons and uncertainty principle.
The maximum number of electrons in any orbit is given by $2n^2$ where, n is the number of the orbit.	The maximum number of electrons present in any orbital is two.

Q.39 Table-tennis ball has mass 10 g and speed of 90 m/s. If speed can be measured within an accuracy of 4%, what will be the uncertainty in speed and position?

Ans. Given that, speed = 90 m/s

$$\text{mass} = 10\ g = 10 \times 10^{-3} kg$$

$$\text{Uncertainty in speed } (\Delta v) = 4\% \text{ of } 90\ ms^{-1} = \frac{4 \times 90}{100} = 3.6\ ms^{-1}$$

From Heisenberg's uncertainty principle,

$$\Delta x \cdot \Delta v = \frac{h}{4\pi m}$$

or

$$\Delta x = \frac{h}{4\pi m \Delta v}$$

$$\text{Uncertainty in position, } \Delta x = \frac{6.626 \times 10^{-34}\ kgm^2 s^{-1}}{4 \times 3.14 \times 10 \times 10^{-3}\ kg \times 3.6\ ms^{-1}}$$

$$= 1.46 \times 10^{-33}\ m$$

Q.40 The effect of uncertainty principle is significant only for motion of microscopic particles and is negligible for the macroscopic particles. Justify the statement with the help of a suitable example.

Ans. If uncertainty principle is applied to an object of mass, say about a milligram (10^{-6} kg), then

$$\Delta v \cdot \Delta x = \frac{h}{4\pi m}$$

$$\Delta v \cdot \Delta x = \frac{6.626 \times 10^{-34}\ \text{kgm}^2\text{s}^{-1}}{4 \times 3.14 \times 10^{-6}\ \text{kg}}$$

$$= 0.527 \times 10^{-28}\ \text{m}^2\text{s}^{-1} \approx 0.53 \times 10^{-28}\ \text{m}^2\text{s}^{-1}$$

The value of $\Delta v \cdot \Delta x$ obtained is extremely small and is insignificant. Therefore, for milligram-sized or heavier objects, the associated uncertainties are hardly of any real consequence.

Q.41 Hydrogen atom has only one electron. So, mutual repulsion between electrons is absent. However, in multielectron atoms mutual repulsion between the electrons is significant. How does this affect the energy of an electron in the orbitals of the same principal quantum number in multielectron atoms?

Ans. In hydrogen atom, the energy of an electron is determined by the value of n only. While, in multielectron atom, it is determined by $(n + l)$. Hence, for a given principal quantum, number of electrons of s, p, d and f-orbitals have different energy (for s, p, d and f, $l = 0, 1, 2$ and 3 respectively).

Matching The Columns

Q.42 Match the following species with their corresponding ground state electronic configuration.

	Atom / Ion		Electronic configuration
A.	Cu	1.	$1s^2 2s^2 2p^6 3s^2 3p^6 3d^{10}$
B.	Cu^{2+}	2.	$1s^2 2s^2 2p^6 3s^2 3p^6 3d^{10} 4s^2$
C.	Zn^{2+}	3.	$1s^2 2s^2 2p^6 3s^2 3p^6 3d^{10} 4s^1$
D.	Cr^{3+}	4.	$1s^2 2s^2 2p^6 3s^2 3p^6 3d^9$
		5.	$1s^2 2s^2 2p^6 3s^2 3p^6 3d^3$

Ans. A. → (3) B. → (4) C. → (1) D. → (5)

A. Cu (Z = 29) : $1s^2 2s^2 2p^6 3s^2 3p^6 3d^{10} 4s^1$ (exception)

B. Cu^{2+} (Z = 29) : $1s^2 2s^2 2p^6 3s^2 3p^6 3d^9$

Zn (Z = 30) : $1s^2 2s^2 2p^6 3s^2 3p^6 3d^{10} 4s^2$

C. Zn^{2+} : $1s^2 2s^2 2p^6 3s^2 3p^6 3d^{10}$

Cr (Z = 24) : $1s^2 2s^2 2p^6 3s^2 3p^6 3d^5 4s^1$

D. Cr^{3+} : $1s^2 2s^2 2p^6 3s^2 3p^6 3d^3$

Q.43 Match the quantum numbers with the information provided by these.

Quantum number	Information provided
A. Principal quantum number	1. Orientation of the orbital
B. Azimuthal quantum number	2. Energy and size of orbital
C. Magnetic quantum number	3. Spin of electron
D. Spin quantum number	4. Shape of the orbital

Ans. **A.** → (2) **B.** → (4) **C.** → (1) **D.** → (3)

A. Principal quantum number is the most important quantum number as it determines the size and to large extent the energy of the orbital.

B. Azimuthal quantum number determines the angular momentum of the electron and defines the three-dimensional shape of the orbital.

C. Magnetic quantum number gives information about the spatial orientation of orbitals with respect to a standard set of coordinate axes.

D. Spin quantum number arises from the spectral evidence that an electron in its motion around the nucleus in an orbit also rotates or spins about its own axis.

Q.44 Match the following rules with their statements.

Rules	Statements
A. Hund's Rule	1. No two electrons in an atom can have the same set of four quantum numbers.
B. Aufbau Principle	2. Half-filled and completely filled orbitals have extra stability.
C. Pauli Exclusion Principle	3. Pairing of electrons in the orbitals belonging to the same subshell does not take place until each orbital is singly occupied.
D. Heisenberg's Uncertainty Principle	4. It is impossible to determine the exact position and exact momentum of a subatomic particle simultaneously.
	5. In the ground state of atoms, orbitals are filled in the order of their increasing energies.

Ans. **A.** → (3) **B.** → (5) **C.** → (1) **D.** → (4)

A. Hund's rule states that pairing of electrons in the orbitals belonging to the same subshell (*p*, *d* or *f*) does not take place until each orbital belonging to that subshell has got one electron each, *i.e.*, it is singly occupied.

B. Aufbau principle states that in the ground state of the atoms, the orbitals are filled in order of their increasing energies.

C. According to Pauli exclusion principle, no two electrons in an atom can have the same set of four quantum numbers.

D. Heisenberg's uncertainty principle states that it is impossible to determine the exact position and exact momentum of a subatomic particle simultaneously.

Q.45 Match the following.

	Column I		Column II
A.	X-rays	1.	$\nu = 10^0 - 10^4$ Hz
B.	Ultraviolet wave (UV)	2.	$\nu = 10^{10}$ Hz
C.	Long radio waves	3.	$\nu = 10^{16}$ Hz
D.	Microwave	4.	$\nu = 10^{18}$ Hz

Ans. **A.** → (4) **B.** → (3) **C.** → (1) **D.** → (2)

Electromagnetic Wave	Frequency	Uses
A. X-rays	$2 \times 10^{16} - 3 \times 10^{19}$ Hz	Medical pictures, material testing
B. Ultraviolet wave (UV)	$7.9 \times 10^{14} - 2 \times 10^{16}$ Hz	Germisidal lamp
C. Long radio waves	$10^0 - 10^4$ Hz	Signal transmission
D. Microwave	$1 \times 10^9 - 5 \times 10^{11}$ Hz	Cooking radar

Q.46 Match the following.

	Column I		Column II
A.	Photon	1.	Value is 4 for *N*-shell
B.	Electron	2.	Probability density
C.	ψ^2	3.	Always positive value
D.	Principal quantum number *n*	4.	Exhibits both momentum and wavelength

Ans. **A.** → (4) **B.** → (4) **C.** → (2, 3) **D.** → (1, 3)

A. Photon has particle nature as well as wave nature. It exhibits both momentum and wavelength.

B. Electron also has particle nature as well as wave nature. Thus, it also exhibits both momentum and wavelength.

C. ψ^2 represents probability density of electron and always has positive values.

D. Principal quantum number, $n = 4$ for N– shell. (It always has positive values)

$$\begin{matrix} & K & L & M & N \\ n = & 1 & 2 & 3 & 4 \end{matrix}$$

Q.47 Match species given in Column I with the electronic configuration given in Column II.

	Column I		Column II
A.	Cr	1.	$[Ar]3d^8 4s^0$
B.	Fe^{2+}	2.	$[Ar]3d^{10} 4s^1$
C.	Ni^{2+}	3.	$[Ar]3d^6 4s^0$
D.	Cu	4.	$[Ar]3d^5 4s^1$
		5.	$[Ar]3d^4 4s^2$

Ans. A. → (4) B. → (3) C. → (1) D. → (2)

A. Cr (Z = 24) = $1s^2 2s^2 2p^6 3s^2 3p^6 3d^5 4s^1$ = [Ar]$3d^5 4s^1$

B. Fe^{2+} (Z = 26) = $1s^2 2s^2 2p^6 3s^2 3p^6 3d^6 4s^0$ = [Ar]$3d^6 4s^0$

C. Ni^{2+}(Z = 28) = $1s^2 2s^2 2p^6 3s^2 3p^6 3d^8 4s^0$ = [Ar]$3d^8 4s^0$

D. Cu (Z = 29) = $1s^2 2s^2 2p^6 3s^2 3p^6 3d^{10} 4s^1$ = [Ar]$3d^{10} 4s^1$

Assertion and Reason

In the following questions a statement of Assertion (A) *followed by a statement of Reason* (R) *is given. Choose the correct option out of the choices given below in each question.*

Q.48 **Assertion** (A) All isotopes of a given element show the same type of chemical behaviour.

Reason (R) The chemical properties of an atom are controlled by the number of electrons in the atom.

(a) Both A and R are true and R is the correct explanation of A
(b) Both A and R are true, but R is not the correct explanation of A
(c) A is true, but R is false
(d) Both A and R are false

Ans. ***(a)*** Both assertion and reason are true and reason is the correct explanation of assertion. Isotopes have the same atomic number *i.e.,* same number of electrons which are responsible for their chemical behaviour. Hence, these exhibit similar chemical properties.

Q.49 **Assertion** (A) Black body is an ideal body that emits and absorbs radiations of all frequencies.

Reason (R) The frequency of radiation emitted by a body goes from a lower frequency to higher frequency with an increase in temperature.

(a) Both A and R are true and R is the correct explanation of A
(b) Both A and R are true, but R is not the correct explanation of A
(c) A is true, but R is false
(d) Both A and R are false

Ans. ***(b)*** Both A and R are true but R is not the correct explanation of A.

A body which absorbs and emits all radiations falling on it is called perfect black body. With rise in temperature, frequency increases.

Q.50 **Assertion** (A) It is impossible to determine the exact position and exact momentum of an electron simultaneously.

Reason (R) The path of an electron in an atom is clearly defined.

(a) Both A and R are true and R is the correct explanation of A
(b) Both A and R are true, but R is not the correct explanation of A
(c) A is true and R is false
(d) Both A and R are false

Ans. ***(c)*** Assertion is true and reason is false. According to Heisenberg's uncertainty principle, the exact position and exact momentum of an electron cannot be determined simultaneously. Thus, the path of electron in an atom is not clearly defined.

Long Answer Type Questions

Q.51 What is photoelectric effect? State the result of photoelectric effect experiment that could not be explained on the basis of laws of classical physics. Explain this effect on the basis of quantum theory of electromagnetic radiations.

Ans. **Photoelectric effect** When radiation with certain minimum frequency (ν_0) strikes the surface of a metal, the electrons are ejected from the surface of the metal. This phenomenon is called photoelectric effect. The electrons emitted are called **photoelectrons.**

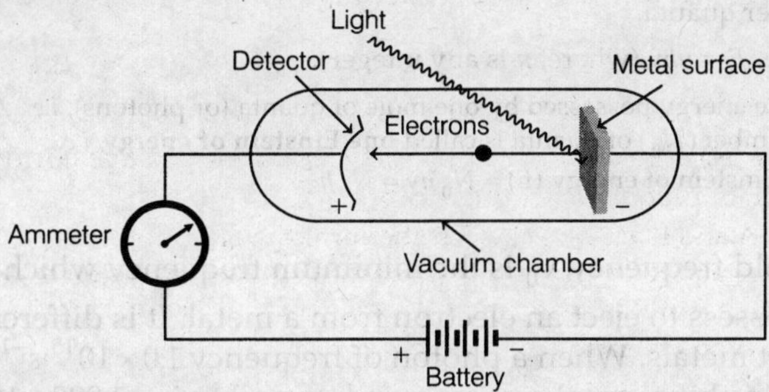

Equipment for studying the photoelectric effect is shown above. Light of a particular frequency strikes a clean metal surface inside a vacuum chamber. Electrons are ejected from the metal and are counted by a detector that measures their kinetic energy.

The result observed in this experiment were :

(i) The electrons are ejected from the metal surface as soon as the beam of light strikes the surface, *i.e.*, there is no time lag between the striking of light beam and the ejection of electrons from the metal surface.

(ii) The number of electrons ejected is directly proportional to the intensity or brightness of light.

(iii) For each metal, there is a characteristic minimum frequency, ν_0 (also known as **threshold frequency**) below which photoelectric effect is not observed. At a frequency $\nu > \nu_0$, the ejected electrons come out with certain kinetic energy. The kinetic energies of these electrons increases with the increase of frequency of the light used.

The above observation cannot be explained by the electromagnetic wave theory or quantum theory of electromagnetic radiations. According to this theory, since radiations were continuous, therefore, it should be possible to accumulate energy on the surface of the metal, irrespective of its frequency and thus, radiations of all frequencies should be able to eject electrons.

Similarly, according to this theory, the energy of the electrons ejected should depend upon the intensity of the incident radiation.

Particle Nature of Electromagnetic Radiation

To explain the phenomena of 'black body radiation' and 'photoelectric effect', Max Planck in 1900, put forward a theory known after his name as Planck's quantum theory. This theory was further extended by Einstein in 1905.

The important points of this theory are as follows

(i) The radiant energy is emitted or absorbed not continuously but discontinuously in the form of small discrete packets of energy. Each such packet of energy is called a **'quantum'**. In case of light, the quantum of energy is called a **'photon'**.

(ii) The energy of each quantum is directly proportional to the frequency of the radiation, *i.e.*, $E \propto \nu$ or $E = h\nu$

where, h is Planck's constant. Its value is approximately equal to 6.626×10^{-27} ergs or 6.626×10^{-34} J s.

(iii) The total amount of energy emitted or absorbed by a body will be some whole number quanta.

Hence, $E = nh\nu$ (where, n is any integer).

Note The energy possessed by one mole of quanta (or photons), *i.e.*, Avogadro's number (N_0) of quanta is called **one Einstein of energy**, *i.e.*,
1 Einstein of energy $(E) = N_0\, h\nu = N_0\, h\dfrac{c}{\lambda}$

Q.52 Threshold frequency, ν_0 is the minimum frequency which a photon must possess to eject an electron from a metal. It is different for different metals. When a photon of frequency $1.0 \times 10^{15}\ \text{s}^{-1}$ was allowed to hit a metal surface, an electron having 1.988×10^{-19} J of kinetic energy was emitted. Calculate the threshold frequency of this metal.

Show that an electron will not be emitted if a photon with a wavelength equal to 600 nm hits the metal surface.

Ans. We know that, $h\nu = h\nu_0 + \text{KE}$

$$h\nu - \text{KE} = h\nu_0$$

or
$$h\nu_0 = (6.626 \times 10^{-34}\ \text{Js} \times 1 \times 10^{15}\ \text{s}^{-1}) - 1.988 \times 10^{-19}\ \text{J}$$
$$h\nu_0 = 6.626 \times 10^{-19} - 1.988 \times 10^{-19}\ \text{J}$$
$$h\nu_0 = 4.638 \times 10^{-19}\ \text{J}$$
$$\nu_0 = \frac{4.638 \times 10^{-19}\ \text{J}}{6.626 \times 10^{-34}\ \text{Js}}$$
$$= 0.699 \times 10^{15}\ \text{s}^{-1} = 6.99 \times 10^{14}\ \text{s}^{-1} \approx 7 \times 10^{14}\ \text{s}^{-1}$$

When,
$$\lambda = 600\ \text{nm} = 600 \times 10^{-19}\ \text{m}$$
$$\nu = \frac{c}{\lambda} = \frac{3.0 \times 10^{8}\ \text{ms}^{-1}}{6.0 \times 10^{-7}\ \text{m}}$$
$$= 0.5 \times 10^{15}\ \text{s}^{-1} = 5.0 \times 10^{14}\ \text{s}^{-1}$$

Thus, $\nu < \nu_0$, hence, no electron will be emitted.

Q.53 When an electric discharge is passed through hydrogen gas, the hydrogen molecules dissociate to produce excited hydrogen atoms. These excited atoms emit electromagnetic radiation of discrete frequencies which can be given by the general formula

$$\bar{\nu} = 109677\left[\frac{1}{n_i^2} - \frac{1}{n_f^2}\right]$$

What points of Bohr's model of an atom can be used to arrive at this formula? Based on these points derive the above formula giving description of each step and each term.

Ans. The two important points of Bohr's model that can be used to derive the given formula are as follows

(i) Electrons revolve around the nucleus in a circular path of fixed radius and energy. These paths are called orbits, stationary states or allowed energy states.

(ii) Energy is emitted or absorbed when an electron moves from higher stationary state to lower stationary state or from lower stationary state to higher stationary state respectively.

Derivation The energy of the electron in the nth stationary state is given by the expression,

$$E_n = -R_H\left(\frac{1}{n^2}\right) \qquad n = 1, 2, 3 \qquad \text{...(i)}$$

where, R_H is called Rydberg constant and its value is 2.18×10^{-18} J. The energy of the lowest state, also called the ground state, is

$$E_n = -2.18 \times 10^{-18}\left(\frac{1}{1^2}\right) = -2.18 \times 10^{-18}\ \text{J} \qquad \text{....(ii)}$$

The energy gap between the two orbits is given by the equation,

$$\Delta E = E_f - E_i \qquad \text{...(iii)}$$

On combining Eqs. (i) and (iii)

$$\Delta E = \left(-\frac{R_H}{n_f^2}\right) - \left(-\frac{R_H}{n_i^2}\right)$$

Where, n_i and n_f stand for initial orbit and final orbit, respectively.

$$\Delta E = R_H\left[\frac{1}{n_i^2} - \frac{1}{n_f^2}\right]$$

$$= 2.18 \times 10^{-18}\ \text{J}\left[\frac{1}{n_i^2} - \frac{1}{n_f^2}\right]$$

Frequency, ν associated with the absorption and emission of the photon can be calculated as follows.

$$\nu = \frac{\Delta E}{h} = \frac{R_H}{h}\left[\frac{1}{n_i^2} - \frac{1}{n_f^2}\right]$$

$$\Rightarrow \quad \nu = \frac{2.18 \times 10^{-18}\,\text{J}}{6.626 \times 10^{-34}\,\text{Js}}\left[\frac{1}{n_i^2} - \frac{1}{n_f^2}\right]$$

$$\nu = 3.29 \times 10^{15}\left[\frac{1}{n_i^2} - \frac{1}{n_f^2}\right]\text{Hz}$$

$$\Rightarrow \quad \bar{\nu} = \frac{\nu}{c} = \frac{3.29 \times 10^{15}}{3 \times 10^8\,\text{ms}^{-1}}\left[\frac{1}{n_i^2} - \frac{1}{n_f^2}\right]$$

$$\bar{\nu} = 1.09677 \times 10^7\left[\frac{1}{n_i^2} - \frac{1}{n_f^2}\right]\text{m}^{-1}$$

$$\bar{\nu} = 109677\left[\frac{1}{n_i^2} - \frac{1}{n_f^2}\right]\text{cm}^{-1}$$

Q.54 Calculate the energy and frequency of the radiation emitted when an electron jumps from $n = 3$ to $n = 2$ in a hydrogen atom.

- **Concept Insight** In hydrogen spectrum, the spectral lines are expressed in terms of wave number ($\bar{\nu}$), which can be calculated by the following formula.

Wave number, $\bar{\nu} = R_H\left(\frac{1}{n_1^2} - \frac{1}{n_2^2}\right)$

(where, R_H = Rydberg constant = 109677 cm^{-1})

Ans. We know that,

$$\bar{\nu} = 109677\ \text{cm}^{-1}\left(\frac{1}{n_1^2} - \frac{1}{n_2^2}\right)$$

$$\bar{\nu} = 109677\ \text{cm}^{-1}\left(\frac{1}{2^2} - \frac{1}{3^2}\right)$$

$$\bar{\nu} = 109677 \times \frac{5}{36} = 15232.9\ \text{cm}^{-1}$$

$$\bar{\nu} = \frac{1}{\lambda}$$

or, $$\lambda = \frac{1}{\bar{\nu}} = \frac{1}{15232.9} = 6.564 \times 10^{-5}\,\text{cm}$$

Wavelength, $$\lambda = 6.564 \times 10^{-7}\ \text{m}$$

Energy, $$E = \frac{hc}{\lambda}$$

$$= \frac{6.626 \times 10^{-34}\ \text{Js} \times 3.0 \times 10^8\ \text{ms}^{-1}}{6.564 \times 10^{-7}\ \text{m}}$$

$$= 3.028 \times 10^{-19}\ \text{J}$$

Frequency, $$\nu = \frac{c}{\lambda} = \frac{3.0 \times 10^8\ \text{ms}^{-1}}{6.564 \times 10^{-7}\ \text{m}}$$

$$= 0.457 \times 10^{15}\ \text{s}^{-1}$$

$$= 4.57 \times 10^{14}\text{s}^{-1}$$

Alternate Method

Energy, $\Delta E = E_3 - E_2$

$$= -2.18 \times 10^{-18}\left[\frac{1}{3^2} - \frac{1}{2^2}\right] = -2.18 \times 10^{18}\left[\frac{1}{9} - \frac{1}{4}\right]$$

$$= 2.18 \times 10^{-18} \times \frac{5}{36} = 3.028 \times 10^{19}\ \text{J}$$

Frequency, $v = \frac{\Delta E}{h} = \frac{3.028 \times 10^{-19}\ \text{J}}{6.626 \times 10^{-34}\ \text{Js}} = 4.569 \times 10^{14}\text{s}^{-1}$

Mistake Alert! *Students may get confused while changing units.*

Q.55 Why was a change in the Bohr Model of atom required? Due to which important development(s), concept of movement of an electron in an orbit was replaced by the concept of probability of finding electron in an orbital? What is the name given to the changed model of atom?

Ans. In Bohr model, an electron is regarded as a charged particle moving in well defined circular orbits about the nucleus. An orbit can completely be defined only if both the position and the velocity of the electron are known exactly at the same time.

This is not possible according to the Heisenberg uncertainty principle. Further more, the wave character of the electron is not considered in Bohr model.

Therefore, concept of movement of an electron in an orbit was replaced by the concept of probabitlity of finding electron in an orbital due to the de-Broglie's concept of dual nature of electron and Heisenberg's uncertainty principle. The changed model is called **quantum mechanical model** of the atom on the basis of quantum mechanics and Schrodinger equation.

Chapter 03

Classification of Elements and Periodicity in Properties

Multiple Choice Questions (MCQs)

Q.1 Consider the isoelectronic species, Na^+, Mg^{2+}, F^- and O^{2-}. The correct order of increasing length of their radii is

(a) $F^- < O^{2-} < Mg^{2+} < Na^+$
(b) $Mg^{2+} < Na^+ < F^- < O^{2-}$
(c) $O^{2-} < F^- < Na^+ < Mg^{2+}$
(d) $O^{2-} < F^- < Mg^{2+} < Na^+$

● **Concept Insight** For isoelectronic species, ionic radii $\propto \frac{1}{\text{atomic number}}$.

Ans. ***(b)*** The ionic radii increases as the positive charge decreases or the negative charge increases.

Ion	Mg^{2+} <	Na^+ <	F^- <	O^{2-}
Atomic number	(12)	(11)	(9)	(8)

Q.2 Which of the following is not an actinoid?

(a) Curium (Z = 96)
(b) Californium (Z = 98)
(c) Uranium (Z = 92)
(d) Terbium (Z = 65)

Ans. ***(d)*** Elements with atomic number, Z = 90 to 103 are called actinoids. Thus, Terbium (Z = 65) is not an actinoid.

Q.3 The order of screening effect of electrons of *s*, *p*, *d* and *f* orbitals of a given shell of an atom on its outer shell electrons is

(a) $s > p > d > f$
(b) $f > d > p > s$
(c) $p < d < s > f$
(d) $f > p > s > d$

Thinking Process To solve this question, keep in mind that shielding effect refers to the reduction in the effective nuclear charge on the valence shell electrons due to the presence of inner shell electrons. These inner electrons partially block the attraction between the nucleus and the outermost electrons, thereby reducing the force of attraction experienced by the valence electrons.

Ans. ***(a)*** For the same shell, screening effect of $s > p > d > f$.

Q.4 The first ionisation enthalpies of Na, Mg, Al and Si are in the order

(a) Na < Mg > Al < Si
(b) Na > Mg > Al > Si
(c) Na < Mg < Al < Si
(d) Na > Mg > Al < Si

Thinking Process All the four elements are of 3rd period and their increasing order of their atomic no. is Na(11), Mg(12), Al(13), Si(14). Now Ionisation enthalpy (I.E.) increase from left to right across a period. But Mg has completely filled $3s^2$ orbital so its, ionization energy is higher than Al which has partially filled *p*-orbitals.

Ans. *(a)* Follow the following steps to solve out such problems

Steps	Method	Apply
Step I	Write the electronic configuration to find position in the periodic table.	${}_{11}Na = [Ne]\, 3s^1$, ${}_{12}Mg = [Ne]\, 3s^2$ ${}_{13}Al = [Ne]\, 3s^2 3p^1$, ${}_{14}Si = [Ne]\, 3s^2 3p^2$
Step II	Arrange them in the order as they are in the periodic table.	11 Na 12 Mg 13 Al 14 Si
Step III	Follow the general trend and also keep in mind the exception.	The I.E. increases along a period from left to right but I.E. of Mg is higher than that of Al due to completely filled 3*s* orbital in Mg.
Step IV	On the above basis find the order.	The order of first I.E. is Na < Mg > Al < Si.

Thus, option (a) is the correct.

Q.5 The electronic configuration of gadolinium (Atomic number 64) is

(a) $[Xe]\, 4f^3\, 5d^5\, 6s^2$
(b) $[Xe]\, 4f^7\, 5d^2\, 6s^1$
(c) $[Xe]\, 4f^7\, 5d^1\, 6s^2$
(d) $[Xe]\, 4f^8\, 5d^6\, 6s^2$

Ans. *(c)* The electronic configuration of La$(Z = 57)$ is $[Xe]\, 4f^0 5d^1\, 6s^2$. Therefore, further addition of electrons occur in the lower energy 4*f*-orbital till it is exactly half-filled $4f^7$ in Eu (Z= 63). Thus, the electronic configuration of Eu is $[Xe]\, 4f^7\, 6s^2$. Thereafter, addition of next electron does not occur in the more stable exactly half-filled $4f^7$ shell but occurs in the little higher energy 5*d*-orbital. Thus, the electronic configuration of Gd (Z = 64) is $[Xe]\, 4f^7 5d^1\, 6s^2$.

Q.6 The statement that is not correct for periodic classification of elements is

(a) The properties of elements are periodic function of their atomic numbers.
(b) Non-metallic elements are less in number than metallic elements.
(c) For transition elements, the 3*d*-orbitals are filled with electrons after 3*p*-orbitals and before 4*s*-orbitals.
(d) The first ionisation enthalpies of elements generally increase with increase in atomic number as we go along a period.

Ans. *(c)* The statement given in option (c) is incorrect. It is because orbitals are filled with electrons in increasing order of energy according to the Aufbau's principle and the order is $3p < 4s < 3d$. Thus, for any element, 4*s* orbital is filled with electron before filling 3*d*-orbitals.

Q.7 Among halogens, the correct order of amount of energy released in electron gain (electron gain enthalpy) is

(a) F > Cl > Br > I (b) F < Cl < Br < I (c) F < Cl > Br > I (d) F < Cl < Br < I

Ans. *(c)* As we move from Cl to I, the electron gain enthalpy (*i.e.*, energy released in electron gain) become less and less negative due to a corresponding increase in the atomic size. However, the electron gain enthalpy of F is less negative than that of Cl due to small size of fluorine which offers strong repulsion to new incoming electron. Thus, the negative electron gain enthalpy follows the order.

$$F < Cl > Br > I$$

Q.8 The period number in the long form of the periodic table is equal to

(a) magnetic quantum number of any element of the period.
(b) atomic number of any element of the period.
(c) maximum principal quantum number of any element of the period.
(d) maximum azimuthal quantum number of any element of the period.

Ans. *(c)* Since each period starts with the filling of electrons in a new principal quantum number, therefore, the period number in the long form of the periodic table refers to the maximum principal quantum number of any element in the period. Period number = maximum n of any element (where, n = principal quantum number).

Q.9 The elements in which electrons are progressively filled in $4f$-orbital are called

(a) actinoids (b) transition elements (c) lanthanoids (d) halogens

● **Concept Insight** Lanthanoids consist of elements from Z = 58 (Cerium) to 71 (Lutetium).

Ans. *(c)* The elements in which electrons are progressively filled in $4f$-orbital are called **lanthanoids** because these are placed after Lanthanum (Z = 57).

Q.10 Which of the following is the correct order of size of the given species :

(a) $I > I^- > I^+$ (b) $I^+ > I^- > I$ (c) $I > I^+ > I^-$ (d) $I^- > I > I^+$

Ans. *(d)* The size of an ion depends on the gain or loss of electrons. When an atom gains an electron to form an anion (I^-), electron–electron repulsion increases, leading to a larger size. In contrast, loss of an electron to form a cation (I^+) increases the effective nuclear charge, pulling electrons closer and decreasing the size. Thus, the correct order of size is $I^- > I > I^+$.

Q.11 The formation of oxide ion O^{2-} (g), from oxygen atom requires first an exothermic and then an endothermic step as shown below

$$O\,(g) + e^- \rightarrow O^-\,(g); \Delta H^\ominus = -141 \text{ kJ mol}^{-1}$$
$$O^-(g) + e^- \rightarrow O^{2}\,(g); \Delta H^\ominus = +780 \text{ kJ mol}^{-1}$$

Thus, process of formation of O^{2-} in gas phase is unfavourable even though O^{2-} is isoelectronic with neon. It is due to the fact that

(a) oxygen is more electronegative.
(b) addition of electron in oxygen results in larger size of the ion.
(c) electronic repulsion outweighs the stability gained by achieving noble gas configuration.
(d) O^- ion has a comparatively smaller size than oxygen atom.

Ans. ***(c)*** Although O^{2-} has noble gas configuration and is isoelectronic with neon but its formation is unfavourable due to the strong electronic repulsion between the negatively charged O^- ion and the second electron being added.

Hence, the electronic repulsion outweighs the stability gained by achieving noble gas configuration.

Q.12 Comprehension given below is followed by some multiple choice questions. Each question has one correct option. Choose the correct option.

In the modern periodic table, elements are arranged in order of increasing atomic numbers which is related to the electronic configuration. Depending upon the type of orbitals receiving the last electron, the elements in the periodic table have been divided into four blocks, *viz* *s*, *p*, *d* and *f*.

The modern periodic table consists of 7 periods and 18 groups. Each period begins with the filling of a new energy shell. In accordance with the Aufbau principle, the seven periods (1 to 7) have 2, 8, 8, 18, 18, 32 and 32 elements respectively.

The seventh period is still incomplete. To avoid the periodic table being too long, the two series of *f*-block elements, called lanthanoids and actinoids are placed at the bottom of the main body of the periodic table.

(i) The element with atomic number 57 belongs to

(a) *s* - block (b) *p* - block (c) *d* - block (d) *f* - block

Ans. ***(c)*** The element with atomic number 57 belongs to *d*-block element as the last electron enters the 5*d*-orbital against the aufbau principle. This anomalous behaviour can be explained on the basis of greater stability of the xenon (inert gas) core. After barium $(Z = 56)$, the addition of the next electron (*i.e.*, 57th) should occur in 4*f*-orbital in accordance with aufbau principle. This will however, tend to destabilize the xenon core $(Z = 54)$, $[Kr](4d^{10}\ 4f^0\ 5s^2\ 5p^6\ 5d^0)$ since the 4*f*-orbitals lie inside the core.

Therefore, the 57th electron prefers to enter 5*d*-orbital which lies outside the xenon core and whose energy is only slightly higher than that of 4*f*-orbital. Thus, the outer electronic configuration of La $(Z = 57)$ is $5d^1\ 6s^2$ rather than the expected $4f^1\ 6s^2$.

(ii) The last element of the *p*-block in 6th period is represented by the outermost electronic configuration.

(a) $7s^2\ 7p^6$ (b) $5f^{14}\ 6d^{10}\ 7s^2\ 7p^0$

(c) $4f^{14}\ 5d^{10}\ 6s^2\ 6p^6$ (d) $4f^{14}\ 5d^{10}\ 6s^2\ 6p^4$

● **Concept Insight** Each period starts with the filling of electrons in a new principal energy shell. Therefore, 6th period starts with the filling of 6*s*-orbital and ends when 6 *p*-orbitals are completely filled.
In between 4*f* and 5*d*-orbitals are filled in accordance with aufbau principle.

Ans. ***(c)*** The outmost electronic configuration of the last element of the *p*-block in the 6th period is $4f^{14}\ 5d^{10}\ 6s^2\ 6p^6$.

(iii) Which of the elements whose atomic numbers are given below, cannot be accommodated in the present set up of the long form of the periodic table?

(a)107 (b) 118 (c) 126 (d) 102

Ans. ***(c)*** The long form of the periodic table contains element with atomic number 1 to 118.

(iv) The electronic configuration of the element which is just above the element with atomic number 43 in the same group is ....

(a) $1s^2\ 2s^2\ 2p^6\ 3s^2\ 3p^6\ 3d^5\ 4s^2$
(b) $1s^2\ 2s^2\ 2p^6\ 3s^2\ 3p^6\ 3d^5\ 4s^3\ 4p^6$
(c) $1s^2\ 2s^2\ 2p^6\ 3s^2\ 3p^6\ 3d^6\ 4s^2$
(d) $1s^2\ 2s^2\ 2p^6\ 3s^2\ 3p^6\ 3d^7\ 4s^2$

Ans. ***(a)*** The fifth period begins with Rb ($Z = 37$) and ends at Xe ($Z = 54$). Thus, the element with $Z = 43$ lies in the 5th period. Since, the 4th period has 18 elements, therefore, the atomic number of the element which lies immediately above the element with atomic number 43 is $43 - 18 = 25$.
Now, the electronic configuration of element with $Z = 25$ is
$1s^2\ 2s^2\ 2p^6\ 3s^2\ 3p^6\ 3d^5\ 4s^2$ (*i.e.*, Mn), or $[Ar]\ 3d^5 4s^2$.

(v) The elements with atomic numbers 35, 53 and 85 are all ....

(a) noble gases (b) halogens
(c) heavy metals (d) light metals

Ans. ***(b)*** Each period ends with a noble gas. The atomic number of noble gases (*i.e.*, group 18 elements) are 2, 10, 18, 36, 54 and 86. Therefore, elements with atomic numbers 35 (36 – 1), 53 (54 – 1), and 85 (86 – 1), lie in a group before noble gases, *i.e.*, halogens (group 17) elements.
Thus, the elements with atomic number 35, 53 and 85 are all belongs to halogens.

Q.13 Electronic configuration of four elements *A*, *B*, *C*, and *D* are given below :

A. $1s^2\ 2s^2\ 2p^6$ B. $1s^2\ 2s^2\ 2p^4$
C. $1s^2\ 2s^2\ 2p^6\ 3s^1$ D. $1s^2\ 2s^2\ 2p^5$

Which of the following is the correct order of increasing tendency to gain electron?

(a) $A < C < B < D$ (b) $A < B < C < D$ (c) $D < B < C < A$ (d) $D < A < B < C$

Ans. ***(a)*** Electronic configuration of elements indicate that *A* is a noble gas (*i.e.*, Ne), *B* is oxygen (group 16), *C* is sodium metal (group 1) and *D* is fluorine (group 17).

(i) Noble gases have no tendency to gain electrons since all their orbitals are completely filled. Thus, element *A* has the least electron gain enthalpy.
(ii) Since, element *D* has one electron less and element *B* has two electrons less than the corresponding noble gas configuration, hence, element *D* has the highest electron gain enthalpy followed by element *B*
(iii) Since, element C has one electron in the *s*-orbital and hence needs one more electron to complete it, therefore, electron gain enthalpy of *C* is less than that of element *B*.

Combining all the facts given above, the electron gain enthalpies of the four elements increase in the order $A < C < B < D$.

Multiple Choice Questions (More Than One Options)

Q.14 Which of the following elements can show covalencey greater than 4?

(a) Be (b) P (c) S (d) B

Ans. *(b, c)* Elements Be and B lie in the 2nd period. They can have a maximum of 8 electrons in the valence shell. In other words, they can have a maximum covalency of 8/2 = 4.

However, elements P and S have **vacant *d*-orbitals** in their respective valence shells and hence can accommodate more than 8 electrons (*e.g.*, 5 in PCl_5, 6 in SF_6) in their respective valence shell. In other words, they can show a covalency of more than 4.

Q.15 Those elements impart colour to the flame on heating in it, the atoms of which require low energy for the ionisation (*i.e.*, absorb energy in the visible region of spectrum). The elements of which of the following groups will impart colour to the flame ?

(a) 2 (b) 13 (c) 1 (d) 17

- **Concept Insight** The elements of group 1 (alkali metals) and group 2 (alkaline earth metals) have 1 and 2 electrons respectively in their valence shells and hence have low ionisation energies.
  Elements of group 1 and 2 imparts colour to the flame,.

Ans. *(a, c)*

Group 1	Colour	Group 2	Colour
Li	Crimson	Ca	Brick-red
Na	Yellow	Sr	Crimson red
K	Pale violet	–	–
Rb	Red violet	Ba	Apple green
Cs	Blue	Ra	Crimson

Q.16 Which of the following sequences contain atomic numbers of only representative elements?

(a) 3, 33, 53, 87 (b) 2, 10, 22, 36
(c) 7, 17, 25, 37, 48 (d) 9, 35, 51, 88

Ans. *(a, d)* Elements of *s* and *p*-block are called representative elements. Elements of *d*-block (Z = 21-30; 39-48; 57 and 72-80; 89 and 104-112) are called transition elements while those of *f*-block (with Z = 58-71 and Z = 90-103) are called inner transition elements.

With reference to this division, elements listed under option (a) and option (*d*) are all representative elements.

Q.17 Which of the following elements will gain one electron more readily in comparison to other elements of their group?

(a) S(*g*) (b) Na(*g*) (c) O(*g*) (d) Cl(*g*)

Ans. *(a, d)* Chlorine has the highest tendency to gain one electron because by doing so, it acquires the stable electronic configuration of the nearest noble gas, *i.e.*, Argon.

Sulphur and oxygen belong to group 16 but the size of oxygen is much smaller than that of sulphur. As a result, when an electron is added to them, the electron-electron repulsions in the smaller $2p$- subshell of oxygen are comparatively stronger than those present in the bigger $3p$-subshell of sulphur. Therefore, S has a higher tendency to gain an electron than O. Na, on the other hand, has only one electron in the valence shell and hence has a strong tendency to lose rather than gain one electron.

Q.18 Which of the following statements are correct?

(a) Helium has the highest first ionisation enthalpy in the periodic table.
(b) Chlorine has less negative electron gain enthalpy than fluorine.
(c) Mercury and bromine are liquids at room temperature.
(d) In any period, atomic radius of alkali metal is the highest.

Ans. *(a, c, d)* Chlorine has more negative electron gain enthalpy than fluorine, even though fluorine is more electronegative. This is because the small size of fluorine leads to strong inter-electronic repulsion in its compact $2p$ subshell, which makes it slightly less favourable for fluorine to accept an additional electron. In contrast, chlorine's larger atomic size ($3p$-subshell) allows better accommodation of the incoming electron with less repulsion, releasing more energy in the process. Hence, statement (b) is incorrect. All other given statements are correct.

Q.19 Which of the following sets contain only isoelectronic ions?

(a) Zn^{2+}, Ca^{2+}, Ga^{3+}, Al^{3+}
(b) K^+, Ca^{2+}, Sc^{3+}, Cl^-
(c) P^{3-}, S^{2-}, Cl^-, K^+
(d) Ti^{4+}, Ar, Cr^{3+}, V^{5+}

Thinking Process Isoelectronic represents those species which have same number of electrons.

Ans. *(b, c)* (a) Zn^{2+} $(30-2=28)$, $Ca^{2+}(20-2=18)$, $Ga^{3+}(31-3=28)$, Al^{3+} $(13-3=10)$.

These species have different number of electrons and hence are not isoelectronic ions.

(b) K^+ $(19-1=18)$, $Ca^{2+}(20-2=18)$, $Sc^{3+}(21-3=18)$, Cl^- $(17+1=18)$.

These are all isoelectronic ions since each one of them has 18 electrons.

(c) P^{3-} $(15+3=18)$, $S^{2-}(16+2=18)$, $Cl^-(17+1=18)$, K^+ $(19-1=18)$.

These are all isoelectronic ions since each one of them has 18 electrons.

(d) Ti^{4+} $(22-4=18)$, Ar(18), $Cr^{3+}(24-3=21)$, V^{5+} $(23-5=18)$.

These have different number of electrons and hence are not isoelectronic ions.

Q.20 In which of the following options order of arrangement does not agree with the variation of property indicated against it?

(a) $Al^{3+} < Mg^{2+} < Na^+ < F^-$ (Increasing ionic size)
(b) $B < C < N < O$ (Increasing first ionisation enthalpy)
(c) $I < Br < Cl < F$ (Increasing electron gain enthalpy)
(d) $Li < Na < K < Rb$ (Increasing metallic radius)

Thinking Process

(i) The ionic size increases as the positive charge on the cation decreases or the negative charge on the anion increases.
(ii) First ionisation enthalpy increases from left to right in the periodic table.
(iii) Electron gain enthalpy increases as the electronegativity of the atom increases.
(iv) The metallic character increases as the size of the metal atom increases.

Ans. ***(b, c)*** Due to greater stability of the half filled *p*-subshell of nitrogen, its ionisation enthalpy is higher than that of oxygen. Thus, option (b) is incorrect.
Due to stronger electron-electron repulsions in the small size of flourine, the negative electron gain enthalpy of fluorine is lower than that of chlorine. Hence, option (c) is incorrect. In options (a) and (d), the remaining variation of property indicated against it are correct.

Q.21 Which of the following have no unit?

(a) Electronegativity
(b) Electron gain enthalpy
(c) Ionisation enthalpy
(d) Metallic character

Ans. ***(a, d)*** Electronegativity and metallic character have no units while electron gain enthalpy and ionisation enthalpy have units of kJ mol^{-1}.

Q.22 Ionic radii vary in :

(a) inverse proportion to the effective nuclear charge.
(b) inverse proportion to the square of effective nuclear charge.
(c) direct proportion to the screening effect.
(d) direct proportion to the square of screening effect.

Ans. ***(a, c)*** Ionic radius decreases as the effective nuclear charge increases.

$$\text{Ionic radius} \propto \frac{1}{\text{effective nuclear charge}}$$

Further, ionic radius increases as the screening effect increases.

$$\text{Ionic radius} \propto \text{screening effect}$$

Q.23 An element belongs to 3rd period and group 13 of the periodic table. Which of the following properties will be shown by the element?

(a) Good conductor of electricity
(b) Liquid, metallic
(c) Solid, metallic
(d) Solid, non-metallic

Ans. ***(a, c)*** Except boron, all elements of groups 13 are metallic. These exists as solid. Being metallic in nature, aluminium is good conductor of electricity.

Short Answer Type Questions

Q.24 Explain why the electron gain enthalpy of fluorine is less negative than that of chlorine?

Ans. It is because Fluorine is smaller in size than chlorine so incoming electron suffers more repulsion by 2*p* electrons in fluorine than by 3*p*-electron in Cl atom (larger size) and hence, incoming electron is weakly attracted in fluorine. This is the reason for the less negative electron gain enthalpy of F than that of Cl.

Q.25 All transition elements are *d*- block elements, but all *d*- block elements are not transition elements. Explain.

Ans. Elements in which the last electron enters in the *d*-orbitals, are called *d*-block elements. Also, the elements having incomplete *d*-orbitals in ground state or in common oxidation state are transition metals. This rule is applicable to all groups 3 to 11 in *d*-block. But elements of Group-12 (Zn, Cd, Hg) in *d*-block do not have incomplete *d*-orbitals in both ground state and common oxidation state so, group-12 metals (Zn, Cd and Hg) are not regarded as transition metals however these are *d*-block elements because last electron enters *d*-orbitals.

Q.26 Identify the group and valency of the element having atomic number 119. Also predict the outermost electronic configuration and write the general formula of its oxide.

Ans. The long form of the periodic table can accommodate maximum 118 elements. Thus, in accordance with aufbau principle, the filling of 8s-orbital will occur. In other words, 119th electron will enter 8s-orbital. As such its outmost electronic configuration will be $8s^1$. Since, it has only one electron in the valence shell, *i.e.*, 8s, therefore, its valency will be 1 and it will lie in the group I along with alkali metals and the formula of its oxide will be M_2O where *M* represents the element.

Q.27 Ionisation enthalpies of elements of second period are given below : Ionisation enthalpy/k cal mol^{-1}: 520, 899, 801, 1086, 1402, 1314, 1681, 2080. Match the correct enthalpy with the elements and complete the graph given in figure. Also write symbols of elements with their atomic number.

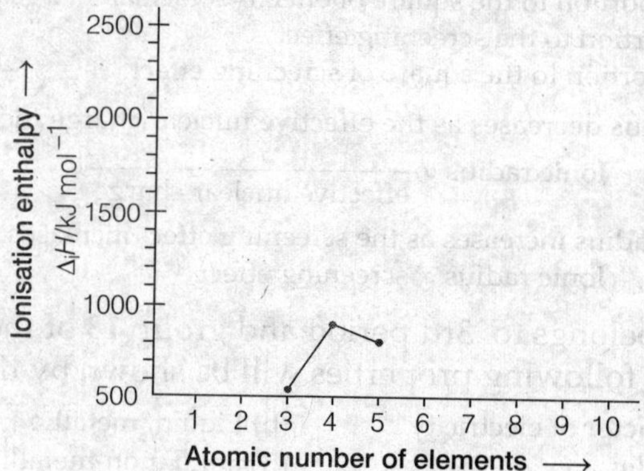

Ans. To match the correct enthalpy with the elements and to complete the graph, the following points are taken into consideration. As we move from left to right across a period, the ionisation enthalpy keeps on increasing due to increased nuclear charge and simultaneous decrease in atomic radius.

However, there are some exceptions given below :

(a) Inspite of increased nuclear charge, the first ionisation enthalpy of B is lower than that of Be. This is due to the presence of fully filled 2s orbital of Be [$1s^2\ 2s^2$] which is a stable electronic arrangement. Thus, higher energy is required to lose the electron from fully filled 2s orbitals, which are more tightly held by the nucleus. While B [$1s^2\ 2s^2\ 2p^1$] contains valence electrons in 2s and 2p orbitals. It can easily lose its one e^- from 2p orbital in order to achieve noble gas configuration. Thus, first ionisation enthalpy of B is lower than that of Be.

(b) The first ionisation enthalpy of N is higher than that of O though the nuclear charge of O is higher than that of N. This is due to the reason that in case of N, the electron is to be removed from a more stable exactly half-filled electronic configuration ($1s^2\ 2s^2\ 2p_x^1\ 2p_y^1\ 2p_z^1$) which is not present in O ($1s^2\ 2s^2\ 2p_x^2\ 2p_y^1\ 2p_z^1$).

Therefore, the first ionisation enthalpy of N is higher than that of O. The symbols of elements along with their atomic numbers are given in the following graph.

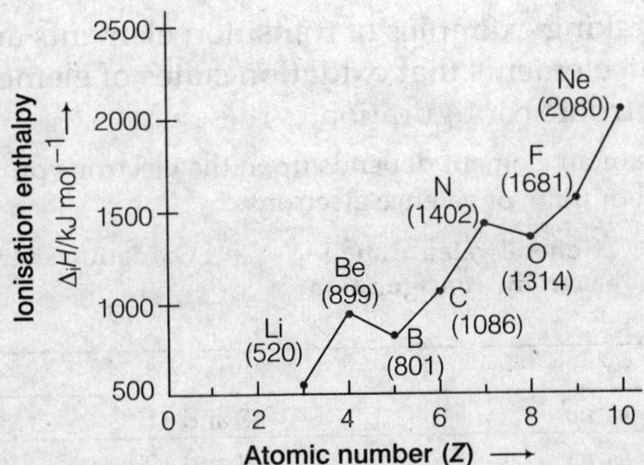

Q.28 Among the elements B, Al, C and Si,

(a) which element has the highest first ionisation enthalpy?

(b) which element has the most metallic character?

Justify your answer in each case.

Ans. The placing of elements are as :

Period	Group-13	Group-14
2nd Period	Boron	Carbon
3rd Period	Aluminium	Silicon

(a) Ionisation enthalpy increases along a period (as we move from left to right in a period) with decrease in atomic size and decreases down the group with increase in atomic size. Hence, carbon has the highest first ionisation enthalpy.

(b) Metallic character decreases across a period but increases on moving down the group. Hence, aluminium has the most metallic character.

Mistake Alert! *Students may get confused regarding the trends in atomic size, ionisation energy and electronegativity across periods and down the groups.*

Q.29 Write four characteristic properties of *p*-block elements.

Ans. The four important characteristic properties of *p*-block elements are the following

(a) *p*-Block elements include both metals and non-metals but the number of non-metals is much higher than that of metals. Further, the metallic character increases from top to bottom within a group and non-metallic character increases from left to right along a period in this block.

(b) Their ionisation enthalpies are relatively higher as compared to *s*-block elements.

(c) They mostly form covalent compounds.

(d) Some of them show variable oxidation states in their compounds. Their oxidising character increases from left to right in a period and reducing character increases from top to bottom in a group.

Q.30 Choose the correct order of atomic radii of fluorine and neon (in pm) out of the options given below and justify your answer.

(a) 72, 160 (b) 160, 160 (c) 72, 72 (d) 160, 72

Ans. ***(a)*** Atomic radius of F is expressed in terms of covalent radius while, atomic radius of neon is usually expressed in terms of van der Waal's radius. **van der Waal's radius of an element is always larger than its covalent radius.** Therefore, atomic radius of F is smaller than atomic radius of Ne (F = 72 pm, Ne = 160 pm).

Q.31 Illustrate by taking examples of transition elements and non-transition elements that oxidation states of elements are largely based on electronic configuration.

Ans. Oxidation state of an element depends upon the electrons present in the outermost shell or 8-no. of valence electrons.

Group	General valence shell electronic configuration	Oxidation state
1	ns^1	+1
2	ns^2	+2
13	$ns^2 np^1$	+3 and +1
14	$ns^2 np^2$	+4 and +2
15	$ns^2 np^3$	+5 and +3, − 3 (except N shows +1, +2, + 4 also)
16	$ns^2 np^4$	+6, + 4, + 2, − 2
17	$ns^2 np^5$	+7, + 5, + 3, + 1, − 1
18	$ns^2 np^6$	0

Transition elements or *d*-block elements General electronic configuration is $(n-1)\, d^{1-10}\, ns^{1-2}$. These elements show variable oxidation states because they have partially filled *d*-orbitals, and both $(n-1)d$ and *ns* electrons can participate in bonding. Their most common oxidation states are + 2 and + 3.

Q.32 Nitrogen has positive electron gain enthalpy whereas oxygen has negative. However, oxygen has lower ionisation enthalpy than nitrogen. Explain.

Ans. Nitrogen has stable half-filled $2s^2\, 2p^3$ electronic configuration. Therefore, addition of extra electron to the 2*p* *p*-orbital requires energy.

Oxygen has less stable configuration than nitrogen, so it readily attracts an incoming electron and releases energy. Thus, oxygen has lower ionisation enthalpy than nitrogen because by removing one electron from 2*p*-orbital, oxygen acquires stable configuration, *i.e.*, $2p^3$. On the other hand, in case of nitrogen it is not easy to remove one of the three 2*p*-electrons due to its stable configuration.

Q.33 First member of each group of representative elements (*i.e.*, *s* and *p*-block elements) shows anomalous behaviour. Illustrate with two examples.

Ans. First member of each group of *s*- and *p*-block shows anomalous behaviour due to (i) **small size** (ii) **high ionisation enthalpy** (iii) **high electronegativity** and (iv) **absence of *d*- orbitals.** *e.g.*, in *s*-block elements, lithium shows anomalous behaviour from rest of the alkali metals.

(a) Compounds of lithium have significant covalent character while compounds of other alkali metals are ionic.

(b) Lithium reacts with nitrogen to form lithium nitride while other alkali metals do not form nitrides.

In *p*-block elements, first member of each group has four orbitals, one 2*s*- orbital and three 2*p*-orbitals in their valence shell. So, these elements show a maximum covalency of four while other members of the same group or different group show a maximum covalency beyond four due to availability of vacant *d*- orbitals.

Q.34 **p-block elements form acidic, basic and amphoteric oxides. Explain each property by giving two examples and also write the reactions of these oxides with water.**

Ans. In *p*-block, when we move from left to right in a period, the acidic character of the oxides increases due to increase in electronegativity. *e.g.*,

(i) **2nd period** $B_2O_3 < CO_2 < N_2O_3$ acidic nature increases.

(ii) **3rd period** $Al_2O_3 < SiO_2 < P_4O_{10} < SO_3 < Cl_2O_7$ acidic nature increases.

On moving down the group, acidic nature decreases and basic nature increases. *e.g.*,

(a) **Nature of oxides of 13 group elements**

B_2O_3	Al_2O_3	Ga_2O_3	In_2O_3	Tl_2O
Weakly acidic	Amphoteric		Basic	Strongly basic

(b) **Nature of oxides of 15 group elements**

N_2O_5	P_4O_{10}	As_4O_{10}	Sb_4O_{10}	Bi_2O_3
Strongly acidic	Moderately acidic	Amphoteric	Amphoteric	Basic

Among the oxides of same element, higher the oxidation state of the element, stronger is the acid. *e.g.*, **SO_3 is a stronger acid than SO_2.**

B_2O_3 is weakly acidic and on dissolution in water, it forms **orthoboric acid.** Orthoboric acid does not act as a protonic acid (it does not ionise) but acts as a weak Lewis acid.

$$\underset{\text{Boron trioxide}}{B_2O_3} + 3H_2O \rightleftharpoons \underset{\text{Orthoboric acid}}{2H_3BO_3}$$

$$B(OH)_3 + H—OH \longrightarrow [B(OH)_4]^- + H^+$$

P_4O_{10} is moderately acidic and on reaction with water gives **orthophosphoric acid.**

$$\underset{\text{Phosphorus pentaoxide}}{P_4O_{10}} + 6H_2O \longrightarrow \underset{\text{Orthophosphric acid}}{4H_3PO_4}$$

Al_2O_3 is amphoteric in nature. It is insoluble in water but dissolves in alkalies and reacts with acids.

$$\underset{\text{Aluminium trioxide}}{Al_2O_3} + 2NaOH \xrightarrow{\Delta} \underset{\text{Sodium meta aluminate}}{2NaAlO_2} + H_2O$$

$$Al_2O_3 + 6HCl \xrightarrow{\Delta} \underset{\text{Aluminium chloride}}{2AlCl_3} + 3H_2O$$

Similarly, PbO_2 is also amphoteric in nature. It dissolves in alkalies and reacts with acids.

$$\underset{\text{Lead oxide}}{PbO_2} + 2NaOH \longrightarrow \underset{\text{Sodium plumbate}}{Na_2PbO_3} + H_2O$$

$$PbO_2 + 4HCl \longrightarrow \underset{\text{Lead chloride}}{PbCl_2} + Cl_2 + 2H_2O$$

Tl_2O is as basic as NaOH due to its lower oxidation state (+1).

$$Tl_2O + 2HCl \longrightarrow 2TlCl + H_2O$$

Bi_2O_3 is basic in nature and its reaction with water is as follows :

$$\underset{\text{Bismuth (III) oxide}}{Bi_2O_3} + 3H_2O \longrightarrow \underset{\text{Bismuth hydroxide}}{2Bi(OH)_3}$$

Cl_2O_7 is strongly acidic in nature and on dissolution in water, it gives **perchloric acid.**

$$\underset{\text{Dichlorine heptoxide}}{Cl_2O_7} + H_2O \longrightarrow \underset{\text{Perchloric acid}}{2HClO_4}$$

Q.35 How would you explain the fact that the first ionisation enthalpy of sodium is lower than that of magnesium but its second ionisation enthalpy is higher than that of magnesium?

Thinking Process The species having exactly half-filled or fully filled orbitals have exceptionally high ionisation enthalpies.

Ans. First ionisation enthalpy of sodium ($Na = 1s^2\ 2s^2\ 2p^6\ 3s^1$) is lower than that of magnesium ($Mg = 1s^2\ 2s^2\ 2p^6\ 3s^2$) because sodium has half filled s – subshell while magnesium has more stable full filled s-orbital. Thus, IE_1 first ionisation enthalpy) sodium is lower than magnesium as lesser energy is required to remove electron from $3s^1$ configuration.

After the removal of first electron Na^+ acquires inert gas (Ne) configuration ($Na^+ = 1s^2\ 2s^2\ 2p^6$) and hence, removal of second electron from sodium is difficult.

While in case of magnesium, after the removal of first electron, the electronic configuration of Mg^+ is $1s^2\ 2s^2\ 2p^6\ 3s^1$. In this case $3s^1$ electron is easy to remove in comparison to remove an electron from inert gas configuration. Therefore, IE_2 (second ionisation enthalpy) of Na is higher than that of magnesium.

Q.36 What do you understand by exothermic reaction and endothermic reaction? Give one example of each type.

Ans. **Exothermic reactions** Reactions in which energy is released are called exothermic reactions. *e.g.,*

$$C(s) + O_2(g) \longrightarrow CO_2(g) + 393.5\ \text{kJ}$$
$$H_2(g) + \frac{1}{2}O_2(g) \longrightarrow H_2O\ (l)\ ; \Delta H = -285.8\ \text{kJ mol}^{-1}$$

Endothermic reactions Reactions in which heat energy is absorbed are called endothermic reactions, *e.g.*

$$C(s) + H_2O(g) \longrightarrow CO\ (g) + H_2(g) - 131.4\ \text{kJ}$$
$$N_2(g) + 3H_2(g) \longrightarrow 2NH_3\ (g)\ ; \Delta H = +92.4\ \text{kJ mol}^{-1}$$

Q.37 Arrange the elements N, P, O and S in the order of

(i) increasing first ionisation enthalpy.
(ii) increasing non-metallic character.

Give reason for the arrangement assigned.

Ans. The placing of elements are as :

Period	Group 15	Group 16
2nd period	N	O
3rd period	P	S

(i) Ionisation enthalpy of nitrogen ($_7N = 1s^2\ 2s^2\ 2p^3$) is greater than oxygen ($_8O = 1s^2\ 2s^2\ 2p^4$) due to extra stable half-filled 2*p*-orbitals in nitrogen. Similarly, ionisation enthalpy of phosphorus ($_{15}P = 1s^2\ 2s^2\ 2p^6\ 3s^2\ 3p^3$) is greater than sulphur ($_{16}S = 1s^2\ 2s^2\ 2p^6\ 3s^2\ 3p^4$).

On moving down the group, ionisation enthalpy decreases with increasing atomic size. So, the order is

$$S < P < O < N \rightarrow \text{First ionisation enthalpy increases.}$$

(ii) Non-metallic character across a period (left to right) increases but on moving down the group it decreases. So, the order is

$$P < S < N < O \rightarrow \text{Non-metallic character increases.}$$

Q.38 Explain the deviation in ionisation enthalpy of some elements from the general trend by using given figure.

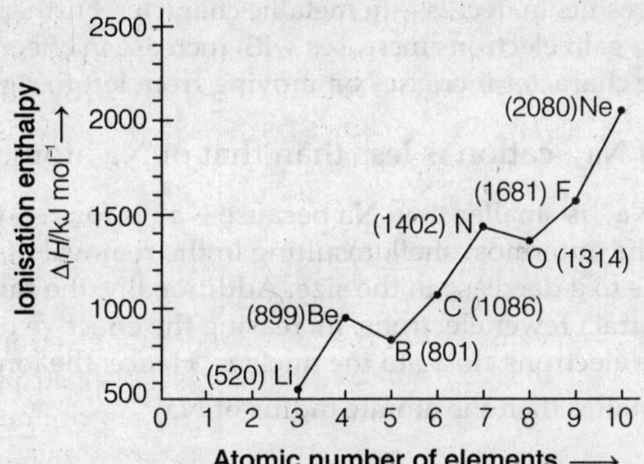

Ans. There is deviation of ionisation enthalpy of some elements from the general trend as shown in figure. The first ionisation enthalpy of B is lower than that of Be and in case of nitrogen, the first ionisation enthalpy is higher than that of O. (Also, refer to Q. 27)

Q.39 Explain the following

(a) Electronegativity of elements increase on moving from left to right in the periodic table.

(b) Ionisation enthalpy decrease in a group from top to bottom.

Ans. (a) Across the period, the nuclear charge increases and the atomic radius decreases. As a result, the tendency of the atom of an element to attract the shared pair of electrons towards itself increases and hence the electronegativity of the element increases. *e.g.*, electronegativity of the elements of the 2nd period increases regularly from left to right as follows

Li (1.0), Be (1.5), B (2.0) , C (2.5), N (3.0), O (3.5) and F (4.0).

(b) The ionisation enthalpy decreases regularly as we move from top to bottom, as explained below

(i) On moving down the group, the atomic size increases gradually due to the addition of a new shell at each succeeding element. As a result, the distance between the nucleus and the valence shell increases.

In other words, the force of attraction of the nucleus for the valence electrons decreases and hence the ionisation enthalpy should decrease.

(ii) With the addition of new shells, the number of inner shells which shield the valence electrons from the nucleus increases. Thus, the shielding or screening effect increases. Therefore, nuclear attraction on the valence electrons decreases and hence, the ionisation enthalpy should decrease. The combined effect of the increase in atomic size and screening effect more than compensate the effect of the increased nuclear charge. Consequently, the valence electrons are weakly held by the nucleus and hence, the ionisation enthalpy gradually decreases as we move down the group.

Q.40 How does the metallic and non-metallic character vary on moving from left to right in a period?

Ans. As we move from left to right in a period, the number of valence electrons increases by one at each succeeding element but the number of shells remain the same. As a result, atomic radius decreases. Hence, the tendency of the element to lose electrons decreases, this results in decrease in metallic character. Further more, the tendency of an element to gain electrons increases with increase in effective nuclear charge, so non-metallic character increases on moving from left to right in a period.

Q.41 The radius of Na^+ cation is less than that of Na atom. Give reason.

Ans. The radius of Na^+ is smaller than Na because Na^+ is formed by the loss of one electron from the outermost shell, resulting in the removal of the entire third shell. This leads to a decrease in the size. Additionally, the same number of protons now attract fewer electrons, increasing the effective nuclear charge, which pulls the electrons closer to the nucleus. Hence, the ionic radius of Na^+ is significantly smaller than the atomic radius of Na.

Q.42 Among alkali metals which element do you expect to be least electronegative and why?

Ans. On moving down the group, electronegativity decreases because atomic size increases. Fr has the largest size, therefore it is least electronegative.

Matching The Columns

Q.43 Match the correct atomic radius with the element.

Element	Atomic radius (pm)
Be	74
C	88
O	111
B	77
N	66

- **Concept Insight**

(i) All the elements given in the question belong to the second period of the periodic table.

(ii) Atomic radius is the distance from the centre of the nucleus to the point upto which the density of the electron cloud (i.e., probability of finding the electron) is maximum.

Ans. All the given elements are of same period and along a period, atomic radii decreases because effective nuclear charge increases. Thus, the order of atomic radii is $O < N < C < B < Be$ or, Be = 111 pm, C = 77 pm, O = 66 pm, B = 88 pm, N = 74 pm.

Q.44 Match the correct ionisation enthalpies and electron gain enthalpies of the following elements.

	Elements		ΔH_1	ΔH_2	$\Delta_{eg} H$
(i)	Most reactive non-metal	A.	419	3051	– 48
(ii)	Most reactive metal	B.	1681	3374	– 328
(iii)	Least reactive element	C.	738	1451	– 40
(iv)	Metal forming binary halide	D.	2372	5251	+ 48

Ans. (i) Most reactive non-metal has high $\Delta_i H_1$ and $\Delta_i H_2$ and most negative $\Delta_{eg} H$. Therefore, the element is B.

(ii) Most reactive metal has low $\Delta_i H_1$ and high $\Delta_i H_2$ (because the second electron has to be lost from noble gas configuration) and has small negative $\Delta_{eg} H$. Therefore, the element is A.

(iii) Noble gases are the least reactive elements. They have very high $\Delta_i H_1$ and $\Delta_i H_2$ and have positive $\Delta_{eg} H$ values. Thus, the element is D.

(iv) Metal forming binary halides are alkaline earth metals. They have $\Delta_i H_1$ and $\Delta_i H_2$ values little higher than those of most reactive metals (such as A) and have comparatively slightly less negative $\Delta_{eg} H$ values. Thus, the element is C.

Q.45 Electronic configuration of some elements is given in Column I and their electron gain enthalpies are given in Column II. Match the electronic configuration with electron gain enthalpy.

	Column I (Electronic configuration)	Column II (Electron gain enthalpy/ kJ mol^{-1})
A.	$1s^2\ 2s^2\ 2p^6$	– 53
B.	$1s^2\ 2s^2\ 2p^6\ 3s^1$	– 328
C.	$1s^2\ 2s^2\ 2p^5$	– 141
D.	$1s^2\ 2s^2\ 2p^4$	+ 48

Ans. A. → (4) B. → (1) C. → (2) D. → (3)

A. This electronic configuration corresponds to the noble gas, *i.e.*, neon. Since, noble gases have positive $\Delta_{eg} H$ values, therefore, electronic configuration (A) corresponds to the $\Delta_{eg} H = +48$ kJ mol^{-1}.

B. This electronic configuration corresponds to the alkali metal, *i.e.*, potassium. Alkali metals have small negative $\Delta_{eg} H$ values, hence, electronic configuration (B) corresponds to $\Delta_{eg} H = -53$ kJ mol^{-1}.

C. This electronic configuration corresponds to the halogen, *i.e.*, fluorine. Since, halogens have high negative $\Delta_{eg} H$ values, therefore, electronic configuration (C) corresponds to $\Delta_{eg} H = -328$ kJ mol^{-1}.

D. This electronic configuration corresponds to the chalcogen *i.e.*, oxygen. Since, chalcogens have $\Delta_{eg} H$ values less negative than those of halogens, therefore, electronic configuration (D) corresponds to $\Delta_{eg} H = -141$ kJ mol^{-1}.

Assertion and Reason

In the following questions a statement of Assertion (A) followed by a statement of Reason (R) is given. Choose the correct option out of the choices given below in each question.

Q.46 **Assertion** (A) Generally, ionisation enthalpy increases from left to right in a period.

Reason (R) When successive electrons are added to the orbitals in the same principal quantum level, the shielding effect of inner core of electrons does not increase very much to compensate for the increased attraction of the electron to the nucleus.

(a) Assertion is correct statement and reason is wrong statement.
(b) Assertion and reason both are correct statements and reason is correct explanation of Assertion.
(c) Assertion and reason both are wrong statements.
(d) Assertion is wrong statement and reason is correct statement.

Ans. *(b)* Assertion and reason both are correct statements and reason is correct explanation of assertion. Ionisation enthalpy increases along a period because effective nuclear charge increases and atomic size decreases.

Q.47 **Assertion** (A) Boron has a smaller first ionisation enthalpy than Beryllium.

Reason (R) The penetration of 2*s* electron to the nucleus is more than the 2*p* electron hence 2*p* electron is more shielded by the inner core of electrons than the 2*s* electrons.

(a) Assertion and reason both are correct statements but reason is not correct explanation for assertion.
(b) Assertion is correct statement but reason is wrong statement.
(c) Assertion and reason both are correct statements and reason is correct explanation for Assertion.
(d) Assertion and reason both are wrong statements.

Ans. *(c)* Assertion and reason both are correct statements and reason is correct explanation for assertion.
Boron has a smaller first ionisation enthalpy than beryllium because the penetration of a 2*s* electron to the nucleus is more than the 2*p* electron. Hence, 2*p* electron is more shielded by the inner core of electron than the 2*s* electron.

Q.48 **Assertion** (A) Electron gain enthalpy becomes less negative as we go down a group.

Reason (R) Size of the atom increases on going down the group and the added electron would be farther from the nucleus.

(a) Assertion and reason both are correct statements but reason is not correct explanation for assertion.
(b) Assertion and reason both are correct statements and reason is correct explanation for assertion.
(c) Assertion and reason both are wrong statements.
(d) Assertion is wrong statement but reason is correct statement.

Ans. *(b)* Assertion and reason both are correct statements and reason is correct explanation for assertion.

Electron gain enthalpy becomes less negative as the size of an atom increases down the group. This is because within a group, screening effect increases on going downward and the added electron would be farther away from the nucleus.

Long Answer Type Questions

Q.49 Discuss the factors affecting electron gain enthalpy and the trend in its variation in the periodic table.

- **Concept Insight** Electron gain enthalpy of an element is the energy change when an electron is added to valence shell of an isolated gaseous atom.

$$A(g) + e^- \longrightarrow A^-(g);\ \Delta_{eg} H = \text{negative}$$

Ans. Factors affecting electron gain enthalpy

(i) **Effective nuclear charge** With increase in nuclear charge, force of attraction between nucleus and incoming electron increases, so value of electron gain enthalpy increases *i.e.,* become more –ve.

(ii) **Atomic size** As atomic size increases, distance between nucleus and incoming electron increases, so electron is weakly attracted by nucleus and hence, electron gain enthalpy decreases.

(iii) **Type of subshell** More closer is the subshell to the nucleus, easier is the addition of electron in that subshell.

Electron gain enthalpy (in decreasing order) for addition of electron in different subshell (for same value of 'n') is $s > p > d > f$.

(iv) **Nature of configuration** Half-filled and completely-filled subshell are stable configurations, so addition of electron in them is not energetically favourable.

(v) **Variation in the periodic table** As a general rule, electron gain enthalpy becomes more and more negative across a period. The effective nuclear charge increases from left to right across a period and consequently, it will be easier to add an electron to a smaller atom.

Electron gain enthalpy becomes less negative down a group because the size of the atom increases and the added electron would be farther from the nucleus.

Q.50 Define ionisation enthalpy. Discuss the factors affecting ionisation enthalpy of the elements and its trends in the periodic table.

Ans. Ionisation enthalpy The minimum amount of energy required to remove the most loosely bound electron from an isolated gaseous atom is called its ionisation enthalpy. It is represented by $\Delta_i H$.

Factors affecting ionisation enthalpy of the elements

Ionisation enthalpy depends upon the following factors :

(i) **Nuclear charge** The ionisation enthalpy increases with increase in nuclear charge. This is because, with increase in nuclear charge, the electrons of the outer shell are more firmly held by the nucleus and thus greater energy is required to pull out an electron from the atom.

e.g., the ionisation enthalpy increases, as we move along a period from left t right due to increased nuclear charge.

$$\text{Li} < \text{Be} > \text{B} < \text{C} < \text{N} > \text{O} < \text{F} < \text{Ne}$$

(ii) **Atomic size or radius** Ionisation enthalpy decreases as the atomic siz increases. As the distance of the outer electrons from the nucleus increases, th attractive force on the outer electron decreases.

Hence, lesser amount of energy is required to lose the electrons *e.g.*, Ionisatio enthalpy is found to decrease on moving down a group.

$$\text{Li} > \text{Na} > \text{K} > \text{Rb} > \text{Cs}.$$

(iii) **Penetration effect of the electrons** Ionisation enthalpy increases as th penetration effect of the electrons increases.

We know that, *s*-electrons of any shell are more penetrating towards th nucleus than *p*-electrons of the same shell. Thus, within the same shell, th penetration effect decreases in the order *s*>*p*>*d*>*f*. Now, more is the penetratio of orbital, higher will be the ionisation energy. *e.g.*, First ionisation enthalpy c aluminium is lower than that of magnesium. This is due to the fact that in cas of aluminium ($1s^2 2s^2 2p^6 3s^2 3p_x^1$), we have to pull out a *p*-electron to form Al ion whereas in case of magnesium ($1s^2, 2s^2 2p^6, 3s^2$), we have to remove a *s*-electron of the same energy shell to produce Mg^+ ion.

(iv) **Shielding *or* screening effect of inner shell electrons** As the shielding or th screening effect of the inner electrons increases, the force of attraction by th nucleus for the valence shell electrons decreases and hence the ionisatio enthalpy decreases.

(v) **Effect of arrangement of electrons** Half filled or completely filled orbitals ha extra stability. Therefore, the removal of an electron from such an ator requires more energy than expected.

e.g., Be ($1s^2 2s^2$) has higher ionisation enthalpy than B($1s^2 2s^2 2p^1$) an N($1s^2 2s^2 2p_x^3$) has higher ionisation enthalpy than O($1s^2 2s^2 2p_x^4$). In general, a we move from left to right in a period, the ionisation enthalpy increases wit increasing atomic numbers. The ionisation enthalpies keep on decreasin regularly as we move down a group from one element to the other.

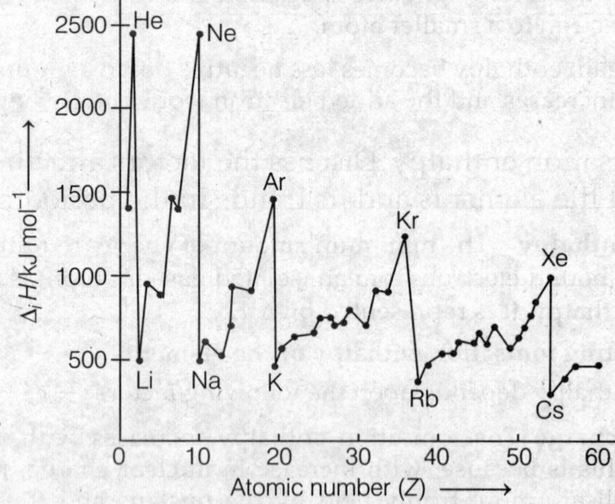

Variation of first ionisation enthalpies ($\Delta_i H$) with atomic number for elements with $Z = 1$ to 60

Q.51 **Justify the given statement with suitable examples–"the properties of the elements are a periodic function of their atomic numbers".**

Ans. The cause of periodicity in properties is the repetition of similar outer electronic configurations after certain regular intervals. *e.g.*, all the elements of 1st group (alkali metals) have similar outer electronic configuration, *i.e.*, ns^1.

$$Li \rightarrow [He]\ 2s^1$$
$$Na \rightarrow [Ne]\ 3s^1$$
$$K \rightarrow [Ar]\ 4s^1$$
$$Rb \rightarrow [Kr]\ 5s^1$$
$$Cs \rightarrow [Xe]\ 6s^1$$
$$Fr \rightarrow [Rn] 7s^1$$

Therefore, due to similar outermost shell electronic configuration, all alkali metals have similar properties.

Similarly, all the elements of 17th group (halogens) have similar outermost shell electronic configuration, *i.e.*, ns^2np^5 and thus possess similar properties.

$${}_{9}F = [He]\ 2s^2 2p^5$$
$${}_{17}Cl = [Ne]\ 3s^2 3p^5$$
$${}_{35}Br = [Ar]\ 3d^{10} 4s^2 4p^5$$
$${}_{53}I = [Kr]\ 4d^{10} 5s^2 5p^5$$
$${}_{85}At = [Xe]\ 5d^{10} 6s^2 6p^5$$

Q.52 **Write down the outermost electronic configurations of alkali metals. How will you justify their placement in group 1 of the periodic table?**

Ans. All the elements of group IA (or I), *i.e.*, alkali metals have the similar outer electronic configuration, *i.e.*, ns^1 where n refers to the number of principal shell. These electronic configurations are given below :

Symbol	Atomic number	Electronic configuration
Li	3	$[He]\ 2s^1$
Na	11	$[Ne]\ 3s^1$
K	19	$[Ar]\ 4s^1$
Rb	37	$[Kr]\ 5s^1$
Cs	55	$[Xe]\ 6d^1$
Fr	87	$[Rn]\ 7s^1$.

Hence, placement of all these elements in group 1 of the periodic table because of similarity in electronic configuration and all the elements have similar properties.

Q.53 **Write the drawbacks in Mendeleev's periodic table that led to its modification.**

Ans. The main drawbacks of Mendeleev's periodic table are :

(i) Some elements having similar properties were placed in different groups whereas some elements having dissimilar properties were placed in the same group.

e.g., alkali metals such as Li, Na, K, etc., (IA group) are grouped together with coinage metals such as Cu, Ag, Au (IB group) though their properties are quite different. Chemically similar elements such as Cu(IB group) and Hg (IIB group) have been placed in different groups.

(ii) Some elements with higher atomic weights are placed before the elements with lower atomic weights in order to maintain the similar chemical nature of elements.

i.e., $^{39.9}_{18}$Ar and $^{39.1}_{19}$K; $^{58.9}_{27}$Co and $^{58.7}_{28}$Ni, etc.

(iii) Isotopes did not find any place in the periodic table. However, according to Mendeleev's classification, these should be placed at different places in the periodic table.

(All the above three defects were however removed when modern periodic law based on atomic number was given).

(iv) Position of hydrogen in the periodic table is not fixed but is controversial.

(v) Position of elements of group VIII could not be made clear which have been arranged in three triads without any justification.

(vi) It could not explain the even and odd series in IV, V and VI long periods.

(vii) Lanthanides and actinides which were discovered later on have not been given proper positions in the main frame of periodic table.

Q.54 In what manner is the long from of periodic table better than Mendeleev's periodic table? Explain with examples.

Ans. The long form of the periodic table is better than Mendeleev's periodic table because it classifies the elements on the basis of electronic configurations of their atoms.

The characteristics of this table are :

(i) The table consists of 9 vertical columns, called the **groups** and 7 horizontal rows, called the **periods.**

(ii) The groups are marked 0 to VIII out of which group I to VII are subdivided into subgroups A and B.

(iii) The group IA elements (Li, Na, K, Rb, Cs and Fr) are known as **alkali metals** and the group IIA elements (Be, Mg, Ca, Sr, Ba and Ra) are known as **alkaline earth metals.** Elements in group VIII A (F, Cl, Br, I and At) are called **halogens** and elements in group VIII (He, Ne, Ar, Kr, Xe and Rn) are called **noble gases** or rare gases.

(iv) The group VIII has three similar elements placed together in one place. These are called **transition triads,** *e.g.*, Fe, Co and Ni; Ru, Rh and Pd; Os, Ir and Pt etc.

(v) In the 6th and 7th period, 14 elements present called as **lanthanides** and **actinides** respectively.

(vi) Based on their electronic configuration, elements have been grouped into *s*-, *p*-, *d*- and *f*-blocks. This has helped us to understand their properties more easily.

(vii) There is gradual change in properties seen from one end to the other.

Q.55 Discuss and compare the trend in ionisation enthalpy of the elements of group 1 with those of group 17 elements.

Ans. The ionisation enthalpies decrease regularly as we move down a group from one element to the other. The first ionisation enthalpies of the elements of group 1 (alkali metals) and group 17 elements as given in table.

Group 1	First ionisation enthalpies (kJ mol^{-1})	Group 17	First ionisation enthalpies (kJ mol^{-1})
H	1312	F	1681
Li	520	Cl	1255
Na	496	Br	1142
K	419	I	1009
Rb	403	At	917
Cs	374		

Given trend can be easily explained on the basis of increasing atomic size and screening effect as follows :

(i) On moving down the group, the atomic size increases gradually due to the addition of one new energy shell at each succeeding element. Hence, the distance of the valence electrons from the nucleus increases.

Consequently, the force of attraction by the nucleus for the valence electrons decreases and hence the ionisation enthalpy should decrease.

(ii) With the addition of new shells, the shielding or the screening effect increases. As a result, the force of attraction of the nucleus for the valence electrons further decreases and hence the ionisation enthalpy should decrease.

(iii) Nuclear charge increases with increase in atomic number. So, force of attraction by the nucleus for the valence electrons should increase and accordingly the ionisation enthalpy should increase.

The combined effect of the increase in the atomic size and the screening effect is more and compensates the effect of the increased nuclear charges. Consequently, the valence electrons become less and less firmly held by the nucleus and hence, the ionisation enthalpies gradually decrease as move down the group.

Chapter

04 Chemical Bonding and Molecular Structure

Multiple Choice Questions (MCQs)

Q.1 Isostructural species are those which have the same shape and hybridisation. Among the given species identify the isostructural pairs.

(a) [NF_3 and BF_3]
(b) [BF_4^- and NH_4^+]
(c) [BCl_3 and $BrCl_3$]
(d) [NH_3 and NO_3^-]

Ans. ***(b)*** (a) NF_3 is pyramidal whereas BF_3 is trigonal planar.

(b) BF_4^- and NH_4^+ ion both are tetrahedral and 'B' and 'N' are sp^3-hybridised.

(c) BCl_3 is trigonal planar whereas $BrCl_3$ is *T* shaped.

(d) NH_3 is pyramidal whereas NO_3^- is trigonal planar.

Thus, BF_4^- and NH_4^+ are isostructural pairs and hence, option (b) is correct.

Q.2 Polarity in a molecule and hence the dipole moment depends primarily on electronegativity of the constituent atoms and shape of a molecule. Which of the following has the highest dipole moment?

(a) CO_2
(b) HI
(c) H_2O
(d) SO_2

Ans. ***(c)*** H_2O is bent shaped with bond angle of 104.5° and electronegativity difference between H and O is quiet high, so H_2O has highest dipole moment. CO_2 is linear and dipole moment of one C—O bond is equal and opposite to other bond. Therefore, dipole moment of CO_2 is zero.

SO_2 and HI have less electronegativity difference between the bonded atoms so these have low dipole moment. The structures of CO_2, HI, H_2O and SO_2 are as follows.

O=C=O $\mu = 0D$

H⇌I $\mu = 0.38D$

H_2O (bent) $\mu = 1.84$ D

SO_2 (bent) $\mu = 1.62$ D

Q.3 The types of hybrid orbitals of nitrogen in NO_2^+, NO_3^- and NH_4^+ respectively are expected to be

(a) *sp*, sp^3 and sp^2
(b) *sp*, sp^2 and sp^3
(c) sp^2, *sp* and sp^3
(d) sp^2, sp^3 and *sp*

Ans. ***(b)*** The type of hybrid orbitals of nitrogen can be decided by using **VSEPR theory** as

$$H = \frac{1}{2}[V + X - C + A]$$

where, V = number of valence electrons in central atom
X = number of monovalent atoms around the central atoms
C = positive charge on the cation
A = negative charge on the anion

NO_2^+, $H = \frac{1}{2}[5 + 0 - 1 + 0] = 2$ so sp

NO_3^-, $H = \frac{1}{2}[5 + 0 - 0 + 1] = 3$ so sp^2

NH_4^+, $H = \frac{1}{2}[5 + 4 - 1 + 0] = 4$ so sp^3

Alternate Method Hybrid orbitals can also be decided by counting bp and lp as

$NO_2^+ = 2bp + 0lp$ = linear = sp hybridised
$NO_3^- = 3bp + 0lp = sp^2$ hybridised
$NH_4^+ = 4bp + 0lp = sp^3$ hybridised

Q.4 Hydrogen bonds are formed in many compounds *e.g.*, H_2O, HF, NH_3. The boiling point of such compounds depends to a large extent on the strength of hydrogen bond and the number of hydrogen bonds. The correct decreasing order of the boiling points of above compounds is :

(a) $HF > H_2O > NH_3$ (b) $H_2O > HF > NH_3$
(c) $NH_3 > HF > H_2O$ (d) $NH_3 > H_2O > HF$

● **Concept Insight** Strength of H-bonding depends on the electronegativity of the atom which follows order H....F > H.....O > H.....N.

Ans. ***(b)*** Strength of H-bonds is in the order H....F > H.....O > H.....N.

But each H_2O molecule is linked to four other H_2O molecules through H-bonds whereas each HF molecule is linked only to two other HF molecules.

Hence, b.p of H_2O > b.p of HF > b.p. of NH_3

Q.5 In PO_4^{3-} ion the formal charge on the oxygen atom of P—O bond is

(a) + 1 (b) – 1 (c) – 0.75 (d) + 0.75

Ans. ***(b)*** The structure of PO_4^{3-} ion is,

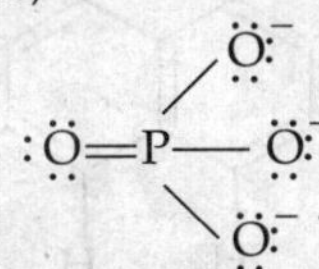

Formal charge on each oxygen atom of P—O bond = No. of valence electrons on oxygen – (No. of unshared electron) $-\frac{1}{2}$ (No. of shared electron)

$$= 6 - 6 - \left(\frac{1}{2} \times 2\right) = -1$$

Q.6 In NO_3^- ion, the number of bond pairs and lone pairs of electrons on nitrogen atom are

(a) 2, 2 (b) 3, 1 (c) 1, 3 (d) 4, 0

Thinking Process To solve this question, we must know the structure of NO_3^- ion, *i.e.*,

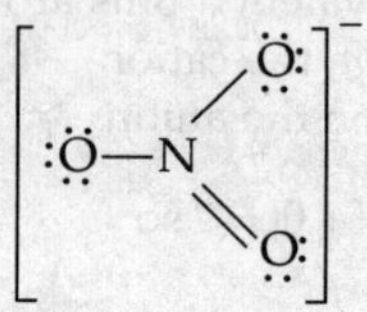

$$\left[:\ddot{O}-N \begin{matrix} \diagup \ddot{O}: \\ \diagdown\!\!\diagdown \ddot{O}: \end{matrix} \right]^-$$

Then, count the bond pairs and lone pairs of electron on nitrogen.

Ans. ***(d)*** On nitrogen atom of NO_3^-,

$\therefore$ Number of bond pairs (or shared pairs) = 4

Number of lone pairs = 0

Q.7 Which of the following species has tetrahedral geometry?

(a) BH_4^- (b) NH_2^- (c) CO_3^{2-} (d) H_3O^+

Ans. ***(a)*** $BH_4^- \Rightarrow$ 4 bond pairs + 0 lone pair $\Rightarrow sp^3$ hybridised = tetrahedral geometry

NH_2^- = 2 bond pairs + 2 lone pairs = bent shape

CO_3^{2-} = 3 bond pairs = trigonal planar

H_3O^+ = 3 bond pairs + 1 lone pair = trigonal pyramidal

Thus, option (a) is correct.

Q.8 Number of π bonds and σ bonds in the following structure is

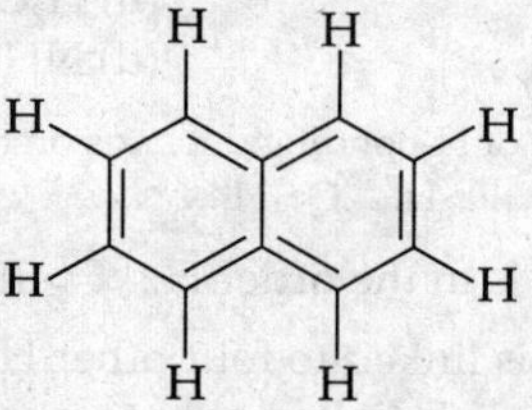

Biphenyl

(a) 6, 19 (b) 4, 20 (c) 5, 19 (d) 5, 20

Ans. ***(c)*** The given compound will have the correct structure as

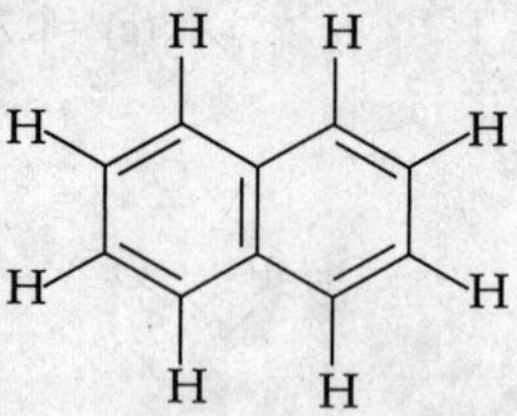

There are 5 π-bonds and 8 C — H + 11C — C σ-bonds, *i.e.*, 19 σ-bonds are present in the above molecule.

Q.9 Which molecule/ion out of the following does not contain unpaired electrons?

(a) N_2^+ (b) O_2 (c) O_2^{2-} (d) B_2

Ans. ***(c)*** The electronic configuration of the given molecules are

$N_2^+ = \sigma 1s^2, \sigma^* 1s^2, \sigma 2s^2, \sigma^* 2s^2, \pi 2p_x^2 = \pi 2p_y^2, \sigma 2p_z^1$

It has one unpaired electron.

$O_2 = \sigma 1s^2, \sigma^* 1s^2, \sigma 2s^2, \sigma^* 2s^2, \sigma 2p_z^2, \pi 2p_x^2 \approx \pi 2p_y^2, \pi^* 2p_x^1 \approx \pi^* 2p_y^1$

O_2 has two unpaired electrons.

$O_2^{2-} = \sigma 1s^2, \sigma^* 1s^2, \sigma 2s^2, \sigma^* 2s^2, \sigma 2p_z^2, \pi 2p_x^2 \approx \pi 2p_y^2, \pi^* 2p_x^2 \approx \pi^* 2p_y^2$

Thus, O_2^{2-} has no unpaired electrons.

$B_2 = \sigma 1s^2, \sigma^* 1s^2, \sigma 2s^2, \sigma^* 2s^2, \pi 2p_x^1 \approx \pi_2 p_y^1$

Thus, B_2 has two unpaired electrons.

Hence, the option (c) is correct.

Mistake Alert ! *Students may misunderstand the relative energy levels of molecular orbitals, particularly in diatomic molecules.*

Q.10 In which of the following molecule/ion all the bonds are not equal?

(a) XeF_4 (b) BF_4^-
(c) C_2H_4 (d) SiF_4

Thinking Process Bond length of double bond is smaller than single bond.

Ans. ***(c)*** $XeF_4 \Rightarrow 4\ bp + 2\ lp \Rightarrow$ square planar $\Rightarrow$ all bonds are equal

$BF_4^- \Rightarrow 4\ bp + 0\ lp \Rightarrow$ tetrahedral (all bonds are equal)

$C_2H_4 \Rightarrow H_2C{=}CH_2 \Rightarrow$ C=C bond is not equal to C—H bond

$SiF_4 \Rightarrow 4\ bp + 0\ lp \Rightarrow$ tetrahedral (all bonds are equal)

Thus, in C_2H_4 all the bonds are not equal.

Q.11 In which of the following substances will hydrogen bond be strongest?

(a) HCl (b) H_2O
(c) HI (d) H_2S

Ans. ***(b)*** HCl, HI and H_2S do not from H-bonds. Only H_2O forms hydrogen bonds. One H_2O molecule forms four H-bonding.

Q.12 If the electronic configuration of an element is $1s^2 2s^2 2p^6 3s^2 3p^6 3d^2 4s^2$, the four electrons involved in chemical bond formation will be

(a) $3p^6$ (b) $3p^6, 4s^2$ (c) $3p^6, 3d^2$ (d) $3d^2, 4s^2$

Ans. ***(d)*** The given electronic configuration shows that an element is vanadium (Z=22). It belongs to *d*-block of the periodic table. In transition elements, *i.e.*, *d*-block elements, electrons of ***ns*** **and** $(\boldsymbol{n-1})\,\boldsymbol{d}$ **subshell** take part in bond formation.

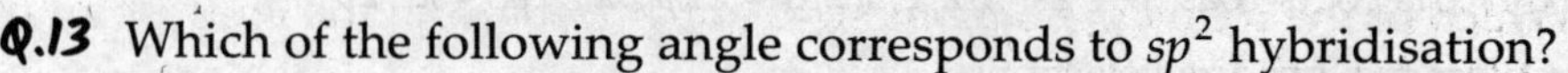

Q.13 Which of the following angle corresponds to sp^2 hybridisation?

(a) 90° (b) 120° (c) 180° (d) 109°

Ans. ***(b)*** For sp^2 hybridisation, the geometry is generally trigonal planar.

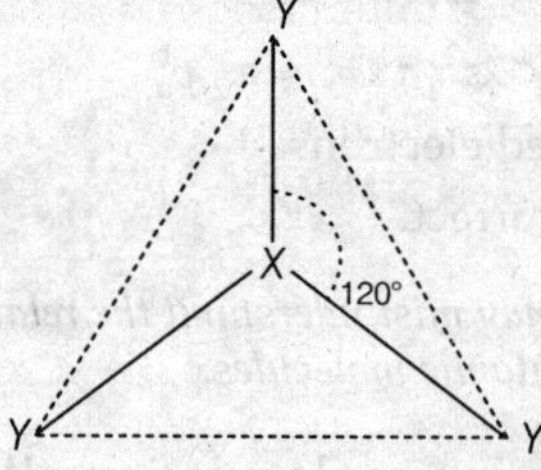

Thus, bond angle is 120°.

Direction (Q. No. 14-17) *The electronic configurations of the elements A, B and C are given below. Answer the questions from 14 to 17 on the basis of these configurations.*

A	$1s^2$	$2s^2$	$2p^6$		
B	$1s^2$	$2s^2$	$2p^6$	$3s^2$	$3p^3$
C	$1s^2$	$2s^2$	$2p^6$	$3s^2$	$3p^5$

Q.14 Stable form of *A* may be represented by the formula :

(a) *A* (b) A_2 (c) A_3 (d) A_4

Ans. ***(a)*** The given electronic configuration shows that *A* is a noble gas (*i.e.*, Ne) because the octet is complete. Thus, it exists as monoatomic.

Q.15 Stable form of C may be represented by the formula :

(a) C (b) C_2 (c) C_3 (d) C_4

Ans. ***(b)*** C requires 1 electron in its outermost shell to acquire stable configuration. Hence, it will share one electron will another C atom and form C_2.

Alternate Method The electronic configuration of C represent chlorine. Its stable form is dichlorine (Cl_2) *i.e.*, C_2.

Q.16 The molecular formula of the compound formed from *B* and *C* will be

(a) *BC* (b) B_2C (c) BC_2 (d) BC_3

Ans. ***(d)*** The electronic configuration show that *B* represents phosphorus and *C* represents chlorine. The stable compound formed is PCl_3, *i.e.*, BC_3.

Q.17 The bond between *B* and *C* will be

(a) ionic (b) covalent (c) hydrogen (d) coordinate

Ans. ***(b)*** Both '*B*' and '*C*' are non-metals, so they share electrons and make covalent bond.

Q.18 Which of the following order of energies of molecular orbitals of N_2 is correct?

(a) $(\pi 2p_y) < (\sigma 2p_z) < (\pi^* 2p_x) \approx (\pi^* 2p_y)$ (b) $(\pi 2p_y) > (\sigma 2p_z) > (\pi^* 2p_x) \approx (\pi^* 2p_y)$
(c) $(\pi 2p_y) < (\sigma 2p_z) > (\pi^* 2p_x) \approx (\pi^* 2p_y)$ (d) $(\pi 2p_y) > (\sigma 2p_z) < (\pi^* 2p_x) \approx (\pi^* 2p_y)$

Ans. ***(a)*** The correct increasing order of energies of molecular orbitals of N_2 is given below $\sigma 1s < \sigma^* 1s < \sigma 2s < \sigma^* 2s < (\pi 2p_x \approx \pi 2p_y) < \sigma 2p_z < (\pi^* 2p_x \simeq \pi^* 2p_y) < \sigma^* 2p_z$

Q.19 Which of the following statement is not correct from the view point of molecular orbital theory?

(a) Be_2 is not a stable molecule
(b) He_2 is not stable but He_2^+ is expected to exist.
(c) Bond strength of N_2 is maximum amongst the homonuclear diatomic molecules belonging to the second period.
(d) The order of energies of molecular orbitals in N_2 molecule is $\sigma 2s < \sigma^* 2s < \sigma 2p_z < (\pi 2p_x \approx \pi 2p_y) < (\pi^* 2p_x \approx \pi^* 2p_y) < \sigma^* 2p_z$

- **Concept Insight** Existence of molecules, bonding nature and energy order of molecular orbitals can be explained on the basis of molecular orbital theory as follows
  (i) Molecules having zero bond order never exists while molecules having non-zero bond order either exists or are expected to exist.
  (ii) Higher the value of bond order, higher will be its bond strength.
  Electrons present in bonding molecular orbital are known as **bonding electrons** (N_b) and electrons present in anti-bonding molecular orbital are known as **anti-bonding electrons** (N_a) and half of their difference is known as **bond order.**

Ans. ***(d)*** (a) Be_2 $(4 + 4 = 8) = \sigma 1s^2, \sigma^* 1s^2, \sigma 1s^2, \sigma^* 2s^2$

Bond order (BO) $= \frac{1}{2} = \frac{4-4}{2} = 0$

$[\because$ BO $= \frac{1}{2}$ Number of bonding electrons (N_b) – Number of anti-bonding electrons (N_a)]

Here, bond order of Be_2 is zero. Thus, it does not exist.

(b) He_2 $(2 + 2 = 4) = \sigma 1s^2, \sigma^* 1s^2$

$$BO = \frac{2-2}{2} = 0$$

Here, bond order of Be_2 is zero. Hence, it does not exist.

$$He_2^+ \ (2 + 2 - 1 = 3) = \sigma 1s^2, \sigma^* 1s^1$$

$$BO = \frac{2-1}{2} = 0.5$$

Since, the bond order is not zero, this molecule is expected to exist.

(c) N_2 $(7 + 7 = 14) = \sigma 1s^2, \sigma^* 1s^2, \sigma 2s^2, \sigma^* 2s^2, \pi 2p_x^2 \approx \pi 2p_y^2, \sigma 2p_z^2$

$$BO = \frac{10-4}{2} = 3$$

Thus, dinitrogen (N_2) molecule contain triple bond and no other molecule of second period have more than double bond. Hence, bond strength of N_2 is maximum amongst the homonuclear diatomic molecules belonging to the second period.

(d) It is incorrect. The correct order of energies of molecular orbitals in N_2 molecule is

$$\sigma 2s < \sigma^* 2s < (\pi 2p_x \simeq \pi 2p_y) < \sigma 2p_z < \pi^* 2p_x \approx \pi^* 2p_y < \sigma^* 2p_z$$

Q.20 Which of the following options represents the correct bond order?

(a) $O_2^- > O_2 > O_2^+$ (b) $O_2^- < O_2 < O_2^+$ (c) $O_2^- > O_2 < O_2^+$ (d) $O_2^- < O_2 > O_2^+$

Thinking Process To calculate bond order, write the molecular orbital configuration of particular species and afterwards using the formula.

Bond order $= \frac{1}{2}$ [Number of bonding electrons (N_b) – Number of anti-bonding electrons (N_a)].

Ans. ***(b)*** Electronic configuration of O_2 (16 electrons)

$$= \sigma 1s^2, \sigma^* 1s^2, \sigma 2s^2, \sigma^* 2s^2, \sigma 2p_z^2, \pi 2p_x^2 \approx \pi 2p_y^2, \pi^* 2p_x^1 \approx \pi^* 2p_y^1$$

Bond order $= \frac{1}{2}(N_b - N_a) = \frac{1}{2}(10 - 6) = 2$

Electronic configuration of O_2^+ (15 electrons)

$$= \sigma 1s^2, \sigma^* 1s^2, \sigma 2s^2, \sigma^* 2s^2, \sigma 2p_z^2, \pi 2p_x^2 \approx \pi 2p_y^2, \pi^* 2p_x^1 \approx \pi^* 2p_y^0$$

Bond order $= \frac{1}{2}(N_b - N_a) = \frac{1}{2}(10 - 5) = 2.5$

Electronic configuration of O_2^- (17 electrons)

$$= \sigma 1s^2, \sigma^* 1s^2, \sigma 2s^2, \sigma^* 2s^2, \sigma 2p_z^2, \pi 2p_x^2 \approx \pi 2p_y^2, \pi^* 2p_x^2 \approx \pi^* 2p_y^1$$

Bond order $= \frac{1}{2}(N_b - N_a) = \frac{1}{2}(10 - 7) = 1.5$

Thus, the order of bond order is $O_2^- < O_2 < O_2^+$

Q.21 The electronic configuration of the outer most shell of the most electronegative elements is

(a) $2s^2 2p^5$ (b) $3s^2 3p^5$

(c) $4s^2 4p^5$ (d) $5s^2 5p^5$

- **Concept Insight** Smaller the atom, more will be electronegativity.

Ans. ***(a)*** The given electronic configuration represents

$2s^2 2p^5$ = fluorine = most electronegative element

$3s^2 3p^5$ = chlorine

$4s^2 4p^5$ = bromine

$5s^2 5p^5$ = iodine

Q.22 Amongst the following elements whose electronic configuration are given below, the one having the highest ionisation enthaply is

(a) [Ne] $3s^2 3p^1$ (b) [Ne] $3s^2 3p^3$ (c) [Ne] $3s^2 3p^2$ (d) [Ar] $3d^{10} 4s^2 4p^3$

Ans. ***(b)*** The electronic configuration of options (b) and (d) have exactly half-filled *p*-orbitals. [Ne] $3s^2 3p^3$ represents phosphorus and [Ar] $3d^{10} 4s^2 4p^3$ represents arsenic but phosphorus is smaller in size than arsenic.

Hence, phosphorus *i.e.*, option (b) has highest ionisation enthalpy. Ionisation enthalpy increases from left to right in the periodic table as the size decreases. While, ionisation energy decreases from top to bottom in the group as the size increases.

Multiple Choice Questions (More Than One Options)

Q.23 Which of the following have identical bond order?

(a) CN^- (b) NO^+ (c) O_2^- (d) O_2^{2-}

Ans. ***(a, b)*** CN^- (number of electrons $= 6 + 7 + 1 = 14$)

NO^+ (number of electrons $= 7 + 8 - 1 = 14$)

O_2^- (number of electrons $= 8 + 8 + 1 = 17$)

O_2^{2-} (number of electrons $= 8 + 8 + 2 = 18$)

Thus, CN^- and NO^+ because of the presence of same number of electrons, have same bond order.

Q.24 Which of the following attain the linear structure?

(a) $BeCl_2$ (b) NCO^+
(c) NO_2 (d) CS_2

Ans. ***(a, d)*** $BeCl_2 (Cl - Be - Cl)$ and CS_2 $(S = C = S)$ both are linear. NCO^+ is non-linear. However, remember that ^-NCO $(^-N = C = O)$ is linear because it is isoelectronic with CO_2. NO_2 is angular with bond angle 132° and each O—N bond length of 1.20 Å (intermediate between single and double bond).

Q.25 CO is isoelectronic with

(a) NO^+ (b) N_2
(c) $SnCl_2$ (d) NO_2^-

Thinking Process Isoelectronic species are those species which have same number of electrons but different nuclear charge.

Ans. ***(a, b)*** Electrons present in CO $= 6 + 8 = 14$

Then, (a) $NO^+ = 7 + 8 - 1 = 14$

(b) $N_2 = 7 + 7 = 14$

(c) $SnCl_2 =$ (very high) $50 + 17 \times 2 = 50 + 34 = 84$

(d) $NO_2^- = 7 + 16 + 1 = 24$

Q.26 Which of the following species have the same shape?

(a) CO_2 (b) CCl_4 (c) O_3 (d) NO_2^-

Ans. ***(c, d)*** The shape of following species are

CO_2 = linear

CCl_4 = tetrahedral

O_3 = bent

NO_2^- = bent

Q.27 Which of the following statements are correct about CO_3^{2-}?

(a) The hybridisation of central atom is sp^3.
(b) Its resonance structure has one C—O single bond and two C=O double bonds.
(c) The average formal charge on each oxygen atom is 0.67 units.
(d) All C—O bond lengths are equal.

Ans. ***(c, d)*** The hybridisation of central atom in CO_3^{2-} is sp^2. Hence, option (a) is incorrect.

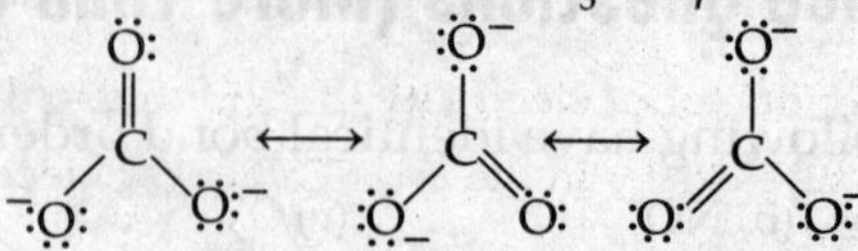

Its resonance structure has two C—O single bond, one C=O double bond. Hence, option (b) is incorrect.

$$\text{Formal charge on each O atom} = \frac{\text{Total charge}}{\text{Number of O atoms}} = \frac{-2}{3} = -0.67 \text{ units.}$$

Hence, option (c) is correct.

Due to resonance, all C—O bond lengths are equal.

Hence, option (d) is correct.

Q.28 Diamagnetic species are those which contain no unpaired electrons. Which among the following are diamagnetic?

(a) N_2 (b) N_2^{2-} (c) O_2 (d) O_2^{2-}

Ans. ***(a, d)*** (a) Electronic configuration of

$N_2 = \sigma 1s^2, \sigma^* 1s^2, \sigma 2s^2, \sigma^* 2s^2, \pi 2p_x{}^2 \approx \pi 2p_y{}^2, \sigma 2p_z{}^2$.

It has no unpaired electron indicating it is diamagnetic species.

Hence, option (a) is correct.

(b) Electronic configuration of N_2^{2-} ion

$= \sigma 1s^2, \sigma^* 1s^2, \sigma 2s^2, \sigma^* 2s^2, \pi 2p_x^2 \approx \pi^2 p_y^2, \sigma 2p_z^2, \pi^* 2p_x^1 \approx \pi^* 2p_y^1$

It has two unpaired electrons, paramagnetic in nature.

(c) Electronic configuration of

$O_2 = \sigma 1s^2, \sigma^* 1s^2, \sigma 2s^2, \sigma^* 2s^2, \sigma 2p_z^2, \pi 2p_x^2 \approx \pi 2p_y^2, \pi^* 2p_x^1 \approx \pi^* 2p_y^1$

The presence of two unpaired electrons shows its paramagnetic nature.

(d) Electronic configuration of O_2^{2-} ion $= \sigma 1s^2, \sigma^* 1s^2, \sigma 2s^2, \sigma 2p_z^2, \pi 2p_x^2 \approx \pi 2p_y^2,$
$\pi^* 2p_x^2 \approx \pi^* 2p_y^2$

It contains no unpaired electron, therefore, it is diamagnetic in nature.

Hence, option (d) is correct.

Q.29 Species having same bond order are :

(a) N_2 (b) N_2^- (c) F_2^+ (d) O_2^-

Ans. ***(c, d)*** Bond order of the following species are calculated using molecular orbital electronic configuration and found as :

$N_2 = 3$

$N_2^- = 2.5$

$F_2^+ = 1.5$

$O_2^- = 1.5$

Q.30 Which of the following statements are not correct?

(a) NaCl being an ionic compound is a good conductor of electricity in the solid state.

(b) In canonical structure there is a difference in the arrangement of atoms.

(c) Hybrid orbitals form stronger bonds than pure orbitals.

(d) VSEPR theory can explain the square planar geometry of XeF_4.

Ans. ***(a, b)*** Statement in option (a) and (b) are incorrect. Their corrected form are as follows.

(a) NaCl is a bad conductor of electricity in solid due to the absence of free ions.

(b) Canonical structures differ in the arrangement of electrons, not in the arrangement of atoms.

Short Answer Type Questions

Q.31 Explain the non-linear shape of H_2S and non-planar shape of PCl_3 using valence shell electron pair repulsion theory.

Ans. In H_2S central atom is S. There are 6 electrons in its valence shell ($_{16}S$ = 2, 8, 6). Two electrons are shared with two H-atoms and the remaining four electrons are present as two lone pairs.

Hence, total pairs of electrons are four (2 bond pairs and 2 lone pairs). Due to the presence of 2 lone pairs, the shape becomes **distorted tetrahedral** or **angular** or **bent** (non-linear).

In PCl_3, central atom is phosphorus. There are 5 electrons in its valence shell ($_{15}P$ = 2, 8, 5). Three electrons are shared with three Cl-atoms and the remaining two electrons are present as one lone pair.

Hence, total pairs of electrons are four (1 lone pair and 3 bond pairs). Due to the presence of one lone pair, the shape becomes **pyramidal (non-planar).**

Mistake Alert ! *Students may overlook the impact of lone pairs on molecular shape and reactivity, which can lead to incorrect geometry predictions.*

Q.32 Using molecular orbital theory, compare the bond energy and magnetic character of O_2^+ and O_2^- species.

Ans. Molecular orbital configurations of O_2^+ and O_2^- are

$O_2^+ : (\sigma 1s)^2(\sigma^* 1s)^2(\sigma 2s)^2(\sigma^* 2s)^2(\sigma 2p_z)^2(\pi 2p_x^2, \pi 2p_y^2)(\pi^* 2p_x^1)$

Bond order of $O_2^+ = \dfrac{10-5}{2} = \dfrac{5}{2} = 2.5$

$O_2^- : (\sigma 1s)^2(\sigma^* 1s^2)(\sigma 2s^2)(\sigma^* 2s^2)(\sigma 2p_z)^2(\pi 2p_x^2, \pi 2p_y^2)(\pi^* 2p_x^2, \pi^* 2p_y^1)$

Bond order of $O_2^- = \dfrac{10-7}{2} = \dfrac{3}{2} = 1.5$

Higher bond order of O_2^+ shows that it is more stable than O_2^-. Both the species have unpaired electrons. So, both are paramagnetic in nature.

Q.33 Explain the shape of BrF_5.

Ans. The central atom Br has seven electrons in its valence shell. Five of these will form bonds with five fluorine atoms and the remaining two electrons are present as one lone pair.

Hence, total pairs of electrons are six (5 bond pairs and 1 lone pair). To minimize repulsion between lone pairs and bond pairs, the shape becomes **square pyramidal.**

Q.34 Structures of molecules of two compounds are given below.

(I) (II)

(a) Which of the two compounds will have intermolecular hydrogen bonding and which compound is expected to show intramolecular hydrogen bonding?

(b) The melting point of compound depends on, among other things, the extent of hydrogen bonding. On this basis explain which of the above two compounds will show higher melting point?

(c) Solubility of compounds in water depends on power to form hydrogen bonds with water. Which of the above compounds will form hydrogen bond easily and be more soluble in it?

Ans. (a)Compound (I) will form intramolecular H-bonding. Intramolecular H-bonding is formed when H-atom, in between the two highly electronegative atoms, is present within the same molecule. In *ortho*-nitrophenol (compound I), H-atom is in between the two oxygen atoms.

intramolecular H—bond

orthonitrophenol
(compound I)

Compound (II) forms intermolecular H-bonding. In *para*-nitrophenol (II), there is a gap between NO_2 and OH group. So, H-bond exists between H-atom of one molecule and O atom of another molecule as depicted below.

para-introphenol (compound II)

(b) Ortho-nitrophenol (Compound I) and para-nitrophenol (Compound II) are positional isomers, but they show different intermolecular interactions, which significantly affect their melting points. Para-nitrophenol has a higher melting point than ortho-nitrophenol due to strong intermolecular hydrogen bonding, which leads to tight crystal packing.

(c) Due to intramolecular H-bonding, compound (I) will not be able to form H-bond with water, so it is less soluble in water. While molecules of compound II form H-bonding with H_2O easily, so it is more soluble in water.

Q.35 Why does type of overlap given in the following figure not result in bond formation?

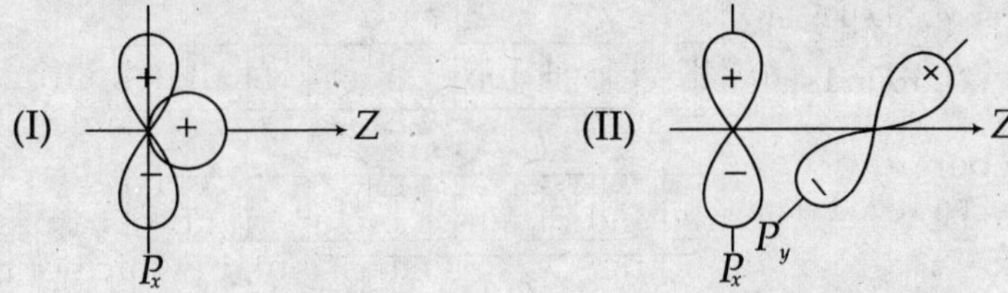

Ans. In the figure (I), area of + + overlap is equal to + – overlap, so net overlap is zero, while in figure (II), there is no overlap due to different symmetry.

Q.36 Explain why PCl_5 is trigonal bipyramidal whereas IF_5 is square pyramidal.

Ans. In PCl_5 'P' share its five valence electrons, each with one 'Cl' atom so there are five bond pairs around 'P' atom which adjust in trigonal bipyramidal shape to minimise repulsion between bond pairs and acquire better stable state.

In IF_5, central 'I' atom has 7 valence electrons, out of which only 5 valence electrons are shared with five fluorine atoms. So, there exists one lone pair and five bond pairs around central I atoms, *i.e.* total six electron pairs adjust in square pyramidal shape as shown below.

Alternate Method The ground state and the excited state outer electronic configurations of phosphorus ($Z = 15$) are represented below

P(ground state) [⥮] [1 | 1 | 1] [| | | |]
3s 3p 3d

P(excited state) [1] [1 | 1 | 1] [1 | | | |]
sp^3d

PCl_5 [⥮] [⥮ | ⥮ | ⥮] [⥮ | | | |]
Cl Cl Cl Cl Cl
sp^3d

Cl, Cl, P—Cl, Cl, Cl

In PCl_5, P is **sp^3d hybridised,** therefore, its shape is **trigonal bipyramidal.**

IF_5–The ground state and the excited state outer electronic configurations of iodine ($Z = 53$) are represented below.

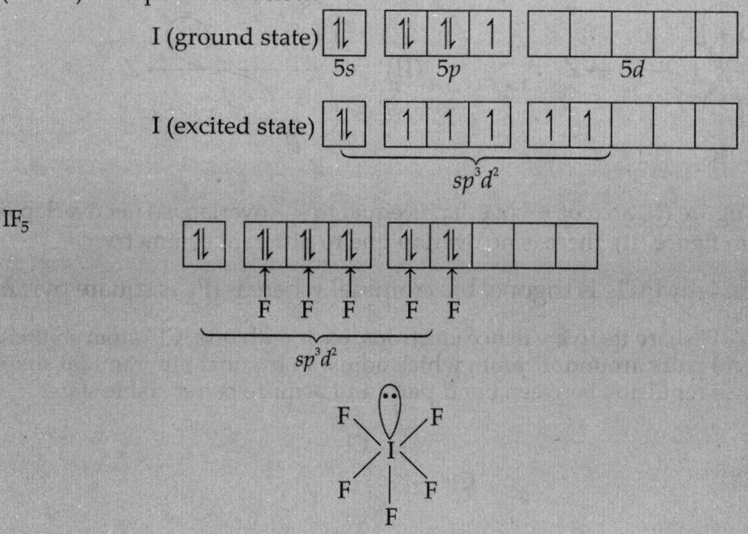

In IF_5, I is **sp^3d^2 hybridised,** therefore, shape of IF_5 is **square pyramidal.**

Q.37 In both water and dimethyl ether ($CH_3—\ddot{O}—CH_3$), oxygen atom is central atom, and has the same hybridisation, yet they have different bond angles. Which one has greater bond angle? Give reason.

Ans. Dimethyl ether has greater bond angle than that of water, however in both the molecules central atom oxygen is sp^3 hybridised with two lone pairs. In dimethyl ether, bond angle is greater (111.7°) due to the greater repulsive interaction between the two bulky methyl groups than that between two H-atoms.

H ‥Ö‥ H
C 111.7° C
H | | H
H H
Dimethyl ether

‥Ö‥
H 104.5° H
Water

Actually C of CH_3 group is attached to three H-atoms through σ-bonds. These three C—H bond pair of electrons increase the electronic charge density on carbon atom.

Q.38 Write Lewis structure of the following compounds and show formal charge on each atom.

$$HNO_3, NO_2, H_2SO_4$$

Thinking Process Formal charge on an atom in a Lewis structure = [total number of valence electrons in free atom] – [total number of non bonding (lone pair) of electrons] $-\frac{1}{2}$ [total number of shared electrons]

Ans. The Lewis structure of the following compounds and formal charge on each atom are as

(i) HNO_3

$$H-\ddot{O}_{(1)}-\overset{+}{N}(=\ddot{O}{:}_{(2)})-\ddot{O}{:}^{-}_{(3)}$$

$$\text{Formal charge on H} = 1 - 0 - \frac{1}{2} \times 2 = 0$$

$$\text{Formal charge on N} = 5 - 0 - \frac{1}{2} \times 8 = 1$$

$$\text{Formal charge on O(1)} = 6 - 4 - \frac{1}{2} \times 4 = 0$$

$$\text{Formal charge on O(2)} = 6 - 4 - \frac{1}{2} \times 4 = 0$$

$$\text{Formal charge on O(3)} = 6 - 6 - \frac{1}{2} \times 2 = -1$$

(ii) NO_2

$$:\ddot{O}{:}_{(1)}=\overset{\cdot +}{N}-:\ddot{O}{:}^{-}_{(2)}$$

$$\text{Formal charge on O(1)} = 6 - 4 - \frac{1}{2} \times 4 = 0$$

$$\text{Formal charge on N} = 5 - 1 - \frac{1}{2} \times 6 = +1$$

$$\text{Formal charge on O(2)} = 6 - 6 - \frac{1}{2} \times 2 = -1$$

(iii) H_2SO_4

$$\underset{(1)}{H}-\underset{(1)}{\ddot{O}}-\overset{2+}{S}(-:\ddot{O}{:}^{-}_{(2)})(-:\ddot{O}{:}^{-}_{(4)})-\underset{(3)}{\ddot{O}}-\underset{(2)}{H}$$

Formal charge on H(1) or H(2) $= 1 - 0 - \frac{1}{2} \times 2 = 0$

Formal charge on O(1) or O(3) $= 6 - 4 - \frac{1}{2} \times 4 = 0$

Formal charge on O(2) or O(4) $= 6 - 6 - \frac{1}{2} \times 2 = -1$

Formal charge on S $= 6 - 0 - \frac{1}{2} \times 8 = +2$

Mistake Alert ! *Students may make errors in calculating formal charges.*

Q.39 The energy of $\sigma 2p_z$ molecular orbital is greater than $\pi 2p_x$ and $\pi 2p_y$ molecular orbitals in nitrogen molecule. Write the complete sequence of energy levels in the increasing order of energy in the molecule. Compare the relative stability and the magnetic behaviour of the following species.

$$N_2, N_2^+, N_2^-, N_2^{2+}$$

- **Concept Insight** From the various rules for filling of molecular orbitals, the electronic configuration of N_2 molecule will be

$$\sigma 1s^2, \sigma^* 1s^2, \sigma 2s^2, \sigma^* 2s^2, \pi 2p_x^2 \approx \pi 2p_y^2, \sigma 2p_z^2$$

Ans. Comparative study of the relative stability and the magnetic behaviour of the following species is as follows :

(i) **N_2 molecule** $\sigma 1s^2, \sigma^* 1s^2, \sigma 2s^2, \sigma^* 2s^2, \pi 2p_x^2 \approx \pi 2p_y^2, \sigma 2p_z^2$

Here, $N_b = 10$, $N_a = 4$.
Hence, bond order $= \frac{1}{2}(N_b - N_a) = \frac{1}{2}(10 - 4) = 3$

Hence, presence of no unpaired electron indicates it is **diamagnetic.**

(ii) **N_2^+ ions** $\sigma 1s^2, \sigma^* 1s^2, \sigma 2s^2, \sigma^* 2s^2, \pi 2p_x^2 \approx \pi 2p_y^2, \sigma 2p_z^1$

Here, $N_b = 9$, $N_a = 4$ so that BO $= \frac{1}{2}(9 - 4) = \frac{5}{2} = 2.5$

Further, as N_2^+ ion has one unpaired electron in the $\sigma(2p_z)$ orbital, so it is **paramagnetic** in nature.

(iii) **N_2^- ions** $\sigma 1s^2, \sigma^* 1s^2, \sigma 2s^2, \sigma^* 2s^2, \pi 2p_x^2 \approx \pi 2p_y^2, \sigma 2p_z^2, \pi^* 2p_x^1$

Here, $N_b = 10$, $N_a = 5$ so that BO $= \frac{1}{2}(10 - 5) = \frac{5}{2} = 2.5$

Again, as it has one unpaired electron in the $\pi^*(2p_x)$ orbital, therefore, it is **paramagnetic.**

(iv) **N_2^{2+} ions** $\sigma 1s^2, \sigma^* 1s^2, \sigma 2s^2, \sigma^* 2s^2, \pi 2p_x^2 \approx \pi 2p_y^2$

Here, $N_b = 8$, $N_a = 4$.
Hence, BO $= \frac{1}{2}(8 - 4) = 2$

Presence of no unpaired electron indicates it to be diamagnetic in nature.
As bond dissociation energies are directly proportional to the bond orders, therefore, the dissociation energies of these molecular species is in the order.

$$N_2 > N_2^- = N_2^+ > N_2^{2+}$$

Greater the bond dissociation energy, greater is the stability. So, the stability of these species is also in the above order.

Q.40 What is the effect of the following processes on the bond order in N_2 and O_2?

(a) $N_2 \longrightarrow N_2^+ + e^-$ (b) $O_2 \longrightarrow O_2^+ + e^-$

Ans. According to molecular orbital theory, electronic configurations and bond order of N_2, N_2^+, O_2 and O_2^+ species are as follows

$$N_2\ (14e^-) = \sigma 1s^2, \overset{*}{\sigma} 1s^2, \sigma 2s^2, \overset{*}{\sigma} 2s^2, (\pi 2p_x^2 \approx \pi 2p_y^2), \sigma 2p_z^2$$

$$\text{Bond order} = \frac{1}{2}[N_b - N_a] = \frac{1}{2}(10-4) = 3$$

$$N_2^+(13e^-) = \sigma 1s^2, \overset{*}{\sigma} 1s^2, \sigma 2s^2, \overset{*}{\sigma} 2s^2, (\pi 2p_x^2 \approx \pi 2p_y^2)\ \sigma 2p_z^1$$

$$\text{Bond order} = \frac{1}{2}[N_b - N_a] = \frac{1}{2}(9-4) = 2.5$$

$$O_2\ (16e^-) = \sigma 1s^2, \overset{*}{\sigma} 1s^2, \sigma 2s^2, \overset{*}{\sigma} 2s^2, \sigma 2p_z^2, (\pi 2p_x^2 \approx \pi 2p_y^2), (\overset{*}{\pi} 2p_x^1 \approx \overset{*}{\pi} 2p_y^1)$$

$$\text{Bond order} = \frac{1}{2}[N_b - N_a] = \frac{1}{2}(10-6) = 2$$

$$O_2^+\ (15e^-) = \sigma 1s^2, \overset{*}{\sigma} 1s^2, \sigma 2s^2, \overset{*}{\sigma} 2s^2, \sigma 2p_z^2, (\pi 2p_x^2 \approx \pi 2p_y^2), (\overset{*}{\pi} 2p_x^1 \approx \overset{*}{\pi} 2p_y^0)$$

$$\text{Bond order} = \frac{1}{2}[N_b - N_a] = \frac{1}{2}(10-5) = 2.5$$

(a) $\underset{\text{B.O.} = 3}{N_2} \longrightarrow \underset{\text{B.O.} = 2.5}{N_2^+} + e^-$

Thus, **bond order decreases.** Hence, bond becomes weaker and longer.

(b) $\underset{\text{B.O} = 2}{O_2} \longrightarrow \underset{\text{B.O} = 2.5}{O_2^+} + e^-$

Thus, bond order increases. Hence, bond becomes stronger and shorter.

Q.41 Give reason for the following.

(a) Covalent bonds are directional bonds while ionic bonds are non-directional.

(b) Water molecule has bent structure whereas carbon dioxide molecule is linear.

(c) Ethyne molecule is linear.

Ans. (a) Covalent bonds are directional because they involve the sharing of electrons between specific atoms in fixed orientations, depending on orbital overlap. Ionic bonds are non-directional as they result from electrostatic attraction, which acts equally in all directions around the oppositely charged ions.

Each positive ion is surrounded by a number of anions in any direction depending upon its size and *vice-versa.* That's why covalent bonds are directional bonds while ionic bonds are non-directional.

(b) In H_2O, oxygen atom is sp^3 hybridised with two lone pairs. The four sp^3 hybridised orbitals acquire a tetrahedral geometry with two corners occupied by hydrogen atoms while other two by the lone pairs.

The bond angle is reduced to 104.5° from 109.5° due to greater repulsive forces between $lp - lp$ and the molecule thus acquires a **V-shape or bent** structure (angular structure).

H 104.5° H (O)

In CO_2 molecule, carbon atom is *sp*-hybridised. The two *sp* hybrid orbitals are oriented in opposite direction forming an angle of 180°.

$$O \overset{\pi}{\underset{\sigma}{=}} C \overset{\pi}{\underset{\sigma}{=}} O$$

That's why H_2O molecule has bent structure whereas CO_2 molecule is linear.

(c) In ethyne molecule, both the carbon atoms are *sp* hybridised, having two unhybridised orbitals, *i.e.*, $2p_x$ and $2p_y$. The two *sp* hybrid orbitals of both the carbon atoms are oriented in opposite direction forming an angle of 180°.

$$H—C\overset{\sigma}{\equiv}C—H$$

2π-bond

That's why ethyne molecule is linear.

Q.42 What is an ionic bond? With two suitable examples expalin the difference between an ionic and a covalent bond?

Ans. Ionic bond The bond formed, as a result of the electrostatic attraction between the positive and negative ions was termed as the electrovalent bond or ionic bond. *e.g.*, the formation of NaCl from sodium and chlorine can be explained as

$$\underset{[Ne]\,3s^1}{Na} \longrightarrow \underset{[Ne]}{Na^+} + e^-$$

$$\underset{[Ne]\,3s^2 3p^5}{Cl} + e^- \longrightarrow \underset{[Ne]\,3s^2 3p^6 \text{ or } [Ar]}{Cl^-}$$

$$Na^+ + Cl^- \longrightarrow NaCl \text{ or } Na^+Cl^-$$

Similarly, the formation of CaF_2 may be shown as

$$\underset{[Ar]4s^2}{Ca} \longrightarrow \underset{[Ar]}{Ca^{2+}} + 2e^-$$

$$\underset{[He]\,2s^2 2p^5}{F} + e^- \longrightarrow \underset{[He]\,2s^2 2p^6 \text{ or } [Ne]}{F^-}$$

$$Ca^{2+} + 2F^- \longrightarrow CaF_2 \text{ or } Ca^{2+}(F^-)_2$$

Covalent bond The bond formed by mutual sharing of electrons between two non-metal atoms is covalent bond. *e.g.*, the formation of chlorine molecule.

$$\underset{2,\,8,\,7}{:\ddot{\underset{..}{Cl}}\cdot} + \underset{2,\,8,\,7}{\cdot\ddot{\underset{..}{Cl}}:} \longrightarrow :\ddot{\underset{..}{Cl}}(:)\ddot{\underset{..}{Cl}}: \text{ or } Cl—Cl$$

Shared pair

Similarly, in the formation of HCl

$$\underset{1}{H\cdot} + \underset{2,\,8,\,7}{\cdot\ddot{\underset{..}{Cl}}:} \longrightarrow H(:)\ddot{\underset{..}{Cl}}: \text{ or } H—Cl$$

Q.43 Arrange the following bonds in order of increasing ionic character giving reason. N—H, F—H, C—H and O—H

Ans. Greater the electronegativity difference between the two bonded atoms, greater will be the ionic character.

Bond	N—H	F—H	C—H	O—H
Electronegativity difference	(3.0 – 2.1) = 0.9	(4.0 – 2.1) = 1.9	(2.5 – 2.1) = 0.4	(3.5 – 2.1) = 1.4

Therefore, increasing order of ionic character of the given bonds is as follows.

C—H < N—H < O—H < F—H

Q.44 Explain why CO_3^{2-} ion cannot be represented by a single Lewis structure. How can it be best represented?

Ans. A single Lewis structure of CO_3^{2-} ion cannot explain all the properties of this ion. It can be represented as a resonance hybrid of the following structures.

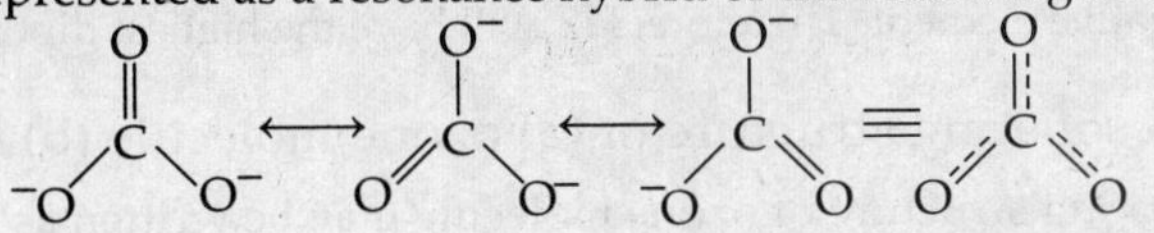

I ⟷ II ⟷ III ≡ Resonance hybrid

Canonical structure

Hence, CO_3^{2-} ion cannot be represented by a single Lewis structure because doing so would localise the double bond to only one C—O bond, while experimental evidence shows that all three C—O bonds are identical in length and strength. This indicates delocalisation of π-electrons across all three oxygen atoms. Therefore, carbonate ion is best represented by three equivalent resonance structures, where the position of the double bond keeps shifting. The actual structure is a resonance hybrid, in which all C—O bonds have equal bond order and partial double bond character.

Q.45 Predict the hybridisation of each carbon in the molecule of organic compound given below. Also indicate the total number of sigma and pi-bonds in this molecule.

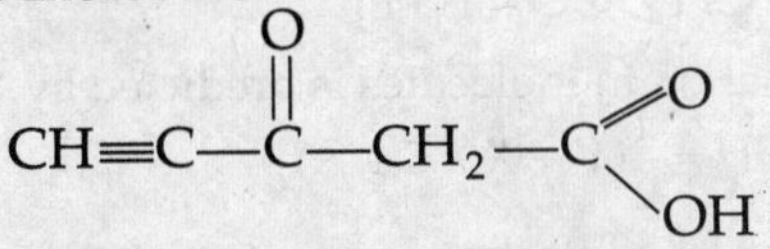

CH≡C—C(=O)—CH₂—C(=O)OH

- **Concept Insight**

  (i) Single bond contains 1σ bond (ii) Double bond contains 1σ and 1π bond.
  (iii) Triple bond contains 1σ and 2π bonds.

Ans. The hybridisation and type of bonds of each carbon in the molecule given below

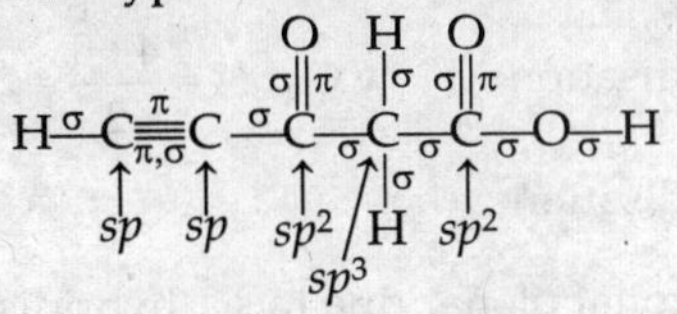

H—C≡C—C(=O)—CH₂—C(=O)—O—H

sp, sp, sp², sp³, sp²

σ-bonds = 11

π-bonds = 4

Q.46 Group the following as linear and non-linear molecules :

H_2O, HOCl, $BeCl_2$, Cl_2O

Ans. The structure of the given molecules are

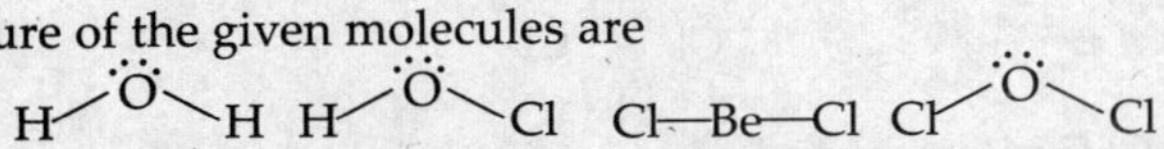

H—Ö—H H—Ö—Cl Cl—Be—Cl Cl—Ö—Cl

Therefore, only $BeCl_2$ is linear and rest of the molecules are non-linear.

Q.47 Elements X, Y and Z have 4, 5 and 7 valence electrons respectively.

(a) Write the molecular formula of the compounds formed by these elements individually with hydrogen.

(b) Which of these compounds will have the highest dipole moment?

Ans. (a)

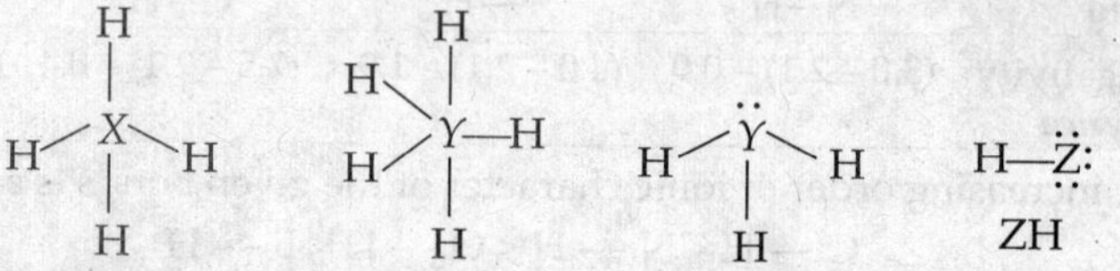

XH_4 $\quad$ YH_5 $\quad$ YH_3 $\quad$ ZH

(b) Dipole moment (μ) is directly related to the difference in electronegativity (ΔEN) between two bonded atoms. Hence, as electronegativity difference increases, dipole moment also increases. Z has seven electrons in its valence shell. It is the most electronegative element. Therefore, HZ will have the highest dipole moment.

Q.48 Draw the resonating structure of (a) ozone molecule (b) nitrate ion

Ans. (a) The resonating structure of ozone molecule may be written as

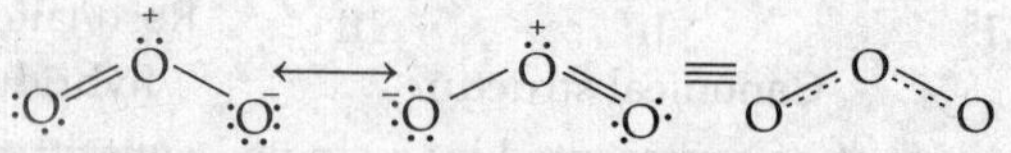

Resonance hybrid

(b) The resonating structure of nitrate ion (NO_3^-) is

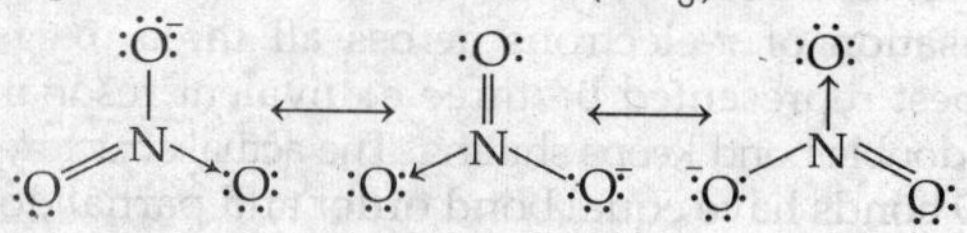

Resonance hybrid

Q.49 Predict the shapes of the following molecules on the basis of hybridisation. BCl_3, CH_4, CO_2, NH_3

Ans. The shape and hybridisation in molecules is predicted by VSEPR Theory using the following formula: $H = \frac{1}{2}(V + X - C + A)$

Where, V = number of valence electrons in central atom

X = number of monovalent atoms around the central atoms

C = poitive charge on the cation, A = negative charge on the anion

BCl_3, H $= \frac{V + S - C + A}{2} = \frac{3+3}{2} = 3$, sp^2 Hybridisation

CH_4, H $= \frac{4+4}{2} = 4$, sp^3 hybridisation $\quad$ CO_2, H $= \frac{4+0}{2} = 2$, sp Hybridisation

NH_3, H $= \frac{5+3}{2} = 4$, sp^3 Hybridisation

In BCl_3, the geometry is trigonal planar due to sp^2 hybridisation.

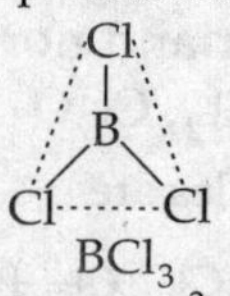

BCl_3

The shape of CH_4 is tetrahedral due to sp^3 hybridisation.

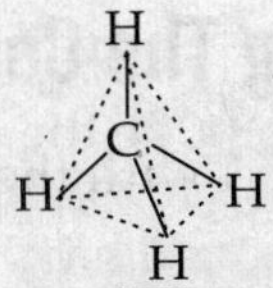

H
C
H H
H
(CH_4)

CO_2 show linear shape because of *sp* hybridisation.

$$:\ddot{O}=C=\ddot{O}:$$
(CO_2)

The geometry of NH_3 is pyramidal shape and has sp^3 hybridisation.

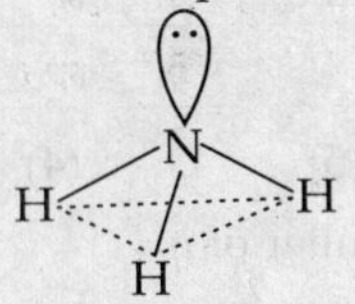

N
H H
H
(NH_3)

Q.50 All the C—O bonds in carbonate ion (CO_3^{2-}) are equal in length. Explain.

Thinking Process To explain the reason of equal length of C—O bonds, one should keep in mind about the resonance. As a result of resonance, the bond length in a molecule become equal.

Ans. Carbonate ion, (CO_3^{2-}) = 3 bond pair + 1 lone pair ⇒ trigonal planar

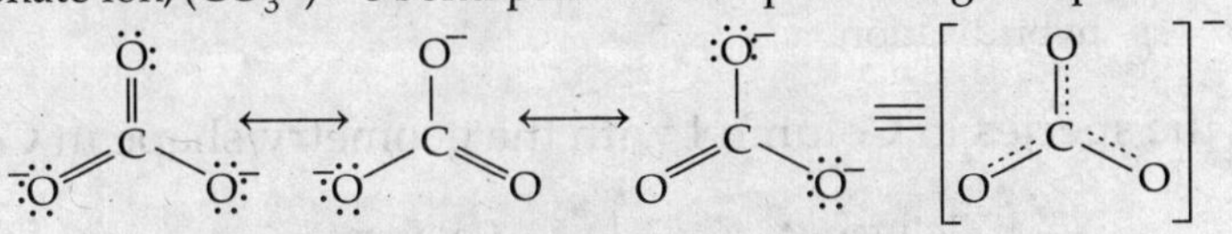

Ö: ‖ C ⁻Ö Ö⁻ ⟷ O⁻ | C ⁻Ö O ⟷ :Ö⁻ | C O Ö⁻ ≡ [O ⋮ C O O]⁻

Due to resonance, all C—O bond length are equal.

Q.51 What is meant by the term average bond enthalpy? Why is there difference in bond enthalpy of O—H bond in ethanol (C_2H_5OH) and water?

Ans. All the similar bonds in a molecule do not have the same bond enthalpies. *e.g.*, in H_2O (H—O—H) molecule after the breaking of first O—H bond, the second O—H bond undergoes some change because of changed electronic environment.

Therefore, in polyatomic molecules average bond enthalpy is used. It is obtained by dividing total bond dissociation enthalpy by the number of bonds broken.

e.g., $H_2O(g) \longrightarrow H^+(g) + {}^-OH(g);\ \Delta_a H_1^\circ = 502\ \text{kJ mol}^{-1}$

$${}^-OH(g) \longrightarrow H^+ + O^{2-}(g);\ \Delta_a H_2^\circ = 427\ \text{kJ mol}^{-1}$$

$$\text{Average O—H bond enthalpy} = \frac{502 + 427}{2} = 464.5\ \text{kJ mol}^{-1}$$

The bond enthalpies of O—H bond in C_2H_5OH and H_2O are different because of the different electronic environment around oxygen atom.

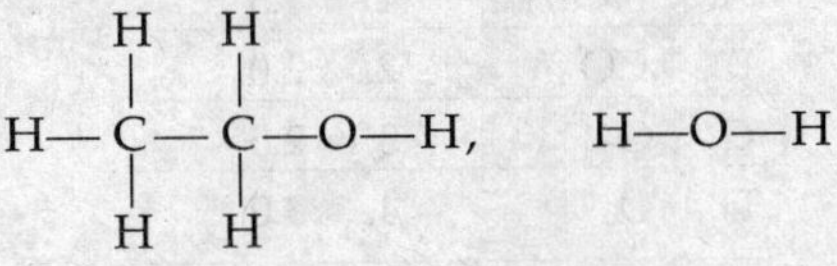

```
    H   H
    |   |
H — C — C — O — H,      H — O — H
    |   |
    H   H
```

(C_2H_5OH) (H_2O)

Matching The Columns

Q.52 Match the species in Column I with the type of hybrid orbitals in Column II.

Column I		Column II	
A.	SF_4	1.	sp^3d^2
B.	IF_5	2.	d^2sp^3
C.	NO_2^+	3.	sp^3d
D.	NH_4^+	4.	sp^3
		5.	sp

Ans. **A.** → (3) **B.** → (1) **C.** → (5) **D.** → (4)

A. SF_4 = number of *bp* (4) + number of *lp* (1)
= sp^3d hybridisation

B. IF_5 = number of *bp* (5) + number of *lp* (1)
= sp^3d^2 hybridisation

C. NO_2^+ = number of *bp* (2) + number of *lp* (0)
= *sp* hybridisation

D. NH_4^+ = number of *bp* (4) + number of *lp* (0)
= sp^3 hybridisation.

Q.53 Match the species in Column I with the geometry/shape in Column II.

Column I		Column II	
A.	H_3O^+	1.	Linear
B.	$HC{\equiv}CH$	2.	Angular
C.	ClO_2^-	3.	Tetrahedral
D.	NH_4^+	4.	Trigonal bipyramidal
		5.	Pyramidal

Ans. **A.** → (5) **B.** → (1) **C.** → (2) **D** → (3)

A. $H_3O^+ = 3bp + 1lp \Rightarrow$ pyramidal shape.
B. $HC{\equiv}CH \Rightarrow$ linear as *sp* hybridised.
C. $ClO_2^- = 2bp + 2lp \Rightarrow$ angular shape.
D. $NH_4^+ = 4bp + 0lp \Rightarrow$ tetrahedral shape.

Q.54 Match the species in Column I with the bond order in Column II.

Column I		Column II	
A.	NO	1.	1.5
B.	CO	2.	2.0
C.	O_2^-	3.	2.5
D.	O_2	4.	3.0

Ans. **A.** → (3) **B.** → (4) **C.** → (1) **D.** → (2)

A. NO $(7 + 8 = 15) = \sigma 1s^2, \sigma^* 1s^2, \sigma 2s^2, \sigma^* 2s^2, \sigma 2p_z^2, \pi 2p_x^2 \approx \pi 2p_y^2, \pi^* 2p_x^1$

$$\text{Bond order} = \frac{1}{2}(N_b - N_a) = \frac{10-5}{2} = 2.5$$

B. CO $(6 + 8 = 14) = \sigma 1s^2, \sigma^* 1s^2, \sigma 2s^2, \sigma^* 2s^2, \sigma 2p_z^2, \pi 2p_x^2 \simeq \pi 2p_y^2$

$$\text{Bond order} = \frac{10-4}{2} = 3$$

C. O_2^- $(8 + 8 + 1 = 17) = \sigma 1s^2, \sigma^* 1s^2, \sigma 2s^2, \sigma^* 2s^2, \sigma 2p_z^2, \pi 2p_x^2 \approx \pi 2p_y^2, \pi^* 2p_x^2 \simeq \pi^* 2p_y^1$

$$\text{Bond order} = \frac{10-7}{2} = 1.5$$

D. $O_2 (8 + 8 = 16) = \sigma 1s^2, \sigma^* 1s^2, \sigma 2s^2, \sigma^* 2s^2, \sigma 2p_z^2, \pi 2p_x^2 \approx \pi 2p_y^2, \pi^* 2p_x^1 \simeq \pi^* 2p_y^1$

$$\text{Bond order} = \frac{10-6}{2} = 2$$

Q.55 Match the items given in Column I with examples given in Column II.

	Column I		Column II
A.	Hydrogen bond	1.	C
B.	Resonance	2.	LiF
C.	Ionic solid	3.	H_2
D.	Covalent solid	4.	HF
		5.	O_3

Ans. A.→ (4) B.→ (5) C.→ (2) D.→ (1)

A. Hydrogen bond → HF B. Resonance → O_3

C. Ionic bond → LiF D. Covalent solid → C

Q.56 Match the shape of molecules in Column I with the type of hybridisation in Column II.

	Column I		Column II
A.	Tetrahedral	1.	sp^2
B.	Trigonal	2.	sp
C.	Linear	3.	sp^3

Ans. A. → (3) B. → (1) C. → (2)

A. Tetrahedral shape – sp^3 hybridisation

B. Trigonal shape – sp^2 hybridisation

C. Linear shape – sp hybridisation

Assertion and Reason

In the following questions, a statement of Assertion (A) followed by a statement of Reason (R) is given. Choose the correct option out of the choices given below in each question.

Q.57 **Assertion** (A) Sodium chloride formed by the action of chlorine gas on sodium metal is a stable compound.

Reason (R) This is because sodium and chloride ions acquire octet in sodium chloride formation.

(a) A and R both are correct and R is the correct explanation of A
(b) A and R both are correct, but R is not the correct explanation of A
(c) A is true, but R is false
(d) A and R both are false

Ans. (a) Assertion and reason both are correct and reason is the correct explanation of assertion.

$$\underset{(2,8,1)}{Na^{\cdot}} + \underset{(2,8,1)}{:\ddot{Cl}:} \longrightarrow \underset{(2,8)\ (2,8,8)}{NaCl}$$

Here both Na^+ and Cl^- have complete octet hence NaCl is stable.

Q.58 **Assertion** (A) Though the central atom of both NH_3 and H_2O molecules are sp^3 hybridised, yet H–N–H bond angle is greater than that of H—O—H.

Reason (R) This is because nitrogen atom has one lone pair and oxygen atom has two lone pairs.

(a) A and R both are correct and R is the correct explanation of A
(b) A and R both are correct but R is not the correct explanation of A
(c) A is true, but R is false
(d) A and R both are false

Ans. (a) Assertion and reason both are correct and reason is the correct explanation of assertion.

H_2O: H–O–H angle 104.5°, *sp*³–hybridised; NH_3: H–N–H angle 107°, *sp*³–hybridised

The bond angle in NH_3 (107.3°) is greater than in H_2O (104.5°) because NH_3 has one lone pair, while H_2O has two. Lone pairs repel bond pairs more strongly, and the greater lone pair repulsion in H_2O reduces its bond angle further compared to NH_3.

Q.59 **Assertion** (A) Among the two O—H bonds in H_2O molecule, the energy required to break the first O—H bond and the other O—H bond is the same.

Reason (R) This is because the electronic environment around oxygen is the same even after breakage of one O—H bond.

(a) A and R both are correct and R is the correct explanation of A
(b) A and R both are correct, but R is not the correct explanation of A
(c) A is true, but R is false
(d) A and R both are false

Ans. (d) A and R both are false.

Correct assertion The bond enthalpies of the two O—H bonds in H—O—H are not equal.

Correct reason This is because electronic environment around O is not same after breakage of one O—H bond.

Long Answer Type Questions

Q.60 (a) Discuss the significance/applications of dipole moment.

(b) Represent diagrammatically the bond moments and the resultant dipole moment in CO_2, NF_3 and $CHCl_3$.

Ans. (a) The applications of dipole moment are

(i) The dipole moment helps to predict whether a molecule is polar or non-polar. As $\mu = q \times d$, greater is the magnitude of dipole moment, higher will be the polarity of the bond. For non-polar molecules, the dipole moment is zero.

(ii) The percentage of ionic character can be calculated as

$$\text{Percentage of ionic character} = \frac{\mu_{\text{observed}}}{\mu_{\text{ionic}}} \times 100$$

(iii) Symmetrical molecules have zero dipole moment although they have two or more polar bonds (in determination of symmetry).

(iv) It helps to distinguish between *cis* and *trans* isomers. Usually *cis*-isomer has higher dipole moment than *trans* isomer.

(v) It helps to distinguish between *ortho, meta* and *para* isomers. Dipole moment of *para* isomer is zero. Dipole moment of ortho isomer is greater than that of *meta* isomer.

(b)

$O \leftrightharpoons C \rightleftharpoons O$, $\mu = 0$

NF_3: $\mu = 0.24$ D

$CHCl_3$: $\mu = 1.03$ D

Q.61 Use the molecular orbital energy level diagram to show that N_2 would be expected to have a triple bond. F_2, a single bond and Ne_2, no bond.

Ans. **Formation of N_2 molecule** Electronic configuration of N- atom

$${}_7N = 1s^2, 2s^2, 2p_x^1, 2p_y^1, 2p_z^1$$

$$N_2 \text{ molecule} = \sigma 1s^2, \sigma^* 1s^2, \sigma 2s^2, \sigma^* 2s^2, \pi 2p_x^2 \approx \pi 2p_y^2, \sigma 2p_z^2$$

$\overset{*}{\sigma}2p_z$

$\overset{*}{\pi}2p_x = \overset{*}{\pi}2p_y$

2p   2p

$\sigma 2p_z$

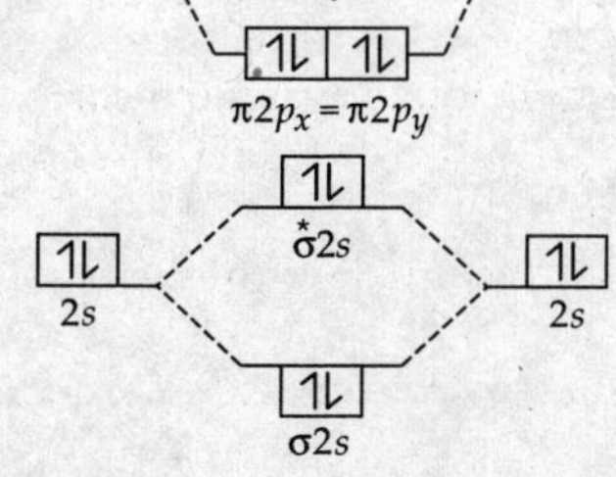

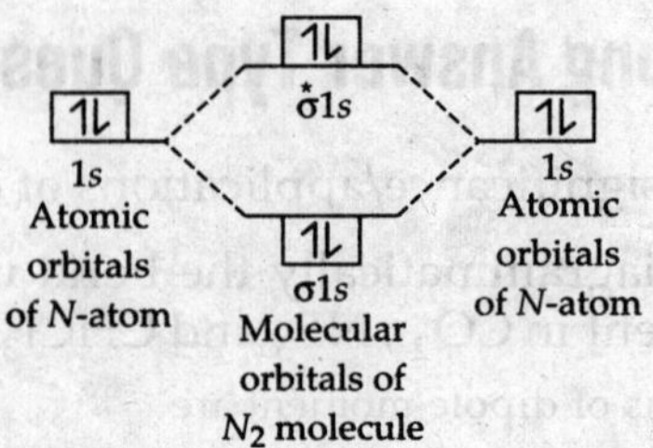

$$\text{Bond order} = \frac{1}{2}[N_b - N_a] = \frac{1}{2}(10-4) = 3.$$

Bond order value of 3 means that N_2 contains a triple bond.

Formation of F_2 molecule, ${}_9F = 1s^2, 2s^2, 2p_x^2, 2p_y^2, 2p_z^1$

$$F_2 \text{ molecule} = \sigma 1s^2, \sigma^* 1s^2, \sigma 2s^2, \sigma^* 2s^2, \sigma 2p_z^{\ 2}, \pi 2p_x^{\ 2} \approx \pi 2p_y^{\ 2}, \pi^* 2p^2{}_x \approx \pi^* 2p^2{}_y$$

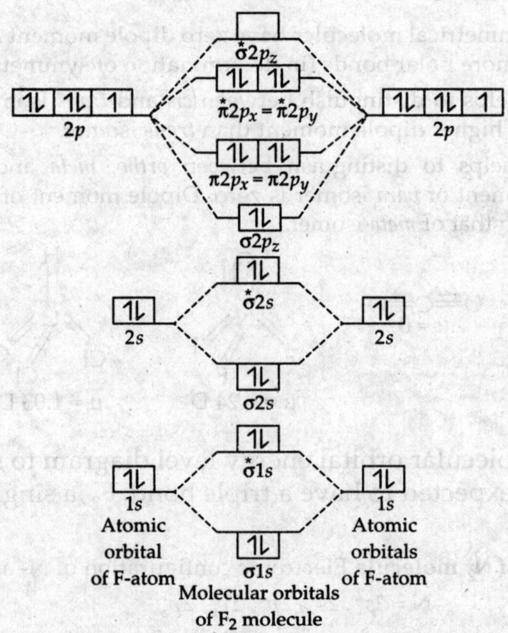

$$\text{Bond order} = \frac{1}{2}[N_b - N_a] = \frac{1}{2}(10-8) = 1$$

Bond order value 1 means that F_2 contains single bond.

Formation of Ne_2 molecule ${}_{10}Ne = 1s^2, 2s^2, 2p_x^2, 2p_y^2, 2p_z^2$

$$Ne_2 \text{molecule} = \sigma 1s^2, \sigma^* 1s^2, \sigma 2s^2, \sigma^* 2s^2, \sigma 2p_z^2, \pi 2p_x^2 \approx \pi 2p_y^2, \pi^* 2p_x^2 \approx \pi^* 2p_y^2, \sigma^* 2p_z^2$$

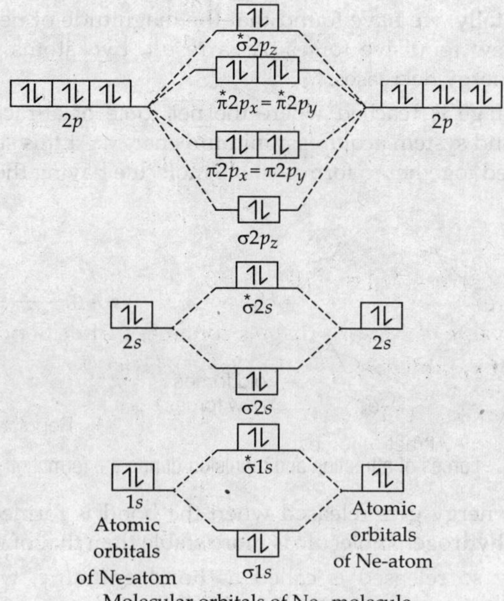

Molecular orbitals of Ne_2 molecule

$$\text{Bond order} = \frac{1}{2}[N_b - N_a] = \frac{1}{2}(10 - 10) = 0$$

Bond order value zero means that there is no formation of bond between two Ne-atoms. Hence, **Ne_2 molecule does not exist.**

Q.62 Briefly describe the valence bond theory of covalent bond formation by taking an example of hydrogen. How can you interpret energy changes taking place in the formation of dihydrogen?

Ans. Valence bond theory (VBT) was introduced by Heitler and London (1927) and developed further by Pauling and other. VBT is based on the knowledge of atomic orbitals, electronic configurations of elements, the overlap criteria of atomic orbitals, the hybridisation of atomic orbitals and the principles of variation and superposition.

Consider two hydrogen atoms A and B approaching each other having nuclei N_A and N_B and electrons present in them are represented by e_A and e_B. When the two atoms are at large distance from each other, there is no interaction between them.

As these two atoms approach each other, new attractive and repulsive forces begin to operate.

Attractive forces arise between

(i) nucleus of one atom and its own electron

i.e., $N_A - e_A$ and $N_B - e_B$

(ii) nucleus of one atom and electron of other atom

i.e., $N_A - e_B$, $N_B - e_A$

Similarly, **repulsive forces arise between**

(i) electrons of two atoms like $e_A - e_B$

(ii) nuclei of two atoms like $N_A - N_B$

Attractive forces tend to bring the two atoms close to each other whereas repulsive forces tend to push them apart.

Experimentally, we have found that the magnitude of new attractive force is more than the new repulsive forces. As a result, two atoms approach each other and potential energy decreases.

Hence, a stage is reached where the net force of attraction balances the force of repulsion and system acquires minimum energy. At this stage, two H-atoms are said to be bonded together to form a stable molecule having the bond length of 74 pm.

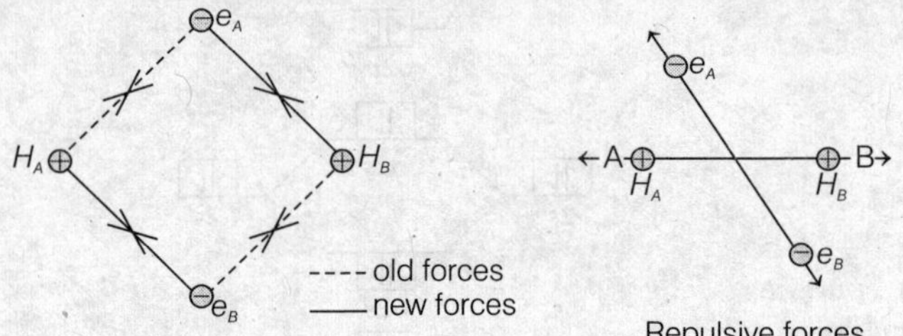

Attractive forces

Forces of attraction and repulsion during the formation of H_2 molecule

Since, the energy gets released when the bond is formed between two hydrogen atoms, the hydrogen molecule is more stable than that of isolated hydrogen atoms.

The energy so released is called as **bond enthalpy,** which is corresponding to minimum in the curve depicted in the given figure. Conversely, 435.8 kJ of energy is required to dissociate one mole of H_2 molecule.

$$H_2(g) + 435.8 \text{kJ mol}^{-1} \longrightarrow H(g) + H(g)$$

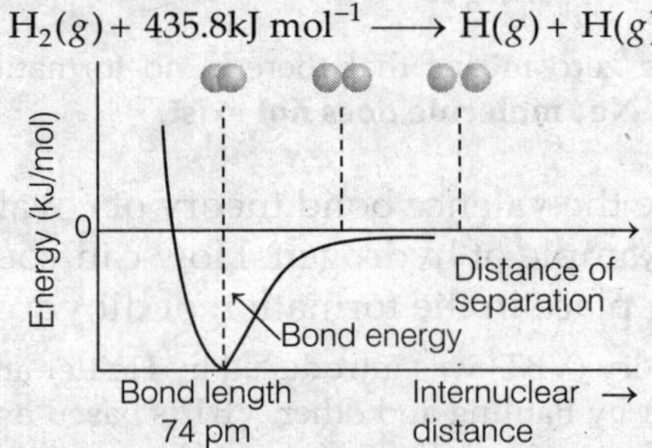

The potential energy curve for the formation of H_2 molecule as a function of internuclear distance of the H-atoms is shown above. The minimum in the curve corresponds to the most stable state of H_2.

Q.63 Describe hybridisation in the case of PCl_5 and SF_6. The axial bonds are longer as compared to equatorial bonds in PCl_5 whereas in SF_6 both axial bonds and equatorial bonds have the same bond length. Explain.

Ans. **Formation of** PCl_5

	3s	3p	3d
Electronic configuration of $_{15}P$ (ground state)	⇅	1 1 1	☐ ☐ ☐ ☐ ☐
Electronic configuration of $_{15}P$ (excited state)	1	1 1 1	1 ☐ ☐ ☐ ☐
PCl_5	⇅	⇅ ⇅ ⇅	⇅ ☐ ☐ ☐ ☐
	Cl	Cl Cl Cl	Cl

sp^3d hybridisation

In PCl_5, phosphorus is sp^3d hybridised to produce a set of five sp^3d hybrid orbitals which are directed towards the five corners of a **trigonal bipyramidal.** These five sp^3d hybrid orbitals overlap with singly occupied p-orbitals of Cl-atoms to form five P—Cl sigma bonds.

(Trigonal bipyramidal)
PCl_5

Three P—Cl bonds lie in one plane and make an angle of 120° with each other. These bonds are called **equatorial bonds.** The remaining two P—Cl bonds, one lying above and other lying below the plane make an angle of 90° with the equatorial plane. These bonds are called **axial bonds. Axial bonds are slightly longer than equatorial bonds** because axial bond pairs suffer more repulsive interaction from the equatorial bond pairs.

Formation of SF_6

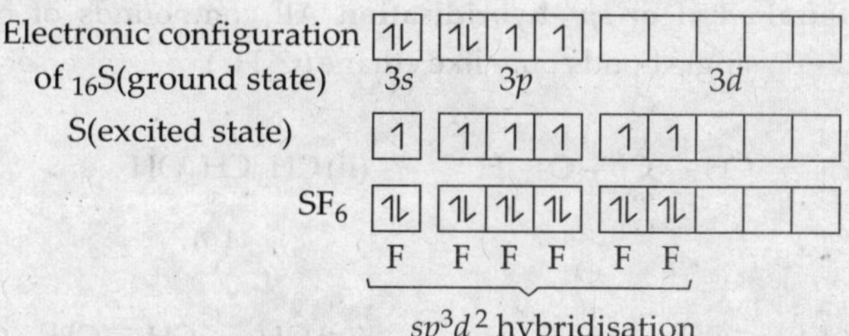

sp^3d^2 hybridisation

In SF_6, sulphur is sp^3d^2 hybridised to produce a set of six sp^3d^2 hybrid orbitals which are directed towards the six corners of a regular octahedron. These six sp^3d^2 hybrid orbitals overlap with singly occupied orbitals of fluorine atoms to form six S—F sigma bonds. Thus, SF_6 molecule has a regular **octahedral geometry** and **all S—F bonds have same bond length.**

Q.64 (a) Discuss the concept of hybridisation. What are its different types in a carbon atom?

(b) What is the type of hybridisation of carbon atoms marked with star?

(i) $\overset{*}{C}H_2{=}CH{-}\overset{*}{C}({=}O){-}O{-}H$ (ii) $CH_3{-}\overset{*}{C}H_2{-}OH$

(iii) $CH_3{-}CH_2{-}C^*({=}O){-}H$ (iv) $\overset{*}{C}H_3{-}CH{=}CH{-}CH_3$

(v) $CH_3{-}\overset{*}{C}{\equiv}CH$

Ans. (a) **Hybridisation** It is defined as intermixing of the orbitals of slightly different energy or of same energy to produce entirely new orbitals of equivalent energy, identical shapes and symmetrically disposed in plane. New orbitals formed are called **hybrid orbitals.**

Only the orbitals of an isolated single atom can undergo hybridisation. The hybrid orbitals generated are equal in number to that of the pure atomic orbitals which mix up.

Hybrid orbitals do not make pi-bonds. If there are π-bonds, equal number of atomic orbitals must be left unhybridised for π-bonding.

Like atomic orbitals, hybrid orbitals cannot have more than two electrons of opposite spins.

Types of hybridisation in carbon atoms are :

(i) **Linear or *sp*-hybridisation** All compounds of carbon containing $C\equiv C$ triple bond like ethyne (C_2H_2).

(ii) **Trigonal or sp^2-hybridisation** All compounds of carbon containing $C=C$ (double bond) like ethene (C_2H_4).

(iii) **Tetrahedral or sp^3-hybridisation** All compounds of carbon containing $C-C$ single bonds only like ethane (C_2H_6).

(b) (i) $\overset{*}{C}H_2 = CH - \overset{O}{\overset{\|}{C^*}} - O - H$ — $\overset{*}{C}H_2$: sp^2 (3σ); C^*: sp^2 (3σ)

(ii) $CH_3\overset{*}{C}H_2OH$ — sp^3 (4σ)

(iii) $CH_3 - CH_2 - \overset{O}{\overset{\|}{C^*}} - H$ — sp^2 (3σ)

(iv) $\overset{*}{C}H_3 - CH = CH - CH_3$ — sp^3 (4σ)

(v) $CH_3 - \overset{*}{C} \equiv CH$ — sp (2σ)

Direction (Q. No. 65-68) *Comprehension given below is followed by some multiple choice questions. Each question has one correct option. Choose the correct option.*

Molecular orbitals are formed by the overlap of atomic orbitals. Two atomic orbitals combine to form two molecular orbitals called bonding molecular orbital (BMO) and anti-bonding molecular orbital (ABMO). Energy of anti-bonding orbital is raised above the parent atomic orbitals that have combined and the energy of the bonding orbital is lowered than the parent atomic orbitals.

Energies of various molecular orbitals for elements hydrogen to nitrogen increase in the order

$$\sigma 1s < \sigma^* 1s < \sigma 2s < \sigma^* 2s < (\pi 2p_x \approx \pi 2p_y) < \sigma 2p_z < (\pi^* 2p_x \approx \pi^* 2p_y) < \sigma^* 2p_z \text{ and}$$

For oxygen and fluorine order of energy of molecular orbitals is given below

$$\sigma 1s < \sigma^* 1s < \sigma 2s < \sigma^* 2s < \sigma 2p_z < (\pi 2p_x \approx \pi 2p_y) < (\pi^* 2p_x \approx \pi^* 2p_y) < \sigma^* 2p_z$$

Different atomic orbitals of one atom combine with those atomic orbitals of the second atom which have comparable energies and proper orientation.

Further, if the overlapping is head on, the molecular orbital is called 'sigma', (σ) and if the overlap is lateral, the molecular orbital is called 'pi', (π). The molecular orbitals are filled with electrons according to the same rules as followed for filling of atomic orbitals. However, the order for filling is not the same for all molecules or their ions. Bond order is one of the most important parameters to compare the strength of bonds.

Q.65 Which of the following statements is correct?

(a) In the formation of dioxygen from oxygen atoms 10 molecular orbitals will be formed

(b) All the molecular orbitals in the dioxygen will be completely filled

(c) Total number of bonding molecular orbitals will not be same as total number of anti-bonding orbitals in dioxygen

(d) Number of filled bonding orbitals will be same as number of filled anti-bonding orbitals

Ans. (a) In the formation of dioxygen from oxygen atoms, ten molecular orbitals will be formed.

$$O_2 = \underset{1}{\underline{\sigma 1s^2}}\ \underset{2}{\underline{\sigma^* 1s^2}}\ \underset{3}{\underline{\sigma 2s^2}}\ \underset{4}{\underline{\sigma^* 2s^2}}\ \underset{5}{\underline{\sigma_2 p_z^2}}\ \underset{6}{\underline{\pi 2p_x^2}}\ \underset{7}{\underline{\pi 2p_y^2}}\ \underset{8}{\underline{\pi^* 2p_x^1}}\ \underset{9}{\underline{\pi^* 2p_y^1}}\ \underset{10}{\underline{\sigma^* 2p_z^0}}$$

Thus, option (a) is correct.

The correct form of other statement are as follows.

(b) All the molecular orbitals in the dioxygen will not be completely filled (*i.e.* $\overset{*}{\pi} 2p_x^1, \pi 2p_{y^1}$)

(c) Total number of bonding molecular orbitals will be same as total number of anti-bonding orbitals in dioxygen.

(d) Number of filled bonding orbitals is 5 and the number of filled anti-bonding orbitals is 4.

Q.66 Which of the following molecular orbitals has maximum number of nodal planes?

(a) $\sigma^* 1s$ (b) $\overset{*}{\sigma} 2p_z$

(c) $\pi 2p_x$ (d) $\overset{*}{\pi} 2p_y$

Ans. ***(d)*** Nodal plane are $\sigma^* 1s = 1$, $\sigma^* 2p_z = 1$, $\pi 2p_x = 1$, $\pi^* 2p_y = 2$

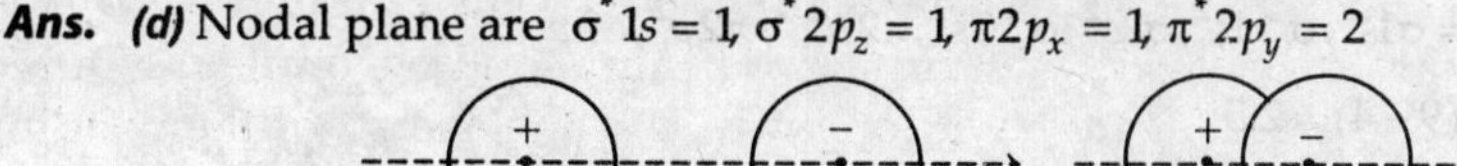

σ* (1s)
Anti-bonding molecular orbital

The molecular orbitals whose number of nodal planes are as

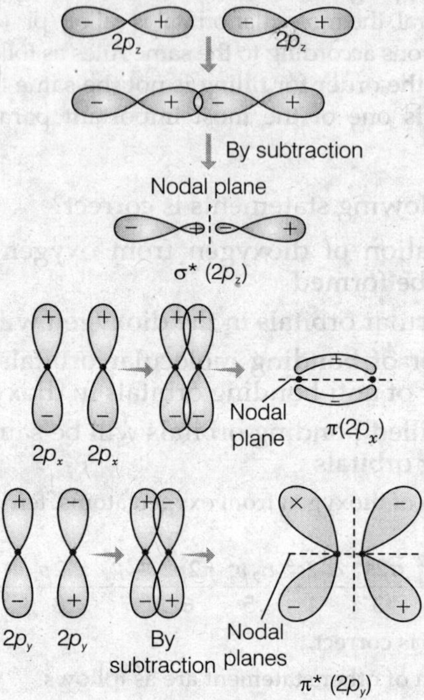

Q.67 Which of the following pair is expected to have the same bond order?

(a) O_2, N_2 (b) O_2^+, N_2^- (c) O_2^-, N_2^+ (d) O_2^-, N_2^-

Ans. ***(b)*** On the basis of molecular orbital theory, we can calculate bond order of molecular ions as

$$BO = \frac{1}{2}(N_b - N_a)$$

Molecular orbital electronic configuration (MOEC) of N_2 is

$$\sigma 1s^2, \sigma^* 1s^2, \sigma 2s^2, \sigma^* 2s^2, \pi 2p_x^2 \simeq \pi 2p_y^2, \sigma 2p_z^2$$

Bond order of $N_2 = \frac{1}{2}(10-4) = 3$

MOEC of $N_2^+ = \sigma 1s^2, \sigma^* 1s^2, \sigma 2s^2, \sigma^* 2s^2, \pi 2p_x^2 \simeq \pi 2p_y^2, \sigma 2p_z^-$

BO of $N_2^+ = \frac{1}{2}(9-4) = 2.5$

MOEC of $N_2^- = \sigma 1s^2, \sigma^* 1s^2, \sigma 2s^2, \sigma^* 2s^2, \pi 2p_x^2 \simeq \pi 2p_y^2, \sigma 2p_z^2, \pi^* 2p_x^1 \simeq \pi^* 2p_y^0$

BO of $N_2^- = \frac{1}{2}(10-5) = 2.5$

MOEC of $O_2 = \sigma 1s^2, \sigma^* 1s^2, \sigma 2s^2, \sigma^* 2s^2, \sigma 2p_z^2, \pi 2p_x^2 \simeq \pi 2p_y{}^2, \pi^* 2p_x^1 \simeq \pi^* 2p_y^1$

BO of $O_2 = \frac{1}{2}(10-6) = 2$

MOEC of $O_2^- = \sigma 1s^2, \sigma^* 1s^2, \sigma 2s^2, \sigma^* 2s^2, \sigma 2p_z^2, \pi 2p_x^2 \simeq \pi 2p_y^2, \pi^* 2p_x^2 \simeq \pi^* 2p_y^1$

BO of $O_2^- = \frac{1}{2}(10-7) = 1.5$

MOEC of $O_2^+ = \sigma 1s^2, \sigma^* 1s^2, \sigma 2s^2, \sigma^* 2s^2, \sigma 2p_z^2, \pi 2p_x^2 \simeq \pi 2p_y^2, \pi^* 2p_x^1 \simeq \pi^* 2p_y$

BO of $O_2^+ = \frac{1}{2}(10-5) = 2.5$

(a) Bond order of O_2 and N_2 are 2 and 3, respectively.

(b) Bond order of both O_2^+ and N_2^- are 2.5.

(c) Bond order of O_2^- and N_2^+ are 1.5 and 2.5, respectively.

(d) Bond order of O_2^- and N_2^- are 1.5 and 2.5 respectively.

Q.68 In which of the following molecules, $\sigma 2p_z$ molecular orbital is filled after $\pi 2p_x$ and $\pi 2p_y$ molecular orbitals?

(a) O_2 (b) Ne_2

(c) N_2 (d) F_2

● **Concept Insight** The increasing order of energies of various molecular orbitals for O_2 and F_2 is given below

$$\sigma 1s<\sigma^* 1s<\sigma 2s<\sigma^* 2s<\sigma 2p_z<(\pi 2p_x \approx \pi 2p_y)<(\pi^* 2p_x \approx \pi^* 2p_y)<\sigma^* 2p_z$$

However, this sequence of energy levels of MO is not correct for the remaining molecules such as Li_2, Be_2, B_2, C_2 and N_2. For these molecules, the increasing order of energies of various MO is

$$\sigma 1s<\sigma^* 1s<\sigma 2s<\sigma^* 2s<(\pi 2p_x \approx \pi 2p_y)<\sigma 2p_z<(\pi^* 2p_x \approx \pi^* 2p_y)<\sigma^* 2p_z$$

Ans. ***(c)*** Total number of electrons present in N_2 molecule is 14.

The electronic configuration of N_2 molecule will be

$$\sigma 1s^2, \sigma^* 1s^2, \sigma 2s^2, \sigma^* 2s^2, \pi 2p_x^2 \approx \pi 2p_y^2, \sigma 2p_z^2$$

Chapter

05

States of Matter*

Multiple Choice Questions (MCQs)

Q.1 A person living in Shimla observed that cooking food without using pressure cooker takes more time. The reason for this observation is that at high altitude.

(a) pressure increases
(b) temperature decreases
(c) pressure decreases
(d) temperature increases

Ans. ***(c)*** Pressure at mountain [or at high altitude] is low. This suggests that boiling takes place at lower temperature and cooking temperature decreases due to which food takes more time to boil.

However, in a pressure cooker, pressure is increased and hence, boiling point increases, allowing food to cook at higher temperature. Thus, food comes to boil in a pressure cooker in a less period of time.

Q.2 Which of the following property of water can be used to explain the spherical shape of rain droplets?

(a) Viscosity
(b) Surface tension
(c) Critical phenomena
(d) Pressure

Ans. ***(b)*** The spherical shape of rain droplets is due to surface tension. The lowest energy state of a liquid will be when the surface area is minimum. Surface tension tries to decrease the surface area of the liquid to the minimum. The rain droplets are spherical because for a given volume, a sphere has minimum surface area.

Q.3 A plot of volume (V) *versus* temperature (T) for a gas at constant pressure is a straight line passing through the origin. The plots at different values of pressure are shown in figure. Which of the following order of pressure is correct for this gas?

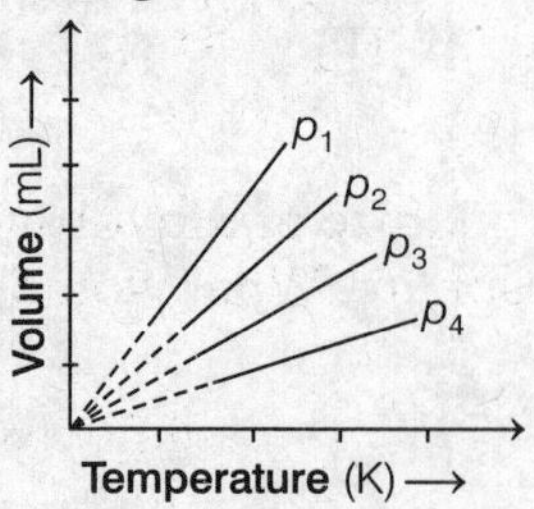

(a) $p_1 > p_2 > p_3 > p_4$
(b) $p_1 = p_2 = p_3 = p_4$
(c) $p_1 < p_2 < p_3 < p_4$
(d) $p_1 < p_2 = p_3 < p_4$

Note (*) *This chapter has been deleted from latest NCERT.*

Thinking Process The question is based upon Boyle's law. It states that at constant temperature, the volume of a given gas is inversely proportional to its pressure, *i.e.*, $V \propto \frac{1}{p}$ or, pV = constant.

Ans. *(c)* At a particular temperature, pV = constant

Thus, $p_1V_1 = p_2V_2 = p_3V_3 = p_4V_4$

As $V_1 > V_2 > V_3 > V_4$

Therefore, $p_1 < p_2 < p_3 < p_4$

Q.4 The interaction energy of London force is inversely proportional to sixth power of the distance between two interacting particles but their magnitude depends upon

(a) charge of interacting particles
(b) mass of interacting particles
(c) polarisability of interacting particles
(d) strength of permanent dipoles in the particles

Ans. *(c)* London dispersion forces operate only over very short distances. The energy of interaction varies as $\frac{1}{(\text{distance between two interacting particles})^6}$.

More complex are the molecules, greater is the magnitude of London forces. This is obviously due to the fact that the large electron clouds are easily distorted or polarised.

Hence, greater the polarisability of the interacting particles, greater is the magnitude of the interaction energy.

Q.5 Dipole-dipole forces act between the molecules possessing permanent dipole. Ends of dipoles possess 'partial charges'. The partial charge is

(a) more than unit electronic charge.
(b) equal to unit electronic charge.
(c) less than unit electronic charge.
(d) double the unit electronic charge.

Ans. *(c)* Partial charges present on ends of a dipole are always less than the unit electronic charge as more electronegative atom attracts charge density of bond pair slightly towards itself.

e.g.,

$\delta\delta-$ on O, $\delta+$ on each H (H—O—H)

$\mu = 1.84\,D$

Q.6 The pressure of a 1 : 4 mixture of dihydrogen and dioxygen enclosed in a vessel is one atmosphere. What would be the partial pressure of dioxygen?

(a) 0.8×10^5 atm
(b) $0.008\ Nm^{-2}$
(c) $8 \times 10^4\ Nm^{-2}$
(d) 0.25 atm

Ans. ***(c)*** Given that, pressure of a 1 : 4 mixture of H_2 and O_2 enclosed in a vessel is one atmosphere. This suggests that the mole ratio of H_2 and O_2 is 1:4. Thus, partial pressure of dioxygen (O_2) is given as

$\therefore$ Partial pressure of O_2 = Mole fraction of O_2 $\times$ total pressure of mixture

$$= \frac{4}{1+4} \times 1 = \frac{4}{5} \times 1\,\text{atm} \qquad \left[\because \text{mole fraction of } O_2 = \frac{4}{1+4}\right]$$

$$= 0.8\,\text{atm}$$

$$= 0.8 \times 10^5\,\text{Nm}^{-2} \qquad [\because 1\,\text{atm} = 1.01 \times 10^5\,\text{Nm}^{-2}]$$

$$= 8 \times 10^4\,\text{Nm}^{-2}$$

Q.7 As the temperature increases, average kinetic energy of molecules increases. What would be the effect of increase of temperature on pressure provided the volume is constant ?

(a) Increases
(b) Decreases
(c) Remains same
(d) Becomes half

Thinking Process This problem is based on Gay-Lussac's law which states that "at constant volume, the pressure of a given mass of a gas is directly proportional to its temperature in degrees Kelvin".

Ans. ***(a)*** From Gay-Lussac's law, at constant volume, as the temperature is increased, pressure of gas increases. Because kinetic energy of gas particles increases with increase in temperature, so molecules strike to the wall of container to more extent.

Q.8 Gases possess characteristic critical temperature which depends on the magnitude of intermolecular forces between the particles. Following are the critical temperatures of some gases.

Gases	H_2	He	O_2	N_2
Critical temperature in Kelvin	33.2	5.3	154.3	126

From the above data what would be the order of liquefaction of these gases? Start writing the order from the gas liquefying first

(a) H_2, He, O_2, N_2
(b) He, O_2, H_2, N_2
(c) N_2, O_2, He, H_2
(d) O_2, N_2, H_2, He

● **Concept Insight** Critical temperature of a gas may be defined as that temperature above which it cannot be liquified howsoever high pressure may be applied on the gas.

Ans. ***(d)*** Higher the critical temperature, more easily is the gas liquified. Hence, order of liquification starting with the gas liquefying first will be O_2, N_2, H_2, He.

Q.9 What is SI unit of viscosity coefficient (η) ?

(a) Pascal
(b) Nsm^{-2}
(c) km^{-2}s
(d) Nm^{-2}

Ans. *(b)* As we know that, $f = \eta A \dfrac{dv}{dx}$

where, f = force

η = viscosity coefficient

A = area

$\dfrac{dv}{dx}$ = velocity gradient

Substitute SI units of f = N, dx = m, $A = \text{m}^2$ and $v = \text{ms}^{-1}$ in above equation, to get,

$$\eta = \frac{\text{N} \times \text{m}}{\text{m}^2 \times \text{ms}^{-1}} = \text{Nm}^{-2}\text{s}$$

Hence, the SI unit of η is Nsm^{-2}.

Q.10 Atmospheric pressures recorded in different cities are as follows

Cities	Shimla	Bangalore	Delhi	Mumbai
p in N/m^2	1.01×10^5	1.2×10^5	1.02×10^5	1.21×10^5

Consider the above data and mark the place at which liquid will boil first.

(a) Shimla (b) Bangalore (c) Delhi (d) Mumbai

Thinking Process A liquid boils when vapour pressure above it becomes equal to the atmospheric pressure. Lower the atmospheric pressure, lower is the boiling point.

Ans. *(a)* Shimla has the lowest atmospheric pressure among all the four cities. Thus, at Shimla liquid will boil first because lower the atmospheric pressure, lower is the boiling point.

Q.11 Which curve in figure represents the curve of ideal gas?

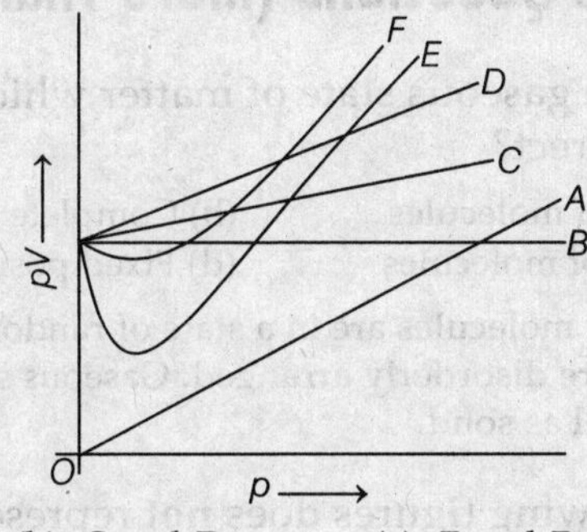

(a) Only B (b) C and D (c) E and F (d) A and B

Thinking Process

(i) The graph given in the question depends upon the Boyle's law.

(ii) At constant temperature, the graph between pV *vs* p at all pressures will be straight line parallel to x-axis for ideal gas.

(iii) At constant temperature pV *vs* p plot for real gases is not straight line.

Ans. *(a)* For ideal gas pV = constant at all pressures. When a gas obeys Boyle's law (i.e., ideal behaviour at constant temperature), the pV *vs* p graph is a straight horizontal line, parallel to x-axis. Therefore, only B represents the curve of an ideal gas.

Q.12 Increase in kinetic energy can overcome intermolecular forces of attraction. How will the viscosity of liquid be affected by the increase in temperature?

(a) Increase (b) No effect
(c) Decrease (d) No regular pattern will be followed

Thinking Process Viscosity is the tendency of a fluid to resist any change in its shape or motion.

Ans. *(c)* With increase of temperature, the kinetic energy of the molecules of liquid increases which can overcome the intermolecular forces. Hence, the liquid starts flowing.

In other words, the viscosity of a liquid decreases with increase in temperature.

Q.13 How does the surface tension of a liquid vary with increase in temperature?

(a) Remains same (b) Decreases
(c) Increases (d) No regular pattern is followed

Concept Insight Surface tension of a liquid is defined as the force acting at right angles to the surface along one centimetre length of the surface. Units of surface tension are dyne per cm (or newtons per metre, *i.e.*, Nm^{-1} in the SI system).

Ans. *(b)* The surface tension of liquids generally decreases with increase of temperature and becomes zero at the critical temperature. The decrease in surface tension with increase of temperature is due to the fact that with increase in temperature, the kinetic energy of the molecules increases and thus, the intermolecular attraction decreases.

Multiple Choice Questions (More Than One Options)

Q.14 With regard to the gaseous state of matter which of the following statements are correct?

(a) Complete order of molecules (b) Complete disorder of molecules
(c) Random motion of molecules (d) Fixed position of molecules

Ans. *(b, c)* In gaseous state, molecules are in a state of random motion, *i.e.*, it is the state in which molecules are disorderly arranged. Gaseous state have higher entropy than the liquid as well as solid.

Q.15 Which of the following figures does **not** represent 1 mole of dioxygen gas at STP?

(a) 16 g of gas (b) 22.4 L of gas
(c) 6.022×10^{23} dioxygen molecules (d) 11.2 L of gas

Ans. *(a, d)* It is known that, 1mole of a gas = gram molecular mass = Avogadro's number of molecules = 22.4 L at STP.

Thus, 1 mole of O_2 gas = 32 g of O_2 = 6.02×10^{23} molecules = 22.4L of O_2 at STP

Q.16 Under which of the following conditions applied together, a gas deviates most from the ideal behaviour?

(a) Low pressure (b) High pressure
(c) Low temperature (d) High temperature

Ans. ***(b, c)*** A gas which obeys the ideal gas equation, $pV = nRT$ under all conditions of temperature and pressure is called an 'ideal gas'. However, there is no gas which obeys the ideal gas equation under all conditions of temperature and pressure. Hence, the concept of ideal gas is only theoretical or hypothetical. The gases are found to obey the gas laws fairly well when the pressure is low or the temperature is high.

Such gases are, therefore, known as **'real gases'.** All gases are real gases. Hence, at **high pressure and low temperature,** a real gas deviates most from ideal behaviour.

Mistake Alert ! *Students may make a mistake of confusing ideal gases with real gases, especially in conditions of high pressure or low temperature, where real gases deviate from ideal behaviour.*

Q.17 Which of the following changes decrease the vapour pressure of water kept in a sealed vessel?

(a) Decreasing the quantity of water
(b) Adding salt to water
(c) Decreasing the volume of the vessel to one-half
(d) Decreasing the temperature of water

Ans. ***(b, d)*** When salt is added, less surface area is available for the water molecules to vaporise because salt molecules occupy the position of water molecules on the surface. Hence, vapour pressure of the water decreases.

Moreover, vapour pressure also decreases with decrease in temperature because kinetic energy of the molecules decrease.

Short Answer Type Questions

Q.18 If 1 g of each of the following gases are taken at STP, which of the gases will occupy (a) greatest volume and (b) smallest volume?

$$CO, H_2O, CH_4, NO$$

Ans. From Avogadro's law, we know that

Volume of 1 mole of the gas = gram molecular mass of the gas = 22.4 L at STP

Volume occupied by 28 g CO (1 mol CO) = 22.4 L at STP

[∵ Molar mass of CO = 12 + 16 = 28 g mol^{-1}]

∴ Volume occupied by 1 g CO $= \frac{22.4}{28}$ L at STP

Similarly, volume occupied by 1 g $H_2O = \frac{22.4}{18}$ L at STP

[∵ Molar mass of $H_2O = (2 \times 1) + 16 = 18$ g mol^{-1}]

$$\text{Volume occupied by 1g } CH_4 = \frac{22.4}{16} \text{ L at STP}$$

[$\because$ Molar mass of $CH_4 = 12 + (4 \times 1) = 16 \text{ g mol}^{-1}$]

$$\text{Volume occupied by 1g NO} = \frac{22.4}{30} \text{ L at STP}$$

[$\because$ Molar mass of NO $= 14 + 16 = 30 \text{ g mol}^{-1}$]

Thus, 1 g CH_4 will occupy maximum volume while 1 g of NO will occupy minimum volume at STP.

Q.19 Physical properties of ice, water and steam are very different. What is the chemical composition of water in all the three states?

Ans. Physical properties of ice, water and steam are very different because they are found in different states. Ice is found in solid state, water is found in liquid state and steam is found in vapour states. The chemical composition of water in all the three states (ice, water and steam) is same, *i.e.*, H_2O.

Q.20 The behaviour of matter in different states is governed by various physical laws. According to you, what are the factors that determine the state of matter ?

Ans. Temperature, pressure, mass and volume are the factors which determine the different states of matter, *i.e.*, solid, liquid and gas.

Q.21 Use the information and data given below to answer the questions (a) to (c),

- Stronger intermolecular forces result in higher boiling point.
- Strength of London forces increases with the number of electrons in the molecule.
- Boiling point of HF, HCl, HBr and HI are 293 K, 189 K, 206 K and 238 K respectively.

(a) Which type of intermolecular forces are present in the molecules HF, HCl, HBr and HI?

(b) Looking at the trend of boiling points of HCl, HBr and HI, explain out of dipole-dipole interaction and London interaction, which one is predominant here.

(c) Why is boiling point of hydrogen fluoride highest while that of hydrogen chloride lowest?

Ans. From the information and data given in the question, we concluded that :

(a) In HCl, HBr and HI, dipole-dipole and London forces of attraction are present because molecules possess permanent dipole. In HF, intermolecular hydrogen bonding are present.

(b) Electronegativity of chlorine, bromine and iodine decreases in the order as follows :

$$Cl > Br > I$$

Therefore, dipole moment should decrease from HCl to HI. Thus, dipole-dipole interaction should decrease from HCl to HI. But boiling point increases on moving from HCl to HI. This means that London forces are predominant. This is so because London forces increase as the number of electrons in a molecule increases and in this case number of electrons is increasing from HCl towards HI.

(c) Hydrogen fluoride (HF) has highest dipole moment due to highest electronegativity of fluorine as well as presence of hydrogen bonding in HF. Therefore, HF has highest boiling point. Hydrogen Chloride (HCl) does not have H-bonding and is attracted by weakest London forces of attraction than HBr and HI, so its boiling point is lowest.

Q.22 What will be the molar volume of nitrogen and argon at 273.15 K and 1 atm?

Ans. When temperature and pressure of a gas is 273.15 K (or 0°C) and 1 atm (or 1 bar or 10^5 pascal), such conditions are called **standard temperature and pressure (STP).** Under these conditions, the volume occupied by 1 mole of each and every gas is 22.4L.

Hence, the molar volume of N_2 and Ar at 273.15 K and 1 atm is 22.4L.

Q.23 A gas that follows Boyle's law, Charle's law and Avogadro's law is called an ideal gas. Under what conditions a real gas would behave ideally?

Ans. At **low pressure and high temperature,** a real gas behaves as an ideal gas. Almost all gases are real gas.

Q.24 Two different gases '*A*' and '*B*' are filled in separate containers of equal capacity under the same conditions of temperature and pressure. On increasing the pressure slightly, the gas '*A*' liquefies but gas *B* does not liquefy even on applying high pressure until it is cooled. Explain this phenomenon.

Ans. The temperature above which a gas cannot be liquefied howsoever high pressure may be applied on the gas is called **critical temperature.** Since, gas '*A*' liquefies easily, this suggests gas '*A*' is below its critical temperature.

On the other hand, gas '*B*' does not liquefy easily even on applying high pressure. This suggests that gas '*B*' is above its critical temperature.

Q.25 Value of universal gas constant (*R*) is same for all gases. What is its physical significance?

Ans. Unit of gas constant (*R*) depends upon those units in which *p*, *V* and *T* are measured as, $R = \frac{pV}{nT}$. If pressure is measured in Pascal, per mole volume is measured in $m^3\ mol^{-1}$ and temperature is measured in Kelvin then units of '*R*' are $Pa\ m^3K^{-1}mol^{-1}$ or $J\ mol^{-1}K^{-1}$. Since, joule is the unit of work done, so '*R*' is work done by the gas per mole per kelvin.

Q.26 **One of the assumptions of kinetic theory of gases states that "there is no force of attraction between the molecules of a gas." How far is this statement correct? Is it possible to liquefy an ideal gas? Explain.**

Ans. This statement is correct only for ideal gases. It is not possible to liquefy an ideal gas because there are no intermolecular forces of attractions present between the molecules of an ideal gas.

Q.27 **The magnitude of surface tension of liquid depends on the attractive forces between the molecules. Arrange the following in increasing order of surface tension:**
Water, alcohol (C_2H_5OH) and hexane [$CH_3(CH_2)_4CH_3$].

Ans. In the above given molecules, only hexane ($CH_3(CH_2)_4CH_3$) is a non-polar molecule in which only London dispersion forces exist. These forces are very weak while both water and alcohol are polar molecules in which dipole-dipole interactions as well as H-bonding exists. However, H-bonding interactions are much stronger in water, therefore, it possesses stronger attractions than alcohol and hexane. Hence, the increasing order of surface tension is

$$\text{hexane} < \text{alcohol} < \text{water}$$

Greater is the attractive forces between the molecules, greater is the magnitude of surface tension of liquid.

Q.28 **Pressure exerted by saturated water vapour is called aqueous tension. What correction term will you apply to the total pressure to obtain pressure of dry gas?**

Ans. Whenever a gas is collected over water, it is moist and saturated with water vapours which exert their own pressure. The pressure due to water vapours is called aqueous tension thus, total pressure of the moist gas is

$$p_{\text{moist gas}} = p_{\text{dry gas}} + \text{aqueous tension}$$

Thus, $p_{\text{dry gas}}$ is given as $p_{\text{dry gas}} = p_{\text{moist gas}} - \text{aqueous tension}$.

Hence, the correction term applied to the total pressure of the gas in order to obtain pressure of dry gas is $p_{\text{moist gas}} - \text{aqueous tension}$.

Q.29 **Name the energy which arises due to motion of atoms or molecules in a body. How is this energy affected when the temperature is increased?**

Ans. The energy which arises due to motion of atoms or molecules in a body is known as **thermal energy.** It is a measure of average kinetic energy of the particles. It increases with increase in temperature.

Q.30 **Name two intermolecular forces that exist between HF molecules in liquid state.**

Ans. H–F is a polar covalent molecule in which **dipole-dipole** interactions exists. Since, it contains an electronegative atom, F bonded to H atom, therefore, hydrogen bonding (H-bond) exists between its molecules. Due to these H-bonds, HF molecules exists in liquid state. Hence, in liquid state, H-bonds as well as dipole dipole interactions exists within HF molecules.

$$\ldots \overset{\delta+}{H} - \overset{\delta-}{F} \ldots \quad \overset{\delta+}{H} \quad - \quad \overset{\delta-}{F} \ldots \overset{\delta+}{H} - \overset{\delta-}{F} \ldots \overset{\delta+}{H} - \overset{\delta-}{F} \ldots$$

solid line
H-bonds →

Q.31 One of the assumptions of kinetic theory of gases is that there is no force of attraction between the molecules of a gas.

State and explain the evidence that shows that the assumption is not applicable for real gases.

Ans. Real gases deviate from ideal behaviour at high pressure and low temperature, where intermolecular forces become significant. For example, real gases can be liquefied, which is only possible if there are attractive forces between molecules. If no such forces existed, gases could never condense to form a liquid. This clearly proves that intermolecular attractions are present in real gases, unlike what is assumed in the kinetic theory.

Q.32 Compressibility factor, Z of a gas is given as $Z = \frac{pV}{nRT}$

(i) What is the value of Z for an ideal gas?

(ii) For real gas what will be the effect on value of Z above Boyle's temperature?

- **Concept Insight** Following important points come out from the compressibility factor, $Z = \frac{pV}{nRT}$.
  (i) For an ideal gas, Z = 1 at all temperatures and pressures because $pV = nRT$.
  (ii) At very low pressure, all gases show $Z \simeq 1$ and behave as ideal gas.
  (iii) At high pressure, all the gases have $Z > 1$. These are more difficult to compress.
  (iv) At intermediate pressures most gases have $Z < 1$.

Ans. (i) For an ideal gas, compressibility factor, Z = 1.

(ii) Above Boyle's temperature, real gases show positive deviation.

So, $Z > 1$

Q.33 The critical temperature (T_c) and critical pressure (p_c) of CO_2 are 30.98°C and 73 atm respectively. Can CO_2 (*g*) be liquefied at 32°C and 80 atm pressure?

Ans. The given critical temperature and pressure of CO_2 gas are 30.98°C and 73 atm respectively. This suggests that CO_2 gas cannot be liquified above 30.98°C and 73 atm, howsoever high temperature and pressure may be applied on CO_2 gas. Hence, CO_2 gas cannot be liquified at 32°C and 80 atm.

Q.34 For real gases the relation between *p*, *V* and *T* is given by van der Waals' equation :

$$\left(p + \frac{an^2}{V^2}\right)(V - nb) = nRT$$

where, '*a*' and '*b*' are van der Waals constants, '*nb*' is approximately equal to the total volume of the molecules of a gas. '*a*' is the measure of magnitude of intermolecular attraction.

(i) Arrange the following gases in the increasing order of '*b*'. Give reason. O_2, CO_2, H_2, He

(ii) Arrange the following gases in the decreasing order of magnitude of '*a*'. Give reason. CH_4, O_2, H_2

Ans. (i) Molar volume occupied by the gas molecules $\propto$ size of the molecules and van der Waals constant 'b' which represents molar volume of the gas molecules. Hence, value of 'b' increases in the following order

$$H_2 < He < O_2 < CO_2$$

(ii) van der Waals constant 'a' is the measure of magnitude of intermolecular attraction. The magnitude of intermolecular attractions increases with increase in size of electron cloud in a molecule. Hence, for the given gases magnitude of 'a' decreases in the following order?

$$CH_4 > O_2 > H_2$$

Greater the size of electron cloud, greater is the polarisability of the molecule and greater is the dispersion forces or London forces.

Q.35 The relation between pressure exerted by an ideal gas (p_{ideal}) and observed pressure (p_{real}) is given by the equation,

$$p_{ideal} = p_{real} + \frac{an^2}{V^2}$$

(i) If pressure is taken in Nm^{-2}, number of moles in mol and volume in m^3, calculate the unit of 'a'.

(ii) What will be the unit of 'a' when pressure is in atmosphere and volume in dm^3?

Ans. Given that, $p_{ideal} = p_{real} + \frac{an^2}{V^2}$

(i) $a = \frac{pV^2}{n^2}$ If units of $p = Nm^{-2}$,

units of $V = m^3$, units of $n =$ mol

then, units of $a = \frac{Nm^{-2}\ (m^3)^2}{(mol)^2} = Nm^4\ mol^{-2}$

(ii) If units of $p =$ atm, units of $V = dm^3$,

units of $n =$ mol

then, units of $a = \frac{pV^2}{n^2} = \frac{atm.\ (dm^3)^2}{(mol)^2} = atm\ dm^6\ mol^{-2}$

Q.36 Name two phenomena that can be explained on the basis of surface tension.

- **Concept Insight** Surface tension is caused by the attraction of the particles in the surface layer by bulk of the liquid which tends to minimise the surface area.

Ans. Two phenomena that can be explained on the basis of surface tension are as following

(i) Rise or fall of the liquid in a capillary-(capillary action).

(ii) Spherical shape of small liquid drops to minimise surface tension.

Q.37 Viscosity of a liquid arises due to strong intermolecular forces existing between the molecules. Stronger the intermolecular forces, greater is the viscosity. Name the intermolecular forces existing in the following liquids and arrange them in the increasing order of their viscosities. Also give reason for the assigned order in one line.

Water, hexane ($CH_3CH_2CH_2CH_2CH_2CH_3$), glycerine ($CH_2OHCH(OH)CH_2OH$)

Thinking Process Stronger the intermolecular forces existing between the liquids, more viscous is the liquid.

Ans. **In water and glycerine,** hydrogen bonding and dipole-dipole interactions exists as both are polar molecules.

In hexane, dispersion forces/London forces are present due its non-polar nature.

The order of intermolecular forces among the given liquids is,

hexane < water < glycerine.

Since, hexane has weakest intermolecular forces and glycerine the strongest (three OH groups) intermolecular forces. Therefore, hexane has minimum viscosity and glycerine has maximum viscosity.

Q.38 Explain the effect of increasing the temperature of a liquid, on intermolecular forces operating between its particles. What will happen to the viscosity of a liquid if its temperature is increased?

Ans. As the temperature of a liquid increases, kinetic energy of the molecules increases which can overcome intermolecular forces. So, the liquid can flow more easily, which results in decrease in viscosity of the liquid.

Q.39 The variation of pressure with volume of the gas at different temperatures can be graphically represented as shown in figure. On the basis of this graph answer the following questions.

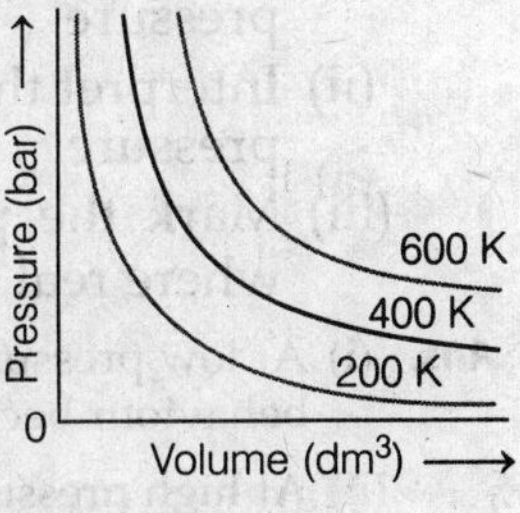

(i) How will the volume of a gas change if its pressure is increased at constant temperature?

(ii) At a constant pressure, how will the volume of a gas change if the temperature is increased from 200 K to 400 K?

Ans. (i) According to **Boyle's law,** pressure of a gas is inversely proportional to its volume if temperature is constant. Thus, the volume of a gas will decrease if the pressure on the gas is increased keeping the temperature constant. *e.g.*, at 200 K when pressure increases from p_1 to p_2, volume of the gas decreases, $V_2 < V_1$.

(ii) According to **Charle's law,** volume of a gas is directly proportional to its temperature if pressure is kept constant.

Thus, on increasing temperature, the volume of a gas will increase if pressure is kept constant. At constant p, when we increase the temperature from 200 K to 400 K, the volume of the gas increases, $V_4 > V_3$.

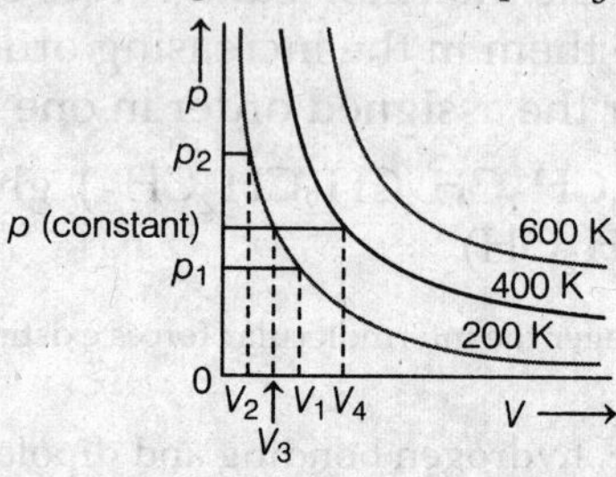

Mistake Alert! *Students may get confused in applying gas laws due to miscalculating variables or not understanding the relationship between them.*

Q.40 Pressure *versus* volume graph for a real gas and an ideal gas are shown in figure. Answer the following questions on the basis of this graph.

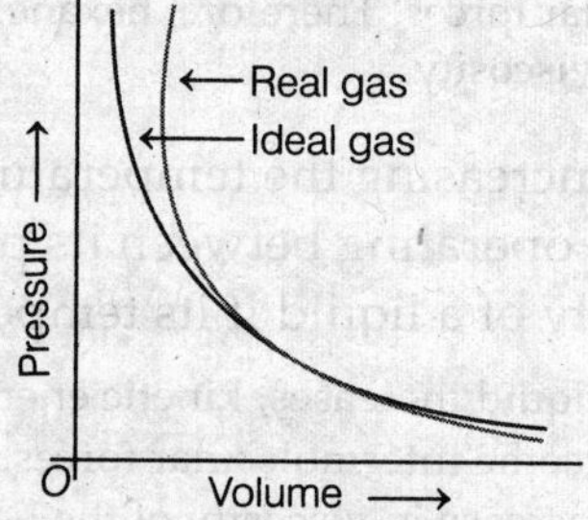

(i) Interpret the behaviour of real gas with respect to ideal gas at low pressure.

(ii) Interpret the behaviour of real gas with respect to ideal gas at high pressure.

(iii) Mark the pressure and volume by drawing a line at the point where real gas behaves as an ideal gas.

Ans. (i) At low pressure, the real gas shows very small deviation from ideal behaviour because the two curves almost coincide at low pressure.

(ii) At high pressure, the real gas show large deviations from ideal behaviour as the curves are far apart.

(iii) At point 'A', both the curves intersect each other. At this point, real gas behaves as an ideal gas. p_1 and V_1 are the pressure and volume which corresponds to this point A.

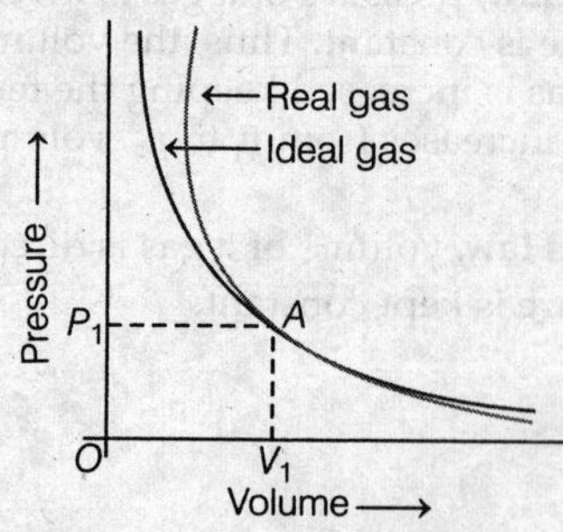

Matching The Columns

Q.41 Match the graphs between the following variables with their names.

	Graps		Names
A.	Pressure vs temperature graph at constant molar volume	1.	Isotherms
B.	Pressure vs volume graph at constant temperature	2.	Constant temperature curve
C.	Volume vs temperature graph at constant pressure	3.	Isochores
		4.	Isobars

Ans. **A.** $\rightarrow$ (3) **B.** $\rightarrow$ (1) **C.** $\rightarrow$ (4)

A. When molar volume is constant, the p-T graph is called **isochore.**

B. When temperature is constant, the p-V graph is called **isotherm.**

C. When pressure is constant, V-T graph is called **isobar.**

Q.42 Match the following gas laws with the equation representing them.

A.	Boyle's law	1.	$V \propto n$ at constant T and p
B.	Charle's law	2.	$p_{Total} = p_1 + p_2 + p_3 + \ldots$ at constant T, V
C.	Dalton's law	3.	$\frac{pV}{T}$ = constant
D.	Avogadro's law	4.	$V \propto T$ at constant n and p
		5.	$p \propto \frac{1}{V}$ at constant n and T

Ans. **A.** $\rightarrow$ (5) **B.** $\rightarrow$ (4) **C.** $\rightarrow$ (2) **D.** $\rightarrow$ (1)

A. Boyle's law, $p \propto \frac{1}{V}$ at constant T and n.

B. Charle's law, $V \propto T$ at constant p and n.

C. Dalton's law, $p_{Total} = p_1 + p_2 + p_3 + \ldots$ at constant T, V.

D. Avogadro's law, $V \propto n$ at constant T and p.

Q.43 Match the following graphs of ideal gas with their coordinates.

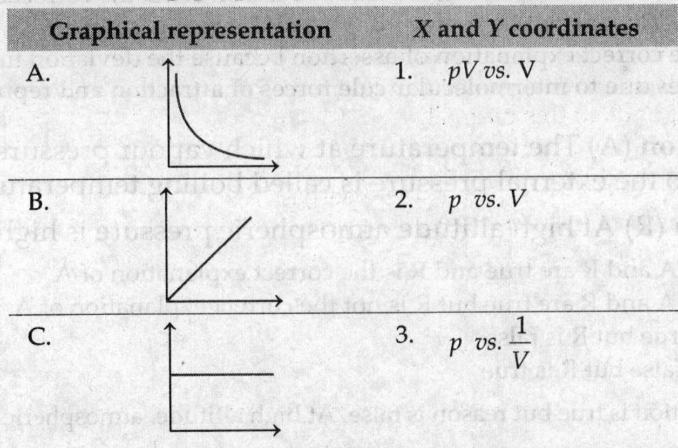

Graphical representation		X and Y coordinates
A.	1.	pV *vs.* V
B.	2.	p *vs.* V
C.	3.	p *vs.* $\frac{1}{V}$

Ans. A. → (2) B. → (3) C. → (1)

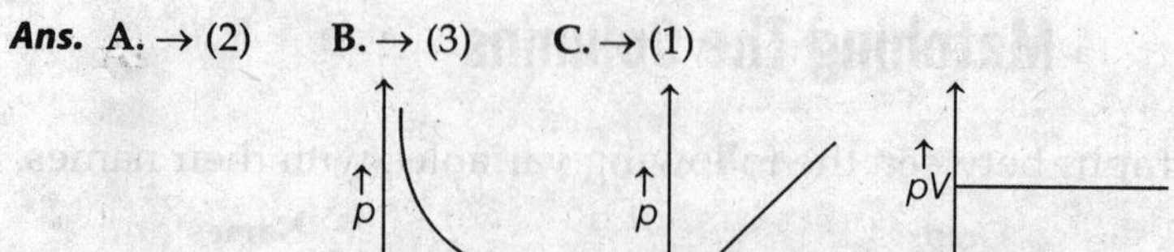

Assertion and Reason

In the following questions a statement of Assertion (A) followed by a statement of Reason (R) is given. Choose the correct option out of the choices given below in each question.

Q.44 **Assertion** (A) Three states of matter are the result of balance between intermolecular forces and thermal energy of the molecules.

Reason (R) Intermolecular forces tend to keep the molecules together but thermal energy of molecules tends to keep them apart.

(a) Both A and R are true and R is the correct explanation of A
(b) Both A and R are true but R is not the correct explanation of A
(c) A is true but R is false
(d) A is false but R is true

Ans. *(a)* Both assertion and reason are true and reason is the correct explanation of assertion. Intermolecular forces and thermal energy decides the states of matter because the former keeps the molecules together but later keeps them apart.

Q.45 **Assertion** (A) At constant temperature, *pV vs V* plot for real gases is not a straight line.

Reason (R) At high pressure all gases have $Z > 1$ but at intermediate pressure most gases have $Z < 1$.

(a) Both A and R are true and R is the correct explanation of A
(b) Both A and R are true but R is not the correct explanation of A
(c) A is true but R is false
(d) A is false but R is true

Ans. *(b)* Both assertion and reason are true but reason is not the correct explanation of assertion. At constant temperature, *pV vs V* for real gases is not a straight line. *R* is not the correct explanation of assertion because the deviation in the *PV* vs *V* plot arises due to intermolecular cule forces of attraction and repulsion.

Q.46 **Assertion** (A) The temperature at which vapour pressure of a liquid is equal to the external pressure is called boiling temperature.

Reason (R) At high altitude atmospheric pressure is high.

(a) Both A and R are true and R is the correct explanation of A
(b) Both A and R are true but R is not the correct explanation of A
(c) A is true but R is false
(d) A is false but R is true

Ans. *(c)* Assertion is true but reason is false. At high altitude, atmospheric pressure is low.

Q.47 **Assertion** (A) Gases do not liquefy above their critical temperature, even on applying high pressure.

Reason (R) Above critical temperature, the molecular speed is high and intermolecular attractions cannot hold the molecules together because they escape because of high speed.

(a) Both A and R are true and R is the correct explanation of A
(b) Both A and R are true but R is not the correct explanation of A
(c) A is true but R is false
(d) A is false but R is true

Ans. ***(a)*** Both assertion and reason are true and reason is the correct explanation of assertion.

Gases do not liquefy above their critical temperature, even on applying high pressure because above critical temperature, the molecular speed is high and intermolecular attractions cannot hold the molecules together.

Q.48 **Assertion** (A) At critical temperature, liquid passes into gaseous state imperceptibly and continuously.

Reason (R) The density of liquid and gaseous phase is equal to critical temperature.

(a) Both A and R are true and R is the correct explanation of A
(b) Both A and R are true but R is not the correct explanation of A
(c) A is true but R is false
(d) A is false but R is true

Ans. ***(a)*** Both assertion and reason are true and reason is the correct explanation of assertion.

At critical temperature, density of liquid and gaseous phase becomes equal. Due to this liquid passes into gaseous state imperceptibly and continuously.

Q.49 **Assertion** (A) Liquids tend to have maximum number of molecules at their surface.

Reason (R) Small liquid drops have spherical shape.

(a) Both A and R are true and R is the correct explanation of A
(b) Both A and R are true but R is not the correct explanation of A
(c) A is true but R is false
(d) A is false but R is true

Ans. ***(d)*** Assertion is false but reason is true.

Liquid tend to reduce number of molecules or surface tension at their surface, that is why small liquid drops have spherical shape.

Long Answer Type Questions

Q.50 Isotherms of carbon dioxide at various temperatures are represented in figure. Answer the following questions based on this figure.

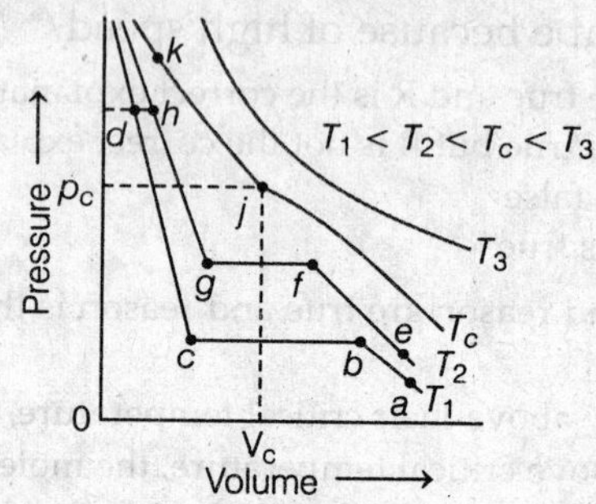

(i) In which state will CO_2 exist between the points *a* and *b* at temperature T_1?

(ii) At what point will CO_2 start liquefying when temperature is T_1?

(iii) At what point will CO_2 be completely liquefied when temperature is T_2?

(iv) Will condensation take place when the temperature is T_3?

(v) What portion of the isotherm at T_1 represent liquid and gaseous CO_2 at equilibrium?

Ans. (i) CO_2 will exist in gaseous state between the points *a* and *b* at temperature T_1.

(ii) At point *b*, the plot becomes linear, this shows phase transition, *i.e.*, liquefication of CO_2 starts and at point *c*, it gets completely liquefied.

(iii) At temperature T_2, *g* is the point at which CO_2 will be completely liquefied.

(iv) Condensation will not take place at T_3 temperature because $T_3 > T_c$ (critical temperature).

(v) Between *b* and *c*, liquid and gaseous states of CO_2 are in equilibrium.

Q.51 The variation of vapour pressure of different liquids with temperature is shown in figure.

(i) Calculate graphically boiling points of liquids *A* and *B*.

(ii) If we take liquid *C* in a closed vessel and heat it continuously. At what temperature will it boil?

(iii) At high altitude, atmospheric pressure is low (say 60 mm Hg). At what temperature liquid *D* boils?

(iv) Pressure cooker is used for cooking food at hill station. Explain in terms of vapour pressure why is it so?

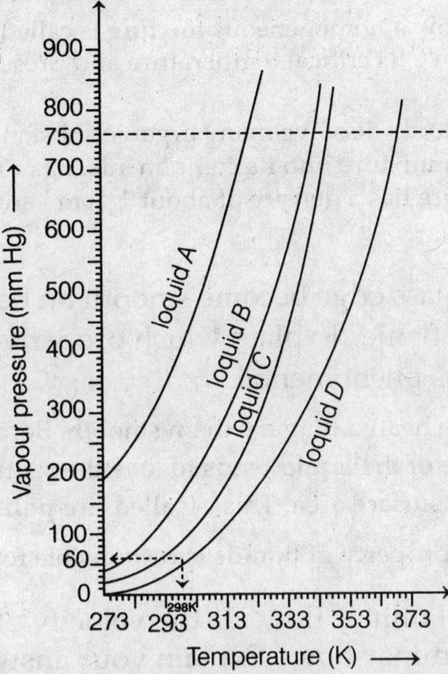

Ans. (i) Boiling point of A = approximately 315 K,

B = approximately 345 K.

(ii) In a closed vessel, liquid C will not boil because pressure inside keeps on increasing.

(iii) Temperature corresponding to 60 mm Hg for liquid D = 313 K.

(iv) A liquid boils when vapour pressure becomes equal to the atmospheric pressure. However at high altitudes, *i.e.*, on, hills, water boils at low temperature due to low atmospheric pressure. But when pressure cooker is used, the vapour pressure of water is increased due to which water boils at higher temperature and within a short period of time.

Q.52 Why does the boundary between liquid phase and gaseous phase disappear on heating a liquid upto critical temperature in a closed vessel? In this situation what will be the state of the substance?

Ans. In a closed vessel, it is essential to know that below the critical point (*i.e.*, critical temperature and critical pressure), the surface of separation between the liquid and its vapour is clearly visible. As we approach towards the critical point, the density of the liquid decreases while that of the vapour increases due to compression.

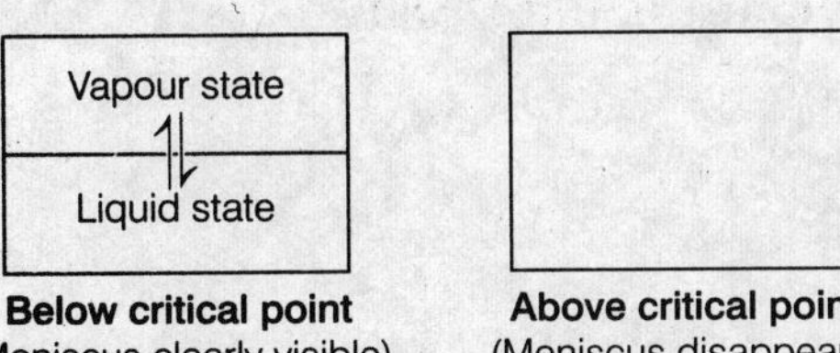

Below critical point (Meniscus clearly visible) **Above critical point** (Meniscus disappears)

At the critical point, the densities of the liquid and that of the vapour become equal and the surface of separation disappears *i.e.*, the liquid and the gaseous state are not separable. In other words, the meniscus is no longer visible.

The fluid which is now a homogeneous mixture is called **supercritical fluid.** Hence, any fluid above its critical temperature and pressure is called a **supercritical fluid.**

These supercritical fluids dissolve many organic substances. They are used for quick separation of a mixture into its components. *e.g.*, CO_2 above 31.1°C and above 600 bar pressure has a density of about $1 g/cm^3$ and it behaves as supercritical fluid.

Q.53 Why does sharp glass edge become smooth on heating it upto its melting point in a flame? Explain which property of liquids is responsible for this phenomenon.

Ans. Sharp glass edges are heated to make them smooth. Because on heating, glass melts and the surface of the liquid tends to take the rounded shape at the edges which has minimum surface area. This is called fire **polishing of glass.**

The **surface tension** property of liquids is responsible for this phenomenon.

Q.54 Explain the term 'laminar flow'. Is the velocity of molecules same in all the layers in laminar flow? Explain your answer.

Ans. When a liquid flows over a fixed surface, the layer of molecules in the immediate contact of surface is stationary. The velocity of the upper layers increases as the distance of layers from the fixed layer increases.

This type of flow in which there is a regular gradation of velocity in passing from one layer to the next is called laminar flow.

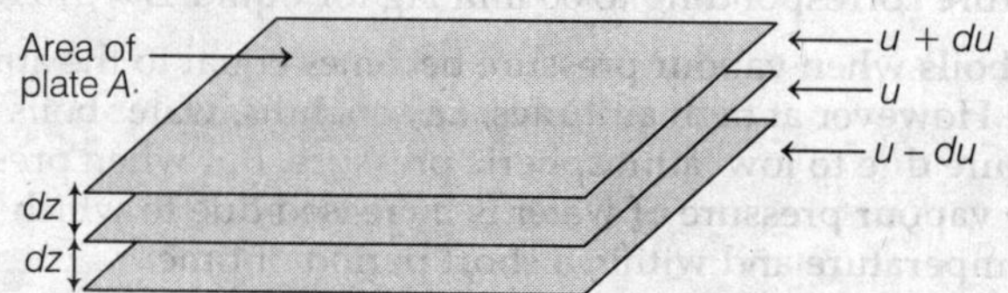

Gradation of velocity in the laminar flow

In laminar flow, the velocity of molecules is not same in all the layers because every layer offers some resistance or friction to the layer immediately below it.

Q.55 Isotherms of carbon dioxide gas are shown in figure. Mark a path for changing gas into liquid such that only one phase (*i.e.*, either a gas or a liquid) exists at any time during the change. Explain how the temperature, volume and pressure should be changed to carry out the change?

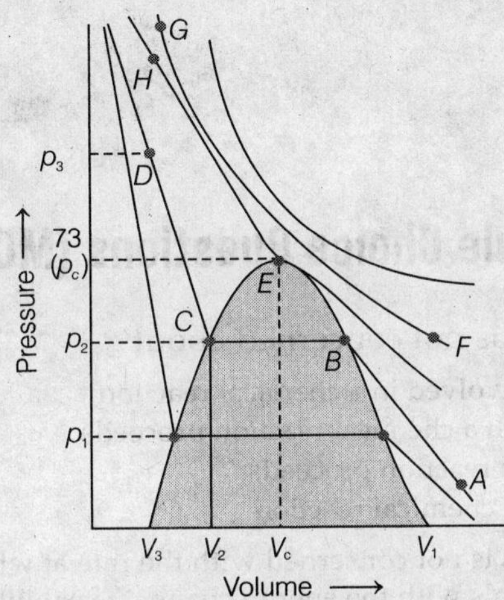

Ans. It is possible to change a gas into a liquid or a liquid into a gas by a process such that there is always a single phase present.

e.g. In figure given above, we can move vertically from *A* to *F* by increasing the temperature, then we can reach the point *G* by compressing the gas at constant temperature along the isotherm (isotherm at 31.1°C). The pressure will increase.

Now, we can move vertically down towards *D* by lowering the temperature. As soon as, we cross the point H on the critical isotherm, we get liquid. Thus, at no stage during the process, we go through two-phase region.

If process is carried out at the critical temperature, substance always remains in one phase. This is called continuity of state between the gaseous and the liquid state.

Chapter 06

Thermodynamics

Multiple Choice Questions (MCQs)

Q.1 Thermodynamics is not concerned about

(a) energy changes involved in a chemical reaction
(b) the extent to which a chemical reaction proceeds
(c) the rate at which a reaction proceeds
(d) the feasibility of a chemical reaction

Ans. *(c)* Thermodynamics is not concerned with the rate at which a reaction proceeds. Thermodynamics deals with the energy change, feasibility and extent of a reaction, but not with the rate and mechanism of a process. Kinetics deals with the rate of chemical reactions, the factors affecting the rate, and the mechanism by which reactions occur.

Q.2 Which of the following statement is correct?

(a) The presence of reacting species in a covered beaker is an example of open system.
(b) There is an exchange of energy as well as matter between the system and the surroundings in a closed system.
(c) The presence of reactants in a closed vessel made up of copper is an example of a closed system.
(d) The presence of reactants in a thermos flask or any other closed insulated vessel is an example of a closed system.

Ans. *(c)* For a closed vessel made of copper, no matter can exchange between the system and the surroundings but energy exchange can occur through its walls. Hence, is an example of closed system.

The corrected form of other statements are as follows.

(a) The presence of reacting species in a covered beaker is an example of **closed system.**
(b) There is an exchange of energy as well as matter between the system and the surroundings in an **open system.**
(d) The presence of reactants in a thermos flask or any other closed insulated vessel is an example of an **isolated system.**

Q.3 The state of a gas can be described by quoting the relationship between ....

(a) pressure, volume, temperature
(b) temperature, amount, pressure
(c) amount, volume, temperature
(d) pressure, volume, temperature, amount

Ans. ***(d)*** The state of a gas can be described by quoting the relationship between pressure, volume, temperature and amount. The ideal gas equation is

$$pV = nRT$$

Thus, p, V, T and n describe the state of the system.

Q.4 The volume of gas is reduced to half from its original volume. The specific heat will be

(a) reduce to half
(b) be doubled
(c) remain constant
(d) increase four times

Ans. ***(c)*** The specific heat will be remain constant because specific heat is an intensive property depending only on the nature of the gas.

Q.5 During complete combustion of one mole of butane, 2658 kJ of heat is released. The thermochemical reaction for above change is

(a) $2C_4H_{10}(g) + 13O_2(g) \rightarrow 8CO_2(g) + 10H_2O(l)\ ; \Delta_c H = -2658.0\ \text{kJ mol}^{-1}$

(b) $C_4H_{10}(g) + \frac{13}{2}O_2\ (g) \rightarrow 4CO_2(g) + 5H_2O(l)\ ; \Delta_c H = -\ 1329.0\ \text{kJ mol}^{-1}$

(c) $C_4H_{10}(g) + \frac{13}{2}O_2(g) \rightarrow 4CO_2(g) + 5H_2O(l)\ ; \Delta_c H = -\ 2658.0\ \text{kJ mol}^{-1}$

(d) $C_4H_{10}(g) + \frac{13}{2}O_2(g) \rightarrow 4CO_2(g) + 5H_2O(l)\ ; \Delta_c H = +\ 2658.0\ \text{kJ mol}^{-1}$

Ans. ***(c)*** Thermochemical reaction of combustion of 1 mole butane is written as

$$C_4H_{10}\ (g) + \frac{13}{2}O_2\ (g) \rightarrow 4CO_2(g) + 5H_2O(l)$$

$$\Delta_C H = -\ 2658.0\ \text{kJ mol}^{-1}$$

$\Delta_c H$ should be negative and have a value of 2658 kJ mol^{-1}, which releases energy.

Q.6 $\Delta_f U^s$ of formation of $CH_4\ (g)$ at certain temperature is–393 kJ mol^{-1}. The value of $\Delta_f H^s$ is

(a) zero
(b) $< \Delta_f U^\ominus$
(c) $> \Delta_f U^\ominus$
(d) equal to $\Delta_f U^\ominus$

- **Concept Insight** The relation between ΔH and ΔU is $\Delta H = \Delta U + \Delta n_g RT$ where, $\Delta n_g = (n_p - n_r)_g$

Ans. ***(b)*** The reaction is $CH_4(g) + 2O_2(g) \longrightarrow CO_2(g) + 2H_2O(l)$

$$\Delta n_g = (n_p - n_r)_g = 1 - 3 = -2$$

$$\Delta_f H° = \Delta_f U^s + \Delta n_g RT$$

Since, $\Delta n_g = -2$

$\therefore$ $\Delta_f H^\ominus < \Delta_f U^\ominus$

Q.7 In an adiabatic process, no transfer of heat takes place between system and surroundings. Choose the correct option for free expansion of an ideal gas under adiabatic condition from the following.

(a) $q = 0, \Delta T \neq 0, W = 0$
(b) $q \neq 0, \Delta T = 0, W = 0$
(c) $q = 0, \Delta T = 0, W = 0$
(d) $q = 0, \Delta T < 0, W \neq 0$

Ans. ***(c)*** Free expansion, $W = 0$

Adiabatic process, $q = 0$

$\Delta U = q + W = 0$, this means that internal energy remains constant. Therefore, $\Delta T = 0$.

In ideal gas there is no intermolecular attraction.

Hence, when such a gas expands under adiabatic conditions into a vacuum, no heat is absorbed or evolved since no external work is done to separate the molecules.

Q.8 The pressure-volume work for an ideal gas can be calculated by using the expression $W = -\int_{V_i}^{V_f} p_{ex}\, dV$. The work can also be calculated from the pV-plot by using the area under the curve within the specified limits. When an ideal gas is compressed (a) reversibly or (b) irreversibly from volume V_i to V_f. Choose the correct option.

(a) W (reversible) = W (irreversible)
(b) W (reversible) < W (irreversible)
(c) W (reversible) > W (irreversible)
(d) W (reversible) = W (irreversible) + $p_{ex} \cdot \Delta V$

Ans. ***(b)*** The correct option is W (reversible) < W (irreversible). This is because area under the curve is always more in irreversible compression as can be seen from given figure.

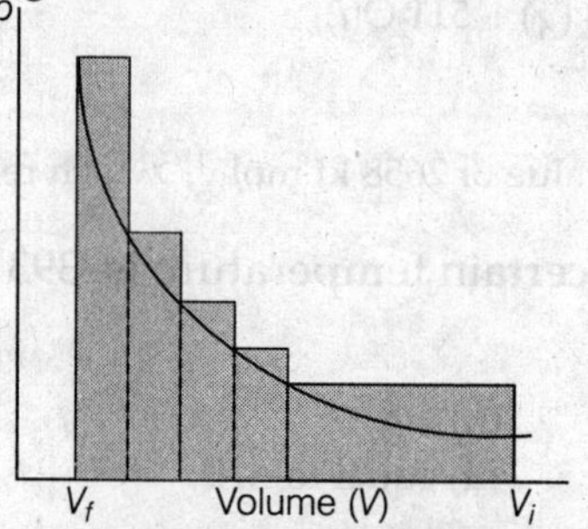

pV-plot when pressure is not constant and changes in finite steps (irreversible conditions) during compression from initial volume, V_i to final volume, V_f. Work done on the gas is represented by the shaded area.

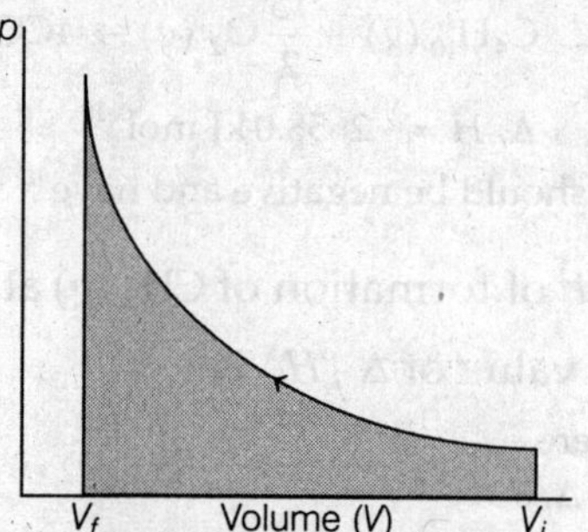

PV-plot when pressure is not constant and changes in infinite steps (reversible conditions) during compression from initial volume, V_i to final volume, V_f. Work done on the gas is represented by the shaded area.

Q.9 The entropy change can be calculated by using the expression $\Delta S = \frac{q_{rev}}{T}$. When water freezes in a glass beaker, choose the correct statement amongst the following.

(a) ΔS (system) decreases but ΔS (surroundings) remains the same
(b) ΔS (system) increases but ΔS (surroundings) decreases
(c) ΔS (system) decreases but ΔS (surroundings) increases
(d) ΔS (system) decreases but ΔS (surroundings) also decreases

Ans. *(c)* The entropy change can be calculated by using the expression

$$\Delta S = \frac{q_{rev}}{T}$$

When water freezes in a glass beaker, ΔS (system) decreases because molecules in solid ice are less random than in liquid water. However, when water freezes to ice, heat is released which is absorbed by the surroundings.

Hence, entropy of the surrounding increases.

Q.10 On the basis of theromochemical equations (1), (2) and (3), find out which of the algebraic relationships given in options (a) to (d) is correct

1. $C\ (\text{graphite}) + O_2\ (g) \rightarrow CO_2\ (g)\ ;\ \Delta_r H = x\ \text{kJ mol}^{-1}$
2. $CO\ (g) + \frac{1}{2} O_2\ (g) \rightarrow CO\ (g)\ ;\ \Delta_r H = y\ \text{kJ mol}^{-1}$
3. $CO\ (g) + \frac{1}{2} O_2\ (g) \rightarrow CO_2\ (g)\ ;\ \Delta_r H = z\ \text{kJ mol}^{-1}$

(a) $z = x + y$ (b) $x = y - z$ (c) $x = y + z$ (d) $y = 2z - x$

Ans. *(c)* The algebraic relationships of the given reaction is

equation (1) – equation (2) = equation (3)

(1) $C\ (\text{graphite}) + O_2(g) \longrightarrow CO_2\ (g)\ ;\ \Delta_r H = x\ \text{kJ mol}^{-1}$

(2) $CO\ (g) \longrightarrow C_{(\text{graphite})} + \frac{1}{2} O_2(g)\ ;\ \Delta_r H = -y\ \text{kJ mol}^{-1}$

(3) $CO\ (g) + \frac{1}{2} O_2(g) \longrightarrow CO_2(g)\ ;\ \Delta_r H = z\ \text{kJ mol}^{-1}$

Hence, $x - y = z$ or $x = y + z$

Q.11 Consider the reactions given below. On the basis of these reactions find out which of the algebraic relationship given in options (a) to (d) is correct?

1. $C\ (g) + 4\ H\ (g) \rightarrow CH_4\ (g);\ \Delta_r H = x\ \text{kJ mol}^{-1}$
2. $C\ (\text{graphite}) + 2H_2(g) \rightarrow CH_4\ (g)\ ;\ \Delta_r H = y\ \text{kJ mol}^{-1}$

(a) $x = y$ (b) $x = 2y$ (c) $x > y$ (d) $x < y$

Ans. *(c)* Same bonds are formed in reaction (1) and (2) but no bonds are broken in reaction (1) whereas bonds in the reactant molecules are broken in reaction (2). As energy is absorbed when bonds are broken, energy released in reaction (1) is greater than that in reaction (2) hence, $x > y$

Q.12 The enthalpies of elements in their standard states are taken as zero. The enthalpy of formation of a compound

(a) is always negative (b) is always positive

(c) may be positive or negative (d) is never negative

Ans. *(c)* Combustion of elements to form a compound can be exothermic or endothermic. e.g. $C_{(\text{graphite})} + O_2(g) \longrightarrow CO_2(g)$ elements should be mentioned in their reference states is exothermic.

whereas, $C_{(\text{graphite})} + 2S \longrightarrow CS_2$ is endothermic.

Hence, enthalpy of formation can be positive or negative.

Q.13 Enthalpy of sublimation of a substance is equal to

(a) enthalpy of fusion + enthalpy of vaporisation
(b) enthalpy of fusion
(c) enthalpy of vaporisation
(d) twice the enthalpy of vaporisation

Ans. ***(a)*** Enthalpy of sublimation of a substance = enthalpy of fusion + enthalpy of vaporisation.

Sublimation is, direct conversion of solid to vapour. solid $\rightarrow$ vapour

Writing in two steps, we have solid $\rightarrow$ liquid $\rightarrow$ vapour,

solid $\rightarrow$ liquid requires enthalpy of fusion

liquid $\rightarrow$ vapour requires enthalpy of vaporisation

Q.14 Which of the following is not correct?

(a) ΔG is zero for a reversible reaction.
(b) ΔG is positive for a spontaneous reaction.
(c) ΔG is negative for a spontaneous reaction.
(d) ΔG is positive for a non-spontaneous reaction.

Ans. ***(b)*** ΔG gives a criteria for spontaneity at constant pressure and temperature.

(i) If ΔG is negative (< 0), the process is spontaneous.
(ii) If ΔG is positive (> 0), the process is non-spontaneous.
(iii) If ΔG is zero then reaction is at equilibrium.

Multiple Choice Questions (More Than One Options)

Q.15 Thermodynamics mainly deals with

(a) interrelation of various forms of energy and their transformation from one form to another.
(b) energy changes in the processes which depend only on initial and final states of the microscopic systems containing a few molecules.
(c) how and at what rate these energy transformations are carried out.
(d) the system in equilibrium state or moving from one equilibrium state to another equilibrium state.

Ans. ***(a, d)*** Thermodynamics deals with interrelation of various forms of energy and their transformation into each other. It also deals with thermal or mechanical equilibrium. However, it does not tell anything about the rate of reaction.

Q.16 In an exothermic reaction, heat is evolved, and system loses heat to the surrounding. For such system

(a) q_p will be negative
(b) $\Delta_r H$ will be negative
(c) q_p will be positive
(d) $\Delta_r H$ will be positive

Ans. ***(a, b)*** Exothermic reactions are those reactions which are accompanied by the evolution of heat.

e.g.,

$$C(s) + O_2(g) \longrightarrow CO_2(g) + 393.5 \text{ kJ}$$

$$H_2(g) + \frac{1}{2} O_2(g) \longrightarrow H_2O(l) + 285.8 \text{ kJ}$$

q_p and $\Delta_r H$ are negative for exothermic reaction.

Q.17 The spontaneity means, having the potential to proceed without the assistance of external agency. The processes which occur spontaneously are

(a) flow of heat from colder to warmer body
(b) gas in a container contracting into one corner
(c) gas expanding to fill the available volume
(d) burning carbon in oxygen to give carbon dioxide

Ans. ***(c, d)*** Options (a) and (b) can neither occur by themselves nor by initiation, (c) can occur by itself, (d) occur on initiation. Flowing of heat from warmer to colder body, expanding of gas and burning of carbon to give carbon dioxide, all are spontaneous process.

Q.18 For an ideal gas, the work of reversible expansion under isothermal condition can be calculated by using the expression $W = -nRT \ln \frac{V_f}{V_i}$.

A sample containing 1.0 mol of an ideal gas is expanded isothermally and reversible to ten times of its original volume, in two separate experiments. The expansion is carried out at 300 K and at 600 K respectively. Choose the correct option.

(a) Work done at 600 K is 20 times the work done at 300 K
(b) Work done at 300 K is twice the work done at 600 K
(c) Work done at 600 K is twice the work done at 300 K
(d) $\Delta U = 0$ in both cases

Ans. ***(c, d)*** Given that, the work of reversible expansion under isothermal condition can be calculated by using the expression

$$W = -nRT \ln \frac{V_f}{V_i}$$

$$V_f = 10\ V_i,\ T_2 = 600\text{ K},\ T_1 = 300\text{ K}$$

Putting these values in above expression, we get

$$W_{600\text{K}} = 1 \times R \times 600\text{ K} \ln \frac{10}{1}$$

$$W_{300\text{K}} = 1 \times R \times 300\text{ K} \ln \frac{10}{1}$$

$$\frac{W_{600\text{K}}}{W_{300\text{K}}} = \frac{1 \times R \times 600\text{ K} \ln \frac{10}{1}}{1 \times R \times 300\text{ K} \ln \frac{10}{1}}$$

$$= \frac{600}{300} = 2$$

$$W_{600\text{ K}} = 2 \times W_{300\text{ K}}$$

For isothermal expansion of ideal gases, $\Delta U = 0$. Since, temperature is constant this means there is no change in internal energy. Therefore, $\Delta U = 0$

Q.19 Consider the following reaction between zinc and oxygen and choose the correct options out of the options given below :

$$2\,Zn\,(s) + O_2\,(g) \rightarrow 2\,ZnO\,(s);\ \Delta H = -\ 693.8\ kJ\ mol^{-1}$$

(a) The enthalpy of two moles of ZnO is less than the total enthalpy of two moles of Zn and one mole of oxygen by 693.8 kJ

(b) The enthalpy of two moles of ZnO is more than the total enthalpy of two moles of Zn and one mole of oxygen by 693.8 kJ

(c) 693.8 kJ mol^{-1} energy is evolved in the reaction

(d) 693.8 kJ mol^{-1} energy is absorbed in the reaction

Ans. *(a, c)* For the reaction, $2Zn(s) + O_2(g) \longrightarrow 2ZnO\,(s); \Delta H = -\ 693.8\ kJ\ mol^{-1}$

As we know that, $\Delta H = H_p - H_R$

A negative value of ΔH shows that $H_R > H_P$, *i.e.*, enthalpy of two moles of ZnO is less than the enthalpy of two moles of zinc and one mole of oxygen by 693.8kJ. As $H_R > H_P$, 693.8 kJ mol^{-1} of energy is evolved in the reaction.

Thus, option (a) and (c) are correct.

Short Answer Type Questions

Q.20 18.0 g of water completely vapourises at 100°C and 1 bar pressure and the enthalpy change in the process is 40.79 kJ mol^{-1}. What will be the enthalpy change for vapourising two moles of water under the same conditions? What is the standard enthalpy of vapourisation for water?

Ans. As we know that, 18.0 g H_2O = 1 mole H_2O

Enthalpy change for vapourising 1 mole of H_2O = 40.79 kJ mol^{-1}

$\therefore$ Enthalpy change for vapourising 2 moles of $H_2O = 2 \times 40.79$ kJ = +81.58 kJ

Standard enthalpy of vapourisation at 100°C and 1 bar pressure,

$$\Delta_{vap}H^{\circ} = +\ 40.79\ kJ\ mol^{-1}$$

Q.21 One mole of acetone requires less heat to vapourise than 1 mole of water. Which of the two liquids has higher enthalpy of vapourisation?

Ans. The enthalpy of vaporisation is the heat required to convert 1 mole of a liquid into vapour at its boiling point. One mole of acetone requires less heat to vapourise than 1 mole of water. Hence, acetone has less enthalpy of vapourisation and water has higher enthalpy of vapourisation.

Q.22 Standard molar enthalpy of formation, $\Delta_f H^{\ominus}$ is just a special case of enthalpy of reaction, $\Delta_r H^{\ominus}$. Is the $\Delta_r H^{\ominus}$ for the following reaction same as $\Delta_f H^{\ominus}$? Give reason for your answer.

$$CaO(s) + CO_2(g) \rightarrow CaCO_3(s);\ \Delta_f H^{\ominus} = -\ 178.3\ kJ\ mol^{-1}$$

Ans. No, $\Delta_r H^{\circ}$ for the given reaction is not same as $\Delta_f H^{\circ}$. Since, standard enthalpy of formation is the enthalpy change when one mole of a substance is formed from its component elements in standard state. In given equation, $CaCO_3(s)$ is not formed from the component elements. It has been formed from compounds

CaO and CO_2. Actual reaction should be

$$Ca(s) + C(\text{grapnite}) + \frac{3}{2} O_2(g) \longrightarrow CaCO_3(s); \Delta_f H°$$

This reaction is different from the given reaction.

Hence, $\Delta_r H° \neq \Delta_f H°$

Q.23 The value of $\Delta_f H^s$ for NH_3 is -91.8 kJ mol^{-1}. Calculate enthalpy change for the following reaction.

$$2NH_3(g) \rightarrow N_2(g) + 3H_2(g)$$

Ans. Given, $\frac{1}{2} N_2(g) + \frac{3}{2} H_2(g) \longrightarrow NH_3(g); \Delta_f H^{\ominus} = -91.8 \text{ kJ mol}^{-1}$

($\Delta_f H^{\ominus}$ means enthalpy of formation of 1 mole of NH_3)

$\therefore$ Enthalpy change for the formation of 2 moles of NH_3

$$N_2(g) + 3H_2(g) \longrightarrow 2NH_3(g); \Delta_f H^s = 2 \times -91.8 = -183.6 \text{ kJ mol}^{-1}$$

And for the reverse reaction,

$$2NH_3(g) \longrightarrow N_2(g) + 3H_2(g); \Delta_r H^s = +183.6 \text{ kJ mol}^{-1}$$

Mistake Alert! *Students may not balance the chemical equation properly which can lead to wrong calculations of ΔH.*

Q.24 Enthalpy is an extensive property. In general, if enthalpy of an overall reaction $A \rightarrow B$ along one route is $\Delta_r H$ and $\Delta_r H_1, \Delta_r H_2, \Delta_r H_3 \ldots$ represent enthalpies of intermediate reactions leading to product B. What will be the relation between $\Delta_r H$ overall reaction and $\Delta_r H_1, \Delta_r H_2 \ldots$ etc for intermediate reactions.

Ans. It is based on **Hess's Law,** according to which

$$\Delta_r H = \Delta_r H_1 + \Delta_r H_2 + \Delta_r H_3 + \ldots$$

Note For a general reaction Hess's law of constant heat summation can be represented as

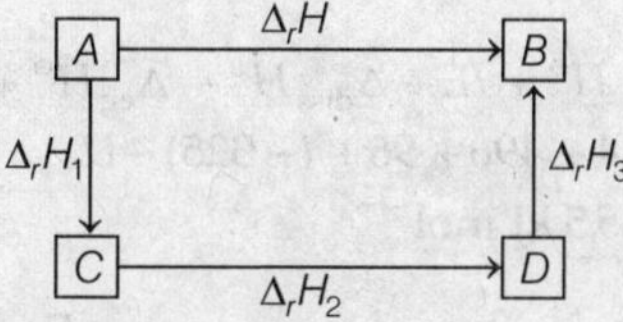

Q.25 The enthalpy of atomisation for the reaction $CH_4(g) \rightarrow C(g) + 4H(g)$ is 1665 kJ mol^{-1}. What is the bond energy of C–H bond?

Thinking Process To solve this problem, keep in mind that in methane all the four C—H bonds are identical in bond length and energy. However, the energies required to break the individual C—H bonds in each successive step differ.

In such cases, we use mean bond enthalpy of C—H bond, *i.e.* $\Delta_{C-H} H^s = \frac{1}{4} (\Delta_a H^{\ominus})$

Ans. In CH_4, there are four C—H bonds. The enthalpy of atomisation of 1 mole of CH_4 means dissociation of four moles of C—H bond.

$$\therefore \quad \text{C—H bond energy per mol} = \frac{1665 \text{ kJ}}{4 \text{ mol}} = 416.25 \text{ kJ mol}^{-1}$$

Q.26 Use the following data to calculate $\Delta_{lattice} H^\ominus$ for NaBr. $\Delta_{sub} H^\ominus$ for sodium metal = 108.4 kJ mol^{-1}, ionisation enthalpy of sodium = 496 kJ mol^{-1}, electron gain enthalpy of bromine = –325 kJ mol^{-1}, bond dissociation enthalpy of bromine = 192 kJ mol^{-1}, $\Delta_f H^\ominus$ for NaBr(s) = – 360.1 kJ mol^{-1}

Thinking Process This question is based upon the concept of **Born-Haber cycle** as well as **Hess's law.** Following steps are used to solve this problem.

(i) $Na(s) \longrightarrow Na(g); \Delta_{sub} H^\ominus$

(ii) $Na(g) \rightarrow Na^+(g) + e^-(g)$; IE (Ionisation enthalpy)

(iii) $\frac{1}{2} Br_2(g) \longrightarrow Br(g); \Delta_{diss} H^\ominus$

(iv) $Br(g) + e^-(g) \longrightarrow Br^-(g); \Delta_{eg} H^\ominus$

(v) Applying Hess's law, $\Delta_f H^\ominus = \Delta_{sub} H^\ominus + IE + \Delta_{diss} H^\ominus + \Delta_{eg} H^\ominus + U$

Ans. Given that, $\Delta_{sub} H^\ominus$ for Na metal = 108.4 k J mol^{-1}

IE of Na = 496 k J mol^{-1}, $\Delta_{eg} H^\ominus$ of Br = – 325 kJ mol^{-1}, $\Delta_{diss} H^\ominus$ of Br = 192 kJ mol^{-1}, $\Delta_f H^\ominus$ for NaBr = – 360.1 kJ mol^{-1}

Born-Haber cycle for the formation of NaBr is as follows

$Na(s) + \frac{1}{2} Br_2(g) \xrightarrow{\Delta_f H^\ominus = -360.1 \text{ kJ}} NaBr(s)$

$\Delta_{sub} H^s = 108.4$ kJ mol^{-1} — $Na(g)$; IE = 496 kJ mol^{-1} — $Na^+(g)$

$\Delta_{diss} H^\ominus = 192/2$ kJ — $Br(g)$; $\Delta_{eg} H^\ominus = -325$ kJ mol^{-1} — $Br^-(g)$

– U (Lattice enthalpy)

By applying Hess's law,

$$\Delta_f H^\ominus = \Delta_{sub} H^\ominus + IE + \Delta_{diss} H^\ominus + \Delta_{eg} H^\ominus + U$$

$$-360.1 = 108.4 + 496 + 96 + (-325) - U$$

$$U = +735.5 \text{ kJ mol}^{-1}$$

Q.27 **Given that $\Delta H = 0$ for mixing of two gases. Explain whether the diffusion of these gases into each other in a closed container is a spontaneous process or not?**

Ans. Even though $\Delta H = 0$ for the mixing of two gases, their diffusion in a closed container is a spontaneous process. This is because the entropy (ΔS), or randomness, increases during mixing. In the equation $\Delta G = \Delta H - T\Delta S$, the positive value of $T\Delta S$ makes ΔG negative. Hence, the process occurs spontaneously.

Q.28 **Heat has randomising influence on a system and temperature is the measure of average chaotic motion of particles in the system. Write the mathematical relation which relates these three parameters.**

Ans. Heat has randomising influence on a system and temperature is the measure of average chaotic motion of particles in the system. The mathematical relation which relates these three parameters is, $\Delta S = \frac{q_{rev}}{T}$

Here, ΔS = change in entropy

q_{rev} = heat of reversible reaction

T = temperature

Q.29 **Increase in enthalpy of the surroundings is equal to decrease in enthalpy of the system. Will the temperature of system and surroundings be the same when they are in thermal equilibrium?**

- **Concept Insight** **Thermal equilibrium** is defined as a condition when two physical systems are brought into contact through a connection that does not allow the transfer of matter but does allow the transfer of energy as heat. Such a connection is called **diathermal.**

  If a diathermal connection is made between two physical systems, and no change of state occurs in either after the connection is established, the systems are said to be in thermal equilibrium. This condition obeys the zeroth law of thermodynamics.

Ans. *Yes,* the temperature of system and surroundings will be the same when they are in thermal equilibrium.

Q.30 **At 298 K, K_p for reaction $N_2O_4\ (g) \rightleftharpoons 2NO_2\ (g)$ is 0.98. Predict whether the reaction is spontaneous or not.**

Ans. For the reaction, $N_2O_4(g) \rightleftharpoons 2NO_2(g),\ K_p = 0.98$

As we know that $\Delta_r G^\ominus = -2.303\ RT \log K_p$

Here, R, T and K_p all have positive value, so $\Delta G = -ve$.

Hence, **reaction is spontaneous.**

Q.31 **A sample of 1.0 mol of a monoatomic ideal gas is taken through a cyclic process of expansion and compression as shown in figure. What will be the value of ΔH for the cycle as a whole?**

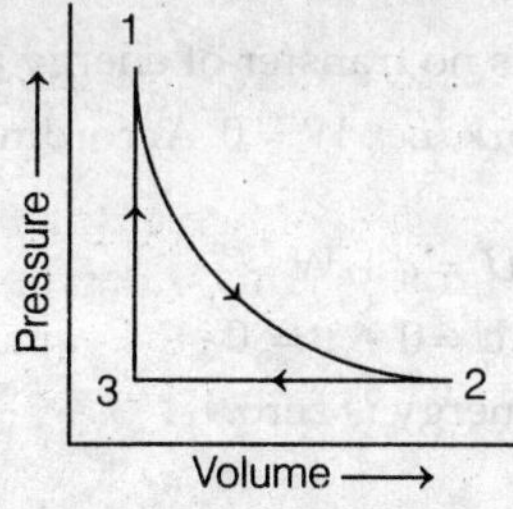

Ans. The net enthalpy change, ΔH for a cyclic process is zero as enthalpy change is a state function, *i.e.* ΔH (cycle) = 0

Q.32 The standard molar entropy of H_2O (*l*) is 70 JK^{-1} mol^{-1}. Will the standard molar entropy of $H_2O(s)$ be more, or less than 70 JK^{-1} mol^{-1}?

Ans. The solid form of H_2O is ice. In ice, molecules of H_2O are less random than in liquid water.

Thus, standard molar entropy of $H_2O(s)$ < molar entropy of H_2O (*l*) i.e. less than 70 JK^{-1} mol^{-1}.

Q.33 Identify the state functions and path functions out of the following: enthalpy, entropy, heat, temperature, work, free energy.

- **Concept Insight** **State functions** are those which depend only on the state of the system and not on how they are reached.
  Path functions are those which depend on the path of the system.

Ans. **State functions** enthalpy, entropy, temperature and free energy.

Path functions Heat and work.

Q.34 The molar enthalpy of vapourisation of acetone is less than that of water. Why?

Thinking Process Amount of heat required to vapourise one mole of a liquid at constant temperature and under standard pressure (1 bar) is called its **molar enthalpy of vaporisation** $\Delta_{vap}H^{\ominus}$.

Ans. Molar enthalpy of vapourisation of water is more than that of acetone because strong hydrogen bonding exist between H_2O molecules which on the other hand, there exist weaker dipole-dipole attraction between acetone molecules.

Q.35 Which quantity out of $\Delta_r G$ and $\Delta_r G^{\ominus}$ will be zero at equilibrium?

Ans. Gibbs energy for a reaction involves all reactants and products in their standard states. $\Delta_r G^{\ominus}$ is related to the equilibrium constant of the reaction as follows :

$$\Delta_r G^{\ominus} = -RT \ln K$$

At equilibrium, $K = 1$

$$\Rightarrow \quad \Delta_r G^{\ominus} = 0$$

Now, $\Delta_r G$ is not zero for any other value of K or when reaction is not in equilibrium.

Q.36 Predict the change in internal energy for an isolated system at constant volume.

Ans. For isolated system, there is no transfer of energy as heat, *i.e.*, $q = 0$ and there is no transfer of energy as work, *i.e.*, $W = 0$. According to the first law of thermodynamics,

$$\Delta U = q + W$$

$$\Delta U = 0 + 0 = 0$$

Hence, change in internal energy is zero.

Q.37 Although heat is a path function but heat absorbed by the system under certain specific conditions is independent of path. What are those conditions? Explain.

Ans. The two conditions under which heat becomes independent of path are

(i) when volume remains constant

(ii) when pressure remains constant

Explanation

(i) **At constant volume** By first law of thermodynamics, $\Delta U = q + W$ or $q = \Delta U - W$. But $W = -p\Delta V$ Hence, $q = \Delta U + p\Delta V$. But as volume remains constant, $\Delta V = 0$

$\therefore$ $q_v = \Delta U$ and since, ΔU is a state function.

Hence, q_V is a state function.

(ii) **At constant pressure** As we know, $q_p = \Delta U + p\Delta V$. But $\Delta U + p\Delta V = \Delta H$.

$\therefore$ $q_p = \Delta H$. As ΔH is a state function therefore, q_p is a state function.

Q.38 Expansion of a gas in vacuum is called free expansion. Calculate the work done and the change in internal energy when 1L of ideal gas expands isothermally into vacuum until its total volume is 5L?

Ans. Work done of a gas in vacuum, $W = -p_{ext}(V_2 - V_1)$. As $p_{ext} = 0$ so, $W = -0(5-1) = 0$ As internal energy of an ideal gas depends only on temperature, therefore, for isothermal expansion of an ideal gas, internal energy remains constant,

i.e. $\Delta U = 0$.

It is to be remember that as $H = U + pV$, $\Delta H = \Delta(U + pV)$ $= \Delta U + p\Delta V = \Delta U + nR(\Delta T)$. For isothermal process, $\Delta T = 0$ and also $\Delta U = 0$, as stated above, therefore, $\Delta H = 0$.

Q.39 Heat capacity (C_p) is an extensive property but specific heat (c) is an intensive property. What will be the relation between C_p and c for 1 mole of water?

Ans. For water, **molar heat capacity,** $C_p = 18 \times$ Specific heat, c

$$C_p = 18 \times c, \text{ Specific heat}$$

where, $c = 4.18\ \text{Jg}^{-1}\text{K}^{-1}$ [for water]

Heat capacity, $C_p = 18 \times 4.18\ \text{JK}^{-1}\text{mol}^{-1} = 75.3\ \text{JK}^{-1}$

Q.40 The difference between C_p and C_v can be derived using the empirical relation $H = U + pV$. Calculate the difference between C_p and C_v for 10 moles of an ideal gas.

Ans. Given that, C_v = heat capacity at constant volume,

C_p = heat capacity at constant pressure

Difference between C_p and C_v is equal to gas constant (R).

$\therefore$ $C_p - C_v = nR$ [where, n = number of moles]

$$= 10 \times 8.314\ \text{J} = 83.14\ \text{J}$$

Q.41 **If the combustion of 1g of graphite produces 20.7 kJ of heat, what will be molar enthalpy change? Give the significance of sign also.**

Ans. Given that, enthalpy of combustion of 1g graphite = 20.7 kJ

Molar enthalpy change for the combustion of graphite,

$$\Delta H = \text{enthalpy of combustion of 1 g graphite} \times \text{molar mass of C (carbon)}$$
$$\Delta H = -20.7 \text{ kJg}^{-1} \times 12 \text{ g mol}^{-1}$$
$$\Delta H = -2.48 \times 10^2 \text{ kJ mol}^{-1}$$

Negative sign in the value of ΔH indicates that the reaction is exothermic.

Q.42 **The net enthalpy change of a reaction is the amount of energy required to break all the bonds in reactant molecules minus amount of energy required to form all the bonds in the product molecules. What will be the enthalpy change for the following reaction?**
$H_2(g) + Br_2(g) \rightarrow 2HBr(g)$.

Given that, bond energy of H_2, Br_2 and HBr is 435 kJ mol^{-1}, 192 kJ mol^{-1} and 368 kJ mol^{-1}, respectively.

Thinking Process To, calculate the enthalpy change, use the following formula when the reactants, and products are in gas phase as

$$\Delta_r H^\ominus = \Sigma \text{ bond energy (reactants)} - \Sigma \text{ bond energy (products)}$$

Ans. For the reaction,

$$H_2(g) + Br_2(g) \longrightarrow 2HBr(g)$$
$$\Delta_r H^\ominus = \Sigma \text{BE (Reactants)} - \Sigma \text{BE (Products)}$$
$$= \text{BE}(H_2) + \text{BE}(Br_2) - 2\text{BE}(HBr)$$
$$= 435 + 192 - (2 \times 368) \text{ kJ mol}^{-1}$$
$$= -109 \text{ kJ mol}^{-1}$$

Q.43 **The enthalpy of vaporisation of CCl_4 is 30.5 kJ mol^{-1}. Calculate the heat required for the vaporisation of 284 g of CCl_4 at constant pressure. (Molar mass of CCl_4 = 154 g mol^{-1})**

Ans. Given that, 1 mol of CCl_4 = [12 + (35.5 × 4)] = 154 g / mol

$$\Delta_{vap} H \text{ for 154 g of } CCl_4 = 30.5 \text{ kJ}$$
$$\therefore \quad \Delta_{vap} H \text{ for 284 g of } CCl_4 = \frac{30.5 \times 284}{154} \text{ kJ} = 56.25 \text{ kJ}$$

Q.44 **The enthalpy of reaction for the reaction :**

$$2H_2(g) + O_2(g) \rightarrow 2H_2O(l) \text{ is } \Delta_r H^\ominus = -572 \text{ kJ mol}^{-1}$$

What will be standard enthalpy of formation of H_2O (*l*)?

Ans. Given that,

$$2H_2(g) + O_2(g) \longrightarrow 2H_2O(l), \ \Delta_r H^\circ = -572 \text{ kJ mol}^{-1}$$

Enthalpy of formation is the enthalpy change of the reaction when 1 mole of the compound is formed from its elements then

$$H_2(g) + \frac{1}{2}O_2(g) \longrightarrow H_2O(l), \Delta_r H^\circ = ?$$

This can be obtained by dividing the given equation by 2.

Therefore, $\Delta_f H^\circ(H_2O) = -\frac{572 \text{ kJmol}^{-1}}{2}$

$= -286 \text{ kJ mol}^{-1}$

Q.45 What will be the work done on an ideal gas enclosed in a cylinder, when it is compressed by a constant external pressure, p_{ext} in a single step as shown in figure? Explain graphically.

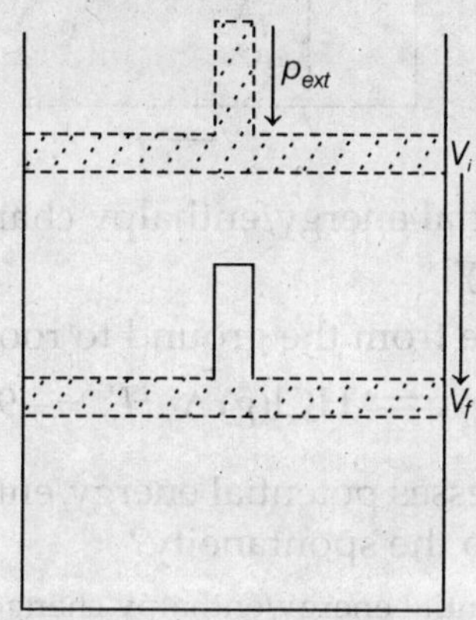

Ans. Suppose initial volume of the gas is V_i and pressure of the gas inside cylinder is p. After compression by constant external pressure, (p_{ext}) in a single step, final volume of the gas becomes V_f.

Then volume change, $\Delta V = (V_f - V_i)$

If W is the work done on the system by movement of the piston, then

$$W = p_{ext}(-\Delta V)$$

$$W = -p_{ext}(V_f - V_i)$$

This can be calculated from $p - V$ graph as shown in the figure. Work done is equal to the shaded area ABV_fV_i

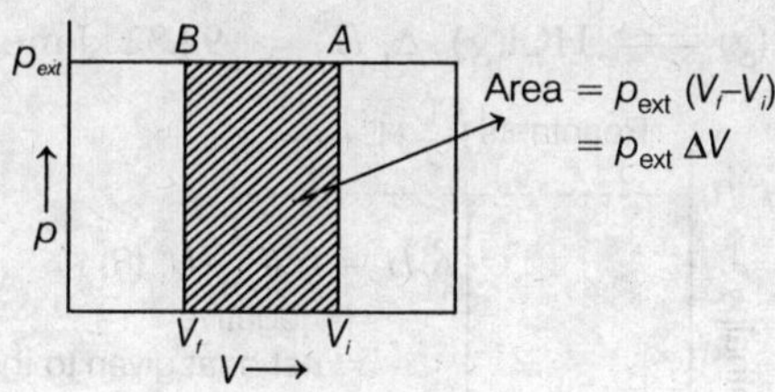

The negative sign in this expression is required to obtain conventional sign for W which will be positive. Because in case of compression work is done on the system, so ΔV will be negative.

Mistake Alert! *Students may get confused with sign conventions for work and heat.*

Q.46 How will you calculate work done on an ideal gas in a compression, when change in pressure is carried out in infinite steps?

Ans. When compression is carried out in infinite steps with change in pressure, it is a **reversible process.** The work done can be calculated from $p-V$ plot as shown in the given figure. Shaded area under the curve represents the work done on the gas.

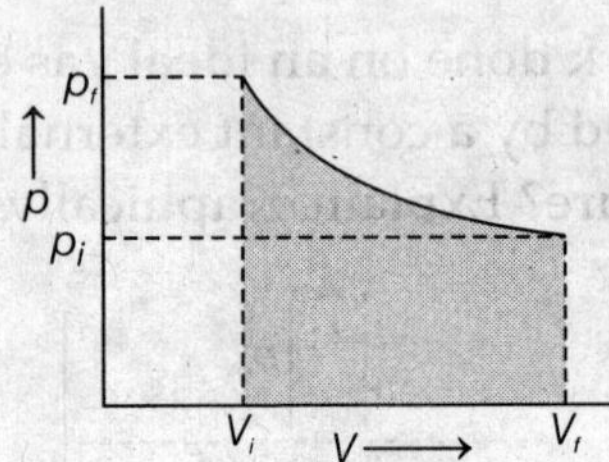

Q.47 Represent the potential energy/enthalpy change in the following processes graphically.

(a) Throwing a stone from the ground to roof.

(b) $\frac{1}{2} H_2(g) + \frac{1}{2} Cl_2(g) \rightleftharpoons HCl(g)\ \Delta_r H^\ominus = -92.32 \text{ kJ mol}^{-1}$

In which of the processes potential energy/enthalpy change is contributing factor to the spontaneity?

Ans. Representation of potential energy/enthalpy change in the following processes :

(a) Throwing a stone from the ground to roof.

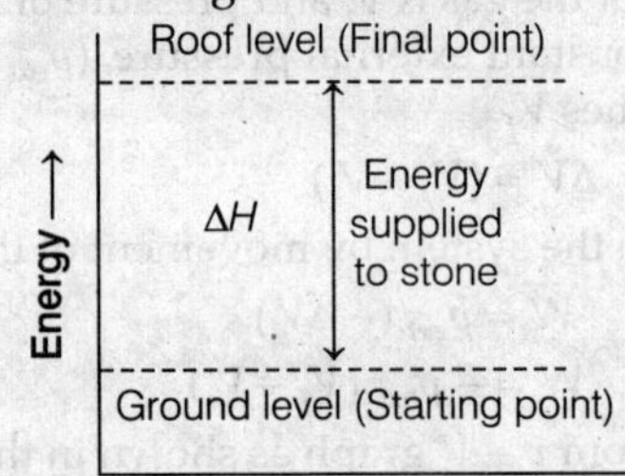

(b) $\frac{1}{2} H_2(g) + \frac{1}{2} Cl_2(g) \rightleftharpoons HCl(g);\ \Delta_r H^\ominus = -92.32 \text{ kJ mol}^{-1}$

Reactants $\left(\frac{1}{2} H_2 + \frac{1}{2} Cl_2\right)$

$H^\circ(R)$

Enthalpy ⟶

$\Delta_r H^\circ = H^\circ(P) - H^\circ(R)$

= negative

= net heat given to the surroundings

$H^\circ(P)$

Product (HCl)

Reaction coordinate ⟶

Energy increases in (a) and it decreases in (b) process. Hence, in process (b), enthalpy change is the contributing factor to the spontaneity.

Q.48 Enthalpy diagram for a particular reaction is given in figure. Is it possible to decide spontaneity of a reaction from given diagram. Explain.

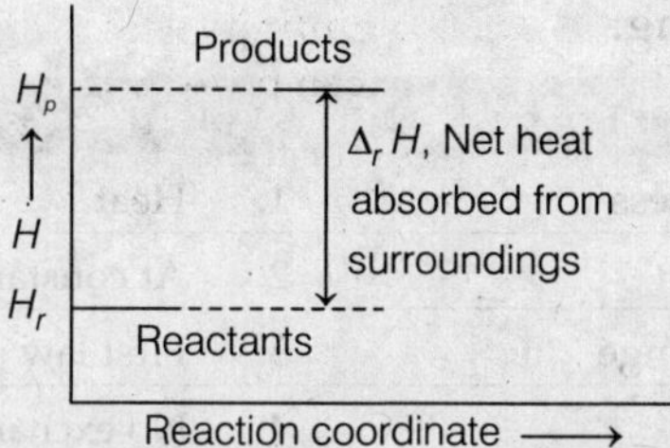

Ans. *No*, enthalpy is not the only contributing factors in deciding spontaneity. Another contributory factor, which is entropy should also to be taken into consideration to decide spontaneity of reaction.

Q.49 1.0 mol of a monoatomic ideal gas is expanded from state (1) to state 2 as shown in figure. Calculate the work done for the expansion of gas from state (1) to state (2) at 298 K.

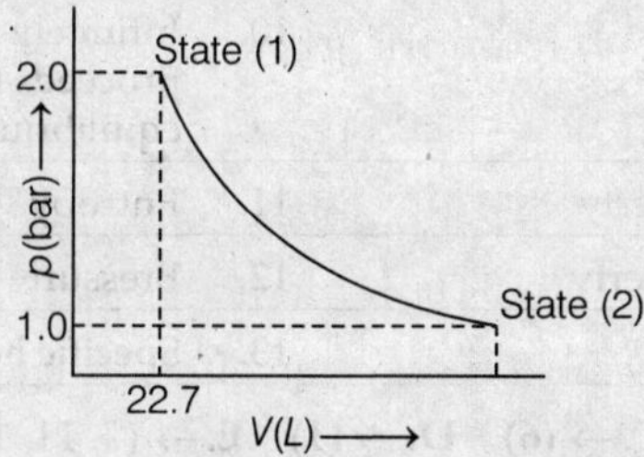

Ans. The given diagram represent that the process is carried out in infinite steps, hence it is an **isothermal reversible expansion** of the ideal gas from pressure 2.0 atm to 1.0 atm at 298 K.

$$W = -2.303\, nRT \log \frac{p_1}{p_2}$$

$$W = -2.303 \times 1\text{ mol} \times 8.314\text{ JK}^{-1}\text{mol}^{-1} \times 298\text{ K} \log 2 \qquad \left[\because \frac{p_1}{p_2} = \frac{2}{1}\right]$$

$$W = -2.303 \times 1 \times 8.314 \times 298 \times 0.3010\text{ J},\ W = -1717.46\text{ J}$$

Q.50 An ideal gas is allowed to expand against a constant pressure of 2 bar from 10 L to 50 L in one step. Calculate the amount of work done by the gas. If the same expansion were carried out reversibly, will the work done be higher or lower than the earlier case?
(Given that, 1L bar = 100 J)

Ans. In the first case, as the expansion is against constant external pressure

$$W = -p_{ext}(V_2 - V_1) = -2\text{bar} \times (50 - 10)\text{ L}$$
$$= -80\text{ L bar} \qquad [1\text{L bar} = 100\text{ J}]$$
$$= -80 \times 100\text{ J} = -8000\text{ J} = -8\text{ kJ}$$

(negative sign indicates work is done by the system)

Work done will be more in reversible expansion because the internal pressure and external pressure remain nearly equal at each infinitesimal step, allowing the gas to perform maximum work throughout the process.

Matching The Columns

Q.51 Match the following.

	List I		List II
A.	Adiabatic process	1.	Heat
B.	Isolated system	2.	At constant volume
C.	Isothermal change	3.	First law of thermodynamics
D.	Path function	4.	No exchange of energy and matter
E.	State function	5.	No transfer of heat
F.	$\Delta U = q$	6.	Constant temperature
G.	Law of conservation of energy	7.	Internal energy
H.	Reversible process	8.	$p_{ext} = 0$
I.	Free expansion	9.	At constant pressure
J.	$\Delta H = q$	10.	Infinitely slow process which proceeds through a series of equilibrium states.
K.	Intensive property	11.	Entropy
L.	Extensive property	12.	Pressure
		13.	Specific heat

Ans. **A.**→ (5) **B.**→ (4) **C.**→ (6) **D.**→ (1) **E.**→ (7, 11, 12) **F.**→ (2) **G.**→ (3) **H.**→ (10) **I.**→ (8) **J.**→ (9) **K.**→ (1, 12, 13) **L.**→ (7,11)

Q.52 Match the following processes with entropy change

	Reaction		Entropy change
A.	A liquid vaporises	1.	$\Delta S = 0$
B.	Reaction is non-spontaneous at all temperatures and ΔH is positive	2.	ΔS = positive
C.	Reversible expansion of an ideal gas	3.	ΔS = negative

Ans. **A.**→ (2) **B.**→ (3) **C.**→ (1)

A. When a liquid vaporises, *i.e.* liquid → vapour, entropy increases, *i.e.*, ΔS = positive

B. When ΔH = positive, *i.e.*, energy factor opposes. The process is non-spontaneous at all temperatures if entropy factor also opposes the process, *i.e.* ΔS = negative. This makes ΔG positive (according to $\Delta G = \Delta H - T\Delta S$) and the reaction non-spontaneous at all temperatures.

C. In the reversible expansion of an ideal gas, the system remains in equilibrium at every stage. Hence, $\Delta S = 0$

Q.53 Match the following parameters with description for spontaneity.

Δ (Parameters) $\Delta_r H^\ominus$	$\Delta_r S^\ominus$	$\Delta_r G^\ominus$		Description
A. +	−	+		1. Non-spontaneous at high temperature
B. −	−	+	(at high T)	2. Spontaneous at all temperatures
C. −	+	−		3. Non-spontaneous at all temperatures

Ans. A. → (3) B. → (1) C. → (2)

A. When $\Delta_r G^\ominus$ is positive, reaction is non-spontaneous at all temperatures

B. When $\Delta_r G^\ominus$ is positive at high temperature means the reaction is non-spontaneous at high temperature.

C. When $\Delta_r H^\ominus$ = negative means it favours, $\Delta_r S^\ominus$ = positive means it also favours. $\Delta_r G^\circ$ = negative means reaction is spontaneous at all temperatures.

Q.54 Match the following

A.	Entropy of vapourisation	1.	decreases
B.	K for spontaneous process	2.	is always positive
C.	Crystalline solid state	3.	lowest entropy
D.	ΔU in adiabatic expansion of ideal gas	4.	$\dfrac{\Delta H_{vap}}{T_b}$

Ans. A. → (2, 4) B. → (2) C. → (3) D. → (1)

A. Entropy of vaporisation is always positive. It is equal to $\Delta H_{vap} / T_b$

B. $\Delta_r G^\circ = -RT \ln K$

If K is positive, $\Delta_r G^\circ$ = negative and reaction is spontaneous.

C. Crystalline solid state has lowest entropy.

D. During adiabatic expansion of an ideal gas, $q = 0$. Hence, $\Delta U = q + W$ gives $\Delta U = W$, *i.e.*, work done is at the cost of internal energy which decreases.

Assertion and Reason

In the following questions a statement of assertion* (A) *followed by a statement of reason* (R) *is given. Choose the correct option out of the choices given below in each question.

Q.55 **Assertion** (A) Combustion of all organic compounds is an exothermic reaction.

Reason (R) The enthalpies of all elements in their standard state are zero.

(a) Both A and R are true and R is the correct explanation of A

(b) Both A and R are true but R is not the correct explanation of A

(c) A is true but R is false

(d) A is false but R is true

Ans. ***(b)*** Both assertion and reason are true but reason is not the correct explanation of assertion.

In a combustion reaction, sum of enthalpies of reactants is greater than the sum of the enthalpies of products. This difference in enthalpy is released as heat. The enthalpy of elements in their standard states is taken as zero by convention and does not explain the heat release during combustion.

Q.56 **Assertion** (A) Spontaneous process is an irreversible process and may be reversed by some external agency.

Reason (R) Decrease in enthalpy is a contributory factor for spontaneity.

(a) Both A and R are true and R is the correct explanation of A
(b) Both A and R are true but R is not the correct explanation of A
(c) A is true but R is false
(d) A is false but R is true

Ans. ***(b)*** Both assertion and reason are true but reason is not the correct explanation of assertion. Spontaneous processes are accompanied by decrease in energy and increase in randomness. While a decrease in enthalpy contributes to spontaneity, it is not the sole criterion. Spontaneity depends on the overall change in Gibbs free energy (ΔG), which includes both enthalpy and entropy changes.

Q.57 **Assertion** (A) A liquid crystallises into a solid and is accompanied by decrease in entropy.

Reason (R) In crystals, molecules organise in an ordered manner.

(a) Both A and R are true and R is the correct explanation of A
(b) Both A and R are true but R is not the correct explanation of A
(c) A is true but R is false
(d) A is false but R is true

Ans. ***(a)*** Both assertion and reason are true and reason is the correct explanation of assertion. When a liquid crystallises, entropy decreases because in crystalline form the molecules are more ordered as compared to the liquid.

Long Answer Type Questions

Q.58 Derive the relationship between ΔH and ΔU for an ideal gas. Explain each term involved in the equation.

Ans. From the first law of thermodynamics, $q = \Delta U + p\Delta V$

If the process carried out at constant volume, $\Delta V = 0$

Hence, $q_v = \Delta U$

[Here, q_v = Heat absorbed at constant volume, ΔU = change in internal energy]

Similarly, $q_p = \Delta H$

Here, q_p = heat absorbed at constant pressure

ΔH = enthalpy change of the system.

Enthalpy change of a system is equal to the heat absorbed or evolved by the system at constant pressure.

As we know that at constant pressure, $\Delta H = \Delta U + p\Delta V$

where, ΔV is the change in volume.

This equation can be rewritten as $\Delta H = \Delta U + p(V_f - V_i) = \Delta U + (pV_f - pV_i)$ ...(i)

where, V_i = initial volume of the system, V_f = final volume of the system

But for the ideal gases, $pV = nRT$

So that $pV_1 = n_1 RT$

and $pV_2 = n_2 RT$

where, n_1 = number of moles of the gaseous reactants

n_2 = number of moles of the gaseous products.

Substituting these values in Eq. (i), we get

$$\Delta H = \Delta U + (n_2 RT - n_1 RT)$$

$$\Delta H = \Delta U + (n_2 - n_1) RT$$

or

$$\Delta H = \Delta U + \Delta n_g RT$$

where, $\Delta n_g = n_2 - n_1$ is the difference between the number of moles of the gaseous products and gaseous reactants.

Q.59 Extensive properties depend on the quantity of matter but intensive properties do not. Explain whether the following properties are extensive or intensive.

Mass, internal energy, pressure, heat capacity, molar heat capacity, density, mole fraction, specific heat, temperature and molarity.

- **Concept Insight** Mole fraction or molarity of a solution is same whether we take a small amount of the solution or large amount of the solution.

Ratio of two extensive properties is always intensive.

$$\frac{\text{Extensive}}{\text{Extensive}} = \text{Intensive}$$

So, mole fraction and molarity are intensive properties.

e.g.,

$$\text{mole fraction} = \frac{\text{Moles of the component}}{\text{Total no. of moles}}$$

$$= \frac{\text{Extensive}}{\text{Extensive}}$$

and

$$\text{molarity} = \frac{\text{Mole}}{\text{Volume}}$$

$$= \frac{\text{Extensive}}{\text{Extensive}}$$

Ans. Extensive properties Those properties whose value depends on the quantity or size of matter present in the system is known as extensive properties.

e.g. mass, internal energy, heat capacity.

Intensive properties Those properties which do not depend on the quantity or size of matter present are known as intensive properties. *e.g.*, pressure, molar heat capacity, density, mole fraction, specific heat, temperature and molarity.

Q.60 **The lattice enthalpy of an ionic compound is the enthalpy when one mole of an ionic compound present in its gaseous state, dissociates into its ions. It is impossible to determine it directly by experiment. Suggest and explain an indirect method to measure lattice enthalpy of NaCl(*s*).**

Ans. The lattice enthalpy of an ionic compound is the enthalpy change which occurs when one mole of an ionic compound dissociates into its ions in gaseous state. For the reaction,

$$Na^+Cl^-(s) \rightarrow Na^+(g) + Cl^-(g);\ \Delta_{lattice}H^\ominus = +788\ \text{kJ mol}^{-1}$$

Lattice enthalpy can not be measured by experiments, so BORN HABER CYCLE is used to measure lattice enthalpy as given below

(i) $Na(s) \rightarrow Na(g)$; Sublimation of sodium metal, $\Delta_{sub}H^\ominus = 108.4$ kJ mol^{-1}

(ii) $Na(g) \rightarrow Na^+(g) + e^-(g)$; The ionisation of sodium atoms, ionisation enthalpy $\Delta_i H^\ominus = 496$ kJ mol^{-1}

(iii) $\frac{1}{2}Cl_2(g) \rightarrow Cl(g)$; The dissociation of chlorine, the reaction enthalpy is half the bond dissociation enthalpy, $\frac{1}{2}\Delta_{bond}H^\ominus = 121$ kJ mol^{-1}

(iv) $Cl(g) + e^-(g) \rightarrow Cl^-(g)$; electron gained by chlorine atoms. The electron gain enthalpy, $\Delta_{eg}H^\ominus = -348.6$ kJ mol^{-1}

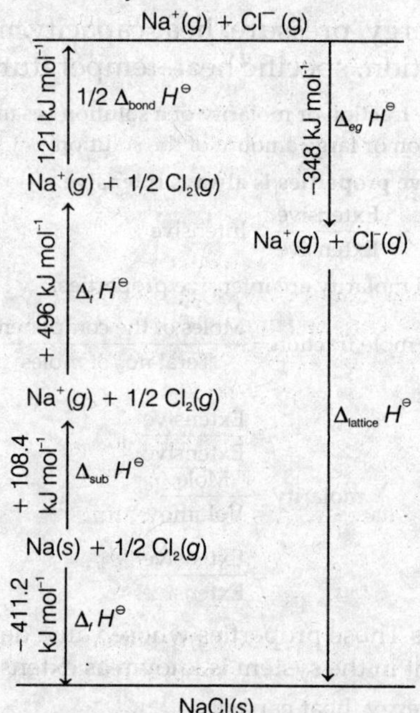

Enthalpy diagram for lattice enthalpy of NaCl

(v) $Na^+(g) + Cl^-(g) \longrightarrow Na^+Cl^-(s)$

The importance of the Born-Haber cycle is that, the sum of the enthalpy changes round a cycle is zero.

Applying Hess's law, we get

$$\Delta_{lattice}H^\ominus = 411.2 + 108.4 + 121 + 496 - 348.6 = +788\ \text{kJ mol}^{-1}$$

Q.61 ΔG is net energy available to do useful work and is thus a measure of "Free energy". Show mathematically that ΔG is a measure of free energy. Find the unit of ΔG. If a reaction has positive enthalpy change and positive entropy change, under what condition will the reaction be spontaneous?

Ans. Gibbs free energy is that thermodynamic quantity of a system, the decrease in whose value during a process is equal to the maximum possible useful work that can be obtained from the system.

Mathematically,this results may be derived as follows :

The relationship between heat absorbed by a system q, the change in its internal energy, ΔU and the work done by the system is given by the equation of the first law of thermodynamics, therefore,

$$\boxed{q = \Delta U + W_{\text{expansion}} + W_{\text{non-expansion}}} \quad \text{...(i)}$$

Under constant pressure condition, the expansion work is given by $p\Delta V$.

$$\therefore \quad q = \Delta U + p\Delta V + W_{\text{non-expansion}} \quad [\because \Delta U + p\Delta V = \Delta H]$$

$$= \Delta H + W_{\text{non-expansion}} \quad \text{...(ii)}$$

For a reversible change taking place at constant temperature,

$$\Delta S = \frac{q_{rev}}{T} \text{ or } q_{rev} = T\Delta S \quad \text{...(iii)}$$

Substituting the value of q from Eq. (iii) in Eq. (ii), we get

$$T\Delta S = \Delta H + W_{\text{non-expansion}}$$

or $$\Delta H - T\Delta S = -W_{\text{non-expansion}} \quad \text{... (iv)}$$

For a change taking place under conditions of constant temperature and pressure,

$$\Delta G = \Delta H - T\Delta S$$

Substituting this value in equation (iv), we get

$$\Delta G = -W_{\text{non-expansion}} \quad \text{...(v)}$$

Thus, free energy change can be taken as a measure of work other than the work of expansion. For most changes, the work of expansion cannot be converted to other useful work, whereas the non-expansion work is convertible to useful work.

Rearranging equation (v), it may write as

$$-\Delta G = W_{\text{non-expansion}}$$

$$= W_{\text{useful}}$$

As $-\Delta G = W_{\text{useful}}$ therefore, ΔG has the same units as those of work, *i.e.*, joule

$$\Delta G = \Delta H - T\Delta S.$$

If ΔH = positive and ΔS = positive, then

ΔG will be negative, i.e., process will be spontaneous only when $T\Delta S > \Delta H$ in magnitude, which will be so when temperature is high.

Alternate Method

$$\Delta S_{total} = \Delta S_{sys} + \Delta S_{surrr}$$

$$\Delta S_{total} = \Delta S_{sys} + \left[\frac{-\Delta H_{sys}}{T}\right]$$

$$T\Delta S_{total} = T\Delta S_{sys} + \Delta H_{sys}$$

For spontaneous change, $\Delta S_{total} > 0$

$\therefore \quad T\Delta S_{sys} - \Delta H_{sys} > 0$

$\Rightarrow \quad -(\Delta H_{sys} - T\Delta_{sys}) > 0$

But, $\quad \Delta H_{sys} - T\Delta_{sys} = \Delta G_{sys}$

$\therefore \quad -\Delta G_{sys} > 0$

$\Rightarrow \quad \Delta G_{sys} = \Delta H_{sys} - T\Delta S_{sys} < 0$

ΔH_{sys} = Enthalpy change of a reaction

$T\Delta S_{sys}$ = Energy which is not available to do useful work.

ΔG_{sys} = Energy available for doing useful work unit of ΔG is joule.

If ΔH is $+ve$ and ΔS is $+ve$ the reaction will be spontaneous at high temperature.

Q.62 Graphically show the total work done in an expansion when the state of an ideal gas is changed reversibly and isothermally from (p_i, V_i) to (p_f, V_f). With the help of a pV plot compare the work done in the above case with that carried out against a constant pressure p_f.

Ans. (i) Total work done in an expansion when the state of an ideal gas is changed reversibly and isothermally from (p_i, V_i) to (p_f, V_f). Reversible work is represented by the combined areas ABC and BCV_iV_f.

(ii) Work against constant pressure, p_f is represented by the area BCV_iV_f.

Work (i) > work (ii)

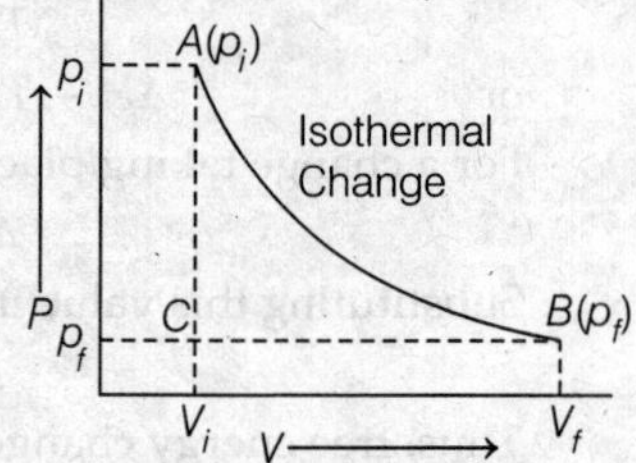

Chapter

07

Equilibrium

Multiple Choice Questions (MCQs)

Q.1 We know that the relationship between K_c and K_p is

$$K_p = K_c(RT)^{\Delta n}$$

What would be the value of Δn for the reaction?

$$NH_4Cl(s) \rightleftharpoons NH_3(g) + HI(g)$$

(a) 1 (b) 0.5
(c) 1.5 (d) 2

Ans. ***(d)*** Δn = (number of moles of gaseous products) – (number of moles of gaseous reactants)

For the reaction, $\Delta n = (1 + 1) - (0) = 2$

Mistake Alert ! *Students sometimes often forget that pure solids and liquids are not included in the calculation of* Δn.

Q.2 For the reaction, $H_2(g) + I_2(g) \rightleftharpoons 2HI(g)$, the standard free energy is $\Delta G^\ominus > 0$. The equilibrium constant (K) would be

(a) $K = 0$ (b) $K > 1$
(c) $K = 1$ (d) $K < 1$

Ans. ***(d)*** $\Delta G^\ominus$ and K are related as :

$$\Delta G^\ominus = - RT \ln K_c$$

when $G^\ominus > 0$ means $\Delta G°$ is positive. This can be so only if ln K_c is negative, *i.e.*, $K_c < 1$.

Q.3 Which of the following is not a general characteristic of equilibria involving physical processes?

(a) Equilibrium is possible only in a closed system at a given temperature
(b) All measurable properties of the system remain constant
(c) All the physical processes stop at equilibrium
(d) The opposing processes occur at the same rate and there is dynamic but stable condition

Ans. ***(c)*** At the stage of equilibria involving physical processes like melting of ice and freezing of water etc., does not stop but forward and reverse process occur at the same rate.

Q.4 PCl_5, PCl_3, and Cl_2 are at equilibrium at 500 K in a closed container and their concentrations are $0 \cdot 8 \times 10^{-3}$ mol L^{-1}, 1.2×10^{-3} mol L^{-1} and 1.2×10^{-3} mol L^{-1}, respectively. The value of K_c for the reaction

$$PCl_5(g) \rightleftharpoons PCl_3(g) + Cl_2(g) \text{ will be}$$

(a) 1.8×10^3 mol L^{-1}
(b) 1.8×10^{-3}
(c) 1.8×10^{-3} mol^{-1} L
(d) 0.55×10^4

Ans. ***(b)*** For the reaction, $PCl_5(g) \rightleftharpoons PCl_3(g) + Cl_2(g)$

At 500 K in a closed container, $[PCl_5] = 0.8 \times 10^{-3}$ mol L^{-1}

$$[PCl_3] = 1.2 \times 10^{-3} \text{ mol L}^{-1}$$

$$[Cl_2] = 1.2 \times 10^{-3} \text{ mol L}^{-1}$$

$$K_c = \frac{[PCl_3][Cl_2]}{[PCl_5]} = \frac{(1.2 \times 10^{-3}) \times (1.2 \times 10^{-3})}{(0.8 \times 10^{-3})}$$

$$= 1.8 \times 10^{-3}$$

Q.5 Which of the following statements is incorrect?

(a) In equilibrium mixture of ice and water kept in perfectly insulated flask, mass of ice and water does not change with time
(b) The intensity of red colour increases when oxalic acid is added to a solution containing iron (III) nitrate and potassium thiocyanate
(c) On addition of catalyst the equilibrium constant value is not affected
(d) Equilibrium constant for a reaction with negative ΔH value decreases as the temperature increases

Ans. ***(b)*** In the reaction, $Fe^{3+}(aq) + 3SCN^-(aq) \rightleftharpoons \underset{\text{(Red colour)}}{[Fe(SCN)_3]}$

When oxalic acid is added, it combines with Fe^{3+} ions so conc. of Fe^{3+} ion decreases and thus equilibrium shifts towards reactant side (*i.e.,* backward direction).

Q.6 When hydrochloric acid is added to cobalt nitrate solution at room temperature, the following reaction takes place and the reaction mixture becomes blue. On cooling the mixture, it becomes pink. On the basis of this information mark the correct answer.

$$\underset{\text{(Pink)}}{[Co(H_2O_6)]^{3+}(aq)} + 4Cl^-(aq) \rightleftharpoons \underset{\text{(Blue)}}{[CoCl_4]^{2-}(aq)} + 6H_2O(l)$$

(a) $\Delta H > 0$ for the reaction
(b) $\Delta H < 0$ for the reaction
(c) $\Delta H = 0$ for the reaction
(d) The sign of ΔH cannot be predicted on the basis of this information

Ans. ***(a)*** In the reaction,

$$\underset{\text{(Pink)}}{[Co(H_2O)_6]^{3+}(aq)} + 4Cl^-(aq) \rightleftharpoons \underset{\text{(Blue)}}{[CoCl_4]^{2-}(aq)} + 6H_2O(l)$$

On cooling, the mixture become pink, *i.e.,* the equilibrium shift to backward direction (reactant side). Similary, at room temperature, the reaction mixture become blue *i.e.,* equilibrium shift to forward direction (product side). Hence, reaction is endothermic, *i.e.,* $\Delta H > 0$.

Q.7 The pH of neutral water at 25°C is 7.0. As the temperature increases, ionisation of water increases, however, the concentration of H^+ ions and OH^- ions are equal. What will be the pH of pure water at 60°C?

(a) Equal to 7.0 (b) Greater than 7.0 (c) Less than 7.0 (d) Equal to zero

Ans. ***(c)*** The pH of neutral water at 25°C is 7.0.

At 25°C, $[H^+] = [OH^-] = 10^{-7}$

and $K_w = [H^+][OH^-] = 10^{-14}$

On heating, K_w increases, i.e. $[H^+][OH^-] > 10^{-14}$

As $[H^+] = [OH^-]$ or, $[H^+]^2 > 10^{-14}$

or, $[H^+] > 10^{-7}$ M

$\therefore$ pH < 7.

With rise in temperature, pH of pure water decreases and it become less than 7 at 60°C.

Q.8 The ionisation constant of an acid, K_a is the measure of strength of an acid. The K_a values of acetic acid, hypochlorous acid and formic acid are 1.74×10^{-5}, 3.0×10^{-8} and 1.8×10^{-4} respectively. Which of the following orders of pH of 0.1 mol dm^{-3} solutions of these acids is correct?

(a) Acetic acid > hypochlorous acid > formic acid
(b) Hypochlorous acid > acetic acid > formic acid
(c) Formic acid > hypochlorous acid > acetic acid
(d) Formic acid > acetic acid > hypochlorous acid

Thinking Process This problem is based upon the relationship between ionisation constant (K_a) and pH, *i.e.*, $K_a \propto \frac{1}{\text{pH}}$. Greater the K_a, lesser the value of pH and vice-versa.

Ans. ***(d)*** As K_a value increases, conc. of H^+ increases, due to dissociation, and hence pH decreases, thus, the order of pH value of the acids is

$$\underset{(3.8 \times 10^{-8})}{\text{Hypochlorous acid}} < \underset{(1.74 \times 10^{-5})}{\text{Acetic acid}} < \underset{(1.8 \times 10^{-4})}{\text{Formic acid}}$$

Q.9 K_{a_1}, K_{a_2} and K_{a_3} are the respective ionisation constants for the following reactions.

$$H_2S \rightleftharpoons H^+ + HS^-$$
$$HS^- \rightleftharpoons H^+ + S^{2-}$$
$$H_2S \rightleftharpoons 2H^+ + S^{2-}$$

The correct relationship between K_{a_1}, K_{a_2}, K_{a_3} is

(a) $K_{a_3} = K_{a_1} \times K_{a_2}$ (b) $K_{a_3} = K_{a_1} + K_{a_2}$
(c) $K_{a_3} = K_{a_1} - K_{a_2}$ (d) $K_{a_3} = K_{a_1} / K_{a_2}$

Thinking Process To find out the correct relationship between three ionisation constants (K_{a_1}, K_{a_2} and K_{a_3}) this must be kept in mind that when two reactions are added, their equilibrium constants are multiplied.

Ans. *(a)* For the reaction, $H_2S \rightleftharpoons H^+ + HS^-$

$$K_{a_1} = \frac{[H^+][HS^-]}{[H_2S]}$$

For the reaction, $HS^- \rightleftharpoons H^+ + S^{2-}$

$$K_{a_2} = \frac{[H^+][S^{2-}]}{[HS^-]}$$

When the above two reactions are added, their equilibrium constants are multiplied, thus

$$K_{a_3} = \frac{[H^+]^2 [S^{2-}]}{[H_2S]} = K_{a_1} \times K_{a_2}$$

Hence, $K_{a_3} = K_{a_1} \times K_{a_2}$

Mistake Alert ! *Students may get confused and add two equilibrium constants also.*

Q.10 Acidity of BF_3 can be explained on the basis of which of the following concepts?

(a) Arrhenius concept
(b) Bronsted Lowry concept
(c) Lewis concept
(d) Bronsted Lowry as well as Lewis concept

Ans. *(c)* According to the Lewis concept species which can accept an electron pair are Lewis acids. Since BF_3 has incomplete octet in B (boron), so it can accept an electron pair and BF_3 is Lewis acid.

Q.11 Which of the following will produce a buffer solution when mixed in equal volumes?

(a) 0.1 mol dm^{-3} NH_4OH and 0.1 mol dm^{-3} HCl
(b) 0.05 mol dm^{-3} NH_4OH and 0.1mol dm^{-3} HCl
(c) 0.1 mol dm^{-3} NH_4OH and 0.05 mol dm^{-3} HCl
(d) 0.1 mol dm^{-3} CH_3COONa and 0.1 mol dm^{-3} NaOH

Ans. *(c)* When the concentration of NH_4OH (weak base) is higher than the strong acid (HCI), a mixture of weak base and its conjugate acid is obtained, which acts as basic buffer. A mixture of NH_4OH and NH_4CI, will be formed when 0.1mol dm^{-3} NH_4OH and 0.05 mol dm^{-3} HCl are mixed.

Q.12 In which of the following solvents is silver chloride most soluble?

(a) 0.1 mol dm^{-3} $AgNO_3$ solution
(b) 0.1 mol dm^{-3} HCl solution
(c) H_2O
(d) Aqueous ammonia

Ans. *(d)* AgCl is most soluble in aqueous ammonia solution. AgCl react with aqueous ammonia to form a complex, $[Ag(NH_3)_2]^+Cl^-$.

$$AgCl + 2NH_3 \longrightarrow [Ag(NH_3)_2]Cl$$

Q.13 What will be the value of pH of 0.01 mol dm^{-3} CH_3COOH ($K_a = 1.74 \times 10^{-5}$)?

(a) 3.4 (b) 3.6 (c) 3.9 (d) 3.0

Ans. (a)

$$\begin{array}{lccc} & CH_3COOH + H_2O & \rightleftharpoons & H_3O^+ + CH_3COO^- \\ \text{Initial conc.} & 0.01 & & 0 \quad\quad 0 \\ \text{At equilibrium} & 0.01-x & & x \quad\quad x \end{array}$$

$$K_a = \frac{[H_3O][CH_3COO]}{[CH_3COOH]} = \frac{x^2}{0.01-x}$$

Since, $x << 0.01$ therefore, $0.01 - x = 0.01$

$$\frac{x^2}{0.01} = 1.74 \times 10^{-5}$$

$$x^2 = 1.74 \times 10^{-7} \text{ or } x = 4.2 \times 10^{-4}$$

$$pH = -\log(4.2 \times 10^{-4}) = 3.37 \sim 3.4$$

Alternate Method

Given that, $K_a = 1.74 \times 10^{-5}$

Concentration of CH_3COOH = 0.01 mol dm^{-3}

$$[H^+] = \sqrt{K_a \cdot C} = \sqrt{1.74 \times 10^{-5} \times 0.01} = 4.17 \times 10^{-4}$$

$$pH = -\log [H^+]$$

$$pH = -\log (4.17 \times 10^{-4}) = 3.376 \sim 3.4$$

Q.14 K_a for CH_3COOH is 1.8×10^{-5} and K_b for NH_4OH is 1.8×10^{-5}. The pH of ammonium acetate will be

(a) 7.005 (b) 4.75 (c) 7.0 (d) Between 6 and 7

- **Concept Insight** The pH of a salt made from a weak acid and a weak base is given as follows.

$$pH = \frac{1}{2}(pK_w + pK_a - pK_b) = 7 + \frac{1}{2}[PK_a - pK_b]$$

Ans. (c) Given that, K_a for $CH_3COOH = 1.8 \times 10^{-5}$

K_b for $NH_4OH = 1.8 \times 10^{-5}$

Ammonium acetate is a salt of weak acid and weak base. For such salts

$$pH = 7 + \frac{pK_a - pK_b}{2}$$

$$= 7 + \frac{[-\log 1.8 \times 10^{-5}] - [-\log 1.8 \times 10^{-5}]}{2} = 7 + \frac{4.74 - 4.74}{2} = 7.00$$

Q.15 Which of the following options will be correct for the stage of half completion of the reaction $A \rightleftharpoons B$?

(a) $\Delta G^\ominus = 0$ (b) $\Delta G^\ominus > 0$ (c) $\Delta G^\ominus < 0$ (d) $\Delta G^\ominus = -RT \ln K$

Ans. (a) As we know that, $\Delta G^\ominus = -RT \ln K$

At the stage of half completion of the reaction,

$A \rightleftharpoons B, [A] = [B]$ (i.e. half of A has been converted to B)

Therefore, $K = 1$

Thus, $\Delta G^\ominus = 0$

Q.16 On increasing the pressure, in which direction will the gas phase reaction proceed to re-establish equilibrium, is predicted by applying the Le-Chatelier's principle. Consider the reaction.

$$N_2(g) + 3H_2(g) \rightleftharpoons 2NH_3(g)$$

Which of the following is correct, if the total pressure at which the equilibrium is established, is increased without changing the temperature?

(a) K will remain same
(b) K will decrease
(c) K will increase
(d) K will increase initially and decrease when pressure is very high

Ans. *(a)* In the reaction, $N_2(g) + 3H_2(g) \rightleftharpoons 2NH_3(g)$

If the total pressure at which the equilibrium is established, is increased without changing the temperature, K will remain same. K changes only with change in temperature.

Q.17 What will be the correct order of vapour pressure of water, acetone and ether at 30°C? Given that among these compounds, water has maximum boiling point and ether has minimum boiling point?

(a) Water < ether < acetone
(b) Water < acetone < ether
(c) Ether < acetone < water
(d) Acetone < ether < water

Ans. *(b)* The given compounds are

Water (Maximum b.p), acetone, ether (Minimum b.p)

The vapour pressure of a liquid at a given temperature is inversely related to its boiling point. A liquid with a lower boiling point has weaker intermolecular forces, so it vaporizes more easily and thus has a higher vapour pressure at a given temperature. Hence, the correct order of vapour pressure will be

Water < acetone < ether

Q.18 At 500 K, equilibrium constant, K_c, for the following reaction is 5.

$$\frac{1}{2}H_2(g) + \frac{1}{2}I_2(g) \rightleftharpoons HI(g)$$

What would be the equilibrium constant K_c for the reaction?

$$2HI(g) \rightleftharpoons H_2(g) + I_2(g)$$

(a) 0.04
(b) 0.4
(c) 25
(d) 2.5

Ans. *(a)* For the reaction, $\frac{1}{2}H_2(g) + \frac{1}{2}I_2(g) \rightleftharpoons HI(g)$

$$K_c = \frac{[HI]}{[H_2]^{1/2}[I_2]^{1/2}} = 5$$

Thus, for the reaction, $2HI(g) \rightleftharpoons H_2(g) + I_2(g)$

$$K_{c_1} = \frac{[H_2][I_2]}{[HI]^2} = \left(\frac{1}{K_c}\right)^2 = \left(\frac{1}{5}\right)^2 = \frac{1}{25} = 0.04$$

Q.19 In which of the following reactions, the equilibrium remains unaffected on addition of small amount of argon at constant volume?

(a) $H_2(g) + I_2(g) \rightleftharpoons 2HI(g)$
(b) $PCl_5(g) \rightleftharpoons PCl_3(g) + Cl_2(g)$
(c) $N_2(g) + 3H_2(g) \rightleftharpoons 2NH_3(g)$
(d) The equilibrium will remain unaffected in all the three cases.

Thinking Process At constant volume, the equilibrium remain unaffected on addition of small amount of inert gas like argon, neon, krypton, etc.

Ans. *(d)* The equilibrium constant (*K*) remains unaffected on addition of inert gas in all the three given cases. At constant volume, adding inert gas (like argon) increases total pressure but does not change the partial pressures of reactants or products. Hence, equilibrium remains unaffected.

Multiple Choice Questions (More Than One Options)

Q.20 For the reaction $N_2O_4(g) \rightleftharpoons 2NO_2(g)$, the value of *K* is 50 at 400 K and 1700 at 500 K. Which of the following option(s) is/are correct?

(a) The reaction is endothermic
(b) The reaction is exothermic
(c) If $NO_2(g)$ and $N_2O_4(g)$ are mixed at 400 K at partial pressures 20 bar and 2 bar respectively, more $N_2O_4(g)$ will be formed
(d) The entropy of the system increases

Ans. *(a, c, d)* For the reaction, $N_2O_4(g) \rightleftharpoons 2NO_2(g)$

At 400 K, $K = 50$

At 500 K, $K = 1700$

(a) As the value of *K* increase with increase of temperature and $K = \frac{K_f}{K_b}$, this means that K_f increases, *i.e.*, forward reaction is favoured. Hence, reaction is endothermic.

(c) At 400 K, $Q = \frac{(P_{NO_2})^2}{P_{N_2O_4}} = \frac{(20)^2}{2} = 200$

As, Q > K hence reaction proceeds in backward direction. Hence, more N_2O_4 will be formed.

(d) As reaction is accompanied by increase in the number of moles, entropy increases.

Q.21 At a particular temperature and atmospheric pressure, the solid and liquid phases of a pure substance can exist in equilibrium. Which of the following term defines this temperature?

(a) Normal melting point
(b) Equilibrium temperature
(c) Boiling point
(d) Freezing point

Ans. *(a, d)* At a particular temperature and atmospheric pressure, the solid and liquid phases of a pure substance can exist as Solid $\rightleftharpoons$ liquid. It represents normal melting point of solid and freezing point of liquid.

Short Answer Type Questions

Q.22 The ionisation of hydrochloric acid in water is given below

$$HCl\ (aq) + H_2O\ (l) \rightleftharpoons H_3O^+\ (aq) + Cl^-\ (aq)$$

Label two conjugate acid-base pairs in this ionisation.

● **Concept Insight** If Bronsted acid is a strong acid then its conjugate base is a weak base and *vice-versa*. Generally, the conjugate acid has one extra proton and each conjugate base has one less proton.

Ans.

Adds proton (from H_2O to H_3O^+)

$$\underset{\text{Acid}}{HCl\ (aq)} + \underset{\text{Base}}{H_2O(l)} \rightleftharpoons \underset{\text{Conjugate acid}}{H_3O^+(aq)} + \underset{\text{Conjugate base}}{Cl^-(aq)}$$

Loses proton (from HCl to Cl^-)

Q.23 The aqueous solution of sugar does not conduct electricity. However, when sodium chloride is added to water, it conducts electricity. How will you explain this statement on the basis of ionisation and how is it affected by concentration of sodium chloride?

Ans. (i) Sugar being a non-electrolyte does not ionise in water whereas NaCl ionises completely in water and produces Na^+ and Cl^- ion which help in the conduction of electricity.

(ii) When concentration of NaCl is increased, more Na^+ and Cl^- ions will be produced. Hence, conductance or conductivity of the solution increases.

Q.24 BF_3 does not have proton but still acts as an acid and reacts with $\ddot{N}H_3$. Why is it so? What type of bond is formed between the two?

Ans. BF_3 is an electron deficient compound as it has incomplete octet (only 6 electrons, valence electrons) and hence acts as **Lewis acid.** $\ddot{N}H_3$ has one lone pair which it can donate the empty *p*-orbital of boron in BF_3 and form a **coordinate bond**. Hence, NH_3 acts as a **Lewis base.** The co-ordinate bond thus formed is shown below.

$$H_3N: \longrightarrow BF_3$$

Q.25 Ionisation constant of a weak base *MOH*, is given by the expression

$$K_b = \frac{[M^+]\,[OH^-]}{[MOH]}$$

Values of ionisation constant of some weak bases at a particular temperature are given below :

Base	Dimethylamine	Urea	Pyridine	Ammonia
K_b	5.4×10^{-4}	1.3×10^{-14}	1.77×10^{-9}	1.77×10^{-5}

Arrange the bases in decreasing order of the extent of their ionisation at equilibrium. Which of the above base is the strongest?

Ans. Given that, ionisation constant of a weak base, MOH

$$K_b = \frac{[M^+][OH^-]}{[MOH]}$$

Larger the ionisation constant (K_b) of a base, greater is its ionisation and stronger the base. Hence, dimethyl amine is the strongest base. The order of extent of ionisation at equilibrium is,

$$\underset{K_b = 5.4\times10^{-4}}{\text{Dimethyl amine}} > \underset{1.77\times10^{-5}}{\text{ammonia}} > \underset{1.77\times10^{-9}}{\text{pyridine}} > \underset{1.3\times10^{-14}}{\text{urea}}$$

Q.26 Conjugate acid of a weak base is always stronger. What will be the decreasing order of basic strength of the following conjugate bases?

$$OH^-, RO^- \; CH_3COO^-, Cl^-$$

Ans. Conjugate acid of the given bases are H_2O, ROH, CH_3COOH and HCl. Order of their acidic strength is

$$HCl > CH_3COOH > H_2O > ROH$$

Hence, order of basic strength of their conjugate bases is

$$Cl^- < CH_3COO^- < OH^- < RO^-$$

Q.27 Arrange the following in increasing order of pH.

$$KNO_3(aq), CH_3COONa\ (aq), NH_4Cl\ (aq), C_6H_5COONH_4(aq)$$

Ans. (i) KNO_3 is a salt of strong acid (HNO_3) and strong base (KOH), hence its aqueous solution is neutral; pH = 7.

(ii) CH_3COONa is a salt of weak acid (CH_3COOH) and strong base (NaOH), hence, its aqueous solution is basic; pH > 7.

(iii) NH_4Cl is a salt of strong acid (HCl) and weak base (NH_4OH) hence, its aqueous solution is acidic; pH < 7.

(iv) $C_6H_5COONH_4$ is a salt of weak acid, C_6H_5COOH and weak base, NH_4OH. But NH_4OH is slightly stronger than C_6H_5COOH. Hence, pH is slightly > 7.

Therefore, increasing order of pH of the given salts is,

$$NH_4Cl < C_6H_5COONH_4 > KNO_3 < CH_3COONa$$

Q.28 The value of K_c for the reaction, $2HI(g) \rightleftharpoons H_2(g) + I_2(g)$ is 1×10^{-4}. At a given time, the composition of reaction mixture is $[HI] = 2\times10^{-5}$ mol, $[H_2] = 1\times10^{-5}$ mol and $[I_2] = 1\times10^{-5}$ mol. In which direction will the reaction proceed?

Ans. Given that,

$$[HI] = 2\times10^{-5}\ \text{mol}$$
$$[H_2] = 1\times10^{-5}\ \text{mol}$$
$$[I_2] = 1\times10^{-5}\ \text{mol}$$

At a given time, the reaction quotient Q_C for the reaction will be given by the expression

$$Q_c = \frac{[H_2][I_2]}{[HI]^2} = \frac{1\times10^{-5} \times 1\times10^{-5}}{(2\times10^{-5})^2} = \frac{1}{4} = 0.25 = 2.5\times10^{-1}$$

As the value of reaction quotient is greater than the value of K_c, *i.e.*, 1×10^{-4} the reaction will proceed in the reverse direction.

Q.29 On the basis of the equation $pH = -\log [H^+]$, the pH of 10^{-8} mol dm^{-3} solution of HCl should be 8. However, it is observed to be less than 7.0. Explain the reason.

Ans. Concentration of 10^{-8} mol dm^{-3} indicates that the solution is very dilute. So, we cannot neglect the contribution of H_3O^+ ions produced from H_2O in the solution. Total $[H_3O^+] = 10^{-8} + 10^{-7}$ M. From this, we get the value of pH close to 7 but less than 7 because the solution is acidic.

Total $[H_3O^+]$ concentration $= 10^{-8} M + 10^{-7} M$

$$= 10^{-8}(1+10) = 11 \times 10^{-8} M$$

$$pH = -\log[H^+] = -\log(11 \times 10^{-8})$$

$$= -\log 11 - \log 10^{-8} = -1.041 + 8 = 6.959$$

Thus, from calculation it is found that pH of 10^{-8} mol dm^{-3} solution of HCl is equal to 6.96.

Q.30 pH of a solution of a strong acid is 5.0. What will be the pH of the solution obtained after diluting the given solution a 100 times?

Ans. Given that,

$$pH = 5$$

$$[H^+] = 10^{-5} \text{ mol } L^{-1}$$

On diluting, the solution 100 times $[H^+] = \frac{10^{-5}}{100} = 10^{-7}$ mol L^{-1}

On calculating the pH using the equation $pH = -\log [H^+]$, value of pH comes out to be 7. It is not possible. This indicates that solution is very dilute.

At very low acid concentrations ($\leq 10^{-6}$ M), the contribution of H^+ ions from water becomes significant. So, total $[H^+]$ is the sum of acidic H^+ and H^+ from water auto-ionization, affecting the final pH.

Hence, Total H^+ ion concentration = H^+ ions from acid + H^+ ion from water

$$[H^+] = 10^{-7} + 10^{-7} = 2 \times 10^{-7} M$$

$$pH = -\log [2 \times 10^{-7}]$$

$$pH = 7 - 0.3010 = 6.699$$

Q.31 A sparingly soluble salt gets precipitated only when the product of concentration of its ions in the solution (Q_{sp}) becomes greater than its solubility product. If the solubility of $BaSO_4$ in water is 8×10^{-4} mol dm^{-3}. Calculate its solubility in 0.01 mol dm^{-3} of H_2SO_4.

Ans. To calculate the solubility of $BaSO_4$ in 0.01 mol dm^{-3} H_2SO_4, we consider the common ion effect due to SO_4^{2-} ions from H_2SO_4, which suppresses the solubility of $BaSO_4$.

	$BaSO_4(s) \rightleftharpoons$	$Ba^{2+}(aq.)$ +	$SO_4^{2-}(aq.)$
At $t = 0$	1	0	0
At equilibrium in water	$1 - s$	s	s
At equilibrium in the presence of sulphuric acid	$1 - s$	s	$(s + 0.01)$

$$K_{sp} \text{ for } BaSO_4 = [Ba^{2+}][SO_4^{2-}] = s \times s = s^2$$

But

$$s = 8 \times 10^{-4} \text{ mol } dm^{-3}$$

$\therefore$

$$K_{sp} = (8 \times 10^{-4})^2 = 64 \times 10^{-8}$$

In the presence of 0.01 MH_2SO_4, the expression for K_{sp} will be

$$K_{sp} = [Ba^{2+}][SO_4^{2-}]$$

$$K_{sp} = (s).(s + 0.01) \qquad (0.01\text{ M } SO_4^{2-} \text{ ions from } 0.01 \text{ M } H_2SO_4)$$

$$64 \times 10^{-8} = s \cdot (s + 0.01)$$

$$s^2 + 0.01s - 64 \times 10^{-8} = 0$$

$$s = \frac{-0.01 \pm \sqrt{(0.01)^2 + (4 \times 64 \times 10^{-8})}}{2} = \frac{-0.01 \pm \sqrt{10^{-4} + (256 \times 10^{-8})}}{2}$$

$$= \frac{-0.01 \pm \sqrt{10^{-4}(1 + 256 \times 10^{-4})}}{2}$$

$$= \frac{-0.01 \pm 10^{-2}\sqrt{1 + 0.0256}}{2} = \frac{10^{-2}(-1 \pm 1.012719)}{2}$$

$$= 5 \times 10^{-3}(-1 + 1.012719) = 6.4 \times 10^{-5} \text{ mol dm}^{-3}$$

Note $s <<< 0.01$, so, $s + 0.01 \approx 0.01$ and $64 \times 10^{-8} = s \times 0.01$

$$s = \frac{64 \times 10^{-8}}{0.01} = 6.4 \times 10^{-5}$$

Q.32 pH of 0.08 mol dm^{-3} HOCl solution is 2.85. Calculate its ionisation constant.

Thinking Process To solve this problem, we use two steps

Step I Find out the concentration of hydrogen ion $[H^+]$ through the formula $pH = -\log[H^+]$.

Step II Then, calculate the K_a of HOCl which is weak monobasic acid by using the formula $K_a = \frac{[H^+]^2}{C}$. where, C is concentration of the solution.

Ans. Given, pH of HOCl = 2.85

But, $-pH = \log[H^+]$

$\therefore$ $-2.85 = \log[H^+]$

$\Rightarrow$ $[H^+] = 1.413 \times 10^{-3}$

For weak monobasic acid, $[H^+] = \sqrt{K_a \times C}$

$$\Rightarrow \quad K_a = \frac{[H^+]^2}{C} = \frac{(1.413 \times 10^{-3})^2}{0.08}$$

$$= 24.957 \times 10^{-6} = 2.4957 \times 10^{-5}$$

Q.33 Calculate the pH of a solution formed by mixing equal volumes of two solutions A and B of a strong acid having pH = 6 and pH = 4 respectively.

Ans. Since, $pH = -\log[H^+]$, pH of solution $A = 6$. Hence, $[H^+] = 10^{-6}$ mol L^{-1}

pH of solution $B = 4$. Hence, $[H^+] = 10^{-4}$ mol L^{-1}

On mixing 1L of each solution, total volume = 1L + 1L = 2L

Amount of H^+ ions in 1L of solution A = concentration × volume, V

$= 10^{-6}$ mol × 1L

Amount of H^+ ions in 1L of solution $B = 10^{-4}$ mol × 1L

$\therefore$ Total amount of H^+ ions in the solution formed by mixing solution A and B is $(10^{-6}\text{ mol} + 10^{-4}\text{ mol})$. This amount is present in 2L solution.

Thus, molar concentration of total H^+ is halved.

Total, $[H^+] = \frac{10^{-6} + 10^{-4}}{2}$ mol L^{-1}

$= \frac{10^{-4}(0.01 + 1)}{2}$ mol L^{-1}

$[H^+] = \frac{1.01 \times 10^{-4}}{2} = 5.05 \times 10^{-5}$ mol L^{-1}

$[H^+] = 5.0 \times 10^{-5}$ mol L^{-1}

$pH = -\log[H^+]$

$\Rightarrow$ $pH = -\log(5.0 \times 10^{-5})$

$pH = -[\log 5 + (-5 \log 10)]$

$\Rightarrow$ $pH = -\log 5 + 5$

$pH = 5 - \log 5 = 5 - 0.6990$

$\Rightarrow$ $pH = 4.3010 \approx 4.3$

Thus, the pH of resulting solution is 4.3.

Q.34 The solubility product of $Al(OH)_3$ is 2.7×10^{-11}. Calculate its solubility in g L^{-1} and also find out pH of this solution. (Atomic mass of Al = 27 u)

Ans. Let S be the solubility of $Al(OH)_3$.

	$Al(OH)_3 \rightleftharpoons$	$Al^{3+}(aq.)$ +	$3OH^-(aq.)$
Concentration at $t = 0$	1	0	0
Concentration at equilibrium	$(1 - s)$	s	$3s$

$K_{sp} = [Al^{3+}][OH^-]^3 = (S)(3S)^3 = 27S^4$

$S^4 = \frac{K_{sp}}{27} = \frac{2.7 \times 10^{-11}}{27} = 1 \times 10^{-12}$

$S = 1 \times 10^{-3}$ mol L^{-1}

(i) **Solubility of $Al(OH)_3$**

Molar mass of $Al(OH)_3$ is 78 g. Therefore,

Solubility of $Al(OH)_3$ in g L^{-1} $= 1 \times 10^{-3} \times 78$ g $L^{-1} = 78 \times 10^{-3}$ g L^{-1}

$= 7.8 \times 10^{-2}$ g L^{-1}

(ii) **pH of the solution** $S = 1 \times 10^{-3}$ mol L^{-1}

$[OH^-] = 3S = 3 \times 1 \times 10^{-3} = 3 \times 10^{-3}$

$pOH = -\log[^-OH]$

$= -\log[3 \times 10^{-3}]$

$pOH = 3 - \log 3$

$pH = 14 - pOH$

$= 11 + \log 3$

$= 11.4771$

Q.35 Calculate the volume of water required to dissolve 0.1 g lead (II) chloride to get a saturated solution.

(K_{sp} of $PbCl_2 = 3.2 \times 10^{-8}$, atomic mass of Pb = 207u)

Ans. Suppose, solubility of $PbCl_2$ in water is s mol L^{-1}

$$\begin{array}{lccc} & PbCl_2(s) \rightleftharpoons & Pb^{2+}(aq) + & 2Cl^-(aq) \\ \text{Concentration at } t = 0 & 1 & 0 & 0 \\ \text{Concentration at equilibrium} & (1-s) & s & 2s \end{array}$$

$$K_{sp} = [Pb^{2+}] \cdot [Cl^-]^2$$

$$K_{sp} = [s][2s]^2 = 4s^3$$

$$3.2 \times 10^{-8} = 4s^3$$

$$s^3 = \frac{3.2 \times 10^{-8}}{4} = 0.8 \times 10^{-8}$$

$$s^3 = 8.0 \times 10^{-9}$$

$$\Rightarrow \quad s = \sqrt[3]{8 \times 10^{-9}} = 2 \times 10^{-3} \text{ mol L}^{-1}$$

Solubility of $PbCl_2$, $s = 2 \times 10^{-3}$ mol L^{-1}

Solubility of $PbCl_2$ in $gL^{-1} = 278 \times 2 \times 10^{-3} = 0.556$ g L^{-1}

[$\because$ Molar mass of $PbCl_2 = 207 + (2 \times 35.5) = 278$]

To get saturated solution, 0.556 g of $PbCl_2$ dissolve in 1 L of water.

$\therefore$ 0.1 g of $PbCl_2$ will dissolve in $= \frac{1 \times 0.1}{0.556}$ L of water = 0.1798 L

To make a saturated solution, dissolution of 0.1g $PbCl_2$ in 0.1798 L $\approx$ 0.2 L of water will be required.

Q.36 A reaction between ammonia and boron trifluoride is given below.

$$:NH_3 + BF_3 \longrightarrow H_3N:BF_3$$

Identify the acid and base in this reaction. Which theory explains it? What is the hybridisation of B and N in the reactants?

Ans. Although BF_3 does not have a proton but acts as Lewis acid as it is an electron deficient compound. It reacts with NH_3 by accepting the lone pair of electrons from NH_3 and complete its octet. The reaction can be represented by

$$BF_3 + :NH_3 \longrightarrow BF_3 \leftarrow NH_3$$

Lewis electronic theory of acids and bases can explain it. Boron in BF_3 is sp^2 hybridised whereas N in NH_3 is sp^3 hybridised.

Q.37 Following data is given for the reaction,

$$CaCO_3(s) \longrightarrow CaO(s) + CO_2(g)$$

$$\Delta_f H^\ominus [CaO(s)] = -635.1 \text{kJ mol}^{-1}$$

$$\Delta_f H^\ominus [CO_2(g)] = -393.5 \text{kJ mol}^{-1}$$

$$\Delta_f H^\ominus [CaCO_3(s)] = -1206.9 \text{kJ mol}^{-1}$$

Predict the effect of temperature on the equilibrium constant of the above reaction.

Ans. In the reaction,

$$CaCO_3(s) \rightleftharpoons CaO(s) + CO_2(g)$$

$$\Delta_f H^\ominus = \Delta_f H^\ominus [CaO(s)] + \Delta_f H^\ominus [CO_2(g)] - \Delta_f H^\ominus [CaCO_3(s)]$$

$$\therefore \quad \Delta_f H^\ominus = -635.1 + (-393.5) - (-1206.9) = 178.3 \text{ kJmol}^{-1}$$

ΔH value is positive, **so forward reaction is endothermic**. Hence, according to Le-Chatelier's principle, reaction will proceed in forward direction on increasing temperature. Thus, the value of equilibrium constant for the reaction increases.

Matching The Columns

Q.38 Match the following equilibria with the corresponding condition.

A.	Liquid $\rightleftharpoons$ Vapour	1.	Saturated solution
B.	Solid $\rightleftharpoons$ Liquid	2.	Boiling point
C.	Solid $\rightleftharpoons$ Vapour	3.	Sublimation point
D.	Solute (s) $\rightleftharpoons$ Solute (solution)	4.	Melting point
		5.	Unsaturated solution

Ans. **A.** → (2) **B.** → (4) **C.** → (3) **D.** → (1)

A. Liquid $\rightleftharpoons$ Vapour, equilibrium exists at the boiling point.

B. Solid $\rightleftharpoons$ Liquid, equilibrium exists at the melting point.

C. Solid $\rightleftharpoons$ Vapour, equilibrium exists at the sublimation point.

D. Solute (*s*) $\rightleftharpoons$ Solute (solution), equilibrium exists at saturated solution.

Q.39 For the reaction, $N_2(g) + 3H_2(g) \rightleftharpoons 2NH_3(g)$

Equilibrium constant, $K_c = \dfrac{[NH_3]^2}{[N_2][H_2]^3}$

Some reactions are written below in Column I and their equilibrium constants in terms of K_c are written in Column II. Match the following reactions with the corresponding equilibrium constant.

	Column I (Reaction)		Column II (Equilibrium constant)
A.	$2N_2(g) + 6H_2(g) \rightleftharpoons 4NH_3(g)$	1.	$2K_c$
B.	$2NH_3(g) \rightleftharpoons 2N_2(g) + 3H_2(g)$	2.	$K_c^{1/2}$
C.	$\frac{1}{2}N_2(g) + \frac{3}{2}H_2(g) \rightleftharpoons NH_3(g)$	3.	$\frac{1}{K_c}$
		4.	K_c^2

Ans. **A.** → (4) **B.** → (3) **C.** → (2)

For the reaction, $N_2(g) + 3H_2(g) \rightleftharpoons 2NH_3(g)$

Equilibrium constant $K_c = \frac{[NH_3]^2}{[N_2][H_2]^3}$

A. The given reaction $[2N_2(g) + 6H_2(g) \rightleftharpoons 4NH_3(g)]$ is twice the above reaction.

Hence, $K = K_c^2$

B. The reaction $[2NH_3(g) \rightleftharpoons N_2(g) + 3H_2(g)]$ is reverse of the above reaction.

Hence, $K = \frac{1}{K_c}$

C. The reaction $\left[\frac{1}{2}N_2(g) + \frac{3}{2}H_2(g) \rightleftharpoons NH_3(g)\right]$ is half of the above reaction.

Hence, $K = \sqrt{K_c} = K_c^{\frac{1}{2}}$.

Q.40 Match standard free energy of the reaction with the corresponding equilibrium constant.

A.	$\Delta G^\ominus > 0$	1.	$K > 1$
B.	$\Delta G^\ominus < 0$	2.	$K = 1$
C.	$\Delta G^\ominus = 0$	3.	$K = 0$
		4.	$K < 1$

Ans. **A.** → (4) **B.** → (1) **C.** → (2)

As we know that, $\Delta G^\ominus = -RT \ln K$

A. If $\Delta G^\ominus > 0$, *i.e.* ΔG° is positive, then K is negative *i.e.* $K < 1$.

B. If $\Delta G^\ominus < 0$, *i.e.* ΔG° is negative then K is positive *i.e.*, $K > 1$.

C. If $\Delta G^\ominus = 0$, $\ln K = 0$, *i.e.*, $K = 1$.

Q.41 Match the following species with the corresponding conjugate acid.

	Species		Conjugate acid
A.	NH_3	1.	CO_3^{2-}
B.	HCO_3^-	2.	NH_4^+
C.	H_2O	3.	H_3O^+
D.	HSO_4^-	4.	H_2SO_4
		5.	H_2CO_3

Ans. **A.** → (2) **B.** → (5) **C.** → (3) **D.** → (4)

As conjugate acid → Base + H^+

A. $NH_3 + H^+ \longrightarrow NH_4^+$

B. $HCO_3^- + H^+ \longrightarrow H_2CO_3$

C. $H_2O + H^+ \longrightarrow H_3O^+$

D. $HSO_4^- + H^+ \longrightarrow H_2SO_4$

Q.42 Match the following graphical variation with their description.

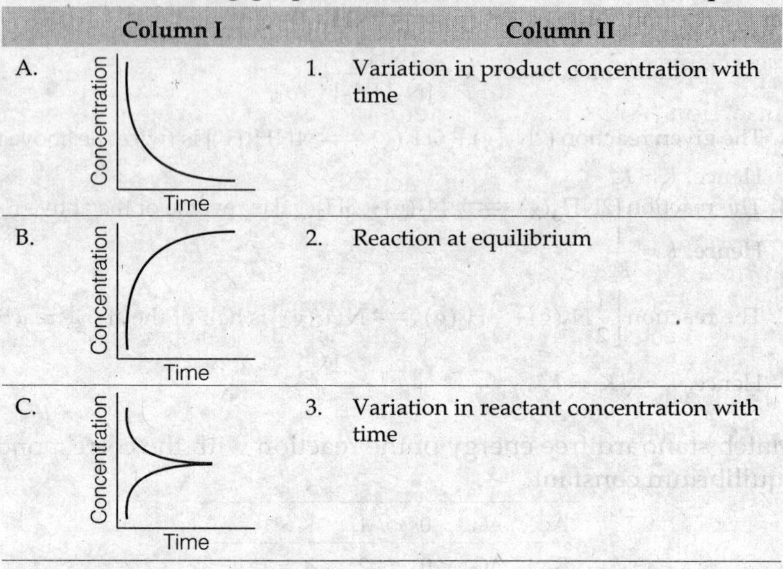

Column I	Column II
A. (Graph: Concentration vs Time)	1. Variation in product concentration with time
B. (Graph: Concentration vs Time)	2. Reaction at equilibrium
C. (Graph: Concentration vs Time)	3. Variation in reactant concentration with time

Ans. A. → (3) B. → (1) C. → (2)

A. Graph (A) represents variation of reactant concentration with time as reactant concentration decrease with passage of time.

B. Graph (B) represents variation of product concentration with time as product concentration increase with passage of time.

C. Graph (C) represents reaction at equilibrium.

Q.43 Match the Column I with Column II.

Column I	Column II
A. Equilibrium	1. $\Delta G > 0, K < 1$
B. Spontaneous reaction	2. $\Delta G = 0$
C. Non-spontaneous reaction	3. $\Delta G^{\ominus} = 0$
	4. $\Delta G < 0, K > 1$

Ans. A. → (2, 3) B. → (4) C. → (1)

A. $\Delta G\ (\Delta G^{\ominus})$ is 0, reaction has achieved equilibrium: at this point, there is no longer any free energy left to drive the reaction.

B. If $\Delta G < 0$, then $K > 1$ which implies a spontaneous reaction or the reaction which proceeds in the forward direction to such an extent that the products are present predominantly.

C. If $\Delta G > 0$, then $K < 1$, which implies a non-spontaneous reaction or a reaction which proceeds in the forward direction to such a small degree that only a very minute quantity of product is formed.

Assertion and Reason

In the following questions a statement of Assertion (A) followed by a statement of Reason (R) is given. Choose the correct option out of the choices given below in each question.

Q.44 **Assertion** (A) Increasing order of acidity of hydrogen halides is HF < HCl < HBr < HI.

Reason (R) While comparing acids formed by the elements belonging to the same group of periodic table, H—A bond strength is a more important factor in determining acidity of an acid than the polar nature of the bond.

(a) Both A and R are true R is the correct explanation of A.
(b) Both A and R are true but R is not the correct explanation of A.
(c) A is true but R is false
(d) Both A and R are false

Ans. ***(a)*** Both assertion and reason are true and reason is the correct explanation of assertion.

In the hydrogen halides, the HI is strongest acid while HF is the weak acid. It is because as halogen atom size increases $H - A$ bond strength decreases, so tendency to release H^+ ion increase thus acidic strength increase from HF to HI.

Q.45 **Assertion** (A) A solution containing a mixture of acetic acid and sodium acetate maintains a constant value of pH on addition of small amounts of acid or alkali.

Reason (R) A solution containing a mixture of acetic acid and sodium acetate acts as buffer solution around pH 4.75.

(a) Both A and R are true and R is the correct explanation of A
(b) Both A and R are true but R is not the correct explanation of A
(c) A is true but R is false
(d) Both A and R are false

Ans. ***(a)*** Both assertion and reason are true and reason is correct explanation of assertion.

A solution containing a mixture of acetic acid and the sodium acetate acts as a buffer solution as it maintains a constant value of pH (= 4.75) and its pH is not affected on addition of small amounts of acid or alkali.

Q.46 **Assertion** (A) The ionisation of hydrogen sulphide in water is low in the presence of hydrochloric acid.

Reason (R) Hydrogen sulphide is a weak acid.

(a) Both A and R are true and R is the correct explanation of A
(b) Both A and R are true but R is not the correct explanation of A
(c) A is true but R is false
(d) Both A and R are false

Ans. ***(b)*** Both assertion and reason are true but reason is not correct explanation of assertion.

The ionisation of hydrogen sulphide (H_2S) in water is suppressed in the presence of hydrochloric acid (HCl) because both release H^+ ions. Due to the common ion effect (H^+ from HCl), the ionisation equilibrium of $H_2S \rightleftharpoons 2H^+ + S^{2-}$ shifts backward, reducing its ionisation.

Q.47 **Assertion** (A) For any chemical reaction at a particular temperature, the equilibrium constant is fixed and is a characteristic property.
Reason (R) Equilibrium constant is independent of temperature.

(a) Both A and R are true and R is the correct explanation of A
(b) Both A and R are true but R is not the correct explanation of A
(c) A is true but R is false
(d) Both A and R are false

Ans. *(c)* Assertion is true but reason is false.
Equilibrium constant of a reaction depends upon temperature.

Q.48 **Assertion** (A) Aqueous solution of ammonium carbonate is basic.
Reason (R) Acidic/basic nature of a salt solution of a salt of weak acid and weak base depends on K_a and K_b value of the acid and the base forming it.

(a) Both A and R are true and R is the correct explanation of A
(b) Both A and R are true but R is not the correct explanation of A
(c) A is true but R is false
(d) Both A and R are false

Ans. *(a)* Both assertion and reason are true and reason is the correct explanation of assertion.

$$(NH_4)_2CO_3 \longrightarrow 2NH_4^+ + CO_3^{2-}$$

$$2H_2O \longrightarrow 2OH^- + 2H^+$$

$$\underset{\text{Weak base}}{NH_4OH} \quad \underset{\text{Weak acid}}{H_2CO_3}$$

If K_b of $NH_4OH > K_a$ of H_2CO_3
So, the solution is basic.
or, if K_a of $H_2CO_3 > K_b$ of NH_4OH; the solution is acidic.

Q.49 **Assertion** (A) An aqueous solution of ammonium acetate can act as a buffer.
Reason (R) Acetic acid is a weak acid and NH_4OH is a weak base.

(a) Both A and R are true and R is the correct explanation of A
(b) Both A and R are true but R is not the correct explanation of A
(c) A is false but R is true
(d) Both A and R are false

Ans. *(b)* Both assertion and reason are true but reason is not correct explanation of assertion.

Ammonium acetate is a salt of weak acid (CH_3COOH) and weak base (NH_4OH). However, the reason does not correctly explain the Assertion because the buffering action arises from the hydrolysis of ammonium acetate, which produces CH_3COO^-. (conjugate base of acetic acid) and NH_4^+ (conjugate acid of NH_4OH). It is this salt and not the separate presence of the weak acid and weak base, that maintains the pH by neutralising added H^+ or OH^- ions.

Q. 50 **Assertion** (A) In the dissociation of PCl_5 at constant pressure and temperature the addition of helium at equilibrium increases the dissociation of PCl_5.

Reason (R) Helium removes Cl_2 from the field of action.

(a) Both A and R are true and R is the correct explanation of A
(b) Both A and R are true but R is not the correct explanation of A
(c) A is true but R is false
(d) Both A and R are false

Ans. *(c)* Assertion is true but reason is false.

$$PCl_5(g) \longrightarrow PCl_3(g) + Cl_2 \uparrow$$

At constant pressure and temperature, the addition of inert helium gas increases the total volume. According to Le Chatelier's Principle, the system will shift in the direction that increases the number of gas molecules — so dissociation of PCl_5 increases. Helium is an inert gas and does not react or remove Cl_2 from the mixture.

Long Answer Type Questions

Q.51 How can you predict the following stages of a reaction by comparing the value of K_c and Q_c?

(i) Net reaction proceeds in the forward direction.
(ii) Net reaction proceeds in the backward direction.
(iii) No net reaction occurs.

Ans. Prediction of the following stages of a reaction by comparing the value of K_c and Q_c are

(i) If $Q_c < K_c$, the reaction will proceed in the direction of the products (forward reaction).
(ii) If $Q_c > K_c$, the reaction will proceed in the direction of reactants (reverse reaction).
(iii) If $Q_c = K_c$, the reaction mixture is already at equilibrium.

Q.52 On the basis of Le-Chatelier principle explain how temperature and pressure can be adjusted to increase the yield of ammonia in the following reaction.

$$N_2(g) + 3H_2(g) \rightleftharpoons 2NH_3(g); \Delta H = -92.38 \text{ kJ mol}^{-1}$$

What will be the effect of addition of argon to the above reaction mixture at constant volume?

Ans.

$$N_2(g) + 3H_2(g) \rightleftharpoons 2NH_3(g); \Delta H = -92.38 \text{ kJ mol}^{-1}$$

It is an exothermic process as ΔH is negative.

Effect of temperature According to Le-Chatelier's principle, low temperature is favourable for high yield of ammonia, but practically very low temperatures slow down the reaction. So, optimum temperature 700 K is favourable in attainment of equilibrium.

Effect of pressure High pressure about 200 atm is favourable for high yield of ammonia. On increasing pressure, reaction goes in the forward direction because the number of moles decreases in the forward direction.

Addition of argon At constant volume addition of argon does not affect the equilibrium because it does not change the partial pressures of the reactants or products involved in the reaction and the equilibrium remains undisturbed.

Q.53 A sparingly soluble salt having general formula $A_x^{p+} B_y^{q-}$ and molar solubility S is in equilibrium with its saturated solution. Derive a relationship between the solubility and solubility product for such salt.

Ans. Given that, a sparingly soluble salt having general formula $A_x^{p+} B_y^{q-}$. Its molar solubility is S mol L^{-1}.

Then, $\underset{S}{A_x^{p+} B_y^{q-}} \rightleftharpoons \underset{xS}{xA^{p+}(aq)} + \underset{yS}{yB^{q-}(aq)}$

S moles of $A_x B_y$ dissolve to give x moles of A^{p+} and y moles of B^{q-}.

Therefore, solubility product $(K_{sp}) = [A^{p+}]^x [B^{q-}]^y = [xS]^x [yS]^y$

$= x^x y^y (S)^{x+y}$

Q.54 Write a relation between ΔG and Q and define the meaning of each term and answer the following.

(a) Why a reaction proceeds forward when $Q < K$ and no net reaction occurs when $Q = K$?

(b) Explain the effect of increase in pressure in terms of reaction quotient Q.
For the reaction, $CO(g) + 3H_2(g) \rightleftharpoons CH_4(g) + H_2O(g)$

Ans. The relation between ΔG and Q is

$$\Delta G = \Delta G^\ominus + RT\ln Q$$

ΔG = change in free energy as the reaction proceeds.

$\Delta G^\ominus$ = standard free energy

Q = reaction quotient

R = gas constant

T = absolute temperature in K

(a) Since, $\Delta G^\ominus = -RT \ln K$

$\therefore$ $\Delta G = -RT \ln K + RT \ln Q$

$$\Delta G = RT \ln \frac{Q}{K}$$

If $Q < K$, ΔG will be negative and the reaction proceeds in the forward direction.

If $Q = K$, $\Delta G = 0$ reaction is in equilibrium and there is no net reaction.

(b) $CO(g) + 3H_2(g) \rightleftharpoons CH_4(g) + H_2O(g)$

$$K_c = \frac{[CH_4][H_2O]}{[CO][H_2]^3}$$

On increasing pressure, volume decreases. If we doubled the pressure, volume will be halved but the molar concentrations will be doubled. Then,

$$Q_c = \frac{2[CH_4] \cdot 2[H_2O]}{2[CO]\{2[H_2]\}^3} = \frac{1}{4}\frac{[CH_4][H_2O]}{[CO][H_2]^3} = \frac{1}{4}K_c$$

Therefore, Q_c is less than K_c, so Q_c will tend to increase to re-establish equilibrium and the reaction will go in forward direction.

Chapter 08

Redox Reactions

Multiple Choice Questions (MCQs)

Q.1 Which of the following is not an example of redox reaction?

(a) $CuO + H_2 \longrightarrow Cu + H_2O$
(b) $Fe_2O_3 + 3CO \longrightarrow 2Fe + 3CO_2$
(c) $2K + F_2 \longrightarrow 2KF$
(d) $BaCl_2 + H_2SO_4 \longrightarrow BaSO_4 + 2HCl$

- **Concept Insight** Redox reactions represent those reactions which involve change in oxidation number of the interacting species. (*i.e.*, oxidation and reduction)

Ans. ***(d)*** $\overset{+2}{Ba}\overset{-1}{Cl_2} + \overset{+1}{H_2}\overset{-2}{SO_4} \longrightarrow \overset{+2}{Ba}\overset{-2}{SO_4} + 2\overset{+1}{H}\overset{-1}{Cl}$

Option (d) is not a redox reaction as oxidation number of various atoms remain same on both sides.

Q.2 The more positive the value of $E^\ominus$, the greater is the tendency of the species to get reduced. Using the standard electrode potential of redox couples given below find out which of the following is the strongest oxidising agent.

$$E^\ominus \text{ values}: Fe^{3+}/Fe^{2+} = +0.77; I_2(s)/I^- = +0.54;$$
$$Cu^{2+}/Cu = +0.34; Ag^+/Ag = 0.80\ V$$

(a) Fe^{3+} (b) $I_2(s)$ (c) Cu^{2+} (d) Ag^+

Ans. ***(d)*** Among the given E°_{Red} values, $E°$ of Ag^+/Ag is the most positive, *i.e.*, 0.80 V, therefore, Ag^+ is the strongest oxidising agent.

Q.3 $^\ominus$ values of some redox couples are given below. On the basis of these values choose the correct option.

$$E^\ominus \text{ values}: Br_2/Br^- = +1.90; Ag^+/Ag(s) = +0.80$$
$$Cu^{2+}/Cu(s) = +0.34; I_2(s)/I^- = +0.54$$

(a) Cu will reduce Br^-
(b) Cu will reduce Ag
(c) Cu will reduce I^-
(d) Cu will reduce Br_2

Ans. ***(d)*** More positive value of $E°$, larger is the tendency of the species to get reduced and stronger is the oxidising agent.

Reduction potential of Br_2/Br^-; Ag^+/Ag and I_2/I^- is more than that of Cu^{2+}/Cu so among the given option (*d*) is correct statement.

Alternate Method

The E° values show that copper will reduce Br_2, if the E° of the following redox reaction is positive.

$$2Cu + Br_2 \longrightarrow CuBr_2$$

Now,
$$Cu \rightarrow Cu^{2+} + 2e^-; E^{\circ} = -0.34 \text{ V}$$
$$Br_2 + 2e^- \rightarrow 2Br^-; E = +1.09 \text{ V}$$
$$Cu + Br_2 \rightarrow CuBr_2; E^{\circ} = E^{\circ}_C - E^{\circ}_A = (+1.09 \text{ V}) - (+0.34) = 0.75 \text{ V}$$

Since, E° of this reaction is positive, therefore, Cu can reduce Br_2.
While, other reaction will give negative value.

Q.4 Using the standard electrode potential, find out the pair between which redox reaction is not feasible.

$$E^{\ominus} \text{ values: } Fe^{3+}/Fe^{2+} = +0.77; I_2/I^- = +0.54;$$
$$Cu^{2+}/Cu = +0.34; Ag^+/Ag = +0.80 \text{ V}$$

(a) Fe^{3+} and I^-
(b) Ag^+ and Cu
(c) Fe^{3+} and Cu
(d) Ag and Fe^{3+}

Thinking Process Calculate the E°_{cell} of the four redox reactions. If E°_{cell} of a reaction is negative, that reaction will not occur.

Ans. (d) $E^{\circ}_{cell} = E^{\circ}_{cathode} - E^{\circ}_{anode}$

Where all E° values are standard reduction potentials.

Cathode where reduction occurs (higher reduction potential).

Anode where oxidation occurs (lower reduction potential).

(a) $2Fe^{3+} + 2e^- \longrightarrow 2Fe^{2+}; E^{\circ} = +0.77V$

$2I^- \longrightarrow I_2 + 2e^-; E^{\circ} = -0.54 \text{ V}$ [sign of E° is reversed]

$2Fe^{3+} + 2I^- \longrightarrow 2Fe^{2+} + I_2; E^{\circ}_{cell} = 0.77 - 0.54 = +0.23 \text{ V}$

This reaction is feasible since E°_{cell} is positive.

(b) $Cu \rightarrow Cu^{2+} + 2e^-; E^{\circ} = -0.34 \text{V}$ [sign of E° has been reversed]

$2Ag^+ + 2e^- \longrightarrow 2Ag; E^{\circ} = +0.80 \text{ V}$

$Cu + 2Ag^+ \longrightarrow Cu^{2+} + 2Ag; E^{\circ} = 0.80 - 0.34 = +0.46 \text{ V}$

This reaction is feasible since E°_{cell} is positive.

(c) $2Fe^{3+} + 2e^- \longrightarrow 2Fe^{2+}; E^{\circ} = +0.77 \text{ V}$

$Cu \longrightarrow Cu^{2+} + 2e^-; E^{\circ} = -0.34 \text{ V}$ [sign of E° is reversed]

$2Fe^{3+} + Cu \longrightarrow 2Fe^{2+} + Cu^{2+}; E^{\circ} = 0.77 - 0.34 = +0.43 \text{ V}$

This reaction is feasible since E°_{cell} is positive.

(d) $Ag \longrightarrow Ag^+ + e^-; E^{\circ} = -0.80 \text{V}$ [sign of E° is reversed]

$Fe^{3+} + e^- \longrightarrow Fe^{2+}; E^{\circ} = +0.77 V$

$Ag + Fe^{3+} \longrightarrow Ag^+ + Fe^{2+}; E^{\circ} = 0.77 - 0.80 = -0.03 \text{ V}$

This reaction is not feasible since E°_{cell} is negative.

Q.5 Thiosulphate reacts differently with iodine and bromine in the reactions given below

$$2S_2O_3^{2-} + I_2 \longrightarrow S_4O_6^{2-} + 2I^-$$
$$S_2O_3^{2-} + 2Br_2 + 5H_2O \longrightarrow 2SO_4^{2-} + 2Br^- + 10H^+$$

Which of the following statements justifies the above dual behaviour of thiosulphate?

(a) Bromine is a stronger oxidant than iodine
(b) Bromine is a weaker oxidant than iodine
(c) Thiosulphate undergoes oxidation by bromine and reduction by iodine in these reactions
(d) Bromine undergoes oxidation and iodine undergoes reduction in these reactions

Ans. ***(a)***

$$2\overset{+2}{S_2}\overset{-2}{O_3^{2-}}(aq) + I_2^0(s) \longrightarrow \overset{2.5}{S_4}O_6^{2-}(aq) + 2I^-(aq)$$
$$\overset{+2}{S_2}\overset{-2}{O_3^{2-}}(aq) + 2\overset{0}{Br_2}(l) + 5H_2O(l) \longrightarrow 2\overset{+6}{S}\overset{2-}{O_4^{2-}}(aq) + 2Br^-(aq) + 10H^+(aq)$$

Bromine being stronger oxidising agent than I_2, oxidises $S_2O_3^{2-}$ to SO_4^{2-} whereas I_2 oxidises it only into $S_4O_6^{2-}$ ion.

Q.6 The oxidation number of an element in a compound is evaluated on the basis of certain rules. Which of the following rules is not correct in this respect?

(a) The oxidation number of hydrogen is always +1
(b) The algebraic sum of all the oxidation numbers in a compound is zero
(c) An element in the free or the uncombined state bears oxidation number zero
(d) In all its compounds, the oxidation number of fluorine is –1

Ans. ***(a)*** Oxidation number of hydrogen is +1 in hydrogen halides, –1 in hydrides and zero in H_2 molecule.

All the other three statements (b), (c) and (d) are correct.

Q.7 In which of the following compounds, an element exhibits two different oxidation states?

(a) NH_2OH (b) NH_4NO_3 (c) N_2H_4 (d) N_3H

Ans. ***(b)*** NH_4NO_3 is an ionic compound containing NH_4^+ and NO_3^- and oxidation number of N is different in both ions.

Let, oxidation number of N in NH_4^+ is x.

$\Rightarrow$ $x + (4 \times 1) = +1$

or $x + 4 = +1$ or $x = -3$

Let, oxidation number of N in NO_3^- is x

$\Rightarrow$ $x + (3 \times -2) = -1$

or $x - 6 = -1$ or $x = +5$

Q.8 Which of the following arrangements represent increasing oxidation number of the central atom ?

(a) CrO_2^-, ClO_3^-, CrO_4^{2-}, MnO_4^-
(b) ClO_3^-, CrO_4^{2-}, MnO_4^-, CrO_2^-
(c) CrO_2^-, ClO_3^-, MnO_4^-, CrO_4^{2-}
(d) CrO_4^{2-}, MnO_4^-, CrO_2^-, ClO_3^-

Ans. ***(a)*** Writing the oxidation number (O.N.) of Cr, Cl and Mn on each species in the four set of ions, then,

(a) $\overset{+3}{Cr}O_2^-, \overset{+5}{Cl}O_3^-, \overset{+6}{Cr}O_4^{2-}, \overset{+7}{Mn}O_4^-$ (b) $\overset{+5}{Cl}O_3^-, \overset{+6}{Cr}O_4^{2-}, \overset{+7}{Mn}O_4^-, \overset{+3}{Cr}O_2^-$

(c) $\overset{+3}{Cr}O_2^-, \overset{+5}{Cl}O_3^-, \overset{+7}{Mn}O_4^-, \overset{+6}{Cr}O_4^{2-}$ (d) $\overset{+6}{Cr}O_4^{2-}, \overset{+7}{Mn}O_4^-, \overset{+3}{Cr}O_2^-, \overset{+5}{Cl}O_3^-$

Only in the arrangement (a), the oxidation number of central atom increases from left to right, therefore, option (a) is correct.

Q.9 **The largest oxidation number exhibited by an element depends on its outer electronic configuration. With which of the following outer electronic configurations the element will exhibit largest oxidation number?**

(a) $3d^1 4s^2$ (b) $3d^3 4s^2$ (c) $3d^5 4s^1$ (d) $3d^5 4s^2$

Ans. ***(d)*** Highest oxidation number of any transition element = $(n-1)\,d$ electrons + ns electrons. Therefore, larger the number of electrons in the $3d$-orbitals, higher is the maximum oxidation number.

(a) $3d^1 4s^2 = 3$ (b) $3d^3 4s^2 = 3 + 2 = 5$

(c) $3d^5 4s^1 = 5 + 1 = 6$ and (d) $3d^5 4s^2 = 5 + 2 = 7$

Thus, option (d) is correct.

Q.10 **Identify disproportionation reaction**

(a) $CH_4 + 2O_2 \longrightarrow CO_2 + 2H_2O$

(b) $CH_4 + 4Cl_2 \longrightarrow CCl_4 + 4HCl$

(c) $2F_2 + 2OH^- \longrightarrow 2F^- + OF_2 + H_2O$

(d) $2NO_2 + 2OH^- \longrightarrow NO_2^- + NO_3^- + H_2O$

● **Concept Insight** Reactions in which the same substance is oxidised as well as reduced are called **disproportionation reactions.**

Ans. ***(d)*** Writing the O.N. of each element above its symbol in the given reactions.

(a) $\overset{-4}{C}\overset{+1}{H_4} + 2\overset{0}{O_2} \longrightarrow \overset{+4}{C}\overset{-2}{O_2} + 2\overset{+1}{H_2}\overset{-2}{O}$

(b) $\overset{-4}{C}\overset{+1}{H_4} + 4\overset{0}{Cl_2} \longrightarrow \overset{+4}{C}\overset{-1}{Cl_4} + 4\overset{+1}{H}\overset{-1}{Cl}$

(c) $2\overset{0}{F_2} + 2\overset{-2}{O}\overset{+1}{H} \longrightarrow 2\overset{-1}{F^-} + \overset{+2}{O}\overset{-1}{F_2} + \overset{+1}{H_2}\overset{-2}{O}$

(d) $2\overset{+4}{N}\overset{-2}{O_2} + 2\overset{-2}{O}\overset{+1}{H^-} \longrightarrow \overset{+3}{N}\overset{-2}{O_2^-} + \overset{+5}{N}\overset{-2}{O_3^-} + \overset{+1}{H_2}\overset{-2}{O}$

Thus, in reaction (d), N is both oxidised as well as reduced since the oxidation number of N increases from +4 in NO_2 to +5 in NO_3^- and decreases from +4 in NO_2 to +3 in NO_2^-.

Q.11 **Which of the following elements does not show disproportionation tendency ?**

(a) Cl (b) Br (c) F (d) I

● **Concept Insight** Disproportionation reactions are a special type of redox reactions, in which an element in one oxidation state is simultaneously oxidised and reduced.

Ans. ***(c)*** Being the most electronegative element, F can only be reduced and always shows an oxidation number of –1. Further, due to the absence of d-orbitals, it cannot be oxidised and hence, it does not show positive oxidation numbers. In other words, F cannot be oxidised as well as reduced simultaneously and hence, does not show disproportionation reactions.

Multiple Choice Questions (More Than One Options)

Q.12 Which of the following statement(s) is/are not true about the following decomposition reaction?

$$2KClO_3 \longrightarrow 2KCl + 3O_2$$

(a) Potassium is undergoing oxidation
(b) Chlorine is undergoing oxidation
(c) Oxygen is reduced
(d) None of the species are undergoing oxidation or reduction

Ans. ***(a, b, c, d)*** Write the oxidation number of each element above its symbol, then

$$2\overset{+1}{K}\overset{+5}{Cl}\overset{-2}{O_3} \longrightarrow 2\overset{+1}{K}\overset{-1}{Cl} + 3\overset{0}{O_2}$$

(a) The oxidation number of K does not change, K undergoes neither reduction nor oxidation. Thus, option (a) is not correct.

(b) The oxidation number of chlorine decreases from +5 in $KClO_3$ to –1 in KCl, hence, Cl undergoes reduction.

(c) Since, oxidation number of oxygen increases from –2 in $KClO_3$ to 0 in O_2, oxygen is oxidised.

(d) This statement is not correct because Cl is undergoing reduction and O is undergoing oxidation.

Q.13 Identify the correct statement (s) in relation to the following reaction :

$$Zn + 2HCl \longrightarrow ZnCl_2 + H_2$$

(a) Zinc is acting as an oxidant
(b) Chlorine is acting as a reductant
(c) Hydrogen ion is acting as an oxidant
(d) Zinc is acting as a reductant

Ans. ***(c, d)*** Writing the oxidation number of each element above its symbol, so that

$$\overset{0}{Zn} + 2\overset{+1}{H}\overset{-1}{Cl} \longrightarrow \overset{+2}{Zn}\overset{-1}{Cl_2} + \overset{0}{H_2}$$

(a) The oxidation number of Zn increases from 0 in Zn to +2 in $ZnCl_2$, therefore, Zn acts as a reductant. Thus, option (a) is incorrect.

(b) The oxidation number of chlorine does not change, therefore, it neither acts as a reductant nor an oxidant. Therefore, option (b) is incorrect.

(c) The oxidation number of hydrogen decreases from +1 in H^+ to 0 in H_2, therefore, H^+ acts as an oxidant. Thus, option (c) is correct.

(d) As explained in option (a), Zn acts as reductant. Thus, option (d) is correct.

Q.14 The exhibition of various oxidation states by an element is also related to the outer orbital electronic configuration of its atom. Atom (s) having which of the following outermost electronic configurations will exhibit more than one oxidation state in its compounds.

(a) $3s^1$
(b) $3d^1 4s^2$
(c) $3d^2 4s^2$
(d) $3s^2 3p^3$

Ans. **(b, c, d)** **Elements** which have only s-electrons in the valence shell do not show more than one oxidation state. Thus, element with $3s^1$ outer electronic configuration shows only one oxidation state of +1.

Transition element such as elements (b), (c) having incompletely filled *d*-orbitals in the penultimate shell show variable oxidation states. Thus, element with outer electronic configuration as $3d^1 4s^2$ shows variable oxidation states of +2 and +3 and the element with outer electronic configuration as $3d^2 4s^2$ shows variable oxidation states of +2, +3 and +4.

***p*-Block elements** also show variable oxidation states due to a number of reason such as availability of vacant of *d*-orbitals and inert pair effect *e.g.*, element (d) with $3s^2 3p^3$ (*i.e.*, P) as the outer electronic configuration shows variable oxidation states of +3 and +5 due to involvement of *d*-orbitals.

Q.15 Identify the correct statements with reference to the given reaction

$$P_4 + 3OH^- + 3H_2O \longrightarrow PH_3 + 3H_2PO_2^-$$

(a) Phosphorus is undergoing reduction only
(b) Phosphorus is undergoing oxidation only
(c) Phosphorus is undergoing oxidation as well as reduction
(d) Hydrogen is undergoing neither oxidation nor reduction

Ans. **(c, d)** Write the oxidation number of each element above its symbol, then

$$\overset{0}{P_4} + 3\overset{-2}{O}\overset{+1}{H^-} + 3\overset{+1}{H_2}\overset{-2}{O} \longrightarrow \overset{-3}{P}\overset{+1}{H_3} + 3\overset{+1}{H_2}\overset{+1}{P}O_2^-$$

In this reaction, oxidation number of P increases from 0 in P_4 to +1 in $H_2PO_2^-$ and decreases to – 3 in PH_3, therefore, P undergoes both oxidation as well as reduction. Thus, options (a) and (b) are incorrect and option (c) is correct.

Further, oxidation number of H remains +1 in all the compounds *i.e.*, H neither undergoes oxidation nor reduction. Thus, option (d) is correct.

Q.16 Which of the following electrodes will act as anodes, which connected to Standard Hydrogen Electrode ?

(a) Al / Al^{3+} $E^\ominus = -1.66$
(b) Fe / Fe^{2+} $E^\ominus = -0.44$
(c) Cu / Cu^{2+} $E^\ominus = +0.34$
(d) $F_2\,(g) / 2F^-\,(aq)$ $E^\ominus = +2.87$

Ans. **(a, b)** Reduction potential of hydrogen is 0.0V. Electrodes having reduction potential lower than hydrogen undergo oxidation and act as anode, so, Al/Al^{3+} and Fe/Fe^{2+} have lower or negative reduction potential, so act as anode.

Short Answer Type Questions

Q.17 The reaction $Cl_2(g) + 2OH^-(aq) \rightarrow ClO^-(aq) + Cl^-(aq) + H_2O(l)$ represents the process of bleaching. Identify and name the species that bleaches the substances due to its oxidising action.

Thinking Process Write the oxidation number of each element above its symbol and then identify the bleaching reagent by observing the change in oxidation number.

Ans. $\overset{0}{Cl_2}(g) + 2\overset{-2\ +1}{OH^-}(aq) \rightarrow \overset{+1\ -2}{ClO^-}(aq) + \overset{-1}{Cl^-}(aq) + \overset{+1\ -2}{H_2O}(l)$

In this reaction, oxidation number of Cl increases from 0 (in Cl_2) to +1 (in ClO^-) as well as decreases from 0 (in Cl_2) to –1 (in Cl^-). So, it acts both reducing as well as oxidising agent. This is an example of disproportionation reaction. In this reaction, ClO^- species bleaches the substances due to its oxidising action. [In hypochlorite ion (ClO^-), Cl can decrease its oxidation number from +1 to 0 or –1.]

Q.18 MnO_4^{2-} undergoes disproportionation reaction in acidic medium but MnO_4^- does not. Give reason.

Ans. In MnO_4^{2-}, the oxidation number of Mn is +6. It can increase its oxidation number (to + 7) or decrease its oxidation number (to + 4, + 3, + 2, 0).

Hence, it undergoes disproportionation reaction in acidic medium.

$$3\overset{+6}{Mn}O_4^{2-} + 4H^+ \longrightarrow 3\overset{+7}{Mn}O_4^- + \overset{+4}{Mn}O_2 + 2H_2O$$

O.N. increases by 1 per atom (oxidation)

O.N. decreases by 2 per atom (reduction)

In MnO_4^-, Mn is in its highest oxidation state, *i.e.*, +7. It can only decrease its oxidation number. Hence, it cannot undergo disproportionation reaction.

Q.19 PbO and PbO_2 react with HCl according to following chemical equations :

$$2PbO + 4HCl \longrightarrow 2PbCl_2 + 2H_2O$$
$$PbO_2 + 4HCl \longrightarrow PbCl_2 + Cl_2 + 2H_2O$$

Why do these compounds differ in their reactivity ?

Ans. Writing the oxidation number of each element above its symbol in the following reactions

(a) $\underset{\text{Basic oxide}}{2\overset{+2\ -2}{PbO}} + \underset{\text{Acid}}{4\overset{+1\ -1}{HCl}} \longrightarrow 2\overset{+2\ -1}{PbCl_2} + 2\overset{+1\ -2}{H_2O}$

In this reaction, oxidation number of each element remains same hence, it is not a redox reaction. In fact, it is an example of **acid-base reaction.**

(b) $\overset{+4\ -2}{PbO_2} + 4\overset{+1\ -1}{HCl} \longrightarrow \overset{+2\ -1}{PbCl_2} + \overset{0}{Cl_2} + 2\overset{+1\ -2}{H_2O}$

In PbO_2, Pb is in +4 oxidation state. Due to inert pair effect, Pb in +2 oxidation state is more stable. So, Pb in +4 oxidation state (PbO_2) acts as an oxidising agent.

It oxidises Cl^- to Cl_2 and itself gets reduced to Pb^{2+}.

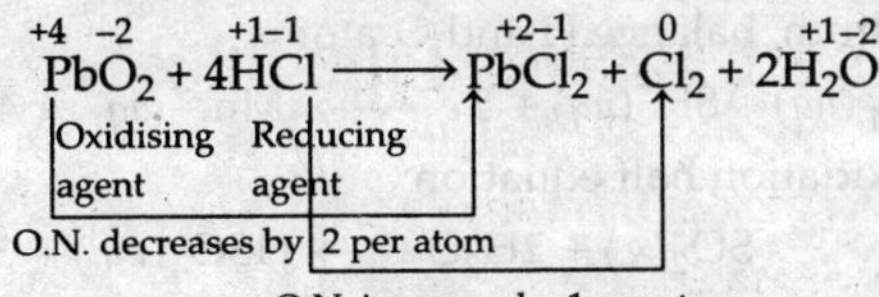

Q.20 Nitric acid is an oxidising agent and reacts with PbO but it does not react with PbO_2. Explain why ?

Ans. Nitric acid (HNO_3) is a strong oxidising agent, meaning it can accept electrons and oxidise other substances. In the case of PbO (lead(II) oxide, also a base), lead is in the +2 oxidation state, and HNO_3 can oxidise it further. So, HNO_3 reacts with PbO, forming soluble $Pb(NO_3)_2$ and water.

$$PbO + 2HNO_3 \longrightarrow \underset{\text{Soluble}}{Pb(NO_3)_2} + H_2O \quad \text{[acid-base reaction]}$$

However, in PbO_2 (lead(IV) oxide), lead is already in the +4 oxidation state, which is its maximum stable oxidation state. Since it cannot be oxidised further, no redox reaction occurs with nitric acid. Thus, PbO_2 does not react with HNO_3 under normal conditions.

Q.21 Write balanced chemical equation for the following reactions :

(a) Permanganate ion (MnO_4^-) reacts with sulphur dioxide gas in acidic medium to produce Mn^{2+} and hydrogen sulphate ion. (Balance by ion electron method)

(b) Reaction of liquid hydrazine (N_2H_4) with chlorate ion (ClO_3^-) in basic medium produces nitric oxide gas and chloride ion in gaseous state. (Balance by oxidation number method)

(c) Dichlorine heptaoxide (Cl_2O_7) in gaseous state combines with an aqueous solution of hydrogen peroxide in acidic medium to give chlorite ion (ClO_2^-) and oxygen gas. (Balance by ion electron method)

Ans. (a) **Ion electron method** Write the skeleton equation for the given reaction.

$$MnO_4^-(aq) + SO_2(g) \longrightarrow Mn^{2+}(aq) + HSO_4^-(aq)$$

Find out the elements which undergo change in O.N.

O.N. of Mn decreases by 5

$$\overset{+7}{2MnO_4^-}(aq) + \overset{+4}{SO_2}(g) \longrightarrow \overset{2+}{Mn}(aq) + \overset{+6}{HSO_4^-}(aq)$$

O.N. of S increases by 2

Divide the given skeleton into two half equations.

Reduction half equation $MnO_4^-(aq) \longrightarrow Mn^{2+}(aq)$

Oxidation half equation $SO_2(g) \longrightarrow HSO_4^-(aq)$

In acidic medium, balance H and O-atoms

$$MnO_4^-(aq) + 8H^+(aq) + 5e^- \longrightarrow Mn^{2+}(aq) + 4H_2O(l)$$

To balance oxidation half equation

$$SO_2(g) + 2H_2O \longrightarrow HSO_4^-(aq.) + 3H^+ + 2e^-$$

To balance the complete reaction

$$2MnO_4^-(aq) + 16H^+(aq) + 10e^- \longrightarrow 2Mn^{2+}(aq) + 8H_2O(l)$$

$$5SO_2(g) + 10H_2O(l) \longrightarrow 5HSO_4^-(aq) + 15H^+(aq) + 10e^-$$

$$2MnO_4^-(aq) + 5SO_2(g) + 2H_2O(l) + H^+(aq) \longrightarrow 2Mn^{2+}(aq) + 5HSO_4^-(aq)$$

(b) **Oxidation number method** Write the skeleton equation for the given reaction.

$$N_2H_4\ (l) + ClO_3^-\ (aq) \longrightarrow NO(g) + Cl^-(g)$$

O.N. increases by 4 per N-atom

$$\overset{-2}{N_2}H_4(l) + \overset{+5}{Cl}O_3^-\ (aq) \longrightarrow \overset{+2}{N}O\ (g) + \overset{-1}{Cl^-}\ (aq)$$

O.N. decreases by 6 per Cl-atom

Multiply NO by 2 because in N_2H_4, there are 2N atoms

$$N_2H_4(l) + ClO_3^-(aq) \longrightarrow 2NO(g) + Cl^-(aq)$$

Total increase in O.N. of N $= 2 \times 4 = 8$ ($8\,e^-$ lost)

Total decrease in O.N. of Cl $= 1 \times 6 = 6$ ($6\,e^-$ gain)

Therefore, to balance increase or decrease in O.N. multiply N_2H_4 by 3, 2NO by 3 and ClO_3^-,Cl^- by 4

$$3N_2H_4(l) + 4ClO_3^-(aq) \longrightarrow 6NO(g) + 4\,Cl^-(aq)$$

Balance O and H-atoms by adding 6 H_2O to RHS

$$3N_2H_4(l) + 4ClO_3^-(aq) \longrightarrow 6NO(g) + 4Cl^-(aq) + 6H_2O(l)$$

(c) **Ion electron method** Write the skeleton equation for the given reaction.

$$Cl_2O_7(g) + H_2O_2(aq) \longrightarrow ClO_2^-(aq) + O_2(g)$$

Find out the elements which undergo a change in O.N.

O. N. of Cl decreases by 4 per Cl-atom

$$\overset{+7}{Cl_2}\overset{-2}{O_7}(g) + \overset{+1}{H_2}\overset{-1}{O_2}\ (aq) \longrightarrow \overset{+3}{Cl}\overset{-2}{O_2^-}(aq) + \overset{0}{O_2}\ (g)$$

O.N. of O increases by 1 per O-atom

Divide the given skeleton equation into two half equations.

Reduction half equation : $Cl_2O_7 \longrightarrow ClO_2^-$

Oxidation half equation : $H_2O_2 \longrightarrow O_2$

To balance the reduction half equation

$$Cl_2O_7(g) + 6\,H^+(aq) + 8\,e^- \longrightarrow 2ClO_2^-(aq) + 3\,H_2O(l)$$

To balance the oxidation half equation

$$H_2O_2(aq) \longrightarrow O_2(g) + 2H^+ + 2\,e^-$$

To balance the complete reaction

$$Cl_2O_7(g) + 6\,H^+(aq) + 8\,e^- \longrightarrow 2ClO_2^-(aq) + 3\,H_2O\ (l)$$

$$4\,H_2O_2(aq) \longrightarrow 4\,O_2(g) + 8\,H^+\ (aq) + 8\,e^-$$

$$Cl_2O_7(g) + 4\,H_2O_2(aq) \longrightarrow 2ClO_2^-\ (aq) + 3\,H_2O\ (l) + 4O_2(g) + 2H^+(aq)$$

This represents the balanced redox reaction.

Mistake Alert ! *Students may does not consider whether the reaction occurs in acidic or basic medium, which affects the balancing process.*

Q.22 Calculate the oxidation number of phosphorus in the following species.

(a) HPO_3^{2-} (b) PO_4^{3-}

Ans. (a) Suppose that the oxidation number of P in HPO_3^{2-} be x.

Then, $1 + x + 3(-2) = -2$ or $x + 1 - 6 = -2$ or $x = +3$

(b) Suppose that the O.N. of P in PO_4^{3-} be x.

Then, $x + 4(-2) = -3$ or $x - 8 = -3$ or $x = +5$

Q.23 Calculate the oxidation number of each sulphur atom in the following compounds.

(a) $Na_2S_2O_3$ (b) $Na_2S_4O_6$ (c) Na_2SO_3 (d) Na_2SO_4

Ans. *The oxidation number of each sulphur atom in the following compounds are given below*

(a) $Na_2S_2O_3$ Let us consider the structure of $Na_2S_2O_3$.

$$\begin{array}{c} S \\ \uparrow \\ Na^+O^- - S - O^-Na^+ \\ \| \\ O \end{array}$$

There is a coordinate bond between two sulphur atoms. The oxidation number of acceptor S-atom is –2. Let, the oxidation number of other S-atom be x.

$$\underset{\text{For Na}}{2(+1)} + \underset{\text{For O-atoms}}{3\times(-2)} + x + \underset{\text{For coordinate S-atom}}{1(-2)} = 0$$

$$x = +6$$

Therefore, the two sulphur atoms in $Na_2S_2O_3$ have –2 and +6 oxidation number.

The average oxidation number of two S-atom $= \frac{-2+6}{2} = +2$

(b) $Na_2S_4O_6$ Let us consider the structure of $Na_2S_4O_6$.

$$\begin{array}{c} \quad O \qquad\qquad\qquad O \\ \quad \| \quad\; 0 \qquad 0 \quad\; \| \\ Na^+O^- - S - S - S - S - O^-Na^+ \\ \quad \| \qquad\qquad\qquad \| \\ \quad O \qquad\qquad\qquad O \end{array}$$

In this structure, two central sulphur atoms have zero oxidation number because electron pair forming the S—S bond remain in the centre. Let, the oxidation number of (remaining S-atoms) S-atom be x.

$$\underset{\text{For Na}}{2(+1)} + \underset{\text{For O}}{6(-2)} + 2x + 2(0) = 0$$

$$2 - 12 + 2x = 0 \text{ or } x = +\frac{10}{2} = +5$$

Therefore, the two central S-atoms have zero oxidation state and two terminal S-atoms have +5 oxidation state each.

(c) Na_2SO_3 Let the oxidation number of S in Na_2SO_3 be x.

$$2(+1) + x + 3(-2) = 0 \text{ or } x = +4$$

(d) Na_2SO_4 Let the oxidation number of S be x.

$$2(+1) + x + 4(-2) = 0 \text{ or } x = +6$$

Mistake Alert ! *Students may find out the oxidation number by normal way but always remember that these are some exceptions also.*

Q.24 Balance the following equations by the oxidation number method.

(a) $Fe^{2+} + H^+ + Cr_2O_7^{-2} \longrightarrow Cr^{3+} + Fe^{3+} + H_2O$

(b) $I_2 + NO_3^- \longrightarrow NO_2 + IO_3^-$

(c) $I_2 + S_2O_3^{2-} \longrightarrow I^- + S_4O_6^{2-}$

(d) $MnO_2 + C_2O_4^{2-} \rightarrow Mn^{2+} + CO_2$

Ans. Oxidation number method

(a)

$$\overset{2+}{Fe^{2+}} + H^+ + \overset{+6}{Cr_2}O_7^{2-} \longrightarrow \overset{+3}{2Cr^{3+}} + \overset{+3}{Fe^{3+}} + H_2O$$

O.N. decreases by 3 per Cr-atom ($3 \times 2 = 6\,e^-$ gain)

O.N. increases by 1 per Fe-atom ($1\,e^-$ loss)

(Multiply Cr^{3+} by 2 because there are 2Cr atoms in $Cr_2O_7^{2-}$ ion.)

Balance increase and decrease in oxidation number.

$$6Fe^{2+} + H^+ + Cr_2O_7^{2-} \longrightarrow 2Cr^{3+} + 6Fe^{3+} + H_2O$$

Balance charge by multiplying H^+ by 14.

$$6Fe^{2+} + 14H^+ + Cr_2O_7^{2-} \longrightarrow 2Cr^{3+} + 6\,Fe^{3+} + H_2O$$

Balance H and O-atoms by multiplying H_2O by 7.

$$6Fe^{2+} + 14H^+ + Cr_2O_7^{2-} \longrightarrow 2Cr^{3+} + 6Fe^{3+} + 7H_2O$$

This represents a balanced redox reaction.

(b)

$$\overset{0}{I_2} + \overset{+5}{N}O_3^- \longrightarrow \overset{+4}{N}O_2 + 2\overset{+5}{I}O_3^-$$

O.N. decreases by 1 per N-atom ($1\,e^-$ gain)

O.N. increases by 5 per I-atom (2×5 electrons loss)

Balance increase and decrease in oxidation number

$$I_2 + 10NO_3^- \longrightarrow 10NO_2 + 2IO_3^-$$

Balance charge by writing 8 H^+ in LHS of the equation.

$$I_2 + 10NO_3^- + 8H^+ \longrightarrow 10NO_2 + 2IO_3^-$$

Balance H-atoms by writing $4H_2O$ in RHS of the equation.

$$I_2 + 10NO_3^- + 8H^+ \longrightarrow 10NO_2 + 2IO_3^- + 4H_2O$$

Oxygen atoms are automatically balanced.

This represents a balanced redox reaction.

(c)

$$\overset{0}{I_2} + 2\overset{+2}{S_2}O_3^{2-} \longrightarrow 2\overset{-1}{I^-} + \overset{2.5}{S_4}O_6^{2-}$$

O.N. decreases by 1 per I-atom ($2 \times 1e^-$ gain)

O.N. increases by 0.5 per S-atom ($4 \times 0.5 = 2e^-$ loss)

(Multiply $S_2O_3^{2-}$ by 2 because there are 4 S-atoms in $S_4O_6^{2-}$ ion.)

Increase and decrease in oxidation number is already balanced. Charge and oxygen atoms are also balanced.

$$I_2 + 2S_2O_3^{2-} \longrightarrow 2I^- + S_4O_6^{2-}$$

This represents a balanced redox reaction.

(d)

$$\overset{+4}{Mn}O_2 + \overset{+3}{C_2}O_4 \longrightarrow Mn^{2+} + 2\,\overset{+4}{C}O_2$$

O.N. decreases by 2 per Mn-atom ($2e^-$ gain)

O.N. increases by 1 per C-atom ($2 \times 1 = 2e^-$ loss)

Increase and decrease in oxidation number is already balanced.

Add 4 H^+ towards LHS of the equation to balance charge.

$$MnO_2 + C_2O_4^{2-} + 4H^+ \longrightarrow Mn^{2+} + 2CO_2$$

Add 2 H_2O towards RHS of the equation to balance H-atoms

$$MnO_2 + C_2O_4^{2-} + 4H^+ \longrightarrow Mn^{2+} + 2CO_2 + 2H_2O$$

This represents a balanced redox reaction.

Q.25 Identify the redox reaction out of the following reactions and identify the oxidising and reducing agents in them.

(a) $3HCl(aq) + HNO_3(aq) \longrightarrow Cl_2(g) + NOCl(g) + 2H_2O(l)$

(b) $HgCl_2(aq) + 2KI(aq) \longrightarrow HgI_2(s) + 2KCl(aq)$

(c) $Fe_2O_3(s) + 3CO(g) \xrightarrow{\Delta} 2Fe(s) + 3CO_2(g)$

(d) $PCl_3(l) + 3H_2O(l) \longrightarrow 3HCl(aq) + H_3PO_3(aq)$

(e) $4NH_3(aq) + 3O_2(g) \longrightarrow 2N_2(g) + 6H_2O(g)$

Ans. (a) Writing the oxidation number on each atom above its symbol, then

$$3\overset{+1}{H}\overset{-1}{Cl}(aq) + \overset{+1}{H}\overset{+5}{N}\overset{-2}{O_3}(aq) \longrightarrow \overset{0}{Cl_2}(g) + \overset{+3}{N}\overset{-2}{O}\overset{-1}{Cl}(g) + 2\overset{+1}{H_2}\overset{-2}{O}(l)$$

Here, the oxidation number of Cl increases from –1 in HCl to 0 in Cl_2, therefore, Cl^- is oxidised and hence, HCl acts as the reducing agent.

The oxidation number of N decreases from +5 in HNO_3 to +3 in NOCl, therefore, HNO_3 acts as the oxidising agent.

Thus, this reaction is a **redox reaction**.

(b) Writing the oxidation number of each atom above its symbol, we have,

$$\overset{+2}{Hg}\overset{-1}{Cl_2}(aq) + 2\overset{+1}{K}\overset{-1}{I}(aq) \longrightarrow \overset{+2}{Hg}\overset{-1}{I_2}(s) + 2\overset{+1}{K}\overset{-1}{Cl^-}(aq)$$

Here, the oxidation number of none of the atoms undergo a change, therefore, this reaction is **not** a **redox reaction**.

(c) $\overset{+3}{Fe_2}\overset{-2}{O_3}(s) + 3\overset{+2}{C}\overset{-2}{O}(g) \xrightarrow{\Delta} 2\overset{0}{Fe}(s) + 3\overset{+4}{C}\overset{-2}{O_2}(g)$

Here, oxidation number of Fe decreases from +3 in Fe_2O_3 to 0 in Fe, therefore, Fe_2O_3 acts as an oxidising agent. Further, oxidation number of C increases from +2 in CO to +4 in CO_2, therefore, CO acts as a reducing agent.

Thus, this reaction is an example of **redox reaction**.

(d) Writing the oxidation number of each atom above its symbol, then

$$\overset{+3\ -1}{PCl_3}(l) + 3\overset{+1\ -2}{H_2O}(l) \longrightarrow 3\overset{+1\ -1}{HCl}(aq) + \overset{+1\ +3\ -2}{H_3PO_3}(aq)$$

Here, O.N. of none of the atoms undergo a change, therefore, this reaction is **not a redox reaction**.

(e) Writing the oxidation number of each atom above its symbol, then

$$4\overset{-3\ +1}{NH_3}(aq) + 3\overset{0}{O_2}(g) \longrightarrow 2\overset{0}{N_2}(g) + 6\overset{+1\ -2}{H_2O}(l)$$

Here, oxidation number of N increases from –3 to 0 in N_2, therefore, NH_3 acts as a reducing agent. Further, O.N. of O decreases from 0 in O_2 to –2 in H_2O, therefore, O_2 acts as a oxidising agent. Thus, this reaction is a **redox reaction**.

Q.26 Balance the following ionic equations.

(a) $Cr_2O_7^{2-} + H^+ + I^- \longrightarrow Cr^{3+} + I_2 + H_2O$

(b) $Cr_2O_7^{2-} + Fe^{2+} + H^+ \longrightarrow Cr^{3+} + Fe^{3+} + H_2O$

(c) $MnO_4^- + SO_3^{2-} + H^+ \longrightarrow Mn^{2+} + SO_4^{2-} + H_2O$

(d) $MnO_4^- + H^+ + Br^- \longrightarrow Mn^{2+} + Br_2 + H_2O$

Ans. (a) Write the O. N. of all atoms above their respective symbols.

O. N. decreases by, 3 per Cr-atom

O.N. decreases by 3 per Cr-atom

$$\overset{+6\ -2}{Cr_2O_7} + H^+ + I^- \longrightarrow \overset{+3}{Cr} + \overset{0}{I_2} + \overset{+1\ -2}{H_2O}$$

O.N. increases by 1 per I-atom

Divide the given equation into two half reactions.

Reduction half reaction : $Cr_2O_7^{2-} \rightarrow Cr^{3+}$

Oxidation half reaction : $I^- \rightarrow I_2$

To balance reduction half reaction.

$$Cr_2O_7^{2-} + 14H^+ + 6e^- \longrightarrow 2Cr^{3+} + 7H_2O$$

To balance oxidation half reaction

$$2I^- \longrightarrow I_2 + 2e^-$$

To balance the reaction by electrons gained and lost

$$Cr_2O_7^{2-} + 14H^+ + 6e^- \longrightarrow 2Cr^{3+} + 7H_2O$$

$$6I^- \longrightarrow 3I_2 + 6e^-$$

$$Cr_2O_7^{2-} + 14H^+ + 6I^- \longrightarrow 2Cr^{3+} + 3I_2 + 7H_2O$$

This gives the final balanced ionic equations.

(b) Write the skeletal equation of the given reaction

$$Cr_2O_7^{2-}(aq) + Fe^{2+}(aq) \longrightarrow Cr^{3+}(aq) + Fe^{3+}(aq)$$

Write the O. N. of all the elements above their respective symbols.

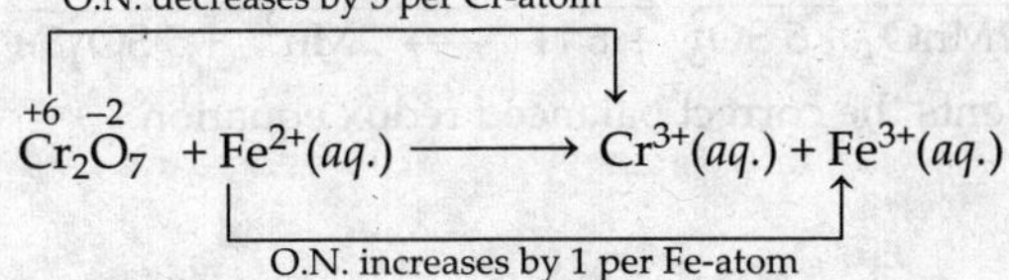

Divide the given equation into two half reactions

Oxidation half reaction $Fe^{2+}(aq) \longrightarrow Fe^{3+}(aq)$

reduction half reaction $Cr_2O_7^{2-}(aq) \longrightarrow Cr^{3+}(aq)$

To balance oxidation half reaction

$$Fe^{2+}(aq) \longrightarrow Fe^{3+}(aq) + e^-$$

To balance reduction half reaction

$$Cr_2O_7^{2-}(aq) + 6e^- \longrightarrow 2Cr^{3+}(aq)$$

Balance charge by adding H^+ ions.

$$Cr_2O_7^{2-}(aq) + 14H^+(aq) + 6e^- \longrightarrow 2Cr^{3+}(aq)$$

Balance O atoms by adding H_2O molecules

$$Cr_2O_7^{2-}(aq) + 14H^+(aq) + 6e^- \longrightarrow 2Cr^{3+}(aq) + 7H_2O(l)$$

To balance the reaction

$$6Fe^{2+}(aq) \longrightarrow 6Fe^{3+}(aq) + 6e^-$$

$$Cr_2O_7^{2-}(aq) + 14H^+(aq) + 6e^- \longrightarrow 2Cr^{3+}(aq) + 7H_2O(l)$$

$$Cr_2O_7^{2-}(aq) + 6Fe^{2+}(aq) + 14H^+(aq) \longrightarrow 2Cr^{3+}(aq) + 7H_2O(l) + 6Fe^{3+}(aq)$$

(c) Write the oxidation number of all atoms above their respective symbols.

O.N. decreases by 5 per Mn-atom

$$\overset{+7\,-2}{MnO_4^-} + \overset{+4\,-2}{SO_3^{2-}} \longrightarrow Mn^{2+} + \overset{+6\,-2}{SO_4^{2-}} + H_2O$$

O.N. increases by 2 per S-atom

Divide the skeleton equation into two half-reactions.

Reduction half reaction $MnO_4^- \longrightarrow Mn^{2+}$

Oxidation half reaction $SO_3^{2-} \longrightarrow SO_4^{2-}$

To balance reduction half reaction

$$MnO_4^- + 8H^+ + 5e^- \longrightarrow Mn^{2+} + 4H_2O$$

To balance oxidation half reaction

$$SO_3^{2-} \longrightarrow SO_4^{2-} + 2e^-$$

Balance charge by adding H^+ ions.

$$SO_3^{2-} \longrightarrow SO_4^{2-} + 2H^+ + 2e^-$$

Balance O-atoms by adding H_2O molecules

$$SO_3^{2-} + H_2O \longrightarrow SO_4^{2-} + 2H^+ + 2e^-$$

To balance the reaction

$$2MnO_4^- + 16H^+ + 10e^- \longrightarrow 2Mn^{2+} + 8H_2O$$

$$5SO_3^{2-} + 5H_2O \longrightarrow 5SO_4^{2-} + 10H^+ + 10e^-$$

$$2MnO_4^- + 5SO_3^{2-} + 6H^+ \longrightarrow 2Mn^{2+} + 5SO_4^{2-} + 3H_2O$$

This represents the correct balanced redox equation.

(d) Write the O. N. of all the atoms above their respective symbols.

O.N. decreases by 5 per Mn-atom

$$\overset{+7}{Mn}\overset{-2}{O_4^-} + H^+ + Br^- \longrightarrow Mn^{2+} + \overset{0}{Br_2} + \overset{+2}{H_2}\overset{-1}{O}$$

O.N. increases by 1 per Br-atom

Divide skeleton equation into two half reactions

Reduction half reaction $MnO_4^- \rightarrow Mn^{2+}$

Oxidation half reaction $Br^- \rightarrow Br_2$

To balance reduction half reaction

$$MnO_4^- + 8H^+ + 5e^- \longrightarrow Mn^{2+} + 4H_2O$$

To balance oxidation half reaction

$$2Br^- \longrightarrow Br_2 + 2e^-$$

To balance the reaction

$$2MnO_4^- + 16H^+ + 10e^- \longrightarrow 2Mn^{2+} + 8H_2O$$

$$10Br^- \longrightarrow 5Br_2 + 10e^-$$

$$\boxed{2MnO_4^- + 10Br^- + 16H^+ \longrightarrow 2Mn^{2+} + 5Br_2 + 8H_2O}$$

This represents the correct balanced ionic equation.

Matching The Columns

Q.27 Match Column I with Column II for the oxidation states of the central atoms.

	Column I		Column II
A.	$Cr_2O_7^{2-}$	1.	+3
B.	MnO_4^-	2.	+4
C	VO_3^-	3.	+5
D.	FeF_6^{3-}	4.	+6
		5.	+7

Ans. A. → (4) B. → (5) C. → (3) D. → (1)

Suppose that x be the oxidation states of central atoms.

A. Oxidation number of Cr in $Cr_2O_7^{2-}$

$$2x + 7(-2) = -2$$
$$2x - 14 = -2$$
$$2x = +12$$
$$x = +6$$

B. Oxidation number of Mn in MnO_4^-

$$x + 4(-2) = -1$$
$$x - 8 = -1$$
$$x = +7$$

C. Oxidation number of V in VO_3^-

$$x + 3(-2) = -1$$
$$x - 6 = -1$$
$$x = +5$$

D. Oxidation number of Fe in FeF_6^{3-}

$$x + 6(-1) = -3$$
$$x - 6 = -3$$
or $$x = +3$$

Q.28 Match the items in Column I with relevant items in Column II.

	Column I		Column II
A.	Ions having positive charge	1.	+7
B.	The sum of oxidation number of all atoms in a neutral molecule	2.	−1
C.	Oxidation number of hydrogen ion (H^+)	3.	+1
D.	Oxidation number of fluorine in NaF	4.	0
E.	Ions having negative charge	5.	Cation
		6.	Anion

Ans. A. → (5) B. → (4) C. → (3) D. → (2) E. → (6)

A. Ions having positive charge — Cation

B. The sum of oxidation number of all atoms in a neutral molecule — Zero

C. Oxidation number of hydrogen ion (H^+) — +1

D. Oxidation number of fluorine in NaF — −1

E. Ions having negative charge — Anion

Assertion and Reason

In the following questions a statement of assertion (A) *followed by a statement of reason* (R) *is given. Choose the correct option out of the choices given below in each question.*

Q.29 **Assertion** (A) Among halogens fluorine is the best oxidant.

Reason (R) Fluorine is the most electronegative atom.

(a) Both A and R are true and R is the correct explanation of A
(b) Both A and R are true but R is not the correct explanation of A
(c) A is true but R is false
(d) Both A and R are false

Ans. ***(b)*** Both assertion and reason are true but reason is not the correct explanation of assertion. Among halogens, F_2 is the best oxidant because it has the highest $E°$ value. (highest standard reduction potential of + 2.87 V)

Q.30 **Assertion** (A) In the reaction between potassium permanganate and potassium iodide, permanganate ions act as oxidising agent.

Reason (R) Oxidation state of manganese changes from +2 to +7 during the reaction.

(a) Both A and R are true and R is the correct explanation of A
(b) Both A and R are true but R is not the correct explanation of A
(c) A is true but R is false
(d) Both A and R are false

Ans. ***(c)*** Assertion is true but reason is false.

$$10KI + 2K\overset{+7}{Mn}O_4 + 8H_2SO_4 \longrightarrow 2\overset{+2}{Mn}SO_4 + 6K_2SO_4 + 8H_2O + 5I_2$$

Oxidation state of Mn decreases from +7 to +2.

Q.31 **Assertion** (A) The decomposition of hydrogen peroxide to form water and oxygen is an example of disproportionation reaction.

Reason (R) The oxygen of peroxide is in −1 oxidation state and it is converted to zero oxidation state in O_2 and −2 oxidation state in H_2O.

(a) Both A and R are true and R is the correct explanation of A
(b) Both A and R are true but R is not the correct explanation of A
(c) A is true but R is false
(d) Both A and R are false

Ans. ***(a)*** Both assertion and reason are true and reason is the correct explanation of assertion.

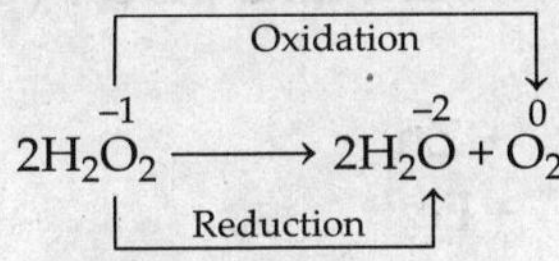

Thus, the above reaction is an example of disproportionation reaction.

Q.32 **Assertion** (A) Redox couple is the combination of oxidised and reduced form of a substance involved in an oxidation or reduction half cell.

Reason (R) In the representation $E^{\ominus}_{Fe^{3+}/Fe^{2+}}$ and $E^{\ominus}_{Cu^{2+}/Cu}$, Fe^{3+}/Fe^{2+} and Cu^{2+}/Cu are redox couples.

(a) Both A and R are true and R is the correct explanation of A
(b) Both A and R are true but R is not the correct explanation of A
(c) A is true but R is false
(d) Both A and R are false

Ans. ***(b)*** Both assertion and reason are true but reason is not the correct explanation of assertion.

Redox couple is the combination of oxidised and reduced form of substance. In the representation $E^{\ominus}_{Fe^{3+}/Fe^{2+}}$ and $E^{\ominus}_{Cu^{2+}/Cu}$, Fe^{3+}/Fe^{2+} and Cu^{2+}/Cu are redox couples.

Long Answer Type Questions

Q.33 **Explain redox reaction on the basis of electron transfer. Given suitable examples.**

Ans. **Reduction** Gain of electron by atom, ion or molecule is called reduction

Oxidation Loss of electron by atom, ion or molecule is called oxidation.

For example

Reduction half equation $Cl_2 + 2e^- \longrightarrow 2Cl^-$

Oxidation half equation $2Na - 2e^- \longrightarrow 2Na^+$

Overall equation of Redox reaction $2Na + Cl_2 \longrightarrow 2Na^+Cl^+$

So, **redox reaction** involve simultaneous occurence of oxidation and reduction reaction. Another example is,

$$Mg + Cl_2 \longrightarrow Mg^{2+}Cl_2^-$$

Oxidation half equation $Mg - 2e^- \longrightarrow Mg^{2+}$

Reduction half equation $Cl_2 + 2e^- \longrightarrow 2Cl^-$

Reducing Agent Species which undergo oxidation act as reducing agent.

Oxidising Agent Species which undergo reduction act as oxidizing agent.

In above example, 'Mg' is oxidised so, act as reducing agent while Cl_2 is gaining electron, so act as oxidising agent.

Q.34 **On the basis of standard electrode potential values, suggest which of the following reactions would take place? (Consult the book for $E^\ominus$ value)**

(a) $Cu + Zn^{2+} \longrightarrow Cu^{2+} + Zn$

(b) $Mg + Fe^{2+} \longrightarrow Mg^{2+} + Fe$

(c) $Br_2 + 2Cl^- \longrightarrow Cl_2 + 2Br^-$

(d) $Fe + Cd^{2+} \longrightarrow Cd + Fe^{2+}$

● **Concept Insight**

The negative value of $E°$ indicates that the reaction is not feasible.
The positive value of $E°$ indicates that the reaction is feasible.

Ans. As we know that, $E°_{Cu^{2+}/Cu} = 0.34$ V, $E°_{Zn^{2+}/Zn} = -0.76$ V,

$E°_{Mg^{2+}/Mg} = -2.37$ V, $E°_{Fe^{2+}/Fe} = -0.74$ V,

$E°_{Br_2/Br^-} = +1.08$ V, $E°_{Cl_2/Cl^-} = +1.36$ V

$E°_{Cd^{2+}/Cd} = -0.44$ V

(a) $E°_{Cu^{2+}/Cu} = +0.34$ V and $E°_{Zn^{2+}/Zn} = -0.76$ V

$$Cu + Zn^{2+} \longrightarrow Cu^{2+} + Zn$$

Here, Cu is oxidised to Cu^{2+}, therefore, Cu^{2+} / Cu couple acts as anode and Zn^{2+} is reduced to Zn, therefore, Zn^{2+} / Zn couple acts as cathode.

$$E^\circ_{cell} = E^\circ_{cathode} - E^\circ_{anode}$$
$$E^\circ_{cell} = -0.76 - (+0.34) = -1.10V$$

Negative value of E°_{cell} indicates that the reaction will not occur.

(b) $Mg + Fe^{2+} \longrightarrow Mg^{2+} + Fe$

$$E^\circ_{Mg^{2+}/Mg} = -2.37V \text{ and } E^\circ_{Fe^{2+}/Fe} = -0.74 \text{ V}$$

In the given cell reaction, Mg is oxidised to Mg^{2+} hence, Mg^{2+} /Mg couple acts as anode and Fe^{2+} is reduced to Fe hence, Fe^{2+} / Fe couple acts as cathode.

$$E^\circ_{cell} = E^\circ_{cathode} - E^\circ_{anode}$$
$$E^\circ_{cell} = -0.74 - (-2.37) = +1.63V$$

Positive value of E°_{cell} indicates that the reaction will occur.

(c) $$Br_2 + 2Cl^- \longrightarrow Cl_2 + 2Br^-$$

$$E^\circ_{Br^-/Br_2} = +1.08 \text{ V and } E^\circ_{Cl^-/Cl_2} = +1.36 \text{ V}$$

In the given cell reaction, Cl^- is oxidised to Cl_2 hence, Cl^-/Cl_2 couple acts as anode and Br_2 is reduced to Br^- hence; Br^-/Br_2 couple acts as cathode.

$$E^\circ_{cell} = E^\circ_{cathode} - E^\circ_{anode}$$
$$E^\circ_{cell} = +1.08 - (+1.36) = -0.28 \text{ V}$$

Negative value of E°_{cell} indicates that the reaction will not occur.

(d) $$Fe + Cd^{2+} \longrightarrow Cd + Fe^{2+}$$

$$E^\circ_{Fe^{2+}/Fe} = -0.74 \text{ V. and } E^\circ_{Cd^{2+}/Cd} = -0.44 \text{ V}$$

Here, Fe is oxidised to Fe^{2+} hence, Fe^{2+} / Fe couple acts as anode and Cd^{2+} is reduced to Cd hence, Cd^{2+} / Cd couple acts as cathode.

$$E^\circ_{cell} = E^\circ_{cathode} - E^\circ_{anode}$$
$$E^\circ_{cell} = -0.44 - (-0.74) = +0.30 \text{ V.}$$

Positive value E°_{cell} indicates that the reaction will occur.

Q.35 Why does fluorine not show disproportionation reaction?

Ans. In a disproportionation reaction, the same species is simultaneously oxidised as well as reduced. Therefore, for such a redox reaction to occur, the reacting species must contain an element which has atleast three oxidation states.

The element, in reacting species, is present in an intermediate state while lower and higher oxidation states are available for reduction and oxidation to occur (respectively).

Fluorine is the strongest oxidising agent. It does not show positive oxidation state and only exhibit oxidation state of –1. That's why fluorine does not show disproportionation reaction.

Q.36 Write redox couples involved in the reactions (a) to (d) given in question 34.

Thinking Process A redox couple represents the oxidised and reduced forms of a substance together taking part in an oxidation or reduction half reaction.

Ans. Given that,

$$Cu + Zn^{2+} \longrightarrow Cu^{2+} + Zn$$
$$Mg + Fe^{2+} \longrightarrow Mg^{2+} + Fe$$
$$Br_2 + 2Cl^- \longrightarrow Cl_2 + 2Br^-$$
$$Fe + Cd^{2+} \longrightarrow Cd + Fe^{2+}$$

(a) Cu^{2+}/Cu and Zn^{2+}/Zn (b) Mg^{2+}/Mg and Fe^{2+}/Fe

(c) Br_2/Br^- and Cl_2/Cl^- (d) Fe^{2+}/Fe and Cd^{2+}/Cd

Q.37 Find out the oxidation number of chlorine in the following compounds and arrange them in increasing order of oxidation number of chlorine.

$NaClO_4, NaClO_3, NaClO, KClO_2, Cl_2O_7, ClO_3, Cl_2O, NaCl, Cl_2, ClO_2$.

Which oxidation state is not present in any of the above compounds?

Ans. Suppose that the oxidation number of chlorine in these compounds be x.

O.N. of Cl in $NaClO_4$ $\therefore$ $+1 + x + 4(-2) = 0$ or, $x = +7$

O.N. of Cl in $NaClO_3$ $\therefore$ $+1 + x + 3(-2) = 0$ or, $x = +5$

O.N. of Cl in $NaClO$ $\therefore$ $+1 + x + 1(-2) = 0$ or, $x = +1$

O.N. of Cl in $KClO_2$ $\therefore$ $+1 + x + 2(-2) = 0$ or, $x = +3$

O.N. of Cl in Cl_2O_7 $\therefore$ $+2x + 7(-2) = 0$ or, $x = +7$

O.N. of Cl in ClO_3 $\therefore$ $x + 3(-2) = 0$ or, $x = +6$

O.N. of Cl in Cl_2O $\therefore$ $2x + 1(-2) = 0$ or, $x = +1$

O. N. of Cl in NaCl $\therefore$ $+1 + x = 0$ or, $x = -1$

O. N. of Cl in Cl_2 $\therefore$ $2x = 0$ or, $x = 0$

O. N. of Cl in ClO_2 $\therefore$ $x + 2(-2) = 0$ or, $x = +4$

None of these compounds have an oxidation number of +2.

Increasing order of oxidation number of chlorine is : –1, 0, +1, +3, +4, +5, +6, +7

Therefore, the increasing order of oxidation number of Cl in compounds is

$$NaCl < Cl_2 < Cl_2O = NaClO < KClO_2 < ClO_2 < NaClO_3 < ClO_3 < Cl_2O_7 = NaClO_4$$

Q.38 Which method can be used to find out strength of reductant/oxidant in a solution? Explain with an example.

Ans. Measure the electrode potential of the given species by connecting the redox couple of the given species with standard hydrogen electrode. If it is positive, the electrode of the given species acts as reductant and if it is negative, it acts as an oxidant.

Find the electrode potentials of the other given species in the same way, compare the values and determine their comparative strength as an reductant or oxidant.

e.g. measurement of standard electrode potential of Zn^{2+}/Zn electrode using SHE as a reference electrode.

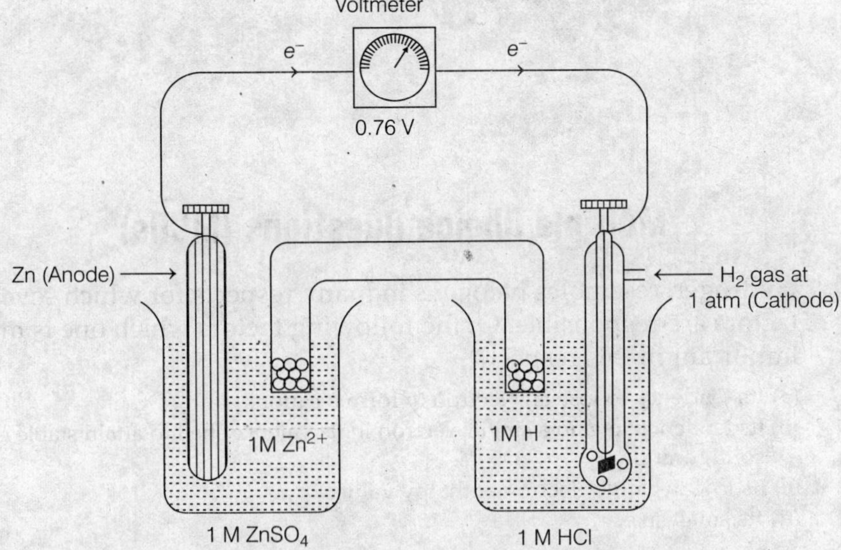

The EMF of the cell comes out to be 0.76 V. (reading of voltmeter is 0.76 V). Zn^{2+}/Zn couple acts as anode and SHE acts as cathode.

$$\therefore \quad E^\circ_{cell} = 0.76 = E^\circ_{cathode} - E^\circ_{anode}$$

$$0.76 = 0 - E^\circ_{anode}$$

$$E^\circ_{anode} = -0.76 \text{ V}$$

$$E^\circ_{Zn^{2+}/Zn} = -0.76\text{V}.$$

Chapter 09

Hydrogen*

Multiple Choice Questions (MCQs)

Q.1 Hydrogen resembles halogens in many respects for which several factors are responsible. Of the following factors which one is most important in this respect?

(a) Its tendency to lose an electron to form a cation.
(b) Its tendency to gain a single electron in its valence shell to attain stable electronic configuration.
(c) Its low negative electron enthalpy value.
(d) Its small size.

Ans. *(b)* The most important factor is that hydrogen like halogens accepts an electron readily to achieve the nearest inert gas configuration. Inspite of the fact that hydrogen, to a certain extent resembles both with alkali metals and halogens.

Q.2 Why does H^+ ion always get associated with other atoms or molecules?

(a) Ionisation enthalpy of hydrogen resembles that of alkali metals.
(b) Its reactivity is similar to halogens.
(c) It resembles both alkali metals and halogens.
(d) Loss of an electron from hydrogen atom results in a nucleus of very small size as compared to other atoms or ions. Due to small size it cannot exist free

Ans. *(d)* H^+ ion always get associated with other atoms or molecules. The reason is that loss of an electron from hydrogen atom results in a nucleus of very small size as compared to other atoms or ions. Due to small size, it cannot exist free and get easily attach with other atoms too.

Q.3 Metal hydrides are ionic, covalent or molecular in nature. Among LiH, NaH, KH, RbH, CsH, the correct order of increasing ionic character is

(a) LiH > NaH > CsH > KH > RbH
(b) LiH < NaH < KH < RbH < CsH
(c) RbH > CsH > NaH > KH > LiH
(d) NaH > CsH > RbH > LiH > KH

Ans. *(b)* Ionic character increases as the size of the atom increases or the electronegativity of the atom decreases. The correct order of increasing ionic character is

$$LiH < NaH < KH < RbH < CsH$$

Mistake Alert ! *Some students mix the concept of hydrogen bonding with ionic character leading to incorrect conclusions.*

Note (*) *This chapter has been deleted from latest NCERT.*

Q.4 Which of the following hydrides is electron-precise hydride?

(a) B_2H_6 (b) NH_3 (c) H_2O (d) CH_4

Ans. ***(d)*** Electron-precise hydrides contain exact number of electrons to form normal covalent bonds. *e.g.*, CH_4 which is tetrahedral in geometry.

Q.5 Radioactive elements emit α, β and γ rays and are characterised by their half-lives. The radioactive isotope of hydrogen is

(a) Protium (b) Deuterium
(c) Tritium (d) Hydronium

Thinking Process To solve this problem, the point kept in mind is, that nuclei with n/p (neutron/proton) ratio > 1.5 are usually radioactive.

Ans. ***(c)*** The radioactive isotope of hydrogen is tritium. For tritium ($n = 3$, $p = 1$), therefore n/p ratio is 3.

Q.6 Consider the reactions

(i) $H_2O_2 + 2HI \longrightarrow I_2 + 2H_2O$

(ii) $HOCl + H_2O_2 \longrightarrow H_3O^+ + Cl^- + O_2$

Which of the following statements is correct about H_2O_2 with reference to these reactions? Hydrogen peroxide is ....

(a) an oxidising agent in both (i) and (ii)
(b) an oxidising agent in (i) and reducing agent in (ii)
(c) a reducing agent in (i) and oxidising agent in (ii)
(d) a reducing agent in both (i) and (ii)

Concept Insight

(i) Reducing agents are those substance (atoms, ions or molecules) which can readily lose electrons to other substance.

(ii) Oxidising agents are those substance (atoms, ions or molecules) which can readily accept electrons from other substance.

Ans. ***(b)***

Reduction

(i) $H_2\overset{-1}{O}_2 + 2H\overset{-1}{I} \longrightarrow \overset{0}{I}_2 + 2H_2\overset{-2}{O}$

Oxidation

Thus, here H_2O_2 oxidises HI into I_2 hence, it behaves as oxidising agent.

Reduction

(ii) $HO\overset{+1}{Cl} + H_2\overset{-1}{O}_2 \longrightarrow H_3O^+ + Cl^- + H_2\overset{0}{O}_2$

Oxidation

Here, H_2O_2 reduces HOCl to Cl^{-1}, thus, it acts as reducing agent.

Q.7 The oxide that gives H_2O_2 on treatment with dilute H_2SO_4 is

(a) PbO_2 (b) $BaO_2 \cdot 8H_2O + O_2$
(c) MnO_2 (d) TiO_2

Ans. *(b)* Oxides such as BaO_2, Na_2O_2 etc; which contain peroxide linkage (i.e., $-O-O$ or O_2^{2-}) on treatment with dilute H_2SO_4 give H_2O_2 but dioxides ($O = M = O$, where M is the metal atom) such as PbO_2, MnO_2, TiO_2 do not give H_2O_2 on treatment with dilute H_2SO_4.

$$\underset{\text{Hydrated barium peroxide}}{BaO_2 \cdot 8H_2O(s)} + H_2SO_4(aq) \longrightarrow BaSO_4(s) + \underset{\text{Hydrogen peroxide}}{H_2O_2(aq)} + 8H_2O(l)$$

Q.8 Which of the following equations depict the oxidising nature of H_2O_2?

(a) $2MnO_4^- + 6H^+ + 5H_2O_2 \longrightarrow 2Mn^{2+} + 8H_2O + 5O_2$
(b) $2Fe^{3+} + 2H^+ + H_2O_2 \longrightarrow 2Fe^{2+} + 2H_2O + O_2$
(c) $2I^- + 2H^+ + H_2O_2 \longrightarrow I_2 + 2H_2O$
(d) $KIO_4 + H_2O_2 \longrightarrow KIO_3 + H_2O + O_2$

Ans. *(c)* The reaction in which H_2O_2 is reduced, *i.e.*, oxidation state of oxygen decreases from -1 to -2 depicts the oxidising nature of H_2O_2. *e.g.*,

Decrease in O.N. (Reduction)

$$2I^- + 2H^+ + \underset{\text{Oxidising agent}}{H_2O_2^{-1}} \longrightarrow \overset{0}{I_2} + 2H_2O^{-2}$$

Increase in O.N. (oxidation)

Q.9 Which of the following equation depicts reducing nature of H_2O_2?

(a) $2[Fe(CN)_6]^{4-} + 2H^+ + H_2O_2 \longrightarrow 2[Fe(CN)_6]^{3-} + 2H_2O$
(b) $I_2 + H_2O_2 + 2OH^- \longrightarrow 2I^- + 2H_2O + O_2$
(c) $Mn^{2+} + H_2O_2 \longrightarrow Mn^{4+} + 2OH^-$
(d) $PbS + 4H_2O_2 \longrightarrow PbSO_4 + 4H_2O$

Ans. *(b)* H_2O_2 acts as an oxidising as well as reducing agent in alkaline media. The given below reaction show the reducing action in basic medium.

$$I_2 + H_2O_2 + 2OH^- \longrightarrow 2I^- + 2H_2O + O_2$$
$$2MnO_4^- + 3H_2O_2 \longrightarrow 2MnO_2 + 3O_2 + 2H_2O + 2OH^-$$

Q.10 Hydrogen peroxide is ....

(a) an oxidising agent (b) a reducing agent
(c) both an oxidising and a reducing agent
(d) neither oxidising nor reducing agent

Ans. *(c)* Hydrogen peroxide acts as an oxidising as well as reducing agent in both acidic and alkaline media because oxygen in H_2O_2 is present in its intermediate oxidation state.

Q.11 Which of the following reactions increases production of dihydrogen from synthesis gas?

(a) $CH_4(g) + H_2O(g) \xrightarrow[\text{Ni}]{1270\text{ K}} CO(g) + 3H_2(g)$

(b) $C(s) + H_2O(g) \xrightarrow{1270\text{ K}} CO(g) + H_2(g)$

(c) $CO(g) + H_2O(g) \xrightarrow[\text{Catalyst}]{673\text{ K}} CO_2(g) + H_2(g)$

(d) $C_2H_6 + 2H_2O \xrightarrow[\text{Ni}]{1270\text{ K}} 2CO + 5H_2$

Ans. ***(c)*** The process of producing syn gas or synthesis gas from coal is called 'coal gasification'.

$$\underset{\text{Coal}}{C(s)} + \underset{\text{Steam}}{H_2O(g)} \xrightarrow[\text{Ni}]{1270\text{ K}} \underbrace{CO(g) + H_2(g)}_{\text{Syn gas}}$$

The production of hydrogen can be increased by reacting carbon monoxide of the syn gas with steam in the presence of iron chromate as a catalyst at 673 K.

$$CO(g) + H_2O(g) \xrightarrow{FeCrO_4,\ 673\text{ K}} CO_2(g) + H_2(g)$$

CO_2 is removed by scrubbing with a solution of sodium arsenite.

Q.12 When sodium peroxide is treated with dilute sulphuric acid, we get ....

(a) sodium sulphate and water
(b) sodium sulphate and oxygen
(c) sodium sulphate, hydrogen and oxygen
(d) sodium sulphate and hydrogen peroxide

Ans. ***(d)*** When sodium peroxide is treated with dilute sulphuric acid, we get sodium sulphate and hydrogen peroxide

$$\underset{\text{Sodium peroxide}}{Na_2O_2} + \text{dil. } H_2SO_4 \longrightarrow \underset{\text{Sodium sulphate}}{Na_2SO_4} + \underset{\text{Hydrogen peroxide}}{H_2O_2}$$

Q.13 Hydrogen peroxide is obtained by the electrolysis of ....

(a) water
(b) sulphuric acid
(c) hydrochloric acid
(d) fused sodium peroxide

Ans. ***(b)*** Peroxodisulphate, obtained by electrolytic oxidation of acidified sulphate solutions at high current density, on hydrolysis yields hydrogen peroxide.

$$2HSO_4^-(aq) \xrightarrow{\text{Electrolysis}} \underset{\text{peroxydisulphuric acid}}{(HO_3SO)_2(aq)} \xrightarrow{\text{Hydrolysis}} 2HSO_4^-(aq) + 2H^+(aq) + H_2O_2(aq)$$

Q.14 Which of the following reactions is an example of use of water gas in the synthesis of other compounds?

(a) $CH_4(g) + H_2O(g) \xrightarrow[\text{Ni}]{1270\text{ K}} CO(g) + H_2(g)$

(b) $CO(g) + H_2O(g) \xrightarrow[\text{Catalyst}]{673\text{ K}} CO_2(g) + H_2(g)$

(c) $C_nH_{2n+2} + nH_2O(g) \xrightarrow[\text{Ni}]{1270\text{ K}} nCO + (2n+1)H_2$

(d) $CO(g) + 2H_2(g) \xrightarrow[\text{Catalyst}]{\text{Cobalt}} CH_3OH(l)$

Ans. ***(d)*** The water gas is the combination of carbon monoxide and hydrogen.

$$CO(g) + 2H_2(g) \xrightarrow[\text{Catalyst}]{\text{Cobalt}} CH_3OH(l)$$

It is an example of water gas used in the synthesis of methanol.

Q.15 Which of the following ions will cause hardness in water sample?

(a) Ca^{2+} (b) Na^{+}
(c) Cl^{-} (d) K^{+}

- **Concept Insight** Hard water forms scum/precipitate with soap. Soap containing sodium stearate ($C_{17}H_{35}COONa$) reacts with hard water to precipitate out Ca/Mg stearate.

$$2C_{17}H_{35}COONa\,(aq) + M^{2+}(aq) \longrightarrow (C_{17}H_{35}COO)_2M \downarrow + 2Na^{+}\,(aq)$$
(where, $M = Ca / Mg$)

It is unsuitable for laundry and boilers.

Ans. ***(a)*** Bicarbonates, chlorides and sulphates of Ca and Mg are responsible for the hardness of water.

Q.16 Which of the following compounds is used for water softening?

(a) $Ca_3(PO_4)_2$ (b) Na_3PO_4
(c) $Na_6P_6O_{18}$ (d) Na_2HPO_4

Ans. ***(c)*** For water softening, sodium hexametaphosphate is used. The chemical formula is

$Na_2[Na_4(PO_3)_6] = Na_6P_6O_{18}$. The trade name is calgon.

$$\underset{\text{(From hard water)}}{2CaCl_2} + \underset{\text{Sodium hexametaphosphate}}{Na_2[Na_4(PO_3)_6]} \rightarrow \underset{\text{Complex salt (soluble)}}{Na_2[Ca_2(PO_3)_6]} + 4\,NaCl$$

Q.17 Elements of which of the following group(s) of periodic table do not form hydrides?

(a) Groups 7, 8, 9 (b) Group 13
(c) Groups 15, 16, 17 (d) Group 14

Ans. ***(a)*** Dihydrogen forms molecular compounds with most of the *p*-block elements. Most familiar examples are CH_4, NH_3, H_2O and HF. Elements of Groups 7, 8, and 9 do not form hydrides due to their low reactivity with hydrogen. This region is called the "hydride gap" as stable hydrides are not formed.

Q.18 Only one element of .... forms hydride.

(a) group 6 (b) group 7
(c) group 8 (d) group 9

- **Concept Insight** Metallic (or interstitial) hydrides are formed by many *d*-block and *f*-block elements. However, the metals of group 7, 8 and 9 do not form hydride. Even from group 6, only chromium forms CrH. These hydrides conduct heat and electricity though not as efficiently as their parent metals do.

Ans. ***(a)*** Only one element of group 6, *i.e.*, Cr forms hydride.

Multiple Choice Questions (More Than One Options)

Q.19 Which of the following statements are not true for hydrogen?

(a) It exists as diatomic molecule.
(b) It has one electron in the outermost shell.
(c) It can lose an electron to form a cation which can freely exist.
(d) It forms a large number of ionic compounds by losing an electron.

Ans. ***(c, d)*** The correct statements for hydrogen are given in option (a) and (b).

The corrected form of statements in option (c) and (d) are as follows.

(c) H^+ does not exist freely and is always associated with other atoms or molecules.

(d) Like alkali metals, hydrogen forms oxides, halides and sulphides. However, unlike alkali metals, it has a very high ionisation enthalpy, so it generally forms covalent compounds.

Q.20 Dihydrogen can be prepared on commercial scale by different methods. In its preparation by the action of steam on hydrocarbons, a mixture of CO and H_2 gas is formed. It is known as ....

(a) Water gas (b) Syn gas (c) Producer gas (d) Industrial gas

Ans. ***(a, b)*** Reaction of steam on hydrocarbons or coke at high temperatures in the presence of catalyst yield hydrogen.

$$C_nH_{2n+2} + nH_2O \xrightarrow[\text{Ni}]{1270\text{ K}} nCO + (2n+1)H_2$$

e.g.,

$$CH_4(g) + H_2O(g) \xrightarrow[\text{Ni}]{1270\text{ K}} CO(g) + 3H_2(g)$$

The mixture of CO and H_2 is called **water gas or syn gas.** As this mixture of CO and H_2 is used for the synthesis of methanol and a number of hydrocarbons.

Q.21 Which of the following statement(s) is/are correct in the case of heavy water?

(a) Heavy water is used as a moderator in nuclear reactor.
(b) Heavy water is more effective as solvent than ordinary water.
(c) Heavy water is more associated than ordinary water.
(d) Heavy water has lower boiling point than ordinary water.

Ans. ***(a, c)*** Heavy water is used as moderator in nuclear reactor. Boiling point of heavy water is higher than ordinary water and it is not as effective in the form of solvent as water due to its low dielectric constant.

Q.22 Which of the following statements about hydrogen are correct?

(a) Hydrogen has three isotopes of which protium is the most common.
(b) Hydrogen never acts as cation in ionic salts.
(c) Hydrogen ion, H^+, exists freely in solution.
(d) Dihydrogen does not act as a reducing agent.

Ans. ***(a, b)*** The correct statements are (a) and (b). Hydrogen has three isotopes — protium, deuterium, and tritium — with protium being the most abundant. In ionic salts, hydrogen does not exist as a free proton (H^+); instead, it forms the hydride ion (H^-) by gaining an electron, especially with highly electropositive metals like Na and Ca.

The corrected form of statements (c) and (d) are as follows:

(c) Hydrogen ion (H.) does not exist freely in solution; it is always associated with molecules like water to form hydronium ion (H_3O.).

(d) Dihydrogen (H_2) does act as a reducing agent, particularly in reactions with metal oxides and non-metals like chlorine and oxygen.

Q.23 Some of the properties of water are described below. Which of them is/are not correct?

(a) Water is known to be a universal solvent.
(b) Hydrogen bonding is present to a large extent in liquid water.
(c) There is no hydrogen bonding in the frozen state of water.
(d) Frozen water is heavier than liquid water.

Ans. ***(c, d)*** There is H-bonding even in frozen state of water, *i.e.*, ice is lighter than liquid water. The crystalline form of water is ice. At atmospheric pressure, ice crystallises in the tetrahedral form having pores thus, density of ice is less than that of water. Therefore, an ice cube floats on water. Hence, frozen water is lighter than liquid water. Thus, statements (c) and (d) are incorrect.

Q.24 Hardness of water may be temporary or permanent. Permanent hardness is due to the presence of

(a) Chlorides of Ca and Mg in water
(b) Sulphates of Ca and Mg in water
(c) Hydrogen carbonates of Ca and Mg in water
(d) Carbonates of alkali metals in water

Ans. ***(a, b)*** Permanent hardness is due to the presence of soluble salts of magnesium (Mg) and calcium (Ca) in the form of chlorides and sulphates in water.

Q.25 Which of the following statements is correct?

(a) Elements of group 15 form electron deficient hydrides
(b) All elements of group 14 form electron precise hydrides
(c) Electron precise hydrides have tetrahedral geometries.
(d) Electron rich hydrides can act as Lewis acids.

Ans. ***(b, c)*** Electron precise compounds have the required number of electrons to write their conventional Lewis structures. All elements of group 14 forms electron-precise compounds e.g., CH_4 which are tetrahedral in geometry. Elements of group 15-17 form electron rich hydrides. They can act as Lewis bases. Elements of group 13 form electron deficient hydrides. They act as Lewis acids. Thus, statements (b) and (c) are correct.

Q.26 Which of the following statements is correct?

(a) Hydrides of group 13 act as Lewis acids.
(b) Hydrides of group 14 are electron deficient hydrides.
(c) Hydrides of group 14 act as Lewis acids.
(d) Hydrides of group 15 act as Lewis bases.

Ans. ***(a, d)*** All elements of group 13 will form electron deficient compounds which acts as Lewis acids. All elements of group 14 will form electron precise compounds.

Electron rich hydrides have excess electrons which are present as lone pairs. Elements of group 15-17 forms such compounds. NH_3 has 1-lone pair, H_2O-2 lone pairs and HF-3 lone pairs act as Lewis bases. Thus, statements (a) and (d) are correct.

Q.27 Which of the following statements is correct?

(a) Metallic hydrides are deficient of hydrogen.
(b) Metallic hydrides conduct heat and electricity.
(c) Ionic hydrides do not conduct electricity in solid state.
(d) Ionic hydrides are very good conductors of electricity in solid state.

Ans. *(a, b, c)* The ionic hydrides are crystalline, non-volatile and non-conducting in solid state. However, their molten state conduct electricity.

Short Answer Type Questions

Q.28 How can production of hydrogen from water gas be increased by using water gas shift reaction?

Ans. Water gas is produced when superheated steam is passed over red hot coke or coal at 1270 K in presence of nickel as catalyst.

$$\underset{\text{Coke}}{C(s)} + \underset{\text{Steam}}{H_2O(g)} + 121.3\,\text{kJ} \xrightarrow[\text{Nickel}]{1270\text{ K}} \underbrace{CO(g) + H_2(g)}_{\text{Water gas}}$$

It is inconvenient to obtain pure H_2 from water gas as CO is difficult to remove. Hence, to increase the production of H_2 from water gas, CO is oxidised to CO_2 by mixing it with more steam and passing the mixture over $FeCrO_4$ catalyst at 673 K.

$$\underbrace{CO(g) + H_2(g)}_{\text{Water gas}} + \underset{\text{Steam}}{H_2O(g)} \xrightarrow[FeCrO_4]{673\text{ K}} CO_2(g) + 2H_2(g)$$

This is called water-gas shift reaction. Carbon dioxide is removed by scrubbing with mixture of sodium arsenite solution or by passing the mixture through water under 30 atm pressure when CO_2 dissolves leaving behind H_2 which is collected.

Q.29 What are metallic/interstitial hydrides? How do they differ from molecular hydrides?

Ans. Metallic/interstitial hydrides are formed by *d*- and *f*-block elements. These hydrides conduct heat and electricity.

These are **non-stoichiometric,** and deficient in hydrogen. e.g. $LaH_{2.87}$, $YbH_{2.55}$, $TiH_{1.5-1.8}$, $ZrH_{1.3-1.75}$, $VH_{0.56}$, $NiH_{0.6-0.7}$, $PdH_{0.6-0.8}$ etc. In such hydrides, the law of constant composition does not hold good.

Comparision between molecular and metallic hydrides

Molecular hydrides	Metallic hydrides
(i) These are mainly formed by *p*-block elements and some *s*-block elements (Be and Mg).	(i) These are formed by group 3, 4, 5 (Sc, Ti, V, Y, Zr, Nb, La, Hf, Ta, Ac etc.,) 10, 11, 12 (Pd, Cu, Zn etc.,) and *f*-block elements (Ce, Eu, Yb, Th, U etc.)
(ii) These are usually volatile compounds having low melting and boiling point.	(ii) These are hard, have a metallic lustre.
(iii) They conduct electricity.	(iii) They do not conduct electricity.

Q.30 Name the classes of hydrides to which H_2O, B_2H_6 and NaH belong.

- **Concept Insight** Molecular hydrides are classified according to the relative number of electrons and bonds in their Lewis structures.

  (i) Electron deficient hydride has too few electrons for writing its conventional Lewis structure.

  (ii) Electron precise compounds have the required number of electrons to write their conventional Lewis structures.

  (iii) Electron rich hydrides have excess electrons which are present as lone pairs.

Ans. H_2O — Covalent or molecular hydride (electron rich hydride).

B_2H_6 — Covalent polymeric hydride (electron deficient hydride).

NaH — Ionic or saline hydride.

Q.31 If same mass of liquid water and a piece of ice is taken, then why is the density of ice less than that of liquid water?

Ans. The density of ice is less than that of liquid water because, in ice, water molecules are arranged in a rigid, open cage-like structure due to **extensive hydrogen bonding.** This structure contains large vacant spaces, making ice less dense. In liquid water, thermal motion causes hydrogen bonds to continuously break and reform, allowing molecules to pack more closely, thereby increasing the density.

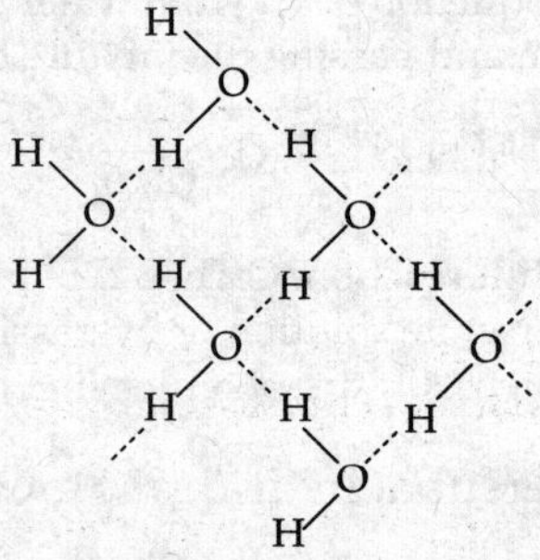

Tetrahedral structure of ice

Q.32 Complete the following equations

(i) $PbS(s) + H_2O_2(aq) \longrightarrow$

(ii) $CO(g) + 2H_2(g) \xrightarrow[\text{Catalyst}]{\text{Cobalt}}$

Ans. (i) $PbS(s) + 4H_2O_2(aq) \longrightarrow PbSO_4(s) + 4H_2O(l)$

The sulphur in PbS is oxidised from –2 to +6 oxidation state.

(ii) $CO(g) + 2H_2(g) \xrightarrow[\text{Catalyst}]{\text{Cobalt}} CH_3OH\ (l)$

This is the catalytic hydrogenation of carbon monoxide to form methanol, an important industrial reaction.

Q.33 Give reasons

(i) Lakes freeze from top towards bottom.

(ii) Ice floats on water.

Ans. (i) At 4°C, water has maximum density and minimum volume. Now, as temperature decreases, the surface of water freezes in severe cold while the water below surface is still at 4°C as it is heavier than water at surface, so top of lake freezes first and water below surface freeze only if temperature is sub-zero.

(ii) Ice floats on water because it is less dense than liquid water. In ice, water molecules are arranged in an open, cage-like structure due to hydrogen bonding, creating large empty spaces.

Q.34 What do you understand by the term 'auto-protolysis' of water? What is its significance?

Ans. Auto-protolysis means **self ionisation of water.**

$$\underset{\text{Acid}_1}{H_2O(l)} + \underset{\text{Base}_2}{H_2O(l)} \rightleftharpoons \underset{\text{Acid}_2}{H_3O^+(aq)} + \underset{\text{Base}_1}{OH^-(aq)}$$

Due to auto-protolysis, water is amphoteric in nature. It reacts with both acids and bases.

e.g.,

$$\underset{\text{Acid}_1}{H_2O(l)} + \underset{\text{Base}_2}{NH_3(aq)} \longrightarrow \underset{\text{Acid}_2}{NH_4^+(aq)} + \underset{\text{Base}_1}{OH^-(aq)}$$

$$\underset{\text{Base}_1}{H_2O(l)} + \underset{\text{Acid}_2}{H_2S(aq)} \longrightarrow \underset{\text{Acid}_1}{H_3O^+(aq)} + \underset{\text{Base}_2}{HS^-(aq)}$$

Q.35 Discuss briefly de-mineralisation of water by ion exchange resin.

Ans. Water free from all soluble mineral salts is called **demineralised water.** Demineralised water is obtained by passing water through a cation exchange and an anion exchange resins.

In cation exchanger, Ca^{2+}, Mg^{2+}, Na^+ and other cations present in water are removed by exchanging them with H^+ ions while in anion exchanger, Cl^-, HCO_3^-, SO_4^{2-}, etc., present in water are removed by exchanging them with OH^- ions.

$$\underset{\text{(Released in cation exchanger)}}{H^+} + \underset{\text{(Released in anion exchanger)}}{OH^-} \longrightarrow H_2O$$

Synthetic ion exchange resins are of two types.

Cation exchange resins contain large organic molecule with SO_3H group and are water soluble. It is changed to *R*Na by treating it with NaCl. The resin *R*Na exchanges Mg^{2+} and Ca^{2+} ions present in hard water to make the water soft.

$$2RNa(s) + M^{2+}(aq) \longrightarrow R_2M(s) + 2Na^+(aq) \quad (M = Ca^{2+} \text{ or } Mg^{2+})$$

The resin can be regenerated by passing NaCl (aqueous solution) in it. Pure demineralised (deionised) water is obtained by passing water successively through a cation exchange and anion exchange resins. In the cation exchange process,

$$2RH(s) + M^{2+}(aq) \rightleftharpoons \underset{\substack{\text{(Cation exchange}\\\text{resin in the } H^+ \text{ form)}}}{MR_2(s)} + 2H^+(aq)$$

H^+ exchanges for Ca^{2+}, Mg^{2+} and other cations present in water.

This process results in proton release and thus, makes the water acidic. In the anion exchange process

$$RNH_2(s) + H_2O(l) \rightleftharpoons R\overset{+}{N}H_3 \cdot OH^-(s)$$

$R\overset{+}{N}H_3 \cdot OH^-$ is substituted ammonium hydroxide anion exchange resin.

$$R\overset{+}{N}H_3 \cdot OH^-(s) + X^-(aq) \rightleftharpoons R\overset{+}{N}H_3 \cdot X^-(s) + OH^-(aq)$$

Q.36 Molecular hydrides are classified as electron deficient, electron precise and electron rich compounds. Explain each type with two examples.

Ans. Molecular hydrides are classified according to the relative numbers of electrons and bonds in Lewis structure as follow

(i) **Electron deficient hydrides** These contain central atom with an incomplete octet. These are formed by 13 group elements, e.g., BH_3, AlH_3, etc. To complele their octet they generally exist in polymeric forms such as B_2H_6, B_4H_{10}, $(AlH_3)_n$ etc. These hydrides act as **Lewis acids.**

(ii) **Electron precise hydrides** These hydrides have exact number of electrons required to form normal covalent bonds. These are formed by 14 group elements, e.g., CH_4, SiH_4, etc. These are tetrahedral in shape.

(iii) **Electron rich hydrides** These hydrides contain central atom with excess electrons, which are present as lone pairs. These are formed by 15, 16 and 17 group elements, *e.g.*, NH_3, H_2O, HF, etc. These hydrides act as **Lewis bases.**

Q.37 How is heavy water prepared? Compare its physical properties with those of ordinary water.

Ans. Heavy water is prepared by prolonged electrolysis of water. Comparison of physical properties of heavy water with those of ordinary water is as follows:

Property	H_2O	D_2O
Molecular mass (g mol^{-1})	18.0151	20.0276
Melting point (K)	273.0	276.8
Boiling point (K)	373.0	374.4
Enthalpy of formation (kJ mol^{-1})	– 285.9	– 294.6
Enthalpy of vaporisation – 373 K (kJ mol^{-1})	40.66	41.61
Enthalpy of fusion (kJ mol^{-1})	6.01	—
Temperature of max. density (K)	276.98	284.2
Density at 298 K (g cm^{-3})	1.0000	1.1059
Viscosity (centipoise)	0.8903	1.107
Dielectric constant (C^2 /Nm^2)	78.39	78.06
Electrical conductivity at 298 K (ohm^{-1} cm^{-1})	5.7×10^{-8}	—

Q.38 Write one chemical reaction for the preparation of D_2O_2.

Ans. D_2O_2 is prepared by the action of D_2SO_4 dissolved in water over BaO_2.

$$BaO_2 + D_2SO_4 \longrightarrow BaSO_4 + D_2O_2$$

Q.39 Calculate the strength of 5 volume H_2O_2 solution.

Ans. 5 volume H_2O_2 solution means that 1 L of this H_2O_2 solution on decomposition produces 5 L of O_2 at STP.

$$2H_2O_2 \longrightarrow 2H_2O + O_2$$
$$2 \times 34 \text{ g} \longrightarrow 22.7 \text{ L at STP}$$

If 22.7 L O_2 at STP will be obtained from $H_2O_2 = 68$ g

$\therefore$ 5 L of O_2 at STP will be obtained from $H_2O_2 = \dfrac{68 \times 5}{22.7}$ g $= 14.98 = 15$ g

$\therefore$ Strength of H_2O_2 in 5 volume H_2O_2 solution $= 15 \text{ g L}^{-1}$.

$\Rightarrow$ Percentage strength of H_2O_2 solution $= \dfrac{15}{1000} \times 100 = 1.5\%$

Therefore, strength of H_2O_2 in 5 volume H_2O_2 solution $= 15$ g/L $= 1.5\%$ H_2O_2 solution.

Q.40 (i) Draw the gas phase and solid phase structure of H_2O_2.
(ii) H_2O_2 is a better oxidising agent than water. Explain.

Ans. (i) H_2O_2 has a non-planar structure. The molecular dimensions in the gas phase and solid phase are given below

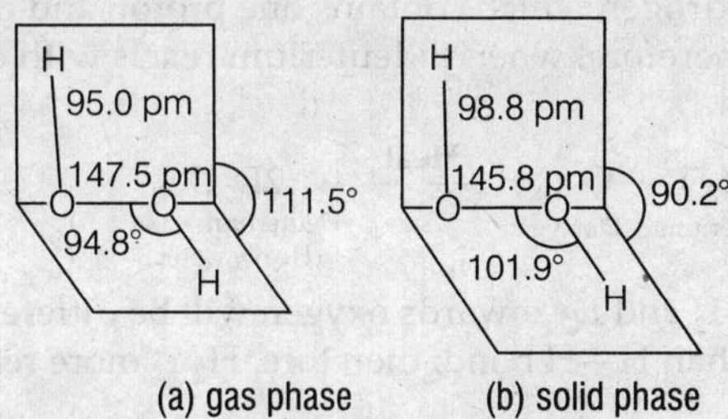

(a) gas phase (b) solid phase

(a) H_2O_2 structure in gas phase, dihedral angle is 111.5°.
(b) H_2O_2 structure in solid phase at 110 K, dihedral angle is 90.2°.

(ii) H_2O_2 is better oxidising agent than water as H_2O_2 is lesser stable and releases oxygen readily and form stable molecule H_2O.

H_2O_2 turns black PbS to white $PbSO_4$ but H_2O does not.

$$PbS(s) + 4H_2O_2(aq) \longrightarrow PbSO_4(s) + 4H_2O(l).$$

Q.41 Melting point, enthalpy of vapourisation and viscosity data of H_2O and D_2O is given below:

	H_2O	D_2O
Melting point/K	373.0	374.4
Enthalpy of vaporisation at (373 K)/kJ mol^{-1}	40.66	41.61
Viscosity/centipoise	0.8903	1.107

On the basis of this data explain in which of these liquids intermolecular forces are stronger?

Thinking Process The data given in the question shows that melting point, enthalpy of vapourisation and viscosity of D_2O is more than that of H_2O. The intermolecular force is directly proportional to these three parameters.

Ans. The given data confirms that D_2O has stronger attraction force than H_2O as melting point. Enthalphy of vapourisation and viscosity are having higher value than for water.

Q.42 Dihydrogen reacts with dioxygen (O_2) to form water. Write the name and formula of the product when the isotope of hydrogen which has one proton and one neutron in its nucleus is treated with oxygen. Will the reactivity of both the isotopes be the same towards oxygen? Justify your answer.

Ans. The isotope of hydrogen which contains one proton and one neutron is deuterium (D). Therefore, when dideuterium reacts with dioxygen, heavy water (D_2O) is produced.

$$\underset{\text{Dideuterium}}{2D_2(g)} + \underset{\text{Dioxygen}}{O_2(g)} \xrightarrow{\text{Heat}} \underset{\substack{\text{Deuterium oxide}\\\text{(Heavy water)}}}{2D_2O}$$

The reactivity of H_2 and D_2 towards oxygen will be different. Since, the D—D bond is stronger than H—H bond, therefore, H_2 is more reactive than D_2.

Q.43 Explain why HCl is a gas and HF is a liquid?

Ans. F is smaller and more electronegative than Cl, so it forms stronger hydrogen bonds as compared to Cl. So, HF molecules are associated due to H-bonding and HF exists as liquid. However, HCl molecules are linked by weaker dipole-dipole attraction, so HCl exists as gas.

Q.44 When the first element of the periodic table is treated with dioxygen, it gives a compound whose solid state floats on its liquid state. This compound has an ability to act as an acid as well as a base. What products will be formed when this compound undergoes autoionisation?

Ans. The first element of the periodic table is hydrogen and its molecular form is dihydrogen (H_2). When H_2 reacts with O_2, water is formed. Water is a liquid at room temperature. When liquid water freezes, it expands to form ice.

Density of ice is lower than that of liquid water and hence ice floats over water. Water is amphoteric in nature. It acts as a base in presence of strong acids and as an acid in presence of strong bases.

$$\underset{\text{Base}_1}{H_2O(l)} + \underset{\text{Acid}_2}{H_2S(aq)} \longrightarrow \underset{\text{Acid}_1}{H_3O^+(aq)} + \underset{\text{Base}_2}{HS^-(aq)}$$

$$\underset{\text{Acid}_1}{H_2O(l)} + \underset{\text{Base}_2}{NH_3(aq)} \longrightarrow \underset{\text{Acid}_2}{NH_4^+(aq)} + \underset{\text{Base}_1}{OH^-(aq)}$$

Due to amphoteric character, water undergoes self ionisation as shown below

$$\underset{\text{Acid}_1}{H_2O(l)} + \underset{\text{Base}_2}{H_2O(aq)} \rightleftharpoons \underset{\substack{\text{Acid}_2\\ \text{(Conjugate}\\ \text{acid)}}}{H_3O^+(aq)} + \underset{\substack{\text{Base}_1\\ \text{(Conjugate}\\ \text{base)}}}{OH^-(aq)}$$

This self ionisation of water is called **auto-protolysis** or **autoionisation.**

Q.45 Rohan heard that instructions were given to the laboratory attendent to store a particular chemical, *i.e.*, keep it in the dark room, add some urea in it, and keep it away from dust. This chemical acts as an oxidising as well as a reducing agent in both acidic and alkaline media. This chemical is important for use in the pollution control treatment of domestic and industrial effluents.

(i) Write the name of this compound.

(ii) Explain why such precautions are taken for storing this chemical.

Ans. (i) The name of the compound is hydrogen peroxide, H_2O_2. It acts as an oxidising agent as well as reducing agent in both acidic and basic medium.

(ii) H_2O_2 decomposes slowly on exposure to light and dust particles. In the presence of metal surfaces or traces of alkali present in glass containers, the decomposition of H_2O_2 is catalysed.

It is, therefore, stored in wax lined glass or plastic vessels in dark. Urea is added as a negative catalyst or stabiliser to check its decomposition.

$$2H_2O_2(l) \xrightarrow{h\nu} 2H_2O(l) + O_2(g)$$

Q.46 Give reasons why hydrogen resembles alkali metals?

Ans. Hydrogen resembles alkali metals, *i.e.*, Li, Na, K, Rb, Cs and Fr of group I of the periodic table in the following respects

(i) Like alkali metals, hydrogen also contain one electron in its outermost (valence) shell and exhibits +1 oxidation state.

(ii) Like alkali metals, hydrogen also loses its only electron to form hydrogen ion, *i.e.*, H^+ (proton).

(iii) Like alkali metals, hydrogen combines with electronegative elements (non-metals) such as oxygen, halogens and sulphur forming their oxides, halides and sulphides respectively.

(iv) Like alkali metals, hydrogen also acts as a strong reducing agent.

Q.47 Hydrogen generally forms covalent compounds. Give reason.

Ans. Hydrogen generally forms covalent compounds because it has high ionisation enthalpy (1312 $kJmol^{-1}$) and a slightly negative electron gain enthalpy (–73 kJ/mol). Due to these properties, it neither easily loses an electron to form H. (like alkali metals) nor easily gains one to form H^- (like halogens). Instead, hydrogen tends to share its single electron with other atoms to attain the stable $1s^2$ configuration, forming covalent bonds.

Q.48 Why is the Ionisation enthalpy of hydrogen higher than that of sodium?

Ans. Both hydrogen and sodium have one electron in the valence shell. But the size of hydrogen is much smaller than that of sodium and hence, the ionisation enthalpy of hydrogen is much higher (1312 kJ mol^{-1}) than that of sodium (496 kJ mol^{-1}).

Q.49 Basic principle of hydrogen economy is transportation and storage of energy in the form of liquid or gaseous hydrogen. Which property of hydrogen may be useful for this purpose? Support your answer with the chemical equation if required.

Ans. Hydrogen is a gas at room temperature. By cooling and applying high pressure, gaseous H_2 can be converted into liquid H_2 which has much smaller volume and hence can be transported easily. Thus, the basic property of hydrogen which is useful for hydrogen economy is that it can be converted into a liquid by cooling under high pressure.

Q.50 What is the importance of heavy water?

Ans. Following are the importance of heavy water

(i) It is extensively used as a moderator in nuclear reactors.

(ii) It is used as a tracer compound in the study of reaction mechanism.

(iii) It is used for the preparation of other deuterium compounds such as CD_4, D_2SO_4, etc.

Q.51 Write the Lewis structure of hydrogen peroxide.

Ans. The Lewis structure of hydrogen peroxide is:

$$H^{\times} + \cdot\ddot{\underset{\cdot\cdot}{O}}\cdot + \cdot\ddot{\underset{\cdot\cdot}{O}}\cdot + {}^{\times}H \longrightarrow H\overset{\times}{\cdot}\ddot{\underset{\cdot\cdot}{O}}:\ddot{\underset{\cdot\cdot}{O}}\overset{\cdot}{\times}H$$

Hydrogen peroxide

Q.52 An acidic solution of hydrogen peroxide behaves as an oxidising as well as reducing agent. Illustrate it with the help of a chemical equation.

Ans. (i) H_2O_2 oxidises acidified KI to iodine, so act as reducing agent.

$$2KI + H_2O_2 + H_2SO_4 \longrightarrow I_2 + K_2SO_4 + 2H_2O$$

(ii) H_2O_2 reduces $KMnO_4$ to MnO_2 in alkaline medium, so H_2O_2 acts as oxidising agent.

$$2KMnO_4 + 3H_2O_2 \longrightarrow 2MnO_2 + 2KOH + 3O_2 + 2H_2O$$

Q.53 With the help of suitable examples, explain the property of H_2O_2 that is responsible for its bleaching action?

Ans. The bleaching action of hydrogen peroxide is due to the nascent oxygen which it liberates on decomposition.

$$H_2O_2 \longrightarrow H_2O + \underset{\text{(nascent oxygen)}}{[O]}$$

The nascent oxygen combines with colouring matter, which gets oxidised. Thus, the bleaching action of H_2O_2 is due to the oxidation of colouring matter by nascent oxygen. It is used for the bleaching of delicate materials like ivory, feathers, silk, wool etc.

$$\text{Colouring matter} + [O] \longrightarrow \text{Colourless matter}$$

Q.54 Why is water molecule polar?

Ans. Oxygen is more electronegative (EN=3.5) than hydrogen (EN = 2.1) hence, O — H bond is polar. In the water molecule, two polar O — H bonds are present which are held together at an angle of 104.5°. Due to the resultant of these two dipoles, water molecule is polar and has a dipole moment of 1.84 Debye.

Q.55 Why does water show high boiling point as compared to hydrogen sulphide? Give reasons for your answer.

Ans. There exist extensive H-bonding between water molecules. So, large amount of energy is required to break these bonds hence, boiling point of H_2O is high.

$$\cdots\cdots \overset{\delta^+}{H}-\overset{\delta^-}{\underset{|\atop H}{O}}\cdots\cdots \overset{\delta^+}{H}-\overset{\delta^-}{\underset{|\atop H}{O}}\cdots\cdots \overset{\delta^+}{H}-\overset{\delta^-}{\underset{|\atop H}{O}}$$

In other words, hydrogen sulphide molecules have weaker dipole-dipole attraction. Hence, boiling point of H_2S is much lower than that of H_2O. Thats why H_2S is a gas at room temperature.

Q.56 Why can dilute solutions of hydrogen peroxide not be concentrated by heating? How can a concentrated solution of hydrogen peroxide be obtained?

Ans. Dilute solutions of H_2O_2 cannot be concentrated by heating because it decomposes much below its boiling point.

$$2H_2O_2 \longrightarrow 2H_2O + O_2$$

1% H_2O_2 is extracted with water and concentrated to ~ 30% (by mass) by distillation under reduced pressure. It can be further concentrated to ~ 85% by careful distillation under low pressure. The remaining water can be frozen out to obtain pure H_2O_2.

Q.57 Why is hydrogen peroxide stored in wax lined bottles?

Ans. Hydrogen peroxide is decomposed by rough surfaces of glass, alkali oxides present in it and light to form H_2O and O_2.

$$2H_2O_2 \longrightarrow 2H_2O + O_2$$

To prevent this decomposition, hydrogen peroxide is usually stored in paraffin wax coated plastic or teflon bottles.

Q.58 Why does hard water not form lather with soap?

Ans. Hard water contains salts of calcium and magnesium ions. These ions combine with soap containing sodium stearate ($C_{17}H_{35}COONa$) to precipitate out as Ca/Mg stearate.

$$2C_{17}H_{35}COONa\,(aq) + M^{2+}(aq) \longrightarrow (C_{17}H_{35}COO)_2M \downarrow + 2Na^+(aq)$$

(where, M is Ca/Mg)

Thus, hard water does not form lather with soap.

Q.59 Phosphoric acid is preferred over sulphuric acid in preparing hydrogen peroxide from peroxides. Why?

Ans. H_2SO_4 acts as a catalyst for decomposition of H_2O_2. Therefore, some weaker acids such as H_3PO_4, H_2CO_3 is preferred over H_2SO_4 for preparing H_2O_2 from peroxides.

$$3BaO_2 + 2H_3PO_4 \longrightarrow \underset{\text{(Insoluble)}}{Ba_3(PO_4)_2} + 3H_2O_2$$

Q.60 How will you account for 104.5° bond angle in water?

Ans. In water, oxygen has sp^3-hybridisation and the bond angle of HOH should have been 109°28′. In H_2O, the oxygen atom is surrounded by two shared bond pairs and two lone pairs of electrons. From VSEPR theory, lone pair - lone pair repulsions are stronger than bond pair–bond pair repulsions.

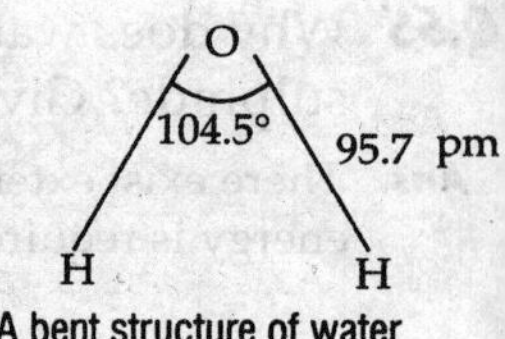

A bent structure of water

As a result, the bond angle of HOH in water slightly decreases from 109°.28′ to 104.5°.

Q.61 Write redox reaction between fluorine and water.

Ans. Fluorine is a strong oxidising agent, it oxidises H_2O to O_2 or O_3. The reactions are as follows

$$2F_2(g) + 2H_2O(l) \longrightarrow O_2(g) + 4H^+(aq) + 4F^-(aq)$$

$$3F_2(g) + 3H_2O(l) \longrightarrow O_3(g) + 6H^+(aq) + 6F^-(aq)$$

Q.62 Write two reactions to explain amphoteric nature of water.

Ans. Water has the ability to act as an acid as well as base, *i.e.*, it behaves as an amphoteric substance. From the Bronsted Lowry theory, it acts as an acid with NH_3 and a base with H_2S.

$$H_2O(l) + NH_3(aq) \longrightarrow OH^-(aq) + NH_4^+(aq)$$

$$H_2O(l) + H_2S(aq) \longrightarrow H_3O^+(aq) + HS^-(aq)$$

The auto-protolysis (self-ionisation) of water takes place. The reaction are as follows

$$\underset{\text{Acid}}{H_2O(l)} + \underset{\text{Base}}{H_2O(l)} \longrightarrow \underset{\text{Conjugate acid}}{H_3O^+(aq)} + \underset{\text{Conjugate base}}{OH^-(aq)}$$

Matching The Columns

Q.63 Correlate the items listed in Column I with those listed in Column II. Find out as many correlations as you can.

	Column I		Column II
A.	Synthesis gas	1.	$Na_2[Na_4(PO_3)_6]$
B.	Dihydrogen	2.	Oxidising agent
C.	Heavy water	3.	Softening of water
D.	Calgon	4.	Reducing agent
E.	Hydrogen peroxide	5.	Stoichiometric compounds of *s*-block elements
F.	Salt like hydrides	6.	Prolonged electrolysis of water
		7.	Zn + NaOH
		8.	Zn + dil. H_2SO_4
		9.	Synthesis of methanol
		10.	Mixture of CO and H_2

Ans. **A.** → (9, 10) **B.** → (4, 5, 7, 8, 9) **C.** → (6) **D.** → (1, 3)
E. → (2, 4) **F.** → (5)

A. Synthesis gas — Synthesis of methanol
— Mixture of CO and H_2

B. Dihydrogen — Reducing agent
— Stoichiometric compounds of *s*-block elements
— Zn + NaOH
— Zn + dil. H_2SO_4
— Synthesis of methanol

C. Heavy water — Prolonged electrolysis of water

D. Calgon — $Na_2[Na_4(PO_3)_6]$
— Softening of water

E. Hydrogen peroxide — Oxidising agent
— Reducing agent

F. Salt like hydrides — Stoichiometric compounds of *s*-block elements.

Q.64 Match Column I with Column II for the given properties/applications mentioned therein.

	Column I		Column II
A.	H	1.	used in the name of perhydrol.
B.	H_2	2.	can be reduced to dihydrogen by NaH.
C.	H_2O	3.	can be used in hydroformylation of olefin.
D.	H_2O_2	4.	can be used in cutting and welding.

Ans. A.→ (4) B. → (3) C. → (2) D. → (1)

A. Atomic hydrogen (H) can be used in cutting and welding.

B. Dihydrogen (H_2) can be used in hydroformylation of olefin.

C. Water (H_2O) can be reduced to dihydrogen by NaH.

D. Hydrogen peroxide (H_2O_2) used in the name of perhydrol.

Q.65 Match the terms in Column I with the relevant item in Column II.

	Column I		Column II
A.	Electrolysis of water produces	1.	atomic reactor
B.	Lithium aluminium hydride is used as	2.	polar molecule
C.	Hydrogen chloride is a	3.	recombines on metal surface to generate high temperature
D.	Heavy water is used in	4.	reducing agent
E.	Atomic hydrogen	5.	hydrogen and oxygen

Ans. A.→ (5) B. → (4) C. → (2) D. → (1) E. → (3)

A. Electrolysis of water produce hydrogen and oxygen.

B. Lithium aluminium hydride is used as reducing agent.

C. Hydrogen chloride is a polar molecule.

D. Heavy water is used in atomic reactor as moderator.

E. Atomic hydrogen recombines on metal surface to generate high temperature.

Q.66 Match the items in Column I with the relevant item in Column II.

	Column I		Column II
A.	Hydrogen peroxide is used as a	1.	zeolite
B.	Used in Calgon method	2.	perhydrol
C.	Permanent hardness of hard water is removed by	3.	sodium hexametaphosphate
		4.	propellant

Ans. A.→ (2, 4) B. → (3) C. → (1, 3)

A. Hydrogen peroxide is used as a perhydrol and propellant.

B. Sodium hexametaphosphate is used in Calgon method.

C. Permanent hardness of hard water is removed by zeolite and sodium hexametaphosphate.

Assertion and Reason

In the following questions a statement of Assertion (A) followed by a statement of Reason (R) is given. Choose the correct option out of the options given below in each question.

Q.67 **Assertion** (A) : Permanent hardness of water is removed by treatment with washing soda.

Reason (R) : Washing soda reacts with soluble magnesium and calcium sulphate to form insoluble carbonates.

(a) Statements A and R both are correct and R is the correct explanation of A.

(b) A is correct but R is not correct.

(c) A and R both are correct but R is not the correct explanation of A.

(d) A and R both are false.

Ans. ***(a)*** Statements of A and R both are correct and R is the correct explanation of A.

$$\underset{}{Na_2CO_3} + \underset{\substack{\text{or} \\ CaSO_4 \\ \text{(from hard} \\ \text{water)}}}{MgSO_4} \longrightarrow Na_2SO_4 + \underset{\substack{\text{or} \\ CaCO_3 \\ \text{(insoluble)}}}{MgCO_3}$$

Q.68 **Assertion** (A) Some metals like platinum and palladium, can be used as storage media for hydrogen.

Reason (R) Platinum and palladium can absorb large volumes of hydrogen.

(a) Statements A and R both are correct and R is the correct explanation of A.

(b) A is correct but R is not correct.

(c) A and R both are correct but R is not the correct explanation of A.

(d) A and R both are false.

Ans. ***(a)*** Statements of A and R both are correct and R is the correct explanation of A. Since, metals like Pd and Pt absorbs a large volume of hydrogen, hence, these are used as a storage media for it.

Long Answer Type Questions

Q.69 Atomic hydrogen combines with almost all elements but molecular hydrogen does not. Explain.

Ans. Atomic hydrogen is highly unstable. Since, the electronic configuration of atomic hydrogen is $1s^1$, it needs one more electron to complete its configuration and gain stability. Therefore, atomic hydrogen is very reactive and combines with almost all the elements.

It, however, reacts in three different ways *i.e.*,

(i) by loss of its single electron to form H^+,

(ii) by gain of one electron to form H^- and

(iii) by sharing its electron with other atoms to form single covalent bonds. In contrast, the bond dissociation energy form H—H bond is very high (435.88 kJ mol^{-1}). As a result, molecular hydrogen is almost inert at room temperature and hence, reacts only with a few elements.

Q.70 How can D_2O be prepared from water? Mention the physical properties in which D_2O differs from H_2O. Give at least three reactions of D_2O showing the exchange of hydrogen with deuterium.

Ans. (i) D_2O can be prepared by prolonged electrolysis of water.

(ii) Physical properties of D_2O are as follows:

(a) D_2O is colourless, odourless, tasteless liquid. It has maximum density – 1.1073 g mL^{-1} at 11.6°C (Maximum density of water at 4°C).

(b) Solubility of salts in heavy water is less than in ordinary water because it is more viscous than ordinary water.

(c) Nearly, all physical constants of D_2O are higher than H_2O. It is due to the greater nuclear mass of deuterium atom than H-atom and stronger H-bonding in D_2O than H_2O.

(iii) Exchange reactions of hydrogen with deuterium

$$NaOH + D_2O \longrightarrow NaOD + HOD$$

$$HCl + D_2O \longrightarrow DCl + HOD$$

$$NH_4Cl + D_2O \longrightarrow NH_3DCl + HOD$$

Q.71 How will you concentrate H_2O_2? Show differences between structures of H_2O_2 and H_2O by drawing their spatial structures. Also mention three important uses of H_2O_2.

Ans. (i) Industrially, H_2O_2 is prepared by the auto-oxidation of **2-alkylanthraquinols.**

$$\text{2-ethylanthraquinol} \underset{H_2/Pd}{\overset{O_2/(air)}{\rightleftharpoons}} H_2O_2 + \text{Oxidised product}$$

In this case, 1% H_2O_2 is formed. It is extracted with water and concentrated to ~ 30% (by mass) by distillation under reduced pressure.

It can be further concentrated to ~ 85% by careful distillation under low pressure. The remaining water can be frozen out to obtain pure H_2O_2.

(ii) H_2O_2 has a non-planar structure or open book structure.

The molecular dimensions in the gas phase and solid phase are shown below:

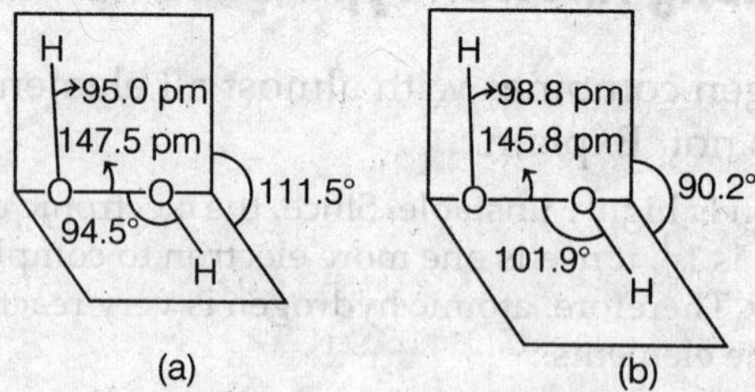

(a) H_2O_2 structure in gas phase, (b) H_2O_2 structure in solid phase

In the gas phase, H_2O is a bent molecule with a bond angle of 104.5° and O—H bond length of 95.7 pm as shown below:

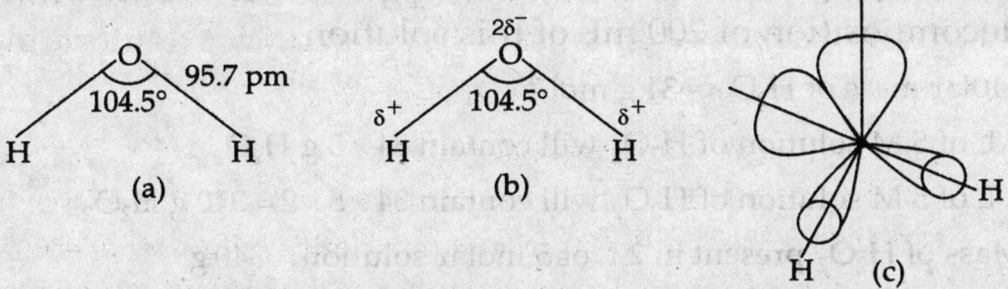

(a) The bent structure of water (b) The water molecule as a dipole (c) The orbital overlap picture in water dipole

(iii) Following are the three important uses of H_2O_2

(a) In daily life, it is used as a hair bleach and as a mild **disinfectant.** As an antiseptic it is sold in the market as **perhydrol.**

(b) It is used in the synthesis of hydroquinone, tartaric acid and certain food products and pharmaceuticals **(cephalosporin)** etc.

(c) It is employed in the industries as a bleaching agent for textiles, paper pulp, leather, oils, fats etc.

Q.72 (i) Give a method for the manufacture of hydrogen peroxide and explain the reactions involved therein.

(ii) Illustrate oxidising, reducing and acidic properties of hydrogen peroxide with equations.

Ans. (i) H_2O_2 is industrially manufactured by the auto-oxidation of 2-alkylanthraquinols.

$$\text{2-ethylanthraquinol} \underset{H_2/Pd}{\overset{O_2/(air)}{\rightleftharpoons}} H_2O_2 + \text{Oxidised product}$$

In this case, 1% H_2O_2 is formed. It is extracted with water and concentrated to ~30% (by mass) by distillation under reduced pressure. It can be further concentrated to ~ 85% by careful distillation under low pressure. The remaining water can be frozen out to obtain pure H_2O_2.

(ii) H_2O_2 acts as an oxidising as well as reducing agent in both acidic and alkaline media.

Following reactions are described below

(a) Oxidising action in acidic medium

$$2Fe^{2+}(aq) + 2H^+(aq) + H_2O_2(aq) \longrightarrow 2Fe^{3+}(aq) + 2H_2O(l)$$

$$PbS(s) + 4H_2O_2(aq) \longrightarrow PbSO_4(s) + 4H_2O(l)$$

(b) Reducing action in acidic medium

$$2MnO_4^- + 6H^+ + 5H_2O_2 \longrightarrow 2Mn^{2+} + 8H_2O + 5O_2$$

$$HOCl + H_2O_2 \longrightarrow H_3O^+ + Cl^- + O_2$$

(c) Oxidising action in basic medium

$$2Fe^{2+} + H_2O_2 \longrightarrow 2Fe^{3+} + 2OH^-$$

$$Mn^{2+} + H_2O_2 \longrightarrow Mn^{4+} + 2OH^-$$

(d) Reducing action in basic medium

$$I_2 + H_2O_2 + 2OH^- \longrightarrow 2I^- + 2H_2O + O_2$$

$$2MnO_4 + 3H_2O_2 \longrightarrow 2MnO_2 + 3O_2 + 2H_2O + 2OH^-$$

Q.73 What mass of hydrogen peroxide will be present in 2 L of a 5 molar solution? Calculate the mass of oxygen which will be liberated by the decomposition of 200 mL of this solution.

Ans. Molar mass of $H_2O_2 = 34 \text{ g mol}^{-1}$

1 L of 5 M solution of H_2O_2 will contain 34×5 g H_2O_2

2 L of 5 M solution of H_2O_2 will contain $34 \times 5 \times 2 = 340$ g H_2O_2

Mass of H_2O_2 present in 2 L of 5 molar solution = 340 g

Alternate Method

$\therefore$ Molarity $= \dfrac{w_B}{m_B \times V_L}$

Mass of H_2O_2 $(w_B) = M \times m_B \times V_L$

$= 5 \times 34 \times 2 = 340$ g

Volume = 200 mL = 0.2 L

Mole of H_2O_2 in 0.2 L = Molarity × Volume = $5 \times 0.2 = 1$ mol

1 mole of H_2O_2 = 34 gm of H_2O_2

From the reaction, $2H_2O_2 \longrightarrow 2H_2O + O_2$

$2 \times 34 = 68$ gm $\quad 2 \times 16 = 32$ gm

68 gm H_2O_2 on decomposition gives 32 gm of O_2

$\therefore$ 34 gm H_2O_2 on decomposition will give $= \dfrac{32 \times 34}{68}$ gm of O_2 = 16 gm of O_2

Q.74 A colourless liquid '*A*' contains H and O elements only. It decomposes slowly on exposure to light. It is stabilised by mixing urea to store in the presence of light.

(i) Suggest possible structure of *A*.

(ii) Write chemical equations for its decomposition reaction in light.

Ans. Since, a colourless liquid 'A' contains only hydrogen and oxygen and decomposes slowly on exposure to light but is stabilised by addition of urea, therefore, liquid *A* is hydrogen peroxide.

(i) The structure of H_2O_2 is

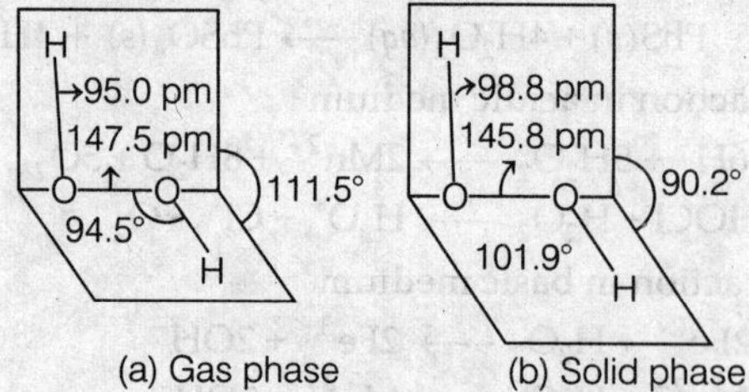

(a) Gas phase (b) Solid phase

(a) H_2O_2 structure in gas phase, dihedral angle is 111.5°.

(b) H_2O_2 structure in solid phase at 110 K, dihedral angle is 90.2°.

(ii) $2H_2O_2 \xrightarrow[\text{Sunlight}]{h\nu} 2H_2O + O_2$

Q.75 An ionic hydride of an alkali metal has significant covalent character and is almost unreactive towards oxygen and chlorine. This is used in the synthesis of other useful hydrides. Write the formula of this hydride. Write its reaction with Al_2Cl_6.

Ans. It is LiH because it has significant covalent character due to the smallest alkali metal, Li. LiH is very stable. It is almost unreactive towards oxygen and chlorine. It reacts with Al_2Cl_6 to form lithium aluminium hydride.

$$8LiH + Al_2Cl_6 \longrightarrow 2LiAlH_4 + 6LiCl$$

Q.76 Sodium forms a crystalline ionic solid with dihydrogen. The solid is non-volatile and non-conducting in nature. It reacts violently with water to produce dihydrogen gas. Write the formula of this compound and its reaction with water. What will happen on electrolysis of the melt of this solid?

Ans. Sodium reacts with dihydrogen to form sodium hydride which is a crystalline ionic solid.

$$2Na + H_2 \longrightarrow 2Na^+H^-$$

It reacts violently with water to produce H_2 gas

$$2NaH + 2H_2O \longrightarrow 2NaOH + 2H_2$$

In solid state, NaH does not conduct electricity. On electrolysis, in its molten state it gives H_2 at anode and Na at cathode.

$$Na^+H^-(l) \xrightarrow{\text{Electrolysis}} \underset{\text{At cathode}}{2Na\,(l)} + \underset{\text{At anode}}{H_2(g)}$$

Chapter 10

The S-Block Elements*

Multiple Choice Questions (MCQs)

Q.1 The alkali metals are low melting. Which of the following alkali metal is expected to melt if the room temperature rises to 30°C?

(a) Na (b) K (c) Rb (d) Cs

- **Concept Insight** The energy binding the atoms in the crystal lattice of the alkali metals is low due to their large atomic radii and especially due to the presence of one valence electron per metal atom as compared to large number of available vacant orbitals. Hence, alkali metals have low melting and boiling points.

Ans. *(d)* The melting point of alkali metals decreases from Li to Cs as cohesive force decreases with increase in atomic size.

Melting point of Cs = 302 K, *i.e.*, 29°C.

Q.2 Alkali metals react with water vigorously to form hydroxides and dihydrogen. Which of the following alkali metals reacts with water least vigorously?

(a) Li (b) Na (c) K (d) Cs

Ans. *(a)* Li has most negative standard reduction potential due to very high enthalpy of hydration. Thus, reaction of Li with water should be most exothermic, but surprisingly Li reacts with water gently, whereas Na and K vigorously.

The explanation is in kinetics and not in thermodynamics of the reaction. No doubt, maximum energy is evolved with Li but its fusion, vapourisation and ionisation consume more energy. As a result, reaction proceeds slowly.

Na or K have low melting points and molten metal spreads over water exposing a larger surface to water, making the reaction more vigorous than Li.

Q.3 The reducing power of a metal depends on various factors. Suggest the factor which makes Li, the strongest reducing agent in aqueous solution.

(a) Sublimation enthalpy (b) Ionisation enthalpy
(c) Hydration enthalpy (d) Electron-gain enthalpy

Thinking Process Standard reduction potential (E°_{RP}) is a measure of tendency of an element to lose electron in aqueous solution. Higher the negative E°_{RP}, greater is the ability to lose electrons.

Note (*) *This chapter has been deleted from latest NCERT.*

Ans. ***(c)*** Standard reduction potential (E°_{RP}) depends on

(i) enthalpy of sublimation

(ii) ionisation enthalpy

(iii) enthalpy of hydration

The formation of $Li^+(aq)$ from Li involves following steps

$$Li(s) \xrightarrow{\Delta H_{sub}} Li(g) \xrightarrow{IE_1} Li^+(g) \xrightarrow{\Delta H \text{ (hydration enthalpy)}} Li^+(aq)$$

For alkali metals, enthalpies of sublimation are almost same. IE_1 value of Li is very high and hydration energy maximum for Li^+ due to small size.

The highly exothermic step (iii) for smallest Li^+ makes it strongest reducing agent.

Thus, hydration enthalpy is the key factor making lithium the strongest reducing agent in aqueous medium.

Q.4 Metal carbonates decompose on heating to give metal oxide and carbon dioxide. Which of the metal carbonates is most stable thermally?

(a) $MgCO_3$ (b) $CaCO_3$ (c) $SrCO_3$ (d) $BaCO_3$

Thinking Process Thermal stability of carbonates depends upon relative stabilities of metal oxide which are formed upon heating. Greater the stability of metal oxide, more will be tendency of carbonate to decompose to metal oxide.

Thermal stability of carbonates increases with increase in atomic number, or atomic size, *i.e.*, on moving down the group $BeCO_3 < MgCO_3 < CaCO_3 < SrCO_3 < BaCO_3$.

Ans. ***(d)*** $BaCO_3$ is thermally most stable because of the small size of resulting oxide ion. With the increase in atomic number, the size of the metal ion, the stability of the metal ion decreases and, hence that of carbonate increases (maximum in case of $BaCO_3$).

Therefore, the increasing size of cation destabilizes the oxides and hence does not favour the decomposition of heavier alkaline earth metal carbonates like $BaCO_3$.

Q.5 Which of the carbonates given below is unstable in air and is kept in CO_2 atmosphere to avoid decomposition?

(a) $BeCO_3$ (b) $MgCO_3$ (c) $CaCO_3$ (d) $BaCO_3$

Ans. ***(a)*** $BeCO_3$ shows reversible reaction because stability of oxide formed is more than carbonates. $BeCO_3 \rightleftharpoons BeO + CO_2$

$BeCO_3$ is unstable due to strong polarising effect of small Be^{2+} ion on the large polarisable carbonate ion. Moreover, an extra stability of the oxide achieved through lattice energy by packing small cation with small oxide ion.

Q.6 Metals form basic hydroxides. Which of the following metal hydroxide is the least basic?

(a) $Mg(OH)_2$ (b) $Ca(OH)_2$ (c) $Sr(OH)_2$ (d) $Ba(OH)_2$

Ans. ***(a)*** Basic character of alkaline metal hydroxide increases from beryllium to barium hydroxide. It is because of decrease in lonisation enthalpy and increase in metal atom size due to which strength of $M-O$ bond in $M(OH)_2$ decreases and hence, tendency to release OH^- ion increases, *i.e.*, basic nature of the metal hydroxides increases. Hence, $Mg(OH)_2$ is least basic among given metal hydroxides.

Q.7 Some of the Group 2 metal halides are covalent and soluble in organic solvents. Among the following metal halides, the one which is soluble in ethanol is

(a) $BeCl_2$ (b) $MgCl_2$ (c) $CaCl_2$ (d) $SrCl_2$

Ans. *(a)* $BeCl_2$ is covalent due to smallest size of Be and high charge density of Be^{2+} so dissolve easily in covalent organic solvents like ethanol, as ("like dissolves like").

Q.8 The order of decreasing ionisation enthalpy in alkali metals is

(a) Na > Li > K > Rb (b) Rb < Na < K < Li (c) Li > Na > K > Rb (d) K < Li < Na < Rb

Thinking Process Ionisation energies depend upon how strongly the valence electron is held by the nucleus. Ionisation energy value will be high if electron is tightly held and if interaction between electron and nucleus is poor then ionisation energy will be low.

Ans. *(c)* On moving down in the group (from Li to Cs), the ionisation energy value decreases from Li to Cs, as size of the atom increases and so the valence electrons are is less tightly held. Increased screening effect from Li to Cs also makes the removal of electron easier.

Q.9 The solubility of metal halides depends on their nature, lattice enthalpy and hydration enthalpy of the individual ions. Amongst fluorides of alkali metals, the lowest solubility of LiF in water is due to

(a) Ionic nature of lithium fluoride
(b) High lattice enthalpy
(c) High hydration enthalpy for lithium ion
(d) Low ionisation enthalpy of lithium atom

● **Concept Insight** Solubilities of alkali metal halides in water can be explained in terms of lattice enthalpy and hydration enthalpy. Lower lattice enthalpies and higher hydration enthalpies favour dissolution.

Ans. *(b)* Among fluorides, the order of solubility is LiF < NaF < KF < RbF < CsF. Low solubility of LiF is due to very **high lattice energy.** On moving down in the group LiF to CsF, solubility increases because lattice energy decreases.

Except LiF, other halides of lithium are highly soluble in water.

Q.10 Amphoteric hydroxides react with both alkalies and acids. Which of the following Group 2 metal hydroxides is soluble in sodium hydroxide?

(a) $Be(OH)_2$ (b) $Mg(OH)_2$ (c) $Ca(OH)_2$ (d) $Ba(OH)_2$

Ans. *(a)* The solubility of hydroxides of alkaline earth metals increases from Be to Ba, in water. $Be(OH)_2$ and $Mg(OH)_2$ are almost insoluble.

Due to high lattice energy $Be(OH)_2$ is not soluble in water.

$Be(OH)_2$ is an amphoteric hydroxide. With acids, $Be(OH)_2$ is neutralised to give a salt.

$$Be(OH)_2 + 2HCl \longrightarrow BeCl_2 + 2H_2O$$

$Be(OH)_2$ reacts with NaOH also forming beryllate.

$$Be(OH)_2 + 2NaOH \longrightarrow Na_2BeO_2 + 2H_2O$$

Beryllium hydroxide $[Be(OH)_2]$ dissolves in sodium hydroxide due to its amphoteric nature, while the other Group 2 hydroxides are purely basic and do not exhibit amphoteric behaviour.

Q.11 In the synthesis of sodium carbonate, the recovery of ammonia is done by treating NH_4Cl with $Ca(OH)_2$. The by-product obtained in this process is

(a) $CaCl_2$ (b) NaCl (c) NaOH (d) $NaHCO_3$

Ans. ***(a)*** Sodium carbonate is synthesised by Solvay ammonia soda process.

The reactions involved are:

$$NH_3 + H_2O + CO_2 \longrightarrow \underset{\text{Ammonium bicarbonate}}{NH_4HCO_3}$$

$$NaCl + NH_4HCO_3 \longrightarrow \underset{\text{Sodium bicarbonate}}{NaHCO_3} \downarrow + NH_4Cl$$

$$2NaHCO_3 \xrightarrow{\Delta} \underset{\text{Sodium carbonate}}{Na_2CO_3} + H_2O + CO_2$$

NH_3 is recovered from NH_4HCO_3 and NH_4Cl formed during the reaction.

$$NH_4HCO_3 \xrightarrow{\text{Heat}} NH_3 + H_2O + CO_2$$

$$\underset{\text{Ammonium chloride}}{2NH_4Cl} + Ca(OH)_2 \longrightarrow \underset{\text{Ammonia}}{2NH_3} + \underset{\text{Calcium chloride}}{CaCl_2} + 2H_2O$$

Hence, the by-product formed in this process is calcium chloride ($CaCl_2$).

Q.12 When sodium is dissolved in liquid ammonia, a solution of deep blue colour is obtained. The colour of the solution is due to

(a) ammoniated electron (b) sodium ion
(c) sodium amide (d) ammoniated sodium ion

Ans. ***(a)*** All alkali metals dissolve in liquid NH_3 giving highly conducting deep blue solution.

$$Na + (x + y)\, NH_3 \longrightarrow \underset{\text{Ammoniated cation}}{[Na\,(NH_3)_x]^+} + \underset{\text{Ammoniated electron}}{[e(NH_3)_y]^-}$$

When light fall on these solutions, the ammoniated electrons excite to a higher energy level by absorbing red wavelengths and so transmitted light is blue.

Hence, the blue colour is due to solvated/ammoniated electrons in the solution.

Q.13 By adding gypsum to cement

(a) setting time of cement becomes less (b) setting time of cement increases
(c) colour of cement becomes light (d) shining surface is obtained

- **Concept Insight** Raw materials for cement-limestone, clay, gypsum. Cement is a dirty greyish heavy powder containing calcium aluminates and silicates.

Ans. ***(b)*** Gypsum ($CaSO_4 \cdot 5H_2O$) is added to the components to increase the setting time of cement so that it gets sufficiently hardened. Setting of cement is an exothermic process and involves hydration of calcium aluminates and silicates.

Q.14 Dead burnt plaster is

(a) $CaSO_4$ (b) $CaSO_4 \cdot \frac{1}{2}H_2O$ (c) $CaSO_4 \cdot H_2O$ (d) $CaSO_4 \cdot 2H_2O$

Ans. ***(a)*** On heating plaster of Paris at 200°C, if forms **anhydrous calcium sulphate,** *i.e.,* dead burnt plaster which has no setting property as it absorbs water very slowly.

$$CaSO_4 \cdot \frac{1}{2}H_2O \xrightarrow{200^\circ C} \underset{\substack{\downarrow \\ \text{dead burnt plaster}}}{CaSO_4} \xrightarrow{1100^\circ C} CaO + SO_3$$

Q.15 Suspension of slaked lime in water is known as

(a) lime water (b) quick lime
(c) milk of lime (d) aqueous solution of slaked lime

Ans. *(c)* Calcium hydroxide is prepared by adding water to quicklime (CaO). It is a white amorphous powder. It is sparingly soluble in water.

$$\underset{\text{Quick lime}}{CaO(s)} + H_2O(l) \longrightarrow \underset{\text{Slaked lime}}{Ca(OH)_2(s)}$$

So, it forms a suspension of slaked lime in water which is called milk of lime and the clear solution obtained after the suspension settles is known as lime water.

Q.16 Which of the following elements does not form hydride by direct heating with dihydrogen?

(a) Be (b) Mg (c) Sr (d) Ba

Ans. *(a)* Except Be, all alkaline earth metals form hydrides (MH_2) on directly heating with H_2. BeH_2 can't be prepared by direct action of H_2 on Be. It is prepared by the action of $LiAlH_4$ on $BeCl_2$.

$$2BeCl_2 + LiAlH_4 \longrightarrow 2BeH_2 + LiCl + AlCl_3$$

NOTE *Beryllium (Be) does not form a hydride by direct combination with dihydrogen because of its small atomic size, high ionization enthalpy, and high lattice energy of the expected hydride.*

Q.17 The formula of soda ash is

(a) $Na_2CO_3 \cdot 10H_2O$ (b) $Na_2CO_3 \cdot 2H_2O$
(c) $Na_2CO_3 \cdot H_2O$ (d) Na_2CO_3

Ans. *(d)* On heating washing soda, it loses its water of crystallisation. Above 373 K, it becomes completely anhydrous white powder called soda ash.

$$\underset{\text{Washing soda}}{Na_2CO_3 \cdot 10H_2O} \xrightarrow{>373\text{ K}} \underset{\text{Soda ash}}{Na_2CO_3}$$

Q.18 A substance which gives brick red flame and breaks down on heating to give oxygen and a brown gas is

(a) magnesium nitrate (b) calcium nitrate
(c) barium nitrate (d) strontium nitrate

Ans. *(b)* Calcium nitrate on heating decomposes into calcium oxide, with evolution of a mixture of NO_2 and O_2.

$$2Ca(NO_3)_2 \longrightarrow 2CaO + NO_2 + O_2$$

NO_2 is brown coloured gas.

Q.19 Which of the following statements is true about $Ca(OH)_2$?

(a) It is used in the preparation of bleaching powder
(b) It is a light blue solid
(c) It does not possess disinfectant property
(d) It is used in the manufacture of cement

Ans. *(a)* Calcium hydroxide is used in the manufacture of bleaching powder.

$$\underset{\text{Slaked lime}}{2Ca(OH)_2} + 2Cl_2 \xrightarrow{\text{Cold}} CaCl_2 + \underset{\text{Bleaching powder}}{Ca(OCl)_2} + 2H_2O$$

Q.20 A chemical *A* is used for the preparation of washing soda to recover ammonia. When CO_2 is bubbled through an aqueous solution of *A*, the solution turns milky. It is used in white washing due to disinfectant nature. What is the chemical formula of *A*?

(a) $Ca(HCO_3)_2$ (b) CaO

(c) $Ca(OH)_2$ (d) $CaCO_3$

Ans. ***(c)*** To recover NH_3 in Solvay ammonia soda process $Ca(OH)_2$ is used.

$$2NH_4Cl + \underset{(A)}{Ca(OH)_2} \longrightarrow 2NH_3 + CaCl_2 + 2H_2O$$

On passing CO_2 through $Ca(OH)_2$, it turns milky due to the formation of $CaCO_3$.

$$\underset{(A)}{Ca(OH)_2} + CO_2 \longrightarrow CaCO_3 \downarrow + H_2O$$

$Ca(OH)_2$ is used for white washing.

Q.21 Dehydration of hydrates of halides of calcium, barium and strontium, *i.e.,* $CaCl_2 \cdot 6H_2O$ $BaCl_2 \cdot 2H_2O$, $SrCl_2 \cdot 2H_2O$, can be achieved by heating.

These become wet on keeping in air. Which of the following statements is correct about these halides?

(a) Act as dehydrating agent

(b) Can absorb moisture from air

(c) Tendency to form hydrate decreases from calcium to barium

(d) All of the above

Ans. ***(d)*** Chlorides of alkaline earth metals are hydrated salts. Due to their hygroscopic nature, they can be used as a dehydrating agent, to absorb moisture from air.

Extent of hydration decreases from Mg to Ba, *i.e.,* $MgCl_2 \cdot 6H_2O$, $CaCl_2 \cdot 6H_2O$, $BaCl_2 \cdot 2H_2O$, $SrCl_2 \cdot 2H_2O$

Thus, all the given statements are correct.

Multiple Choice Questions (More Than One Options)

Q.22 Metallic elements are described by their standard electrode potential, fusion enthalpy, atomic size, etc. The alkali metals are characterised by which of the following properties?

(a) High boiling point

(b) High negative standard electrode potential

(c) High density

(d) Large atomic size

Ans. ***(b, d)*** Alkali metals are the first members in a period. Alkali metals have largest atomic radii in their period due to least effective nuclear charge.

They have low density because size is large and mass is least in a period. Alkali metals are soft metals to cut with a knife, *i.e.,* low boiling point.

Due to '*ns*' electronic configuration, they lose electron easily and have high negative standard electrode potential.

Q.23 Several sodium compounds find use in industries. Which of the following compounds are used for textile industry?

(a) Na_2CO_3 (b) $NaHCO_3$ (c) NaOH (d) NaCl

Ans. ***(a, c)*** Na_2CO_3 is used in manufacture of soap powders, in laundry for washing. NaOH is used in manufacture of rayon.

Thus, Na_2CO_3 and NaOH are used for textile industry.

Q.24 Which of the following compounds are readily soluble in water?

(a) $BeSO_4$ (b) $MgSO_4$ (c) $BaSO_4$ (d) $SrSO_4$

Ans. ***(a, b)*** Solubility of sulphates of alkaline earth metals in water decreases from Be to Ba · $BeSO_4$ are fairly soluble while $BaSO_4$ is almost completely insoluble. The decreasing solubility of $BeSO_4$ to $BaSO_4$ is due to decreasing hydration energy from Be^{2+} to Ba^{2+} (as size increases). For $BeSO_4$ and $MgSO_4$, hydration energy is more than lattice energy and so they are readily soluble.

Q.25 When zeolite, which is hydrated sodium aluminium silicate is treated with hard water, the sodium ions are exchanged with which of the following ion(s)?

(a) H^+ ions (b) Mg^{2+} ions
(c) Ca^{2+} ions (d) SO_4^{2-} ions

Ans. ***(b, c)*** To make hard water soft, sodium zeolite or sodium alumino silicate ($Na_2Al_2SiO_3 \cdot xH_2O$) is used. It exchange Ca^{2+} and Mg^{2+} ion in hard water for sodium ion.

Q.26 Identify the correct formula of halides of alkaline earth metals from the following.

(a) $BaCl_2 \cdot 2H_2O$ (b) $BaCl_2 \cdot 4H_2O$ (c) $CaCl_2 \cdot 6H_2O$ (d) $SrCl_2 \cdot 4H_2O$

Ans. ***(a, c)*** All the chlorides of alkaline earth metals are hydrated to different extent and extent of hydration decreases from Mg to Ba *e.g.* $MgCl_2 \cdot 6H_2O, CaCl_2 \cdot 6H_2O, BaCl_2 \cdot 2H_2O, SrCl_2 \cdot 2H_2O$.

Q.27 Choose the correct statements from the following.

(a) Beryllium is not readily attacked by acids because of the presence of an oxide film on the surface of the metal.
(b) Beryllium sulphate is readily soluble in water as the greater hydration enthalpy of Be^{2+} overcomes the lattice enthalpy factor.
(c) Beryllium exhibits coordination number more than four.
(d) Beryllium oxide is purely acidic in nature.

Concept Insight The anomalous behaviour of Be is mainly due to its very small size and partly due to its high electronegativity. These two factors increase the polarising power of Be^{2+} ions to such extent that it becomes significantly equal to the polarising power of Al^{3+} ions. Therefore, these two elements, Be and Al resemble (diagonal relationship) very much.

$$\text{Polarising power} = \frac{\text{Ionic chgarge}}{(\text{Ionic radii})^2}$$

Ans. ***(a, b)*** Due to diagonal relationship, beryllium is similar to aluminium. It also forms an oxide film which is very stable on the surface of the metal, thus does not readily attacked by acids.

Beryllium sulphate is soluble in water due to high hydration energy. Beryllium does not exhibit coordination number more than four. Like Al_2O_3, BeO is amphoteric in nature.

Thus, statements in options (a) and (b) are correct.

Q.28 Which of the following are the correct reasons for anomalous behaviour of lithium?

(a) Exceptionally small size of its atom
(b) Its high polarising power
(c) It has high degree of hydration
(d) Exceptionally low ionisation enthalpy

Ans. ***(a, b)*** Although Li exhibits, the characteristic properties of alkali metals but it dffers at same time in many of its properties from alkali metals.

The anomalous behaviour of lithium is due to extremely small size of lithium and its cation.

On account of small size and high nuclear charge, lithium exerts the greatest polarising effect among all alkali metals on negative ions.

Short Answer Type Questions

Q.29 How do you account for the strong reducing power of lithium in aqueous solution?

Ans. Strong reducing power of lithium in aqueous solution is due to its very high oxidation potential. Electrode potential is a measure of the tendency of an element to lose electrons in the aqueous solution. It mainly depends upon the following three factors i.e.

(i) $Li(s) \xrightarrow[\text{Enthalpy}]{\text{Sublimation}} Li(g)$

(ii) $Li(g) \xrightarrow[\text{Enthalpy}]{\text{Ionisation}} Li^+(g) + e^-$

(iii) $Li^+(g) + aq \longrightarrow Li^+(aq) + \text{enthalpy of hydration}$

Due to small size of ion, lithium has the highest hydration enthalpy. However, ionisation enthalpy of Li is highest among alkali metals but hydration enthalpy predominates over ionisation enthalpy.

Therefore, lithium is the strongest reducing agent in aqueous solution mainly because of its high enthalpy of hydration.

Q.30 When heated in air, the alkali metals form various oxides. Mention the oxides formed by Li, Na and K.

Ans. The reactivity of alkali metals towards oxygen increases on moving down the group with the increase in atomic size. Thus, Li forms only lithium oxide (Li_2O), sodium forms mainly sodium peroxide (Na_2O_2) along with a small amount of sodium oxide while potassium forms only potassium superoxide (KO_2).

$$4Li + O_2 \xrightarrow{\Delta} 2Li_2O$$

$$6Na + 2O_2 \xrightarrow{\Delta} \underset{\text{(major)}}{\underset{\text{Sodium peroxide}}{Na_2O_2}} + \underset{\text{(minor)}}{\underset{\text{Monoxide}}{\underset{\text{Sodium}}{2Na_2O}}}$$

$$K + O_2 \xrightarrow{\Delta} \underset{\text{superoxide}}{\underset{\text{Potassium}}{KO_2}} + \underset{\text{Peroxide}}{\underset{\text{Potassium}}{K_2O_2}} + \underset{\text{Monoxide}}{\underset{\text{Potassium}}{K_2O}}$$

The superoxide, O_2^- ion is stable only in presence of large cations such as K, Rb etc.

Q.31 Complete the following reactions

(i) $O_2^{2-} + H_2O \longrightarrow$ (ii) $O_2^- + H_2O \longrightarrow$

● **Concept Insight** O_2^{2-} represents a peroxide ion and O_2^- represents a superoxide ion.

Ans. (i) Peroxide ion react with water to form H_2O_2

$$O_2^{2-} + 2H_2O \longrightarrow 2OH^- + \underset{\text{peroxide}}{\underset{\text{Hydrogen}}{H_2O_2}}$$

(ii) Superoxide ion react with water to form H_2O_2 and O_2

$$2O_2^- + 2H_2O \longrightarrow 2OH^- + \underset{\text{peroxide}}{\underset{\text{Hydrogen}}{H_2O_2}} + O_2$$

Mistake Alert ! *Some students may get confused between peroxide and superoxide ions.*

Q.32 Lithium resembles magnesium in some of its properties. Mention two such properties and give reasons for this resemblance.

Ans. Lithium resembles with magnesium as its charge/size ratio is closer to Mg. Its resemblance with Mg is known as **diagonal relationship.**

Period	Group I	Group II
2	Li ↘	Be
3	Na	→ Mg

Following characteristics are same for Li and Mg,

(i) Due to covalent nature, chlorides of Li and Mg are deliquescent and soluble in alcohol and pyridine.

(ii) Carbonates of Li and Mg decompose on heating and liberate CO_2

$$Li_2CO_3 \longrightarrow Li_2O + CO_2$$

$$MgCO_3 \longrightarrow MgO + CO_2$$

Q.33 Name an element from group 2 which forms an amphoteric oxide and a water soluble sulphate.

Ans. An element from group 2 which forms an amphoteric oxide and a water soluble sulphate is beryllium.

Beryllium forms oxide BeO, which is amphoteric in nature as it reacts with acids and bases both.

$$Al_2O_3 + 2NaOH \longrightarrow 2NaAlO_2 + H_2O$$

$$Al_2O_3 + 6HCl \longrightarrow 2AlCl_3 + 3H_2O$$

Sulphate of beryllium is a white solid which crystallises as hydrated salts ($BeSO_4 \cdot 4H_2O$) while oxides of all other group 2 metals are basic in nature.

$BeSO_4$ is fairly soluble in water due to highest hydration energy in the group (small size).

For $BeSO_4$, hydration energy is more than lattice energy and so, they are readily soluble.

Q.34 Discuss the trend of the following

(i) Thermal stability of carbonates of Group 2 elements.

(ii) The solubility and the nature of oxides of Group 2 elements.

Ans. (i) All the alkaline earth melals form carbonates (MCO_3). These carbonates decompose on heating to give CO_2 and metal oxide. The thermal stability of these carbonates increases down the group, i.e. from Be to Ba.

$$BeCO_3 < MgCO_3 < CaCO_3 < SrCO_3 < BaCO_3$$

$BeCO_3$ is stable only in atmosphere of CO_2. These carbonates however show reversible decomposition in closed container.

$$BeCO_3 \rightleftharpoons BeO + CO_2$$

Hence, more is the stability of oxide formed, less will be stability of carbonates. Stability of oxides decreases down the group, so stability of carbonates increases from 'Be' to 'Ba'.

(ii) All the alkaline earth metals form oxides of formula, *MO*. The oxides are very stable due to high lattice energy and are used as refractory material.

Except BeO (predominantly covalent) all other oxides are ionic and their lattice energy decreases as the size of cation increases.

The oxides are basic and basic nature increases from BeO to BaO (due to increasing ionic nature).

$$\underbrace{BeO <}_{\text{Amphoteric}} \; \underbrace{MgO <}_{\text{Weakly basic}} \; \underbrace{CaO < SrO < BaO}_{\text{Strongly basic}}$$

BeO dissolves both in acid and alkalies to give salts and is amphoteric

The oxides of the alkaline earth metals (except BeO and MgO) dissolve in water to form basic hydroxides and evolve a large amount of heat. BeO and MgO possess high lattice energy and thus insoluble in water.

Q.35 **Why are $BeSO_4$ and $MgSO_4$ readily soluble in water while $CaSO_4$, $SrSO_4$ and $BaSO_4$ are insoluble?**

Ans. The lattice energy of alkaline earth metal sulphates is almost constant due to large size of sulphate ion. Thus, their solubility is decided by hydration energy which decreases on moving down the group.

The greater hydration enthalpies of Be^{2+} and Mg^{2+} ions overcome the lattice enthalpy factor and therefore, their sulphates are soluble in water.

However, hydration enthalpy is low for Ca^{2+}, Sr^{2+} ions and cannot overcome the lattice energy factor. Hence, these are insoluble.

Q.36 **All compounds of alkali metals are easily soluble in water but lithium compounds are more soluble in organic solvents. Explain.**

Ans. Smallest size of Li^+ ion (among all alkali metals) and its high polarising power are the two factors which develop covalent character in the lithium compounds (Fajan's rule).

So, these are soluble in alcohol and other organic solvents in accordance with "like dissolves like" principle while other alkali metal compounds are ionic in nature, so soluble in water.

Q.37 **In the Solvay process, can we obtain sodium carbonate directly by treating the solution containing $(NH_4)_2CO_3$ with sodium chloride? Explain.**

Ans. No, $(NH_4)_2CO_3$ reacts with NaCl as

$$(NH_4)_2CO_3 + 2NaCl \rightleftharpoons Na_2CO_3 + 2NH_4Cl$$

Because the products obtained, Na_2CO_3 and NH_4Cl are highly soluble and the equilibrium will not shift in forward direction.

That's why in the Solvay process, we cannot obtain sodium carbonate directly by treating the solution containing $(NH_4)_2CO_3$ with sodium chloride.

Q.38 **Write Lewis structure of O_2^- ion and find out oxidation state of each oxygen atom? What is the average oxidation state of oxygen in this ion?**

Ans. The Lewis structure of O_2^- is

$$[:\dot{\underset{\cdot\cdot}{O}} - \ddot{\underset{\cdot\cdot}{O}}:]^-$$

(1) (2)

Oxygen atom (1) carrying no charge has six electrons, so its oxidation number is zero. But oxygen atom (2) carrying – 1 charge has 7 electrons, so its oxidation number is – 1.

Average oxidation number of each oxygen atom $= \frac{1}{2}$

$$O_2^- = 2x = -1$$

$$x = -\frac{1}{2}$$

Q.39 Why do beryllium and magnesium not impart colour to the flame in the flame test?

- **Concept Insight** All alkaline earth metals (except Be and Mg) impart a characteristic colour to the Bunsen flame. The different colours arise due to different energies required for electronic excitation and de-excitation.

Ans. Be and Mg atoms due to their small size, bind their electrons more strongly (because of higher effective nuclear charge). Hence, require high excitation energy and are not excited by the energy of the flame due to which no flame colour is shown by them.

Q.40 What is the structure of $BeCl_2$ molecule in gaseous and solid state?

Ans. Beryllium chloride has different structures in solid and vapour state. In solid state, it exists in the form of polymeric chain structure in which each Be-atom is surrounded by four chlorine atoms having two of the chlorine atoms covalently bonded while the other two by coordinate bonds. The resulting bridge structure contains infinite chains.

202 pm, 92°, 82°, ← 263 pm →

Structure of $BeCl_2$ in solid state

In vapour or gaseous state, above 1200 K, it exists as a monomer having linear structure and zero dipole moment. But below 1200 K, it exists as dimer structure even in vapour state.

Cl—Be—Cl

Above 1200 K
Monomer

Below 1200 K
Dimer

Matching The Columns

Q.41 Match the elements given in Column I with the properties mentioned in Column II.

Column I	Column II
A. Li	1. Insoluble sulphate
B. Na	2. Strongest monoacidic base
C. Ca	3. Most negative $E^{\ominus}$ value among alkali metals
D. Ba	4. Insoluble oxalate
	5. $6s^2$ outer electronic configuration

Ans. A.→ (3) B.→ (2) C.→ (4) D.→ (1, 5)

A. Li—Most negative $E^{\ominus}$ value among alkali metals

[Due to very high hydration energy the resulting $E^{\ominus}$ is most negative].

B. Na—Strongest monoacidic base

[Alkalies are more acidic than alkaline earth metals. LiOH has covalent character].

C. Ca—insoluble oxalate

[Calciuim oxalate is insoluble in water]

D. Ba—Insoluble sulphate

[Hydration energy decreases as size of cation increases].

$6s^2$ outer electronic configuration

$[_{56}Ba = 1s^2, 2s^2, 2p^6, 3s^2, 3p^6, 3d^{10}, 4s^2, 4p^6, 4d^{10}, 5s^2, 5p^6, 6s^2]$

Q.42 Match the compounds given in Column I with their uses mentioned in Column II.

Column I	Column II
A. $CaCO_3$	1. Dentistry, ornamental work
B. $Ca(OH)_2$	2. Manufacture of sodium carbonate from caustic soda
C. CaO	3. Manufacture of high quality paper
D. $CaSO_4$	4. Used in white washing

Ans. A.→ (3) B.→ (4) C.→ (2) D.→ 1

A. $CaCO_3$ — Manufacture of high quality paper

B. $Ca(OH)_2$ — Used in white washing

C. CaO — Manufacture of sodium carbonate from caustic soda

D. $CaSO_4$ — Dentistry, ornamental work

Q.43 Match the elements given in Column I with the colour they impart to the flame given in Column II.

Column I	Column II
A. Cs	1. Apple green
B. Na	2. Violet
C. K	3. Brick red
D. Ca	4. Yellow
E. Sr	5. Crimson red
F. Ba	6. Blue

Ans. A.→ (6) B.→ (4) C.→ (2) D.→ (3) E.→ (5) F.→ 1

Elements with the characteristic flame colour are as follows

A. Cs – Blue B. Na – Yellow C. K – Violet

D. Ca – Brick red E. Sr – Crimson red F. Ba – Apple green

Flame colours are produced from the movement of the electrons in the metal ions present in the compounds. These movement of electrons (electronic excitation-de-excitation) requires energy.

Each atom has particular energy gap between ground and excited energy level therefore each of these movements involves a specific amount of energy emitted as light energy, and each corresponds to a particular colour. As we know energy gap between ground and excited state energy level increases wavelength decreases and complementary colour is observed as a result.

Assertion and Reason

In the following questions a statement of Assertion (A) followed by a statement of Reason (R) is given. Choose the correct option out of the choices given below in each question.

Q.44 **Assertion** (A) The carbonate of lithium decomposes easily on heating to form lithium oxide and CO_2.

Reason (R) Lithium being very small in size polarises large carbonate ion leading to the formation of more stable Li_2O and CO_2.

(a) Both A and R are correct and R is the correct explanation of A
(b) Both A and R are correct but R is not the correct explanation of A
(c) Both A and R are not correct
(d) A is not correct but R is correct

Ans. ***(a)*** Both A and R are correct and R is the correct explanation of A. The thermal stability of carbonates increases down the group. Hence, Li_2CO_3 is least stable. Due to small size of Li^+, its strong polarising power distorts the electron cloud of CO_3^{2-} ion. High lattice energy of Li_2O than Li_2CO_3 also favours the decomposition of Li_2CO_3 to form Li_2O and CO_2.

Q.45 **Assertion** (A) Beryllium carbonate is kept in the atmosphere of carbon dioxide.

Reason (R) Beryllium carbonate is unstable and decomposes to give beryllium oxide and carbon dioxide.

(a) Both A and R are correct and R is the correct explanation of A
(b) Both A and R are correct but R is not the correct explanation of A
(c) Both A and R are not correct
(d) A is not correct but R is correct

Ans. ***(a)*** Both A and R are correct and R is the correct explanation of A. BeO is more stable than $BeCO_3$ due to small size and high polarising power of Be^{2+}.

So, $BeCO_3$ is unstable when $BeCO_3$ is kept in an atmosphere of CO_2, a reversible process takes place and stability of $BeCO_3$ increases.

$$BeCO_3 \rightleftharpoons BeO + CO_2$$

Long Answer Type Questions

Q.46 The *s*-block elements are characterised by their larger atomic sizes, lower ionisation enthalpies, invariable +1 oxidation state and solubilities of their oxosalts. In the light of these features describe the nature of their oxides, halides and oxosalts.

Ans. Due to low ionisation energy and large atomic size, alkali metals form cation readily and so their compounds are ionic.

Oxides

Due to +1 oxidation state, alkali metals form normal oxides of general formula, M_2O. Only Li forms normal oxide Li_2O when heated in air. Other form peroxide and superoxide.

Oxides of alkali metals are strongly basic and are soluble in water.

Group-2 metals form oxide of type *MO*. These are basic in nature and except BeO and MgO all other oxides are water soluble and form hydroxide.

The basic character of oxide increases gradually from Li_2O to Cs_2O due to increased ionic character.

Halides

Except lithium halides, all other alkali metal halides are ionic. Due to high polarising power of Li^+ lithium halide is covalent in nature. Due to +1 oxidation states alkali metal halides have general formula *MX*. Low ionisation enthalpy allows formation of ionic halides.

Group-2 metals forms halides of type MX_2. Beryllium halides are covalent due to small size and high polarising power of Be^{2+} ion while other Group-2 metal halides are ionic in nature.

Oxo salts

All alkali metals form solid carbonates of general formula M_2CO_3. Carbonates are stable except Li_2CO_3 due to high polarising capacity of Li^+ which is unstable and decomposes. All the alkali metals (except Li) form solid bicarbonates $MHCO_3$. All alkali metals form nitrates having formula MNO_3. They are colourless, water soluble, electrovalent compounds.

Q.47 Present a comparative account of the alkali and alkaline earth metals with respect to the following characteristics.

(a) Tendency to form ionic/covalent compounds
(b) Nature of oxides and their solubility in water
(c) Formation of oxosalts
(d) Solubility of oxosalts
(e) Thermal stability of oxosalts

Ans. (a) The compounds of alkali metals are more ionic than alkaline earth metals and this ionic character increases down the group due to increasing ionic size and decreasing ionization enthalpy. 'Li' and 'Be' compounds are covalent in nature due to their smallest size and high polarising power.

(b) Oxides of alkaline earth metals are less basic than corresponding oxides of alkali metals.

The oxides dissolve in water to form basic hydroxides and evolve a large amount of heat. The alkaline earth metal hydroxides, are however less basic and less stable than alkali metal hydroxides.

(c) Alkaline earth metals form oxoacids as alkali metals. The formation of alkali metal oxoacids is much more faster and stronger than their corresponding alkaline earth metals due to increased nuclear charge and small size.

(d) Solubility of alkaline oxoacids is more than alkali oxoacids because alkaline earth metals have small size of cation and higher hydration energy. Salts like $CaCO_3$ are insoluble in water.

(e) Oxosalts of alkali metals are thermally more stable than those of alkaline earth metals. As the electropositive character increases down the group, the stability of carbonate and hydrogen carbonates of alkali metal increases. Whereas for alkaline earth metals, carbonate decomposes on heating to give carbon dioxide and oxygen.

Q.48 When a metal of group 1 was dissolved in liquid ammonia, the following observations were obtained

(a) Blue solution was obtained initially.

(b) On concentrating the solution, blue colour changed to bronze colour.

How do you account for the blue colour of the solution? Give the name of the product formed on keeping the solution for some time.

Ans. (a) The reaction that takes place when alkali metal is dissolved in liquid ammonia is

$$M + (x + y)NH_3 \longrightarrow [M(NH_3)_x]^+ + [e(NH_3)_y]^-$$

The blue colour of the solution is due to the presence of ammoniated electrons which absorb energy in the visible region of light and thus, impart blue colour to the solution.

(b) In concentrated solution, the blue colour changes to bronze colour due to the formation of cluster of metal ion. The blue solution on been kept for some time liberates hydrogen slowly with the formation of amide.

$$\underset{\text{Ammoniacal}}{M^+ + e^-} + NH_3 \longrightarrow \underset{\text{Amide}}{MNH_2} + \frac{1}{2}H_2$$

Q.49 The stability of peroxide and superoxide of alkali metals increase as we go down the group. Explain giving reason.

Ans. The stability of peroxide or superoxide increases as the size of metal ion increases, *i.e.*,

$$KO_2 < RbO_2 < CsO_2$$

The reactivity of alkali metals toward oxygen to form different oxides is due to strong positive field around each alkali metal cation. Li^+ is the smallest, it does not allow O^{2-} ion to react with O_2.

Further, Na^+ is larger than Li, its positive field is weaker than Li^+. It cannot prevent the conversion of O^{2-} into O_2^{2-}.

The largest K^+, Rb^+ and Cs^+ ions permit O_2^{2-} ion to react with O_2 forming superoxide ion O_2^-.

$$\underset{\text{Oxide}}{O_2^{2-}} \xrightarrow{\frac{1}{2}O_2} \underset{\text{Peroxide}}{O^{2-}} \xrightarrow{O_2} \underset{\text{Superoxide}}{2O_2^-}$$

Futhermore, increased stability of the peroxide or superoxide with increase in the size of metal ion is due to the stabilisation of large anions by larger cations through lattice energy effect.

Q.50 When water is added to compound (*A*) of calcium, solution of compound (*B*) is formed. When carbon dioxide is passed into the solution, it turns milky due to the formation of compound (*C*). If excess of carbon dioxide is passed into the solution milkiness disappears due to the formation of compound (*D*). Identify the compounds *A*, *B*, *C* and *D*. Explain why the milkiness disappears in the last step.

Ans. Appearance of milkiness on passing CO_2 through the solution of compound *B* indicates that compound *B* is lime water and compound *C* is $CaCO_3$. Since, compound *B* is obtained by adding H_2O to compound *A*, therefore, compound *A* is quicklime, CaO.

The reactions are as follows.

(i) $$\underset{\substack{\text{Calcium}\\\text{oxide}\\(A)}}{CaO} + H_2O \longrightarrow \underset{\substack{\text{Lime water}\\(B)}}{Ca(OH)_2}$$

(ii) $$\underset{(B)}{Ca(OH)_2} + CO_2 \longrightarrow \underset{\substack{\text{Calcium carbonate}\\\text{(Milky)}\\(C)}}{CaCO_3} + H_2O$$

(iii) When excess of CO_2 is passed, milkiness disappears due to the formation of soluble calcium bicarbonate (*D*).

$$\underset{\substack{\text{Milkiness}\\(C)}}{CaCO_3} + CO_2 + H_2O \longrightarrow \underset{\substack{\text{Calcium bicarbonate}\\(\text{Soluble in } H_2O)\\(D)}}{Ca(HCO_3)_2}$$

Q.51 Lithium hydride can be used to prepare other useful hydrides. Beryllium hydride is one of them. Suggest a route for the preparation of beryllium hydride starting from lithium hydride. Write chemical equations involved in the process.

Ans. BeH_2 can be prepared from the corresponding halides by the reduction with complex alkali metal hydrides such as lithium aluminium hydride, $LiAlH_4$.

$$8LiH + Al_2Cl_6 \longrightarrow 2LiAlH_4 + 6LiCl$$

$$2BeCl_2 + LiAlH_4 \longrightarrow 2BeH_2 + LiCl + AlCl_3$$

Q.52 An element of group 2 forms covalent oxide which is amphoteric in nature and dissolves in water to give an amphoteric hydroxide. Identify the element and write chemical reactions of the hydroxide of the element with an alkali and an acid.

Ans. The element is 'Be' and its oxide is BeO.

BeO is amphoteric while other oxides are basic in nature and react with water to form sparingly soluble hydroxides.

BeO dissolves both in acid and alkalis to give salt and is amphoteric.

$$BeO + H_2O \longrightarrow \underset{\substack{\text{Beryllium}\\\text{hydroxide}}}{Be(OH)_2}$$

$Be(OH)_2$ is an amphoteric hydroxide, dissolving in both acids and alkalies.

With alkalies, it dissolves to form the tetrahydroxidoberyllate anion with sodium hydroxide solution.

$$2\,NaOH(aq) + Be(OH)_2(s) \longrightarrow \underset{\text{Sodium tetrahydroxidoberyllate}}{Na_2Be(OH)_4(aq)}$$

With acids, it forms beryllium salts.

$$Be(OH)_2 + \underset{\text{Sulphuric acid}}{H_2SO_4} \longrightarrow \underset{\text{Beryllium sulphate}}{BeSO_4} + 2H_2O$$

Q.53 Ions of an element of group 1 participate in the transmission of nerve signals and transport of sugars and amino acids into cells. This element imparts yellow colour to the flame in flame test and forms an oxide and a peroxide with oxygen. Identify the element and write chemical reaction to show the formation of its peroxide. Why does the element impart colour to the flame?

Ans. Yellow colour flame in flame test indicates that the alkali metal must be sodium. It reacts with O_2 to form a mixture of sodium peroxide, Na_2O_2 and sodium oxide, Na_2O.

$$4Na + O_2 \xrightarrow{\Delta} 2Na_2O \text{ (Minor)}$$

$$2Na_2O + O_2 \xrightarrow{\Delta} 2\,Na_2O_2 \text{ (Major)}$$

$$2Na + O_2 \xrightarrow{\Delta} Na_2O_2$$

Ionisation enthalpy of sodium is low. When sodium metal or its salt is heated on Bunsen flame, the flame energy causes an excitation of the outermost electron which on reverting back to its initial position gives out the absorbed energy as visible light and complementary colour of absorbed colour from the light radiation is seen.

That's why sodium imparts yellow colour to the flame.

Chapter

11 The *p*-Block Elements*

Multiple Choice Questions (MCQs)

Q.1 The element which exists in liquid state for a wide range of temperature and can be used for measuring high temperature is

(a) B (b) Al (c) Ga (d) In

Ans. ***(c)*** In gallium, the crystal structure is different, suggesting that Ga consists of almost discrete Ga_2 molecule, that's why its melting point is lowest. Ga exists as liquid from 30°C upto 2000°C and hence, it is used in high temperature thermometry.

Q.2 Which of the following is a Lewis acid?

(a) $AlCl_3$ (b) $MgCl_2$ (c) $CaCl_2$ (d) $BaCl_2$

- **Concept Insight** Lewis acid represents those substances in which octet remains incomplete and act as electron acceptors.

Ans. ***(a)*** Alkaline earth metals form ionic chloride whereas aluminium chloride is covalent. Despite of sharing electrons with chlorine, the octet of aluminium is incomplete. To complete the octet, it needs electrons and thus, acts as a Lewis acid.

$$_{13}Al = 2, 8, 3 \text{ and } _{17}Cl = 2, 8, 7$$

```
      Cl
      |
Cl — Al — Cl
      ↑
Octet incomplete
```

Q.3 The geometry of a complex species can be understood from the knowledge of type of hybridisation of orbitals of central atom. The hybridisation of orbitals of central atom in $[B(OH_4)]^-$ and the geometry of the complex are respectively

(a) sp^3, tetrahedral (b) sp^3, square planar

(c) sp^3d^2, octahedral (d) dsp^2, square planar

Thinking Process Hybridisation and geometry of a complex can be found by counting number of bond pairs and lone pairs present in a central atom.

Note (*) *This chapter has been deleted from latest NCERT.*

Ans. ***(a)*** Structure of $[B(OH)_4]^-$ is

$$\begin{array}{c} OH \\ | \\ HO-B^--OH \\ | \\ OH \end{array}$$

4 bond pair + 0 lone pair

Hybridisation — sp^3
Geometry — Tetrahedral

Q.4 Which of the following oxides is acidic in nature?

(a) B_2O_3 (b) Al_2O_3 (c) Ga_2O_3 (d) In_2O_3

Ans. ***(a)*** The acidic nature of oxides changes from acidic to basic through amphoteric on moving down the group.

$$\underbrace{B_2O_3}_{\text{More acidic less basic}},\ \underbrace{Al_2O_3 \text{ and } Ga_2O_3}_{\text{Amphoteric}},\ \underbrace{In_2O_3 \text{ and } Tl_2O_3}_{\text{Basic}}$$

Hence, B_2O_3 is acidic in nature.

Q.5 The exhibition of highest coordination number depends on the availability of vacant orbitals in the central atom. Which of the following elements is not likely to act as central atom in MF_6^{3-}?

(a) B (b) Al (c) Ga (d) In

Ans. ***(a)*** Boron does not have vacant *d*-orbital. The element *M* in the complex ion MF_6^{3-} has a coordination number of six. Boron can show maximum coordination number of 4. Thus, B cannot form complex of the type MF_6^{3-}.

Q.6 Boric acid is an acid because its molecule

(a) contains replaceable H^+ ion
(b) gives up a proton
(c) accepts OH^- from water releasing proton
(d) combines with proton from water molecule

Ans. ***(c)*** Lewis acids are substances whose octet is incomplete and accepts electrons.

Boric acid [H_3BO_3 or $B(OH)_3$] is a monobasic weak acid. It does not liberate H^+ ion but accepts electrons from OH^- ion i.e. behaves as Lewis acid.

$$H_3BO_3 + H_2O \longrightarrow [B(OH)_4]^- + H^+$$

or,

$$B(OH)_3 + 2H_2O \longrightarrow [B(OH)_4]^- + H_3O^+$$

The structure of H_3BO_3 is as shown below, where the octet of boron in H_3BO_3 is incomplete.

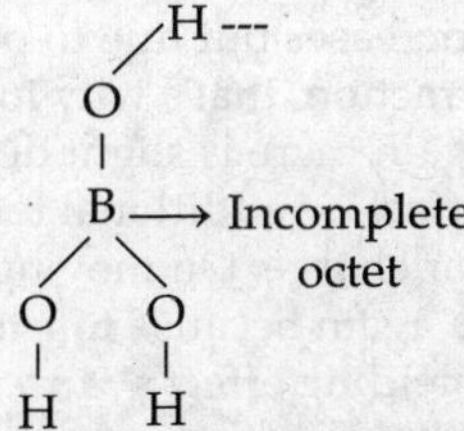

Q.7 Catenation, *i.e.*, linking of similar atoms depends on size and electronic configuration of atoms. The tendency of catenation in group 14 elements follows the order :

(a) C > Si > Ge > Sn (b) C >> Si > Ge ≈ Sn (c) Si > C > Sn > Ge (d) Ge > Sn > Si > C

Ans. ***(b)*** Catenation is the ability of an element to form covalent bonds with atoms of the same element to form long chains or rings. This property is especially prominent in carbon, which can form stable single, double, or triple bonds with other carbon atoms, resulting in a wide variety of compounds. Catenation depends on the strength of the element-element bond, and it decreases down the group in the periodic table.

$$C >> Si > Ge \approx Sn > Pb$$

This is due to high bond energy of C—C bonds. Down the group, size increases and electronegativity decreases, thereby, tendency to show catenation decreases.

Q.8 Silicon has a strong tendency to form polymers like silicones. The chain length of silicone polymer can be controlled by adding

(a) $MeSiCl_3$ (b) Me_2SiCl_2 (c) Me_3SiCl (d) Me_4Si

Ans. ***(c)*** The chain length of silicon polymer can be controlled by adding Me_3SiCl which block the ends as shown below

$$n\left(HO-\underset{CH_3}{\overset{CH_3}{\underset{|}{\overset{|}{Si}}}}-OH\right) + HO-\underset{CH_3}{\overset{CH_3}{\underset{|}{\overset{|}{Si}}}}-CH_3 \xrightarrow[-H_2O]{\text{Polymerisation}} -O\left(-\underset{CH_3}{\overset{CH_3}{\underset{|}{\overset{|}{Si}}}}-O-\right)_n\underset{CH_3}{\overset{CH_3}{\underset{|}{\overset{|}{Si}}}}-CH_3$$

Silicone

Q.9 Ionisation enthalpy ($\Delta_i H$ $kJmol^{-1}$) for the elements of group 13 follows the order.

(a) B > Al > Ga > In > Tl (b) B < Al < Ga < In < Tl

(c) B < Al > Ga < In > Tl (d) B > Al < Ga > In < Tl

Thinking Process Ionisation enthalpy ($\Delta_i H$) is the energy required to remove a valence electron. On moving down the group 13, due to an increase in atomic size and screening effect, ionization enthalpy changes irregularly.

Ans. ***(d)*** On moving from B to Al, the ionisation enthalpy decreases due to an increase in atomic size and decreasing nuclear attraction. On moving from Al to Ga, the ionisation enthalpy increases slightly, because on moving from Al to Ga, nuclear charge on valence electron increases but due to poor shielding by *d*-electron in Ga, resulting in *d*-block contraction, that's why ionisation enthalpies increase. On moving from Ga to In, again there is slight decrease in ionisation enthalpies due to increased shielding effect by additional ten 4*d* electrons, which outweighs the effect of increased nuclear charge. On moving from In to Tl, ionisation enthalpies show the increase again because fourteen 4*f* electrons shield valence electron poorly (order of shielding effect $s > p > d > f$) and so effective nuclear charge increases, consequently ionisation enthalpies increase.

Q.10 In the structure of diborane,

(a) All hydrogen atoms lie in one plane and boron atoms lie in a plane perpendicular to this plane
(b) 2 boron atoms and 4 terminal hydrogen atoms lie in the same plane and 2 bridging hydrogen atoms lie in the perpendicular plane
(c) 4 bridging hydrogen atoms and boron atoms lie in one plane and two terminal hydrogen atoms lie in a plane perpendicular to this plane
(d) All the atoms are in the same plane

Ans. ***(b)*** Boron is trivalent, so form simple hydride, BH_3. However, BH_3 is not stable. Due to incomplete octet, so BH_3 dimerises to form B_2H_6 molecule with covalent bond containing three centre 2-electron bond. The simplest boron hydride is diborane B_2H_6.

The geometry of B_2H_6 can be represented as

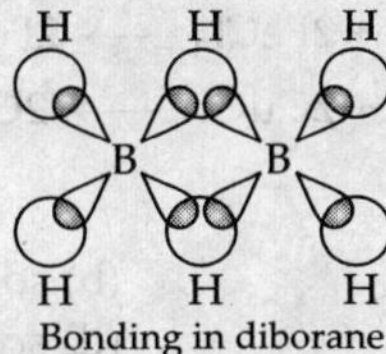

Bonding in diborane

The four terminal hydrogen atoms and two boron atoms lie one plane. Above and below the plane, there are two bridging hydrogen atoms. Each boron atom forms four bonds even though it has only three electrons. The terminal B—H bonds are regular bonds but the bridge B—H bonds are different.

Each bridged hydrogen is bonded to the two boron atoms only by sharing of two electrons. Such covalent bond is called three centre electron pair bond or a multi centre bond or banana bond.

Q.11 A compound *X*, of boron reacts with NH_3 on heating to give another compound *Y* which is called inorganic benzene. The compound *X* can be prepared by treating BF_3 with lithium aluminium hydride. The compounds *X* and *Y* are represented by the formulas.

(a) B_2H_6, $B_3N_3H_6$
(b) B_2O_3, $B_3N_3H_6$
(c) BF_3, $B_3N_3H_6$
(d) $B_3N_3H_6$, B_2H_6

Ans. ***(a)*** (i) Reaction of ammonia with diborane gives initially $B_2H_6 \cdot 2NH_3$ which is formulated as $[BH_2(NH_3)_2]^+[BH_4^-]$ further heating gives borazine, $B_3N_3H_6$ also called borazole.

$$\underset{\substack{\text{Diborane}\\(X)}}{3B_2H_6} + 6NH_3 \xrightarrow{473\text{ K}} \underset{\substack{\text{Borazine}\\(Y)}}{2B_3N_3H_6} + 12H_2$$

Borazole has cyclic structure and is isoelectronic and isosteric with benzene and thus called inorganic benzene or triborine triammine or borazine.

(ii) Diborane can be prepared by the reduction of BF_3 with lithium aluminium hydride in diethyl ether.

$$4BF_3 + 3LiAlH_4 \longrightarrow \underset{(X)}{2B_2H_6} + 3AlF_3 + 3LiF$$

Q.12 Quartz is extensively used as a piezoelectric material, it contains ....

(a) Pb (b) Si (c) Ti (d) Sn

- **Concept Insight** Quartz, cristobalite and tridymite are some of the crystalline forms of silica and they are interconvertable at suitable temperature.

Ans. *(b)* Quartz is extensively used as a piezoelectric material, it contains Si.

Q.13 The most commonly used reducing agent is

(a) $AlCl_3$ (b) $PbCl_2$
(c) $SnCl_4$ (d) $SnCl_2$

Thinking Process Reducing agents are those substances which reduces other substances and oxidises itself.

Ans. *(d)* In $SnCl_2$, Sn exists in +2 oxidation state, thus, acts as a strong reducing agent, *i.e.*

$$SnCl_2 + 2FeCl_3 \longrightarrow 2FeCl_2 + SnCl_4$$
$$SnCl_2 + 2CuCl_2 \longrightarrow 2CuCl + SnCl_4$$

Q.14 Dry ice is

(a) solid NH_3 (b) solid SO_2
(c) solid CO_2 (d) solid N_2

- **Concept Insight** Dry ice is also called cardice. It is obtained when CO_2 is cooled under pressure (50-60 atm). Dry ice is used for making cold baths in the laboratory by mixing it with volatile organic solvents. It is also used as a coolant for preserving perishable articles in food industry, curing local burns and in hospitals for surgical operation of sores.

Ans. *(c)* Carbon dioxide can be obtained as a solid in the form of dry ice allowing the liquified CO_2 to expand rapidly.

Q.15 Cement, the important building material is a mixture of oxides of several elements. Besides calcium, iron and sulphur, oxides of elements of which of the group (*s*) are present in the mixture?

(a) Group 2 (b) Groups 2, 13 and 14
(c) Groups 2 and 13 (d) Groups 2 and 14

Ans. *(b)* Cement is a product obtained by combining a material rich in lime, CaO with other material like clay which contains silica, SiO_2 alongwith the oxides of aluminium, iron and magnesium. The average composition of Portland cement is

CaO (50 – 60%)
SiO_2 (20 – 25%)
Al_2O_3 (5 – 10%)
Fe_2O_3 (1 – 2%)
SO_2 (1 – 2%)
MgO (2 – 3%).

Thus, it contains elements of group 2 (Ca), group 13 (Al) and group 14 (Si).

Multiple Choice Questions (More Than One Options)

Q.16 The reason for small radius of Ga compared to Al is ....

(a) poor screening effect of d and f-orbitals
(b) increase in nuclear charge
(c) presence of higher orbitals
(d) higher atomic number

Ans. ***(a, b)*** On moving down the group from Al to Ga, atomic radius decreases (exception) due to poor shielding or screening effect of d-electrons. On moving from Al to Ga, shielding effect in d-electrons is unable to compensate increased nuclear charge.

Hence, successive increase of atomic radius as expected is not observed.

Q.17 The linear shape of CO_2 is due to ....

(a) sp^3 hybridisation of carbon
(b) sp hybridisation of carbon
(c) $p\pi - p\pi$ bonding between carbon and oxygen
(d) sp^2 hybridisation of carbon

● **Concept Insight** Sigma bond is formed by $s-s$ overlap, $s-p$ overlap and $p-p$ overlapping. pi (π) bond is formed by $p-p$ overlapping.

Ans. ***(b, c)*** The structure of CO_2 is

$$\underset{sp-p\,(\sigma)}{\overset{p-p\,(\pi)}{O=C}}\;\underset{sp-p(\sigma)}{\overset{p-p\,(\pi)}{=O}}$$ is 2 sigma bonds and 2 pi bonds.

Hybridisation of CO_2 is sp and the shape is linear. Due to pi bond, it has $p\pi - p\pi$ bonding between carbon and oxygen.

Q.18 Me_3SiCl is used during polymerisation of organo silicones because

(a) chain length of organo silicone polymers can be controlled by adding Me_3SiCl
(b) Me_3SiCl blocks the end terminal of silicone polymer
(c) Me_3SiCl improves the quality and yield of the polymer
(d) Me_3SiCl acts as a catalyst during polymerisation

Ans. ***(a, b)*** The chain length of the polymer can be controlled by adding $(CH_3)_3SiCl$ which blocks the ends as shown below

$$(CH_3)_3SiCl \xrightarrow[-HCl]{H_2O} (CH_3)_3SiOH$$

$$n\left(HO-\underset{CH_3}{\overset{CH_3}{Si}}-OH\right) + HO-\underset{CH_3}{\overset{CH_3}{Si}}-CH_3 \xrightarrow[-H_2O]{\text{Polymerisation}} -O\left(\underset{CH_3}{\overset{CH_3}{Si}}-O\right)_n\underset{CH_3}{\overset{CH_3}{Si}}-CH_3$$

Silicone

Q.19 Which of the following statements are correct ?

(a) Fullerenes have dangling bonds
(b) Fullerenes are cage-like molecules
(c) Graphite is thermodynamically most stable allotrope of carbon
(d) Graphite is slippery and hard and therefore used as a dry lubricant in machines.

Ans. ***(b, c)*** Fullerene an allotrope of carbon with finite number of carbon atoms with closed cage structure. The C_{60} isotope is more dominants. The structure is nearly spherical, like football.

Sphere is formed by the combination of 20 hexagons and 12 pentagons. Graphite is thermodynamically more stable than all allotropes of carbon.

Q.20 Which of the following statements are correct? Answer on the basis of given figure.

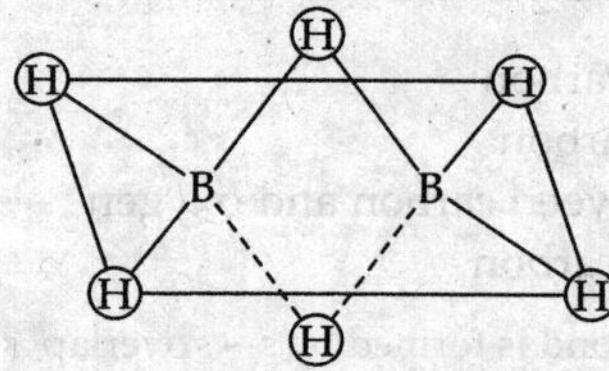

(a) The two bridged hydrogen atoms and the two boron atoms lie in one plane
(b) Out of six B—H bonds two bonds can be described in terms of 3 centre 2 electron bonds
(c) Out of six B—H bonds four B—H bonds can be described in terms of 3 centre 2 electron bonds
(d) The four terminal B—H bonds are two centre-two electron regular bonds

Ans. ***(a, b, d)*** In diborane, there are 12 valence electrons, three from each B-atom and six from H-atoms. Electron structure of diborone is shown in figure below.

H H H
B 1.34Å B 1.19Å
H H H

The two bridging H-atoms are in a plane perpendicular to the rest of the molecule and prevent rotation between the two B-atoms.

The terminal B—H distances are the same as the bond lengths measured in non-electron deficient compounds. These are assumed to be normal covalent bonds, with two electrons shared between two atoms. We can describe these bonds as two centre two electron bond ($2c—2e$).

Obviously, they are abnormal bonds as the two bridges involve only one electron, each from one of the boron atoms and hydrogen atoms, making a total of four electrons.

According to molecular orbital theory, each B-atom uses sp^3-hybrid orbitals for bonding. Out of the four sp^3-hybrid orbitals on each B-atom, one is without an electron shown in broken lines.

The terminal B—H bonds are normal 2 centre—2 electron bonds but the two bridge bonds are 3 centre—2 electron bonds. The 3-centre—2 electron bridge bonds are also called **banana bonds.**

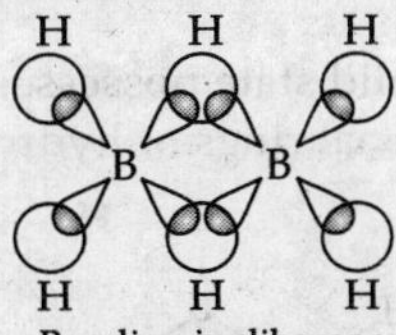

Bonding in diborane

Thus, statements in options (a), (b) and (d) are correct.

Q.21 Identify the correct resonance structures of carbon dioxide from the ones given below

(a) $O—C\equiv O$ (b) $O=C=O$ (c) $^{-}O\equiv C—O^{+}$ (d) $^{-}O—C\equiv O^{+}$

Thinking Process Resonance is the phenomenon in which a molecule or ion is represented by two or more Lewis structures, called resonating structures, which differ only in the arrangement of electrons (not atoms).

Ans. ***(b, d)*** The resonating structure of CO_2 are

$$O=C=O \leftrightarrow {}^{+}O\equiv C—O^{-} \leftrightarrow {}^{-}O—C\equiv O^{+}$$

Short Answer Type Questions

Q.22 Draw the structures of $BCl_3 \cdot NH_3$ and $AlCl_3$ (dimer).

Ans. In the BCl_3, due to small size of B^{3+}, BCl_3 is covalent (Fajan's rule). Still, the octet of B remains incomplete. In NH_3, N has a lone pair of electrons. Hence, N shares lone pair of electrons with B to complete the octet and BCl_3 acts as Lewis acid while NH_3 acts as Lewis bases.

Thus, when boron trichloride (BCl_3) reacts with ammonia (NH_3), it forms a **coordinate covalent compound** through Lewis acid-base interaction.

$$H_3N: + BCl_3 \longrightarrow H_3N \xrightarrow[\text{co-ordinate bond}]{} BCl_3 \text{ or } BCl_3 \cdot NH_3$$

$AlCl_3$ forms dimer by completing octet of Al involving *p*-orbitals to accept electron pair from chlorine.

Cl, Cl — Al — $\ddot{C}l$: + :$\ddot{C}l$ — Al — Cl, Cl ⟶ Cl, Cl — Al(—Cl—)$_2$Al — Cl, Cl (221pm, 206pm)

Q.23 Explain the nature of boric acid as a Lewis acid in water.

Ans. Orthoboric acid or boric acid is less soluble in cold water but highly soluble in hot water. It is a monobasic acid. It does not liberate H^+ ion but accepts OH^- from water, behaving as a Lewis acid.

$$H_3BO_3 + H_2O \longrightarrow [B(OH)_4]^- + H^+$$

The structure of H_3BO_3 is H—O—B(O—H)(O—H)

Octet of boron remains incomplete. Oxygen atom contains lone pair of electrons in water molecule. Hence, instead of donating proton (H^+), boric acid accepts OH^- from water forming $[B(OH)_4]^-$ to complete octet. Since, electron acceptor substance behaves as Lewis acid, therefore, boric acid acts as a Lewis acid in water.

Q.24 Draw the structure of boric acid showing hydrogen bonding. Which species is present in water ? What is the hybridisation of boron in this species ?

Ans. Orthoboric acid H_3BO_3, in solid state possesses a layer structure made up of $B(OH)_3$ units forming hexagonal rings of hydrogen-bonding as given below

Each H-atom acts as a bridge between two oxygen atoms of different BO_3^{3-} units.

Boric acid when dissolved in water, acts as Lewis acid forming $[B(OH)_4]^-$

$$H_3BO_3 + H_2O \longrightarrow [B(OH)_4]^- + H^+$$

The hybridisation of boron in $[B(OH)_4]^-$ is sp^3.

Q.25 Explain why the following compounds behave as Lewis acids ?

(a) BCl_3

(b) $AlCl_3$

Ans. As both (a) BCl_3 and (b) $AlCl_3$ hance an incomplete octet in their respective chlorides. Therefore, to complete the octet, both have the tendency to accept one lone pair from electron rich molecules to achieve stable electronic configuration and thus, act as a Lewis acids.

Q. 26 Give reasons for the following

(a) CCl_4 is immiscible in water, whereas $SiCl_4$ is easily hydrolysed.

(b) Carbon has a strong tendency for catenation compared to silicon.

Ans. (a) Carbon tetrachloride (CCl_4) is a covalent compound while H_2O is a polar compound. CCl_4 does not form hydrogen-bond with water molecule. Hence, it is immiscible in water like dissolves like.

Furthermore, CCl_4 is not hydrolysed by water because of the absence of *d*-orbitals in carbon while $SiCl_4$ is readily hydrolysed by water.

$$SiCl_4 + 4H_2O \longrightarrow \underset{\text{Silicic acid}}{Si(OH)_4} + 4HCl$$

The hydrolysis of $SiCl_4$ occurs due to coordination of OH^- with empty 3*d* orbitals in silicon atom of $SiCl_4$ molecule.

$$SiCl_4 + H_2\ddot{O} \longrightarrow Cl_4Si \leftarrow OH_2 \xrightarrow{-HCl} SiCl_3(OH) \xrightarrow[-3HCl]{+3H_2O} Si(OH)_4$$

(b) Carbon atoms have the tendency to link with one another through covalent bonds to form chains and rings. This property is called **catenation**. This is because C – C bonds are very strong. Down the group, the size increases, electronegativity decreases and thereby, tendency to show catenation decreases. Thus, carbon has a strong tendency for catenation as compared to silicon.

Q.27 Explain the following.

(a) CO_2 is a gas whereas SiO_2 is a solid.

(b) Silicon forms SiF_6^{2-} ion whereas corresponding fluoro compound of carbon is not known.

Ans. (a) Carbon has small size and high electronegativity, So its satisfies its tetravalancy by making one σ bond and one pπ – pπ bond with each oxygen atom in CO_2. Further CO_2 is linear shaped and has zero dipole moment. The CO_2 molecules are held together by weak vander walls forces so, CO_2 exists as a gas at room temperature.

(Si) has large size and low electrongativity, so it can not make pπ - pπ bond with oxygen atom. Now, to satisfy its tetravalency, each Si link to four oxygen atom (two oxygen atom of its (SiO_2) molecules and two oxygen atom of two other SiO_2 molecules) by single bond. As a result SiO_2 makes a 3-D network structure, making it a hard crystalline solid due to its extended covalent network.

(b) In silicon, vacant 3*d* orbitals are available due to which it can accomodate electrons from 6 fluorine atoms, thereby, forming SiF_6^{2-} ion. However, in case of Carbon, *d*-orbitals are not available and thus , it cannot expand its covalency more than 4. Thus, CCl_6^{2-} is not known.

Q.28 The +1 oxidation state in group 13 and +2 oxidation state in group 14 becomes more and more stable with increasing atomic number. Explain.

Ans. In Group 13, elements generally show a +3 oxidation state, but the +1 oxidation state becomes more stable as we move down the group from B→Tl. Similarly, in Group 14, the common oxidation state is +4, but the +2 oxidation state becomes more stable as we go from C→Pb.

This trend is due to the inert pair effect, which refers to the reluctance of the *s*-electrons (ns^2) in the valence shell to participate in bonding as atomic size increases. In heavier elements like Tl (Group 13) and Pb (Group 14), the ns^2 electrons remain non-bonding (inert) due to poor shielding by intervening d- and *f*-orbitals and increased effective nuclear charge. This makes the lower oxidation states (+1 for Group 13 and +2 for Group 14) more stable than the expected higher ones.

Q.29 Carbon and silicon both belong to the group 14, but inspite of the stoichiometric similarity, the dioxides, (*i.e.* carbon dioxide and silicon dioxide), differ in their structures . Comment.

Ans. All members of group 14 form dioxides of formula, MO_2, *i.e.*, for carbon, CO_2 and silica, SiO_2. CO_2 has a linear structure since, its dipole moment is zero. Both the oxygen atoms are linked by double bonds. The C-atom is *sp* hybridised.

$$\overset{p-p\,(\pi)}{\underset{sp-p\,(\sigma)}{O=}}C\overset{p-p(\pi)}{\underset{sp-p(\sigma)}{=O}}$$

However, C—O bond length is 1.15 Å, which is less than calculated value of C=O bond. Hence, it shows resonance hybrid of following structures.

$$O=C=O \longleftrightarrow O^{-}-C\equiv O^{+} \longleftrightarrow O\equiv C-O^{-}$$

But, the structure of silica is entirely different from that of CO_2. Si — O bonds have a considerable ionic character due to large electronegative difference between Si and O. As a result, silica has a three dimensional structure in which silica atom is tetrahedrally bonded to four oxygen atoms and each oxygen atom is bonded to two silicon atoms by covalent bonds.

There is no discrete SiO_2 molecule but entire crystal as a giant molecule. Si—O bonds are strong making it solid having high melting point.

Q.30 If a trivalent atom replaces a few silicon atoms in three dimensional network of silicon dioxide, what would be the type of charge on overall structure?

Ans. The structure of SiO_2 crystal is as

```
       |        |        |
     —Si — O — Si — O — Si—
       |        |        |
       O        O        O
       |        |        |
     —Si — O — Si — O — Si—
       |        |        |
```

When some Si-atoms are replaced by trivalent impurity, holes are created, which are equivalent to positive charge. These holes make the crystal structure as conductor of electricity.

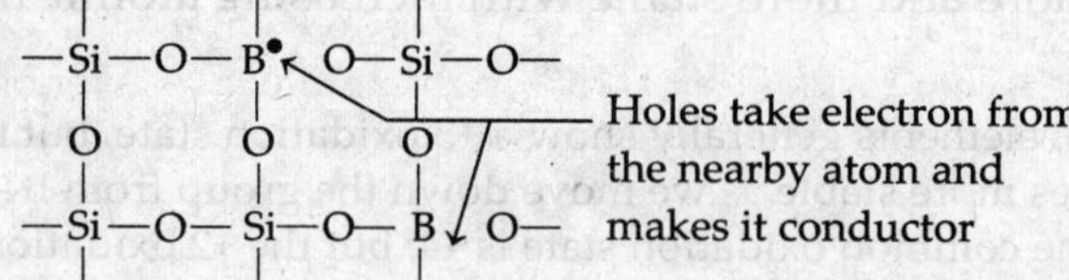

The resultant negative charge will be present on the overall structure.

An electron from a neighbouring atom can come and fill the electron hole, but in doing so it would leave an electron hole at its original position. If it happens, the electron hole has moved in the direction opposite to that of the electron.

Under the influence of electric field, electrons would move towards the positively charged plate through electronic holes, but it would appear as if electron holes are positively charged and are moving towards negatively charged plate. This type of semiconductors are called *p*-type semiconductors.

Q.31 When BCl_3 is treated with water, it hydrolyses and forms $[B[OH]_4]^-$ only whereas $AlCl_3$ in acidified aqueous solution forms $[Al[H_2O]_6]^{3+}$ ion. Explain what is the hybridisation of boron and aluminium in these species?

Ans. BCl_3 on hydrolysis in water form $[B(OH)_4]^-$ species, the hybridisation state of B is sp^3.

$$BCl + 3H_2O \longrightarrow B(OH)_3 + 3HCl$$

$$B(OH)_3 + H_2O \longrightarrow [B(OH)_4]^- + H^+$$

$AlCl_3$ in acidified aqueous solution form octahedral $[Al(H_2O)_6]^{3+}$ ion. In this complex, the 3*d* orbitals of Al are involved and the hybridisation state of Al is sp^3d^2.

$$AlCl_3 + H_2O \xrightarrow{HCl} [Al(H_2O)_6]^{3+} + 3Cl^- \ (aq)$$

	1s	2s	2p	3s	3p	3d
Electronic configuration of Al^{3+}	⇅	⇅	⇅ ⇅ ⇅	☐	☐ ☐ ☐	☐ ☐ ☐ ☐ ☐
Formation of $[Al(H_2O)_6]^{3+}$	⇅	⇅	⇅ ⇅ ⇅	×	× × ×	× × ☐ ☐ ☐

sp^3d^2 hybridisation

Q.32 Aluminium dissolves in mineral acids and aqueous alkalies and thus shows amphoteric character. A piece of aluminium foil is treated with dilute hydrochloric acid or dilute sodium hydroxide solution in a test tube and on bringing a burning matchstick near the mouth of the test tube, a pop sound indicates the evolution of hydrogen gas.

The same activity when performed with concentrated nitric acid, reaction doesn't proceed. Explain the reason.

Ans. Aluminium being amphoteric in nature dissolves both in acids and alkalies evolving H_2 gas which burns with a pop sound.

$$2Al + 6HCl \longrightarrow 2AlCl_3 + 3H_2$$

$$2Al + 2NaOH + 2H_2O \longrightarrow \underset{\text{Sodium meta aluminate}}{2NaAlO_2} + 3H_2$$

But when Al is treated with conc. HNO_3, a thin protective layer of Al_2O_3 is formed on its surface which prevents further action.

$$2Al + 6HNO_3 \longrightarrow Al_2O_3 + 6NO_2 + 3H_2O$$

Q.33 Explain the following.

(a) Gallium has higher ionisation enthalpy than aluminium.

(b) Boron does not exist as B^{3+} ion.

(c) Aluminium forms $[AlF_6]^{3-}$ ion but boron does not form $[BF_6]^{3-}$ ion.

(d) PbX_2 is more stable than PbX_4.

(e) Pb^{4+} acts as an oxidising agent but Sn^{2+} acts as a reducing agent.

(f) Electron gain enthalpy of chlorine is more negative as compared to fluorine.

(g) $Tl(NO_3)_3$ acts as an oxidising agent.

(h) Carbon shows catenation property but lead does not.

(i) BF_3 does not hydrolyse.

(j) Why does the element silicon, not form a graphite like structure whereas carbon does?

Ans. (a) In gallium, there is poor shielding of valence electrons by the 3*d* electrons. Thus, the nuclear charge becomes effective, thus, atomic radius decreases and hence, the ionisation enthalpy of gallium is higher than that of aluminium.

(b) Due to small size of boron, the sum of its first three ionisation enthalpies is very high. This prevents it to form +3 ions and forces it to form only covalent compound. That's why boron does not exist as B^{3+} ion.

(c) Aluminium forms $[AlF_6]^{3-}$ ion because of the presence of vacant *d*-orbitals, hence it can expand its coordination number from 4 to 6. In this complex, Al undergoes sp^3d^2 hybridisation.

On the other hand, boron does not form $[BF_6]^{3-}$ ion, because of the unavailability of *d*-orbitals as it cannot expand its coordination number beyond four. Hence, it can form $[BF_4]^-$ ion (sp^3 hybridisation).

(d) Due to inert pair effect, Pb in +2 oxidation state is more stable than in +4 oxidation state hence PbX_2 is more stable than PbX_4.

(e) Due to inert pair effect, tendency to form +2 ions increases down the group, hence Pb^{2+} is more stable than Pb^{4+}. That's why Pb^{4+} acts as an oxidising agent while Sn^{2+} is less stable than Sn^{4+} and hence, Sn^{2+} acts as a reducing agent.

$$\underset{\text{Reducing agent}}{Sn^{2+}} \longrightarrow Sn^{4+} + 2e^-$$

$$\underset{\text{Oxidising agent}}{Pb^{4+}} + 2e^- \longrightarrow Pb^{2+}$$

(f) Electron gain enthalpy of (Cl) chlorine is more negative than electron gain enthalpy of fluorine (F) because when an electron is added to F, the added electron goes to the smaller $n = 2$ quantum level and suffers significant repulsion from other electrons present in this level.

For $n = 3$ quantum level (in Cl) the added electron occupies a larger region of space and the electron-electron repulsion is much less.

(g) Due to inert pair effect, Tl in +1 oxidation state is more stable than that of+3 oxidation state. Therefore, $Tl(NO_3)_3$ acts as an oxidising agent.

(h) Property of catenation depends upon the atomic size of the element. Down the group, size increases and electronegativity decreases, thus the tendency to show catenation decreases. As the size of C is much smaller than Pb, therefore, carbon show property of catenation but lead does not show catenation.

(i) Unlike other boron halides, BF_3 does not hydrolyse completely. However, it form boric acid and fluoroboric acid. This is because the HF first formed reacts with H_3BO_3.

$$BF_3 + 3H_2O \longrightarrow H_3BO_3 + 3HF] \times 4$$
$$H_3BO_3 + 4HF \longrightarrow H^+[BF_4]^- + 3H_2O] \times 3$$
$$4BF_3 + 3H_2O \longrightarrow H_3BO_3 + 3[BF_4]^- + 3H^+$$

(j) In graphite, C is sp^2 hybridised. Carbon due to its smallest size and highest electronegativity among group 14 elements has strong tendency to form $p\pi - p\pi$ multiple bonds while silicon due to its larger size and less electronegativity has poor ability to form $p\pi - p\pi$ multiple bonds. That's why the element silicon does not form a graphite like structure.

Q.34 Identify the compounds *A*, *X* and *Z* in the following reactions.

$$A + 2HCl + 5H_2O \longrightarrow 2NaCl + X$$
$$X \xrightarrow[370\text{ K}]{\Delta} HBO_2 \xrightarrow[>370\text{ K}]{\Delta} Z$$

Ans. (i) $\underset{\text{Borax }(A)}{Na_2B_4O_7} + 2HCl + 5H_2O \longrightarrow 2NaCl + \underset{\text{Orthoboric acid }(X)}{4H_3BO_3}$

(ii) $\underset{(X)}{H_3BO_3} \xrightarrow{D,\ 370\text{ K}} \underset{\text{Metaboric acid}}{HBO_2} + H_2O$

(iii) $4HBO_2 \xrightarrow[-H_2O]{\Delta,\ >370\text{ K}} \underset{\text{Tetraboric acid}}{[H_2B_4O_7]} \xrightarrow[\text{Heat}]{\text{Red}} \underset{\text{Boron trioxide }(Z)}{2B_2O_3} + H_2O$

Q.35 Complete the following chemical equations.

$$Z + 3LiAlH_4 \longrightarrow X + 3LiF + 3AlF_3$$
$$X + 6H_2O \longrightarrow Y + 6H_2$$
$$X + 3O_2 \xrightarrow{\Delta} B_2O_3 + 3H_2O$$

Ans. (i) $\underset{(Z)}{4BF_3} + 3LiAlH_4 \longrightarrow \underset{\text{Diborane }(X)}{2B_2H_6} + 3LiF + 3AlF_3$

(ii) $\underset{(X)}{B_2H_6} + 6H_2O \longrightarrow \underset{\text{Orthoboric acid }(Y)}{2H_3BO_3} + 6H_2$

(iii) $\underset{(X)}{B_2H_6} + 3O_2 \xrightarrow{\Delta} B_2O_3 + 3H_2O$

Mistake Alert! *Students make mistake in balancing of chemical reactions.*

Matching The Columns

Q.36 Match the species given in Column I with the properties mentioned in Column II.

Column I	Column II
A. BF_4^-	1. Oxidation state of central atom is +4
B. $AlCl_3$	2. Strong oxidising agent
C. SnO	3. Lewis acid
D. PbO_2	4. Can be further oxidised
	5. Tetrahedral shape

Ans. **A.** → (5) **B.** → (3) **C.** → (4) **D.** → (1, 2)

A. BF_4^- → Tetrahedral shape with sp^3 hybridisation and regular geometry.

B. $AlCl_3$ → Octet not complete of Al, act as Lewis acid.

C. SnO → Sn^{2+} can show +4 oxidation state.

D. PbO_2 → Oxidation state of Pb in PbO_2 is +4. Due to inert pair effect Pb^{4+} is less stable than Pb^{2+}, acts as strong oxidising agent.

Q.37 Match the species given in Column I with properties given in Column II.

Column I	Column II
A. Diborane	1. Used as a flux for soldering metals
B. Gallium	2. Crystalline form of silica
C. Borax	3. Banana bonds
D. Aluminosilicate	4. Low melting, high boiling, useful for measuring high temperatures
E. Quartz	5. Used as catalyst in petrochemical industries

Ans. **A.** → (3) **B.** → (4) **C.** → (1) **D.** → (5) **E.** → (2)

A. BH_3 is unstable forms diborane B_2H_6 by 3 centre—2 electron bond show banana bond.

B. Gallium with low melting point and high boiling point makes it useful to measure high temperatures.

C. Borax is used as a flux for soldering metals for heat, scratch resistant coating in earthernwares.

D. Aluminosilicate used as catalyst in petrochemical industries.

E. Quartz is a crystalline form of silica.

Q.38 Match the species given in Column I with the hybridisation given in Column II.

	Column I		Column II
A.	Boron in $[B(OH_4)]^-$	1.	sp^2
B.	Aluminium in $[Al(H_2O)_6]^{3+}$	2.	sp^3
C.	Boron in B_2H_6	3.	sp^3d^2
D.	Carbon in buckminster fullerene		
E.	Silicon in SiO_4^{4-}		
F.	Germanium in $[GeCl_6]^{2-}$		

Ans. A.→ (2) B.→ (3) C.→ (2) D.→ (1) E.→ (2) F.→ (3)

A. Boron in $[B(OH)_4]^-$, sp^3 hybridised.
B. Aluminium in $[Al(H_2O)_6]^{3+}$, sp^3d^2 hybridised.
C. Boron in B_2H_6 sp^3, hybridised.
D. Carbon in Buckminster fullerene, sp^2 hybridised.
E. Silicon in SiO_4^{4-}, sp^3 hybridised.
F. Germanium in $[GeCl_6]^{2-}$, sp^3d^2 hybridised.

Assertion and Reason

In the following questions a statement of Assertion (A) *followed by a statement of Reason* (R) *is given. Choose the correct option out of the choices given below in each question.*

Q.39 **Assertion** (A) If aluminium atoms replace a few silicon atoms in three dimensional network of silicon dioxide, the overall structure acquires a negative charge.

Reason (R) Aluminium is trivalent while silicon is tetravalent.

(a) Both A and R are correct and R is the correct explanation of A
(b) Both A and R are correct but R is not the correct explanation of A
(c) Both A and R are not correct
(d) A is not correct but R is correct

Ans. ***(a)*** Both assertion and reason are correct and reason is the correct explanation of assertion.

In silicon dioxide (SiO_2), silicon is tetravalent (valency = 4). If some Si^{4+} ions are replaced by Al^{3+}. ions (which are trivalent), there is a deficiency of one positive charge for each substitution. To maintain electrical neutrality, the structure develops a net negative charge, usually balanced by extra cations like Na. or K.. This is the basis for formation of aluminosilicates (like zeolites).

Q. 40 **Assertion** (A) Silicones are water repelling in nature.

Reason (R) Silicones are organosilicon polymers, which have (—R_2SiO—) as repeating unit.

(a) A and R both are correct and R is the correct explanation of A
(b) Both A and R are correct but R is not the correct explanation of A
(c) A and R both are correct
(d) A is not correct but R is correct

Ans. *(b)* Both A and R are correct but R is not the correct explanation of A. Silicones are a group of organosilicon polymers which have (—R_2SiO—) as a repeating unit. This suggests that silicones are surrounded by non-polar alkyl groups that are water repelling in nature. They have wide applications. It is used for water proofing of fabrics.

Long Answer Type Questions

Q. 41 Describe the general trends in the following properties of the elements in groups 13 and 14.

(a) Atomic size (b) Ionisation enthalpy (c) Metallic character
(d) Oxidation states (e) Nature of halides

Ans. **For Group 13**

(a) **Atomic Size** On moving down the group for each successive member, one extra shell of electrons is added and therefore, atomic radius is expected to increase. However, a deviation can be seen.

Atomic radius of Ga is less than that of Al due to presence of additional 10*d* - electrons, which offer poor screening effect to the outer electron.

(b) **Ionisation Enthalpy** The ionisation enthalpy values as expected from general trends do not decrease smoothly down the group. The decrease from B to Al is associated with increase in size. The observed discontinuity between Al and Ga and between In and Tl is due to poor screening effect of *d* and *f*-electrons which compensates increased nuclear charge.

(c) **Metallic or Electropositive Character** Boron is a metalloid due to very high ionisation enthalpy. All others are metals and metallic character first increases from B to Al as size increases. From Al to Tl decrease due to poor shielding of *d*- and *f*-electrons.

(d) **Oxidation States** As we move down the group, the stability of +3 oxidation state decreases while that of + 1 oxidation state progressively increases. In other words, the order of stability of + 1 oxidation state increase in the order, Al < Ga < In < Tl. Infact, in Ga, In and Tl, both + 1 and + 3 oxidation states are observed.

(e) **Nature of Halides** These elements react with halogens to form trihalides (except TlI_3) $2E(s) + 3X_2(g) \longrightarrow 2EX_3\ (s)$ [X = F, Cl, Br, I]

Boron in halides are electron deficient molecules and behave as Lewis acids. The Lewis character decreases in the order : $BI_3 > BBr_3 > BCl_3 > BF_3$

For Group 14

(a) **Atomic Size** There is considerable increase in covalent radius from C to Si. Thereafter from Si to Pb a small increase in radius is observed. This is due to the presence of completely filled *d* and *f*- orbitals in heavier members.

(b) **Ionisation Enthalpy** The first ionisation enthalpy of group 14 members is higher than the corresponding members of group 13. The influence of inner core electrons is visible here. In general the ionisation enthalpy decreases down the group. Small decrease in ionisation enthalpy from Si to Ge to Sn and slight increase in ionisation enthalpy from Sn to Pb is the consequence of poor shielding effect of intervening *d* and *f*-orbitals and increase in size of the atom.

(c) **Metallic Character** Metallic character increases down the group C (non-metal) ,Si, Ge (metalloid), Sn, Pb (metals).

(d) **Oxidation States** The group 14 elements have four electrons in the outermost shell. The common oxidation states exhibited by these elements are +4 and +2. Carbon also exhibits negative oxidation states (for eg. in metal carbides). Since, the sum of the first four ionisation enthalpies is very high, compounds in +4 oxidation states are generally covalent in nature. In heavier members, the tendency to show +2 oxidation state increases in the order, Ge < Sn < Pb due to inert pair effect.

(e) **Nature of Halides** These elements can form halides of formula MX_2 and MX_4 (where, X = F, Cl, Br, I). Except carbon, all other members react directly with halogen under suitable condition to make halides. Most of MX_4 are covalent with sp^3 hybridisation and tetrahedral in structure. Exceptions are SnF_4 and PbF_4 which are ionic in nature. Heavier members Ge to Pb are able to make halides of formula MX_2. Stability of halides increases down the group.

Q. 42 Account for the following observations.

(a) $AlCl_3$ is a Lewis acid.

(b) Though fluorine is more electronegative than chlorine yet BF_3 is a weaker Lewis acid than Cl_3.

(c) PbO_2 is a stronger oxidising agent than SnO_2.

(d) The +1 oxidation state of thallium is more stable than its +3 state.

Ans. (a) In $AlCl_3$, Al has only six electrons in its valence shell an incomplete octet. This makes it electron-deficient and capable of accepting an electron pair from a donor (Lewis base) to complete its octet. Therefore, it acts as a Lewis acid (electron acceptor).

(b) In BF_3, boron has a vacant 2*p*-orbital and fluorine has one 2*p*-completely filled unutilised orbital. Both of these orbitals belong to same energy level therefore, they can overlap effectively and form $p\pi - p\pi$ bond. This type of bond formation is known as **back bonding.** While back bonding is not possible in BCl_3, because there is no effective overlapping between the 2*p*-orbital of boron and 3*p*-orbital of chlorine, which is larger and higher in energy. This size and energy mismatch leads to poor orbital overlap, making back bonding much less effective. Therefore, electron deficiency of B is higher in BCl_3 than that of BF_3. That's why BF_3 is a weaker Lewis acid than BCl_3.

2*p* orbital (Vacant) 2*p* orbital (Completely filled)

(c) In PbO_2 and SnO_2, both lead and tin are present in + 4 oxidation state. But due to stronger inert pair effect, Pb^{2+} ion is more stable than Sn^{2+} ion. In other words, Pb^{4+} ions, *i.e.* PbO_4 is more easily reduced to Pb^{2+} ions than Sn^{4+} ions reduced to Sn^{2+} ions. Thus, PbO_2 acts as a stronger oxidising agent than SnO_2.

(d) Tl^+ is more stable than Tl^{3+} because of inert pair effect. This is because the $6s^2$ electrons in thallium are held tightly by the nucleus due to poor shielding by inner *d*- and *f*-electrons, making them reluctant to participate in bonding. This reluctance to lose the *s*-electrons is known as the inert pair effect. Therefore, thallium commonly forms compounds in the +1 state, and its +3 compounds are relatively less stable and more oxidising, tending to revert to the +1 state.

Q.43 **When aqueous solution of borax is acidified with hydrochloric acid, a white crystalline solid is formed which is soapy to touch. Is this solid acidic or basic in nature ? Explain.**

Ans. When an aqueous solution of borax is acidified with HCl, boric acid is formed.

$$Na_2B_4O_7 + 2HCl + 5H_2O \longrightarrow 2NaCl + \underset{\text{Boric acid}}{4H_3BO_3}$$

Boric acid is a white crystalline solid. It is soapy to touch because of its planar layered structure. Boric acid is a weak monobasic acid. It is not a protonic acid but acts as a Lewis acid by accepting electrons from a hydroxyl ion.

$$B(OH)_3 + 2HOH \longrightarrow [B(OH)_4]^- + H_3O^+$$

Q. 44 **Three pairs of compounds are given below. Identify that compound in each of the pairs which has group 13 element in more stable oxidation state. Given reason for your choice. State the nature of bonding also.**

(a) $TlCl_3$, TlCl

(b) $AlCl_3$, AlCl

(c) $InCl_3$, InCl

Ans. (a) TlCl more stable than $TlCl_3$ due to inert pair effect. $TlCl_3$ is less stable and covalent in nature but TlCl is more stable and ionic in nature.

(b) Due to absence of *d*-orbitals, Al does not show inert pair effect. Hence, its most stable oxidation state is + 3. Thus, $AlCl_3$ is much more stable than AlCl. Further, in the solid or the vapour state, $AlCl_3$ is covalent in nature but in aqueous solutions, it ionises to form Al^{3+} (*aq*) and Cl^- (*aq*) ions.

(c) Due to inert pair effect, indium exists in both +1 and +3 oxidation states out of which +3 oxidation state is more stable than +1 oxidation state. In other words, $InCl_3$ is more stable than InCl. Being unstable, InCl undergoes disproportionation reaction.

$$3\,InCl\,(aq) \longrightarrow 2In(s) + In^{3+}(aq) + 3Cl^-(aq)$$

Q.45 **BCl_3 exists as monomer whereas $AlCl_3$ is dimerised through halogen bridging. Give reason. Explain the structure of the dimer of $AlCl_3$ also.**

Ans. Boron halides do not exist as dimer due to small size of boron atom which makes it unable to accommodate four large sized halide ions. $AlCl_3$ exists as dimer. Al makes use of vacant $3p$—orbital by coordinate bond, *i.e.* Al atoms complete their octet by forming dimers.

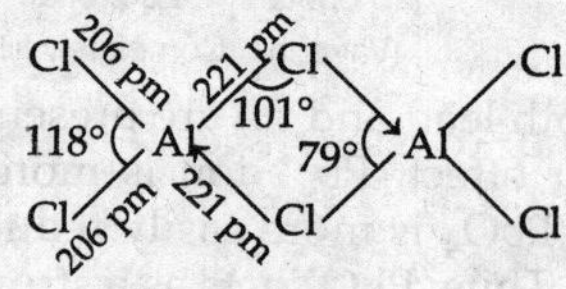

Dimer structure of $AlCl_3(Al_2Cl_6)$

Q.46 Boron fluoride exists as BF_3 but boron hydride doesn't exist as BH_3. Give reason. In which form does it exist ? Explain its structure.

Ans. Due to $p\pi - p\pi$ back bonding, the lone pair of electrons of F is donated to the empty *p*-orbital of B-atom. This delocalisation reduces the deficiency of electrons on B thereby increasing the stability of BF_3 molecule. Due to absence of lone pair of electrons on H-atom, in BH_3, electron deficiency is not compensated in BH_3. Hence, to reduce its electron deficiency, BH_3 dimerises to form B_2H_6.

In B_2H_6, four terminal hydrogen atoms and two boron atoms lie in one plane. Above and below this plane there are two bridging H–atoms. The four terminal B—H bonds are regular while the two bridge (B — H — B) bonds are three centre-two electron bonds.

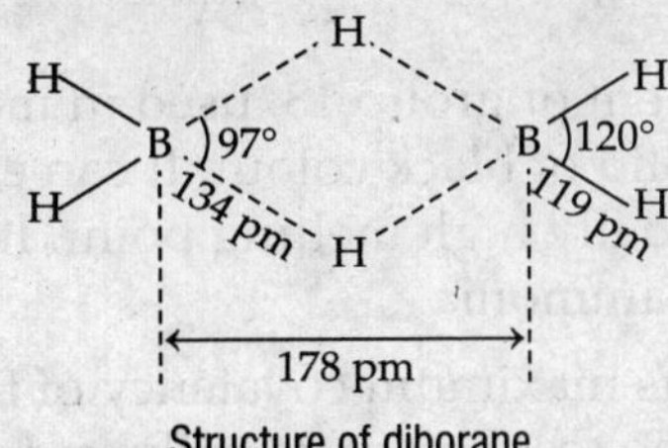

Structure of diborane

Q.47 (a) What are silicones? State the uses of silicones.

(b) What are boranes ? Give chemical equation for the preparation of diborane.

Ans. (a) Silicones are a group of organosilicon polymers, which have (R_2SiO) as a repeating unit. These may be linear silicones, cyclic silicones and cross-linked silicones.

These are prepared by the hydrolysis of alkyl or aryl derivatives of $SiCl_4$, like $RSiCl_3$, R_2SiCl_2, and R_3SiCl and polymerisation of alkyl or aryl hydroxy derivatives obtained by hydrolysis.

$$2CH_3Cl + Si \xrightarrow[570\text{ K}]{\text{Cu powder}} (CH_3)_2SiCl_2 \xrightarrow[+2H_2O,-2HCl]{\text{Hydrolysis}} (CH_3)_2Si(OH)_2$$

$$HO-\underset{CH_3}{\overset{CH_3}{Si}}-HO + HO-\underset{CH_3}{\overset{CH_3}{Si}}-OH \xrightarrow[-H_2O]{\text{Polymerisation}} -O\left(\underset{CH_3}{\overset{CH_3}{Si}}-O\right)_n\underset{CH_3}{\overset{CH_3}{Si}}-OH$$

Silicone

Uses

These are used as sealant, greases, electrical insulators and for water proofing of fabrics. These are also used in surgical and cosmetic plants.

(b) Boron forms a number of covalent hydrides with general formulae B_nH_{n+4} and B_nH_{n+6}. These are called boranes. B_2H_6 and B_4H_{10} are the representative compounds of the two series respectively.

Preparation of Diborane

It is prepared by treating boron trifluoride with $LiAlH_4$ in diethyl ether.

$$4BF_3 + 3LiAlH_4 \longrightarrow 2B_2H_6 + 3LiF + 3AlF_3$$

On industrial scale, it is prepared by the reaction of BF_3 with sodium hydride.

$$2BF_3 + 6NaH \xrightarrow{450\text{ K}} B_2H_6 + 6NaF$$

Q.48 A compound (A) of boron reacts with NMe_3 to give an adduct (B) which on hydrolysis gives a compound (C) and hydrogen gas. Compound (C) is an acid. Identify the compounds A, B, and C. Give the reactions involved.

Ans. Since, compound (A) of boron reacts with NMe_3 to form an adduct (B) thus, compound (A) is a Lewis acid. Since, adduct (B) on hydrolysis gives an acid (C) and hydrogen gas, therefore, (A) must be B_2H_6 and (C) must be boric acid.

$$\underset{\text{Diborane }(A)}{B_2H_6} + \underset{\text{Adduct }(B)}{2NMe_3} \longrightarrow \underset{\text{Adduct }(B)}{2BH_3NMe_3}$$

$$\underset{(B)}{BH_3 \cdot NMe_3} + 3H_2O \longrightarrow \underset{\text{Boric acid }(C)}{H_3BO_3} + NMe_3 + 6H_2$$

Q.49 A non-metallic element of group 13, used in making bullet proof vests is extremely hard solid of black colour. It can exist in many allotropic forms and has unusually high melting point. Its trifluoride acts as Lewis acid towards ammonia.

The element exihibits maximum covalency of four. Identify the element and write the reaction of its trifluoride with ammonia. Explain why does the trifluoride act as a Lewis acid?

Ans. The only non-metallic element of group 13 is boron. It is an extremely hard substance and is used in making bullet proof vests. It exists in many allotropic forms and has high melting point. Since B has only s and p-orbitals but no d-orbitals. The maximum covalency of boron is 4.
In trivalent state, the number of electrons around the central atom in a molecule will be six as in case of BF_3. Such electron deficient molecules have tendency to accept a pair of electron to achieve stable electronic configuration and behave as Lewis acid. BF_3 easily accepts lone pair of electron from NH_3 (Lewis base).

$$BF_3 + \ddot{N}H_3 \longrightarrow F_3B \leftarrow NH_3$$

Q.50 A tetravalent element forms monoxide and dioxide with oxygen. When air is passed over heated element (1273 K), producer gas is obtained. Monoxide of the element is a powerful reducing agent and reduces ferric oxide to iron.
Identify the element and write formulae of its monoxide and dioxide. Write chemical equations for the formation of producer gas and reduction of ferric oxide with the monoxide.

Ans. Producer gas is a mixture of CO and N_2, therefore, the tetravalent element is carbon and its monoxide and dioxide are CO and CO_2 respectively.

$$2C(s) + \underbrace{O_2(s) + 4N_2(g)}_{\text{Air}} \xrightarrow{1273\text{ K}} \underbrace{2CO(g) + 4N_2(g)}_{\text{Producer gas}}$$

The carbon monoxide is a strong reducing agent and reduces ferric oxide to iron.

$$Fe_2O_3(s) + 3CO(g) \xrightarrow{\Delta} 2Fe(s) + 3CO_2(g)$$

Chapter

12

Organic Chemistry : Some Basic Principles and Techniques

Multiple Choice Questions (MCQs)

Q.1 Which of the following is the correct IUPAC name?

(a) 3-ethyl-4, 4-dimethylheptane
(b) 4,4-dimethyl-3-ethylheptane
(c) 5-ethyl-4, 4-dimethylheptane
(d) 4,4-bis(methyl)-3-ethylheptane

Thinking Process Prefix di, tri, tetra are not included in alphabetical order.

Ans. *(a)* The structure is

$$CH_3—CH_2—CH_2—\underset{CH_3}{\overset{CH_3}{\overset{|}{\underset{|}{C}}}}—\underset{C_2H_5}{\underset{|}{CH}}—CH_2—CH_3$$

3-ethyl-4, 4-dimethylheptane

While writing IUPAC name, alkyl groups are written in alphabetical priority, thus lower locant 3 is assigned to ethyl.

Q.2 The IUPAC name for $CH_3—\overset{\overset{O}{\|}}{C}—CH_2—CH_2—\overset{\overset{O}{\|}}{C}—OH$ is

(a) 1-hydroxypentane-1,4-dione
(b) 1,4-dioxopentanol
(c) 1-carboxybutan-3-one
(d) 4-oxopentanoic acid

- **Concept Insight** When more than one functional group is present, then the main chain, nomenclature is done according to that functional group which has higher priority. Carboxylic acid (— COOH) has more priority than ketone ($>C=O$)

Ans. *(d)* $\overset{5}{C}H_3—\overset{\overset{O}{\|}}{\overset{4}{C}}—\overset{3}{C}H_2—\overset{2}{C}H_2—\overset{\overset{O}{\|}}{\overset{1}{C}}—OH$

4-oxopentanoic acid

Q.3 The IUPAC name for

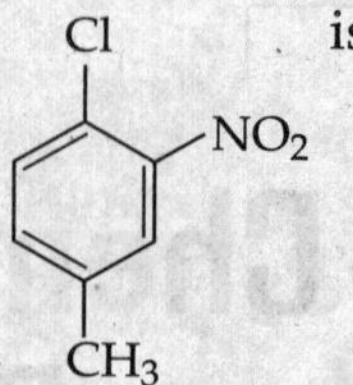

is

(a) 1-chloro-2-nitro-4-methylbenzene (b) 1-chloro-4-methyl-2-nitrobenzene
(c) 2-chloro-1-nitro-5-methylbenzene (d) *m*-nitro-*p*-chlorotoluene

Ans. ***(b)*** For tri or higher substituted benzene derivatives, the compounds are named by identifying substituent, positions on the ring by following the lowest locant rule.

Substituent of the base compound is assigned number 1 and then the direction of numbering is chosen such that the next substituent gets the lowest number. The substituents appear in the name in alphabetical order.

Cl
1
NO_2
2
3
4
CH_3

1-chloro-4-methyl-2-nitrobenzene

Mistake Alert ! *Students may not numbering the carbon chain correctly to give the lowest possible locants to functional groups.*

Q.4 Electronegativity of carbon atoms depends upon their state of hybridisation. In which of the following compounds, the carbon marked with asterisk is most electronegative?

(a) $CH_3—CH_2—{}^*CH_2—CH_3$ (b) $CH_3—{}^*CH{=}CH—CH_3$
(c) $CH_3—CH_2—C{\equiv}CH$ (d) $CH_3—CH_2—CH{=}{}^*CH_2$

Ans. ***(c)*** Electronegativity of carbon atom depends on percentage of *s*-character in hybrid orbital. More *s*-character, more will be the electronegativity.

$$sp^3 < sp^2 < sp$$
$$25\%\ s \quad 33\%\ s \quad 50\%\ s$$

Carbon-linked to a triple bond is *sp* hybridised and *sp*-carbon has the highest electronegativity, *i.e.*, option (c) ($CH_3—CH_2—C\equiv{}^*CH$) is correct.

Q.5 In which of the following, functional group isomerism is not possible?

(a) Alcohols (b) Aldehydes (c) Alkyl halides (d) Cyanides

● **Concept Insight** Two or more compounds having the same molecular formula but different functional groups are called functional isomers.

Ans. ***(c)*** Functional isomer of alcohol is ether.
Functional isomer of aldehyde is ketone.
Functional isomer of cyanide is isocyanide
However, alkyl halides do not show functional isomerism. Hence, option (c) is correct.

Q.6 The fragrance of flowers is due to the presence of some steam volatile organic compounds called essential oils. These are generally insoluble in water at room temperature but are miscible with water vapour in vapour phase. A suitable method for the extraction of these oils from the flowers is

(a) distillation
(b) crystallisation
(c) distillation under reduced pressure
(d) steam distillation

Thinking Process Steam distillation technique is applied to separate substances which are steam volatile and immiscible with water.

Ans. ***(d)*** Essential oils are insoluble in water and have high vapour-pressure at 373K but are miscible with water-vapour in vapour phase, it means these are steam volatile. Hence, steam distillation technique is used for the extraction of essential oils.

Q.7 During hearing of a court case, the judge suspected that some changes in the documents had been carried out. He asked the forensic department to check the ink used at two different places. According to you which technique can give the best results?

(a) Column chromatography
(b) Solvent extraction
(c) Distillation
(d) Thin layer chromatography

Ans. ***(d)*** Thin layer chromatography (TLC) involves separation of substances of a mixture over a thin layer of an adsorbent coated on a glass plate.

A thin layer of an adsorbent is spread over a glass plate and glass plate is placed in an eluant. As eluant rises, components of the mixture move up along with the eluant to different distances depending on their degree of adsorption and separation takes place.

Therefore, TLC technique will give best results in identifying the different types of ink used at different places in the documents.

Q.8 The principle involved in paper chromatography is

(a) adsorption (b) partition
(c) solubility (d) volatility

Ans. ***(b)*** Partition chromatography is based on continuous differential partioning of components of a mixture between stationary and mobile phases. Paper chromatography is a type of partition chromatography.

Hence, the principle involved in paper chromatography is partition.

Q.9 What is the correct order of decreasing stability of the following cations.

$$\underset{\text{I}}{CH_3-\overset{\oplus}{C}H-CH_3} \qquad \underset{\text{II}}{CH_3-\overset{\oplus}{C}H-OCH_3}$$

$$\underset{\text{III}}{CH_3-\overset{\oplus}{C}H-CH_2-OCH_3}$$

(a) II > I > III (b) II > III > I (c) III > I > II (d) I > II > III

Ans. *(a)* Stability of the given cations can be understood by the following structures

$$\underset{\text{I}}{CH_3 \rightarrow \overset{+}{C}H \leftarrow CH_3} \; ; \; \underset{\text{II}}{CH_3-\overset{+}{C}H \curvearrowleft \ddot{\underset{\cdot\cdot}{O}}-CH_3} \; ; \; \underset{\text{III}}{CH_3-\overset{+}{C}H \rightarrow CH_2 \rightarrow OCH_3}$$

Weak + *I*-effect of the two methyl groups stabilises carbocation (I)

Strong + *R*-effect of $-OCH_3$ group stabilises carbocation (II)

$-I$-effect of $-OCH_3$ group destabilises the carbocation (III)

Hence, the stability of carbocation decreases in the order II > I > III

Q.10 Correct IUPAC name for $H_3C-\underset{C_2H_5}{\underset{|}{C}H}-\underset{C_2H_5}{\underset{|}{C}H}-CH_3$ is ....

(a) 2-ethyl-3-methylpentane (b) 3, 4-dimethylhexane

(c) 2-*sec*-butylbutane (d) 2, 3-dimethylbutane

- **Concept Insight** "Apply IUPAC rules to identify the longest carbon chain and number it such that substituents get the lowest possible locants."

Ans. *(b)*

$$H_3C-\overset{4}{C}H-\overset{3}{C}H-\overset{1}{C}H_3$$

with $\overset{5}{C}H_2-\overset{6}{C}H_3$ on C-4 and $\overset{2}{C}H_2-\overset{1}{C}H_3$ on C-3

3, 4-dimethylhexane

Q.11 In which of the following compounds the carbon marked with asterisk is expected to have greatest positive charge?

(a) $^*CH_3-CH_2-Cl$ (b) $^*CH_3-CH_2-Mg^+Cl^-$

(c) $^*CH_3-CH_2-Br$ (d) $^*CH_3-CH_2-CH_3$

Thinking Process When a more electronegative atom is attached to carbon, the shared pair of electron moves towards more electronegative atom. Carbon has less electron density and gains partial positive charge.

Ans. *(a)* Electronegativity of Cl, Br, C and Mg follows the order Cl > Br > C > Mg

$$^*CH_3 \rightarrow CH_2 \rightarrow Cl \qquad [-I\text{-effect}]$$

$$^*CH_3 \leftarrow CH_2 \leftarrow Mg^+Cl^-$$

$$^*CH_3 \rightarrow CH_2 \rightarrow Br \qquad [-I\text{-effect}]$$

$$^*CH_3-CH_2-CH_3 \qquad [+I\text{-effect}]$$

–I effect of Cl > Br.

Hence, CH_3-CH_2-Cl has the greatest positive charge.

Q.12 Ionic species are stabilised by the dispersal of charge. Which of the following carboxylate ion is the most stable?

(a) $CH_3—\overset{O}{\overset{||}{C}}—O^-$ (b) $Cl—CH_2—\overset{O}{\overset{||}{C}}—O^-$

(c) $F—CH_2—\overset{O}{\overset{||}{C}}—O^-$ (d) $\begin{matrix}F \\ F\end{matrix}\rangle CH—\overset{O}{\overset{||}{C}}—O^-$

● **Concept Insight** "Electronegative substituents with stronger –*I* effect increase charge delocalization, thus making the ion more stable."

Ans. ***(d)*** In all the given carbocations, the negative charge is dispersed which stabilises these carbocations. Here, the negative charge is dispersed by two factors, *i.e.*, +*R*-effect of the carboxylate ion (conjugation) and *I*-effect of the halogens.

These effects are shown below in the carbocations

(a) $CH_3 \rightarrow \overset{O}{\overset{||}{C}} - O^{\ominus} \longleftrightarrow CH_3 \rightarrow \overset{O^{\ominus}}{\overset{|}{C}}=O \equiv CH_3 \rightarrow C\overset{O}{\underset{O}{\ominus}}$

(b) $Cl \leftarrow CH_2 \leftarrow \overset{O}{\overset{||}{C}} - O^{\ominus} \longleftrightarrow Cl \leftarrow CH_2 \leftarrow \overset{O^{\ominus}}{\overset{|}{C}}=O \equiv Cl \leftarrow CH_2 \leftarrow C\overset{O}{\underset{O}{\ominus}}$

(c) $F \leftarrow CH_2 \leftarrow \overset{O}{\overset{||}{C}} - O^{\ominus} \longleftrightarrow F \leftarrow CH_2 \leftarrow \overset{O^{\ominus}}{\overset{|}{C}}=O \equiv F \leftarrow CH_2 \leftarrow C\overset{O}{\underset{O}{\ominus}}$

(d) $\begin{matrix}F \\ F\end{matrix}\rangle CH \leftarrow \overset{O}{\overset{||}{C}} - O^{\ominus} \longleftrightarrow \begin{matrix}F \\ F\end{matrix}\rangle CH \leftarrow \overset{O^{\ominus}}{\overset{|}{C}}=O \equiv \begin{matrix}F \\ F\end{matrix}\rangle CH \leftarrow C\overset{O}{\underset{O}{\ominus}}$

As it is clear from the above structures, that +*R*-effect is common in all the four structures, therefore, overall dispersal of negative charge depends upon the number of halogen atoms and electronegativity. Since, F has the highest electronegativity and two F-atoms are present in option (d), thus, dispersal of negative charge is maximum in option (d).

Note In above structure (a), methyl group (CH_3) increases the density on C-atom.

Q.13 Electrophilic addition reactions proceed in two steps. The first step involves the addition of an electrophile. Name the type of intermediate formed in the first step of the following addition reaction.

$H_3C—HC=CH_2 + H^+ \longrightarrow ?$

(a) 2° carbanion (b) 1° carbocation (c) 2° carbocation (d) 1° carbanion

● **Concept Insight** Stability of carbocations is the basis of Markovnikov's rule.

Ans. ***(c)*** When electrophile attacks $CH_3—CH=CH_2$ delocalisation of electrons can take place, in two possible ways

$$CH_3—CH=CH_2 + H^+ \longrightarrow \underset{2^\circ \text{ carbocation}}{CH_3—\overset{\oplus}{C}H—CH_3} + \underset{1^\circ \text{ carbocation}}{CH_3—CH_2—\overset{\oplus}{C}H_2}$$

As 2° carbocation is more stable than 1° carbocation thus, first addition is more feasible. The type of intermediate formed in the first step of the following addition reaction is a 2° carbocation.

Q.14 Covalent bond can undergo fission in two different ways. The correct representation involving a heterolytic fission of $CH_3—Br$ is

(a) $CH_3—Br \longrightarrow \overset{\oplus}{C}H_3 + Br^{\ominus}$ (b) $CH_3—Br \longrightarrow \overset{\oplus}{C}H_3 + Br^{\ominus}$

(c) $CH_3—Br \longrightarrow \overset{\ominus}{C}H_3 + Br^{\oplus}$ (d) $CH_3—Br \longrightarrow \dot{C}H_3 + \dot{B}r$

Thinking Process Homolytic fission gives free radical whereas heterolytic fission gives carbocation or carbanion.

Ans. ***(b)*** Arrow denotes the direction of movement of electrons in the options. Since, Br is more electronegative than carbon, hence heterolytic fission occurs towards Br. So, CH_3 gets the positive charge and Br gets the negative charge. Thus, option (b) is correct.

Q.15 The addition of HCl to an alkene proceeds in two steps. The first step is the attack of H^+ ion to $>C=C<$ portion which can be shown as

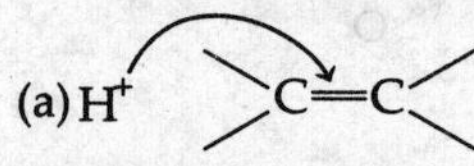

(b) $H^+ \leftarrow >C=C<$

(a) $H^+ >C=C<$ (d) All of these are possible

Ans. ***(b) Step*** I π-bonds creates an electron cloud, which attacks over electrophile (H^+). And, a carbocation is formed.

$$H^+ \; >C=C< \;\longleftrightarrow\; >\overset{+}{C}-\underset{\underset{H}{|}}{C}<$$

Step II The chloride anion attacks the carbocation.

$$>\overset{\oplus}{C}-\underset{\underset{H}{|}}{C}< + Cl^- \longrightarrow >\underset{\underset{Cl}{|}}{C}-\underset{\underset{H}{|}}{C}<$$

Multiple Choice Questions (More Than One Options)

Q.16 Which of the following compounds contain all the carbon atoms in the same hybridisation state?

(a) $H—C\equiv C—C\equiv C—H$ (b) $CH_3—C\equiv C—CH_3$

(c) $CH_2=C=CH_2$ (d) $CH_2=CH—CH=CH_2$

Ans. ***(a, d)*** Hybridisation of carbon atoms in different compounds is shown below

(a) $\underset{sp}{HC}\equiv\underset{sp}{C}-\underset{sp}{C}\equiv\underset{sp}{CH}$ (b) $\underset{sp^3}{CH_3}-\underset{sp}{C}\equiv\underset{sp}{C}-\underset{sp^3}{CH_3}$

(c) $\underset{sp^2}{CH_2}=\underset{sp}{C}=\underset{sp^2}{CH_2}$ (d) $\underset{sp^2}{CH_2}=\underset{sp^2}{CH}-\underset{sp^2}{CH}=\underset{sp^2}{CH_2}$

In options (a) and (d), all carbon atoms are in same hybridisation state, *i.e.*, in *sp* and sp^2 hybridisation respectively.

Q.17 In which of the following representations given below spatial arrangement of group/atom different from that given in structure '*A*'?

(A) [C with CH_3 up, Cl (dashed), H, Br (wedge)]

(a) [C with CH_3 up, Cl (dashed), Br, H (wedge)]
(b) [C with CH_3 up, H (dashed), Br, Cl (wedge)]
(c) [C with CH_3 up, Br (dashed), H, Cl (wedge)]
(d) [C with Br up, Cl (dashed), H, H_3C (wedge)]

Thinking Process The spatial arrangement of group/atom can be checked by doing two interchanges of groups/atoms and then by bringing H below the plane of the paper. Then find out the sequence of the remaining groups in a particular order whether clockwise or anti-clockwise starting from atom with highest atomic number towards atoms with lower atomic numbers.

Ans. (a, c, d)

(A) [CH_3, Cl, H, Br] — 1st interchange (Cl ⟶ H) → [CH_3, H, Cl, Br] — 2nd interchange (Br ⟶ Cl) → [CH_3, H, Br, Cl] (Clockwise)

Now, check all the options.

(a) [CH_3, Cl, Br, H] — 1st interchange (Cl ⟶ H) → [CH_3, H, Br, Cl] — 2nd interchange (Cl ⟶ Br) → [CH_3, H, Cl, Br] (Anti-clockwise)

(b) [CH_3, H, Br, Cl] No need of interchange, as it is already arranged, clockwise.

(c) [CH_3, Br, H, Cl] — 1st interchange (Br ⟶ H) → [CH_3, H, Br, Cl] — 2nd interchange (Cl ⟶ Br) → [CH_3, H, Cl, Br] (Anti-clockwise)

(d)

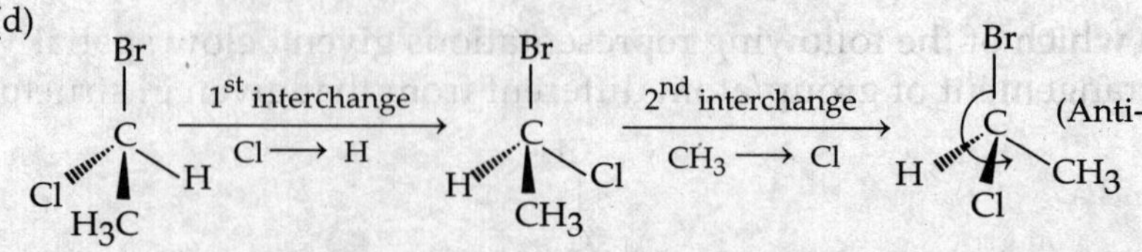

$$\text{Br-C(Cl)(H)(H_3C)} \xrightarrow[\text{Cl} \longrightarrow \text{H}]{1^{st}\text{ interchange}} \text{Br-C(H)(Cl)(CH_3)} \xrightarrow[\text{CH}_3 \longrightarrow \text{Cl}]{2^{nd}\text{ interchange}} \text{Br-C(H)(CH_3)(Cl)} \text{ (Anti-clockwise)}$$

Hence, only option (b) has same spatial arrangement of group/atom as in (A), *i.e.*, clockwise, while in rest of the options (a), (c) and (d) it is different, *i.e.*, anti-clockwise.

Q.18 Electrophiles are electron seeking species. Which of the following groups contain only electrophiles?

(a) BF_3, NH_3, H_2O (b) $AlCl_3, SO_3, NO_2^+$

(c) $NO_2^+, CH_3^+, CH_3-C^+{=}O$ (d) $C_2H_5^-, \dot{C}_2H_5, C_2H_5^+$

Thinking Process Electrophiles are electron deficient species. Hence, they are molecules with incomplete octet and ions with positive charge.

Ans. ***(b, c)*** All $AlCl_3, SO_3$ (Lewis acids), $NO_2^+, CH_3^+, CH_3-\overset{+}{C}=O$ are electron deficient species. Hence, these are electrophiles.

Direction (Q. No. 19-20) Consider the following four compounds.

$$\text{(I) } CH_3-CH_2-CH_2-CH_2-\overset{O}{\overset{\|}{C}}-H$$

$$\text{(II) } CH_3-CH_2-CH_2-\overset{O}{\overset{\|}{C}}-CH_3$$

$$\text{(III) } CH_3-CH_2-\underset{O}{\underset{\|}{C}}-CH_2-CH_3$$

$$\text{(IV) } CH_3-\underset{CH_3}{\underset{|}{CH}}-CH_2-\underset{O}{\underset{\|}{C}}-H$$

Q.19 Which of the following pairs are position isomers?

(a) I and II (b) II and III (c) II and IV (d) III and IV

Ans. ***(b)*** When two or more compounds differ in the position of substituent atom or functional group on the carbon skeleton, they are called position isomers.

$$CH_3-CH_2-CH_2-\overset{O}{\overset{\|}{C}}-CH_3 \quad \text{(II)}$$

$$CH_3-CH_2-\underset{O}{\underset{\|}{C}}-CH_2-CH_3 \quad \text{(III)}$$

Here, position of $-\underset{O}{\underset{\|}{C}}-$ varies. Thus, II and III are position isomers.

Q.20 Which of the following pairs are not functional group isomers?

(a) II and III (b) II and IV
(c) I and IV (d) I and II

Ans. ***(a, c)*** Two or more compounds having the same molecular formula but different functional groups are called functional isomers.

I. Aldehyde II. Ketone
III. Ketone IV. Aldehyde

Here, II and III; I and IV are not functional group isomers. Thus, option (a) and (c) are correct.

Q.21 Nucleophile is a species that should have

(a) a pair of electrons to donate
(b) positive charge
(c) negative charge
(d) electron deficient species

Ans. ***(a, c)*** Nucleophile (nucleus-loving) are chemical species that donates an electron pair to an electrophile (electron-loving). Hence, a nucleophile should have either a negative charge or an electron pair to donate. Thus, option (a) and (c) are correct.

Q.22 Hyperconjugation involves delocalisation of ....

(a) electrons of carbon-hydrogen σ bond of an alkyl group directly attached to an atom of unsaturated system.
(b) electrons of carbon-hydrogen σ bond of alkyl group directly attached to the positively charged carbon atom.
(c) π-electrons of carbon-carbon bond
(d) lone pair of electrons.

Ans. ***(a, b)*** Hyperconjugation is the delocalisation of sigma electron also known as **sigma-pi conjugation.** Presence of $\alpha - H$ with respect to double bond, triple bond or carbon containing positive charge (in carbonium ion) or unpaired electron (in free radical) is a condition for hyperconjugation.

$$H-\underset{H}{\overset{H}{\underset{|}{\overset{|}{C}}}}-CH=CH_2 \leftrightarrow H-\underset{H}{\overset{H^{\oplus}}{\underset{|}{C}}}=CH-\overset{\ominus}{C}H_2 \leftrightarrow H^{\oplus}\ \underset{H}{\overset{H}{\underset{|}{\overset{|}{C}}}}=CH-\overset{\ominus}{C}H_2 \leftrightarrow$$

$$H-\underset{H^{\oplus}}{\overset{H}{\overset{|}{C}}}=CH-\overset{\ominus}{C}H_2$$

Short Answer Type Questions

Direction (Q. No. 23 to 26) Consider structures I to VII.

I. $CH_3—CH_2—CH_2—CH_2—OH$

II. $CH_3—CH_2—\underset{\displaystyle OH}{\underset{|}{CH}}—CH_3$

III. $CH_3—\overset{\displaystyle CH_3}{\overset{|}{\underset{\displaystyle OH}{\underset{|}{C}}}}—CH_3$

IV. $CH_3—\underset{\displaystyle CH_3}{\underset{|}{CH}}—CH_2—OH$

V. $CH_3—CH_2—O—CH_2—CH_3$

VI. $CH_3—O—CH_2—CH_2—CH_3$

VII. $CH_3—O—\underset{\displaystyle CH_3}{\underset{|}{CH}}—CH_3$

Q.23 Which of the above compounds form pairs of metamers?

Ans. Metamerism arises due to different alkyl chains on either side of the functional group in the molecule. In the given structures V and VI or VI and VII form a pair of metamers because they differ in carbon atoms on the either side of the functional group, *i.e.*, O-atom.

$$\left.\begin{array}{ll} \text{V. } CH_3—CH_2—O—CH_2—CH_3 & \text{ethoxy ethane} \\ \text{VI. } CH_3—O—CH_2—CH_2—CH_3 & \text{methoxy propane} \end{array}\right\}\text{Metamers}$$

$$\left.\begin{array}{ll} \text{VI. } CH_3—O—CH_2—CH_2—CH_3 & \text{methoxy propane} \\ \text{VII. } CH_3—O—\underset{\displaystyle CH_3}{\underset{|}{CH}}—CH_3 & \text{methoxy isopropane} \end{array}\right\}\text{Metamers}$$

Q.24 Identify the pairs of compounds which are functional group isomers.

Ans. Two or more compounds having the same molecular formula but different functional groups are called functional isomers.

In the given structure I, II, III, IV represent alcohols as functional group, whereas V, VI, VII are ethers.

Hence, I and V, I and VI, I and VII, II and V, II and VI, II and VII, III and V, III and VI, III and VII, IV and V, IV and VI, IV and VII all are functional group isomers.

Q.25 Identify the pairs of compounds that represents position isomerism.

- **Concept Insight** When two or more compounds differ in position of substituent atom or functional group on the carbon skeleton, they are position isomers.

Ans. In the given structures, I and II; III and IV, and VI and VII are position isomers.

I. $CH_3-CH_2-CH_2-CH_2-OH$ (butan-1-ol) and II. $CH_3-CH_2-CH(OH)-CH_3$ (butan-2-ol)

III. $CH_3-C(CH_3)(OH)-CH_3$ (2-methylpropan-2-ol)

IV. $CH_3-CH(CH_3)-CH_2-OH$ (2-methylpropan-1-ol)

VI. $CH_3-O-CH_2-CH_2-CH_3$ (Methoxypropane) and VII. $CH_3-O-CH(CH_3)-CH_3$ (Methoxyisopropane or methoxy 1-methylethane)

Q.26 Identify the pairs of compounds that represents chain isomerism.

Ans. When two or more compounds have similar molecular formula but different skeletons, these are referred to as chain isomer.

In the following structure

I. $CH_3-CH_2-CH_2-CH_2-OH$ (Butan-1-ol)

III. $CH_3-C(CH_3)(OH)-CH_3$ (2-methylpropan-2-ol)

II. $CH_3-CH_2-CH(OH)-CH_3$ (Butan-2-ol)

IV. $CH_3-CH(CH_3)-CH_2-OH$ (2-methylpropan-1-ol)

I and III, I and IV, II and III, II and IV are chain isomers.

Q.27 For testing halogens in an organic compound with $AgNO_3$ solution, sodium extract (Lassaigne's test) is acidified with dilute HNO_3. What will happen if a student acidifies the extract with dilute H_2SO_4 in place of dilute HNO_3?

Thinking Process Nitrogen, sulphur, halogens and phosphorous present in an organic compound are detected by Lassaigne's test. The elements in compound are converted from covalent to ionic form fused with sodium metal.

Ans. On adding dilute H_2SO_4 for testing halogens in an organic compound with $AgNO_3$, white precipitate of Ag_2SO_4 is formed. This will interfere with the test of chlorine and this Ag_2SO_4 may be mistaken for white precipitate of chlorine as AgCl. Hence, dilute HNO_3 is used instead of dilute H_2SO_4.

$$2AgNO_3 + H_2SO_4 \longrightarrow Ag_2SO_4 + 2HNO_3$$

Q.28 What is the hybridisation of each carbon in $H_2C{=}C{=}CH_2$?

Ans. The given structure is of allene (C_3H_4)

$$\overset{1}{H_2C}{=}\overset{2}{C}{=}\overset{3}{CH_2}$$

In allene, carbon atoms 1 and 3 are sp^2-hybridised as each one of them is joined by one double bond. And, carbon atom 2 is *sp*-hybridised as it has two double bonds at each of its side. Therefore, the two π-bonds are perpendicular to each other, in allene, as shown below.

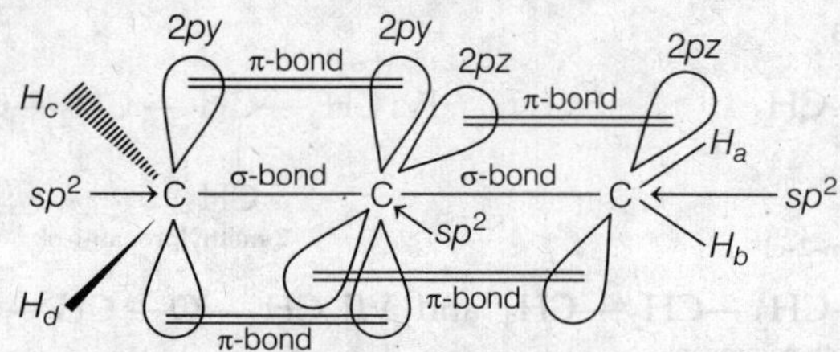

H_a and H_b lie in the plane of paper while H_c and H_d lie in a plane perpendicular to the plane of the paper. Hence, the allene molecule as a whole is non-planar.

Q.29 Explain, how is the electronegativity of carbon atoms related to their state of hybridisation in an organic compound?

Ans. Electronegativity of carbon atom, also depends on the hybridisation of the carbon atom. Since, *s*-electrons are more strongly attracted by the nucleus than *p*-electrons, thus, electronegativity increases with increase in *s*-character of the hybridised orbital, *i.e.*,

25%	33.3%	50%	s-character
sp^3 <	sp^2 <	sp	Hybridisation

Increasing order of % *s*-character →
Increasing order of electronegativity

Thus, *sp*-hybridised carbon is the most electronegative carbon.

Q.30 Show the polarisation of carbon-magnesium bond in the following structure.

$$CH_3—CH_2—CH_2—CH_2—Mg—X$$

Ans. Carbon (2.5) is more electronegative than magnesium (1.2) therefore, Mg acquires a partial positive charge while carbon attached to it acquires a partial negative charge.

$$CH_3—CH_2—CH_2—\overset{-\delta}{C}H_2 \leftarrow \overset{+\delta}{Mg}—X$$

Q.31 Compounds with same molecular formula but differing in their structures are said to be structural isomers. What type of structural isomerism is shown by

$$CH_3-S-CH_2-CH_2-CH_3 \text{ and } CH_3-S-CH{<}^{CH_3}_{CH_3}$$

Ans. The two isomers which differ in the position of the functional group on the carbon skeleton are called position isomers and this phenomenon is known as position isomerism.

Thus, (*A*) and (*B*) may be regarded as position isomers.

$$\underset{\text{Methyl-n-propylthioether (A)}}{CH_3-S-\overset{1}{C}H_2-\overset{2}{C}H_2-\overset{3}{C}H_3} \qquad \underset{\text{Isopropylthioether (B)}}{CH_3-S-\overset{2}{C}H(\overset{1}{C}H_3)-\overset{3}{C}H_3}$$

Q.32 Which of the following selected chains is correct to name the given compound according to IUPAC system?

$$CH_3-CH(CH_2-CH_3)-CH_2-CH(CH_2-CH_2-OH)-C(=O)-OH$$

4 carbon chain

7 carbon chain

5 carbon chain

6 carbon chain

Ans. Among the following given compounds, according to IUPAC, the longest carbon chain having maximum number of functional group is being selected. Thus, 4 carbon chain is selected for IUPAC naming.

$$CH_3-CH(CH_2-CH_3)-CH_2-\boxed{CH(CH_2-CH_2-OH)-C(=O)-OH}$$

Q.33 In DNA and RNA, nitrogen atom is present in the ring system. Can Kjeldahl method be used for the estimation of nitrogen present in these? Give reasons.

Ans. DNA and RNA have nitrogen in the heterocyclic rings. Nitrogen present in rings, azo and nitro groups cannot be converted into $(NH_4)_2SO_4$. That's why Kjeldahl method cannot be used for the estimation of nitrogen present in DNA and RNA.

Q.34 If a liquid compound decomposes at its boiling point, which method (s) can you choose for its purification. It is known that the compound is stable at low pressure, steam volatile and insoluble in water.

Ans. If a compound decomposes at its boiling point but is steam volatile, water-insoluble and stable at low pressure, steam distillation can be used for its purification. This technique is applied to separate substances which are steam volatile and immiscible with water.

Direction (Q. No. 35-38) On the basis of information given below "Stability of carbocations depends upon the electron releasing inductive effect of groups adjacent to positively charged carbon atom involvement of neighbouring groups in hyperconjugation and resonance."

Q.35 Draw the possible resonance structures for $CH_3—\ddot{\underset{\cdot\cdot}{O}}—\overset{+}{C}H_2$ and predict which of the structures is more stable. Give reason for your answer.

Ans. The given carbocation has two resonance structures.

$$\underset{\text{I}}{CH_3—\ddot{\underset{\cdot\cdot}{O}}—\overset{+}{C}H_2} \longleftrightarrow \underset{\text{II}}{CH_3—\overset{+}{\underset{\cdot\cdot}{O}}{=}CH_2}$$

Structure (II) is more stable because both the carbon atoms and the oxygen atom have octet of electrons.

Q.36 Which of the following ions is more stable? Use resonance to explain your answer.

(A) $\overset{\oplus}{C}H_2$ attached to cyclohexene ring (endocyclic double bond) $\longleftrightarrow$ (B) CH_2 exocyclic double bond with $\oplus$ on ring carbon

Ans. Carbocation (A) is more stable than carbocation (B). Carbocation (A) is more planar and double bond is present in ring endocyclic. So, 'A' is stable while (B) has double bond outside ring exocyclic.

(A) $\overset{+}{C}H_2$ on cyclohexene $\longleftrightarrow$ (B) $=CH_2$ exocyclic, $+$ on ring

Q.37 The structure of triphenylmethyl cation is given below. This is very stable and some of its salts can be stored for months. Explain the cause of high stability of this cation.

$\overset{\oplus}{C}$

Ans. In triphenylmethyl cation, due to resonance, the positive charge can move at both the *o*- and *p*-position of each benzene ring. This is illustrated below

I

+ Six more such structures are possible due to other two benzene rings.

II III

Since, there are three benzene rings, hence, there are, in all, nine resonance structures.

Thus, triphenylmethyl cation is highly stable due to these nine resonance structures.

Q.38 Write structures of various carbocations that can be obtained from 2-methylbutane. Arrange these carbocations in order of increasing stability.

Ans. 2-methylbutane has four different sets of equivalent H-atoms.

$$CH_3-\underset{\underset{CH_3}{|}}{CH}-CH_2-CH_3$$

Removal of 1-1-1 atom from any of these equivalent sets gives four different carbocations.

$$CH_3 \rightarrow \underset{\underset{CH_3}{\uparrow}}{\overset{b}{CH}} \rightarrow \overset{a}{CH_2} \rightarrow \overset{+}{CH_2} \quad \text{(I) (1°)}$$

$$CH_3 \rightarrow \underset{\underset{CH_3}{|}}{CH} \rightarrow \overset{+}{CH} \leftarrow CH_3 \quad \text{(II) (2°)}$$

$$CH_3 \rightarrow \underset{\underset{CH_3}{\uparrow}}{\overset{+}{C}} \leftarrow CH_2-CH_3 \quad \text{(III) (3°)}$$

$$\overset{+}{CH_2} \leftarrow \underset{\underset{CH_3}{\uparrow}}{CH} \leftarrow CH_2-CH_3 \quad \text{(IV) (1°)}$$

Stability of carbocation decreases in the order 3°> 2°> 1°. So, III D 3° carbocation is most stable followed by II (2°carbocation). Out of I and IV (both are 1° carbocation) I has a —CH_3 group at β-carbon while II has a —CH_3 group at α-carbon. As +*I*-effect decreases with distance, hence IV is more stable than I. Therefore, the overall stability of these four carbocations increases in the order.

I < IV < II < III

Q.39 Three students, Manish, Ramesh and Rajni were determining the extra elements present in an organic compound given by their teacher. They prepared the Lassaigne's extract (L.E.) independently by the fusion of the compound with sodium metal. Then they added solid $FeSO_4$ and dilute sulphuric acid to a part of Lassaigne's extract. Manish and Rajni obtained prussian blue colour but Ramesh got red colour.

Ramesh repeated the test with the same Lassaigne's extract, but again got red colour only. They were surprised and went to their teacher and told him about their observation. Teacher asked them to think over the reason for this. Can you help them by giving the reason for this observation. Also, write the chemical equations to explain the formation of compounds of different colours.

Ans. If the organic compound contains both N and S, then while fusion it may form either a mixture of sodium cyanide (NaCN) and sodium sulphide (Na_2S) or sodium thiocyanate (NaSCN) depending on the amount of Na metal used.

If less sodium metal is used, only NaSCN is obtained which gives red colour on reacting with Fe^{3+} ions (produced by oxidation of Fe^{2+} ions while preparing Lassaigne's extract) due to the formation of ferric thiocyanate.

$$Fe^{2+} \xrightarrow{\text{Aerial oxidation}} Fe^{3+}$$

$$Fe^{3+} + 3NaSCN \longrightarrow \underset{\substack{\text{Ferric thiocyanate} \\ \text{(red)}}}{Fe(SCN)_3} + 3Na^{+}$$

In case, excess of sodium metal is used, the initally formed sodium thiocyanate decomposes as follows:

$$\underset{\substack{\text{Sodium} \\ \text{thiocyanate}}}{NaSCN} + 2Na \xrightarrow{\Delta} \underset{\substack{\text{Sodium} \\ \text{cyanide}}}{NaCN} + \underset{\substack{\text{Sodium} \\ \text{sulphide}}}{Na_2S}$$

This NaCN then reacts with $FeSO_4$, Fe^{3+} ions and NaCN, it gives prussian blue colour due to the formation of ferric ferrocyanide or iron (III) hexacyanoferrate (II).

$$2NaCN + FeSO_4 \longrightarrow Na_2SO_4 + Fe(CN)_2$$

$$Fe(CN)_2 + 4NaCN \longrightarrow \underset{\substack{\text{Sodium hexacyano–} \\ \text{ferrate (II).}}}{Na_4[Fe(CN)_6]}$$

$$3Na_4[Fe(CN)_6] + 4Fe^{3+} \longrightarrow \underset{\substack{\text{Iron (III) hexacyanoferrate} \\ \text{(II) (prussian blue)}}}{Fe_4[Fe(CN)_6]_3} + 12\,Na^{+}$$

On the basis of above results, it is clear that Ramesh used less sodium and hence NaSCN formed in the Lassaigne's extract which gave red colouration due to $Fe(SCN)_3$ formation while Manish and Rajni used excess sodium and hence, NaCN formed in the Lassaigne's extract which gave prussian blue colour of $Fe_4[Fe(CN)_6]_3$.

Q.40 Name the compounds whose line formulae are given below :

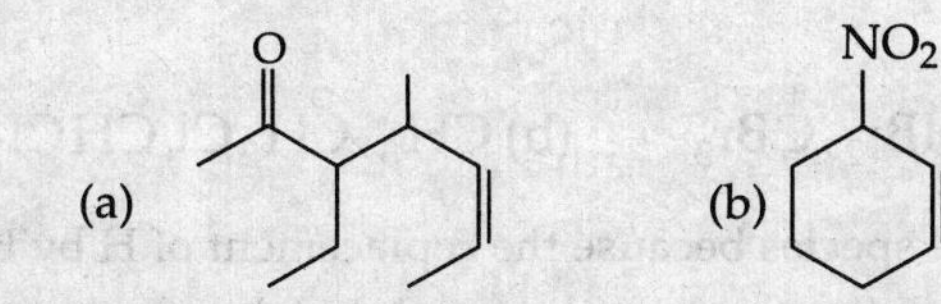

Ans.

(a) 3-ethyl-4-methylhept-5-en-2-one (longest possible chain are numbered in a way that the functional group, >C = O, gets the lowest possible locant)

(b) 3-nitrocyclohex-1-ene (C-atoms of the ring are numbered in such a manner that double bond gets the lowest possible locant followed by the $-NO_2$ group)

Q.41 Write structural formulae for compounds named as

(a) 1-bromoheptane (b) 5-bromoheptanoic acid

Ans. (a) $\overset{7}{C}H_3-\overset{6}{C}H_2-\overset{5}{C}H_2-\overset{4}{C}H_2-\overset{3}{C}H_2-\overset{2}{C}H_2-\overset{1}{C}H_2-Br$

1-bromoheptane

(b) $\overset{7}{C}H_3-\overset{6}{C}H_2-\overset{5}{C}H(Br)-\overset{4}{C}H_2-\overset{3}{C}H_2-\overset{2}{C}H_2-\overset{1}{C}(=O)-O-H$

5-bromoheptanoic acid

Q.42 Draw the resonance structures of the following compounds.

(a) $CH_2=CH-\ddot{\underset{..}{Cl}}:$

(b) $CH_2=CH-CH=CH_2$

(c) $CH_2=CH-C(H)=O$

Ans.

(a) $CH_2=CH-\ddot{Cl}: \longleftrightarrow :\bar{C}H_2-CH=\overset{+}{Cl}:$

(b) $CH_2=CH-CH=CH_2 \longleftrightarrow \overset{+}{C}H_2-CH=CH-\bar{C}H_2 \longleftrightarrow :\bar{C}H_2-CH=CH-\overset{+}{C}H_2$

(c) $CH_2=CH-C(=O)-H \longleftrightarrow \overset{+}{C}H_2-CH=C(-\ddot{O}:^-)-H$

Q.43 Identify the most stable species in the following set of ions giving reasons :

(a) $\overset{+}{C}H_3, \overset{+}{C}H_2Br, \overset{+}{C}HBr_2, \overset{+}{C}Br_3$ (b) $\overset{\ominus}{C}H_3, \overset{\ominus}{C}H_2Cl, \overset{\ominus}{C}HCl_2, \overset{\ominus}{C}Cl_3$

Ans. (a) $\overset{+}{C}H_3$ is the most stable species because the replacement of H by Br increases positive charge (–*I*-effect) on carbon atom and destabilises the species and, more the number of Br-atoms, less stable is the species.

(b) $\overset{\ominus}{C}Cl_3$ is the most stable species because on replacing H by Cl, negative charge on carbon is dispersed due to –*I*-effect of Cl and thus, get reduced and species is stabilised. Further, more the number of Cl atoms, more is the dispersal of the negative charge and hence, more stable is the species.

Q.44 Give three points of differences between inductive effect and resonance effect.

Ans. Difference between inductive effect and resonance effect is as follows

S.No.	Inductive effect	Resonance effect
1.	Inductive effect involves σ – electrons displacement and occurs only in saturated compounds.	It involves π – electrons or lone pair of electrons and occurs only in unsaturated and conjugated system.
2.	Inductive effect can move upto 3 – carbon atoms.	It is applicable all along the length of conjugated system.
3.	In inductive effect, there is a slight displacement of electrons and thus only partial positive and negative charges appear.	In resonance effect, there is complete transfer of electrons and thus, full positive and negative charges appear.

Q.45 Which of the following compounds will not exist as resonance hybrid. Give reason for your answer.

(a) CH_3OH
(b) $R—CONH_2$
(c) $CH_3CH=CHCH_2NH_2$

Ans. (a) $\mathbf{CH_3OH}$ As it lacks π-electrons, hence, it will not exist as resonance hybrid.

(b) $\mathbf{R-CONH_2}$ Due to the presence of electrons on nitrogen and π-electrons on bond, amide can be represented as a resonance hybrid of the following three resonating structures.

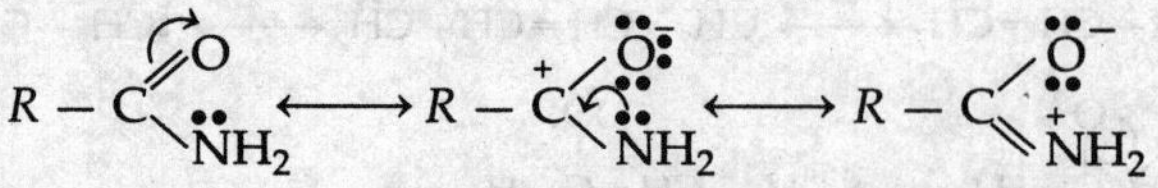

$$R-C(=O)-\ddot{N}H_2 \longleftrightarrow R-\overset{+}{C}(-\ddot{O}:^-)-\ddot{N}H_2 \longleftrightarrow R-C(-O^-)=\overset{+}{N}H_2$$

I II III

(c) $\mathbf{CH_3CH=CHCH_2NH_2}$ As the lone pair of electrons on the N-atom is not conjugated with the π-electrons of the double bond, thus, resonance is not possible and hence, no resonance hybrid will exist.

Q.46 Why does SO_3 act as an electrophile?

Ans. Three highly electronegative oxygen atoms are attached to sulphur atom in SO_3 which makes sulphur atom electron-deficient.

Further, due to resonance, sulphur acquires positive charge. Both these factors, make SO_3 an electrophile.

$$O{=}S({=}O){=}O \longleftrightarrow O{=}\overset{+}{S}({=}O)\text{–}\overset{-}{O} \longleftrightarrow \overset{-}{O}\text{–}\overset{+}{S}({=}O)\text{–}O \longleftrightarrow O{=}\overset{+}{S}(\text{–}\overset{-}{O}){=}O$$

Q.47 Resonance structures of propenal are given below. Which of these resonating structures is more stable? Give reason for your answer.

$$\underset{\text{I}}{CH_2{=}CH{-}CH{=}O} \longleftrightarrow \underset{\text{II}}{\overset{\oplus}{C}H_2{-}CH{=}CH{-}\overset{\ominus}{O}}$$

Ans. Structure I is more stable. The structure having more covalent bonds in a resonating structure, has more stability. Further, there is charge separation in structure (II) and the terminal carbon has only a sextet of electrons in (II), i.e., an incomplete octet. These two factors makes structure (II) less stable.

$$\underset{\text{I}}{CH_2{=}CH{-}CH{=}O} \longleftrightarrow \underset{\text{II}}{\overset{\oplus}{C}H_2{-}CH{=}CH{-}\overset{\ominus}{O}}$$

Hence, I > II in terms of stability.

Q.48 By mistake, an alcohol (boiling point 97°C) was mixed with a hydrocarbon (boiling point 68°C). Suggest a suitable method to separate the two compounds. Explain the reason for your choice.

Ans. To separate a mixture of an alcohol (b.p. 97°C) and a hydrocarbon (b.p. 68°C), the most suitable method is simple distillation. This method relies on the principle that the component with the lower boiling point vaporises first. Here, the hydrocarbon will vaporise and condense before the alcohol, which remains in the distillation flask. Since the boiling point difference exceeds 25°C, simple distillation allows efficient and effective separation. This ensures a clean separation with no contamination of one component by the other.

Q.49 Which of the two structures (*A*) and (*B*) given below is more stabilised by resonance. Explain

$$\underset{(A)}{CH_3COOH} \text{ and } \underset{(B)}{CH_3CO\overset{\ominus}{O}}$$

Ans. Resonating structures of (*A*) and (*B*) are as follows

$$\text{(A)}\ CH_3-\overset{\overset{\ddot{O}:}{\|}}{C}-\ddot{O}H \longleftrightarrow CH_3-\overset{\overset{:\ddot{O}:^-}{|}}{C}=\overset{+}{\ddot{O}}H$$

$$\text{I} \qquad\qquad \text{II}$$

$$\text{(B)}\ CH_3-\overset{\overset{\ddot{O}:^-}{\|}}{C}-\ddot{O}: \longleftrightarrow CH_3-\overset{\overset{:\ddot{O}:^-}{|}}{C}=\ddot{O}:$$

$$\text{III} \qquad\qquad \text{IV}$$

Structure (II) is less stable than structure (I) because later carries separation of positive and negative charges. Therefore, contribution of structure (II) is less than that of (I) towards the resonance hybrid of compound (*A*), *i.e.* CH_3COOH which is nautral hence more stable. On contrary, structure (III) and (IV) are of equal energy and hence, contribute equally towards the resonance hybrid of compound (*B*). Therefore, structure (*B*), *i.e.*, CH_3COO^- is more stable than structure (*A*), as it does not involve charge separation and shows equivalent resonance.

Note ***Equivalent resonance*** *structures are those which have the same energy, same arrangement of atoms, and differ only in the position of electrons (p or lone pairs). These structures contribute equally to the resonance hybrid and provide maximum resonance stabilization.*

Matching The Columns

Q.50 Match the type of mixture of compounds in Column I with the technique of separation/purification given in column II.

	Column I		Column II
A.	Two solids which have different solubilities in a solvent and which do not undergo reaction when dissolved in it	1.	Steam distillation
B.	Liquid that decomposes at its boiling point	2.	Fractional distillation
C.	Steam volatile liquid	3.	Simple distillation
D.	Two liquids which have boiling points close to each other	4.	Distillation under reduced pressure
E.	Two liquids with large difference in boiling points.	5.	Crystallisation

Ans. **A.** → (5) **B.** → (4) **C.** → (1) **D.** → (2) **E.** → (3)

	Column I		Column II
A.	Two solids which have different solubilities in a solvent and which do not undergo reaction when dissolved in it	5.	Crystallisation
B.	Liquid that decomposes at its boiling point	4.	Distillation under reduced pressure
C.	Steam volatile liquid	1.	Steam distillation
D.	Two liquids which have boiling points close to each other.	2.	Fractional distillation
E.	Two liquids with large difference in boiling points.	3.	Simple distillation

Q.51 Match the terms mentioned in Column I with the terms in Column II.

Column I	Column II
A. Carbocation	1. Cyclohexane and 1- hexene
B. Nucleophile	2. Conjugation of electrons of C—H σ bond with empty p-orbital present at adjacent positively charged carbon
C. Hyperconjugatio n	3. sp^2 hybridised carbon with empty p-orbital
D. Isomers	4. Ethyne
E. *sp*-hybridisation	5. Species that can receive a pair of electrons
F. Electrophile	6. Species that can supply a pair of electrons.

Ans. A.→ (3) B.→ (6) C.→ (2) D.→ (1) E.→ (4) F.→ (5)

Column I	Column II	Explanation
A. Carbocation	3. sp^2-hybridised carbon with empty p-orbital	H_3C^+ is carbocation. Loss of e^- makes its p-orbitals empty (sp^2-hybridised carbon)
B. Nucleophile	6. Species that can supply a pair of electron	Nucleus loving, *i.e.*, having negative charge or excess of electrons
C. Hyperconjugation	2. Conjugation of electrons of C—H σ bond with empty p-orbital present at adjacent positively charged carbon	The delocalization of C–H σ-bond electrons spreads electron density and stabilizes the carbocation without forming new bonds.
D. Isomers	1. Cyclohexane and 1-hexene	Same molecular formula but different structures
E. *sp*-hybridisation	4. Ethyne	$HC \equiv CH$ (*sp*-hybridisation)
F. Electrophile	5. Species that receive a pair of electron	Electron loving, *i.e.*, positive charge or lack of electrons

Q.52 Match Column I with column II.

Column I	Column II
A. Dumas method	1. $AgNO_3$
B. Kjeldahl's method	2. Silica gel
C. Carius method	3. Nitrogen gas
D. Chromatography	4. Free radicals
E. Homolysis	5. Ammonium sulphate

Ans. **A.**→ (3) **B.**→ (5) **C.**→ (1) **D.**→ (2) **E.**→ (4)

Column I	Column II	Explanation
A. Dumas method	3. Nitrogen gas	Used for N containing compounds
B. Kjeldahl's method	5. Ammonium sulphate	Nitrogen converts to ammonium sulphate
C. Carius method	1. $AgNO_3$	Compound is heated in presence of $AgNO_3$
D. Chromatography	2. Silica gel	Adsorbent used is silica gel
E. Homolysis	4. Free radicals	Free radicals are formed by homolytic fission

Q.53 Match the intermediates given in Column I with their probable structure in Column II.

Column I	Column II
A. Free radical	1. Trigonal planar
B. Carbocation	2. Pyramidal
C. Carbanion	3. Linear

Ans. **A.**→ (1) **B.**→ (1) **C.**→ (2)

Column I	Column II	Explanation
A. Free radical	1. Trigonal planar	Free radicals are formed by homolytic fission *e.g.*, $\dot{C}H_3$ hybridisation, *sp*^{2}
B. Carbocation	1. Trigonal planar	Formed by heterolytic fission when carbon is attached to a more electronegative atom *e.g.*, $\overset{+}{C}H_3$: hybridisation, *sp*^{2}
C. Carbanion	2. Pyramidal	Formed by heterolytic fission when carbon is attached to more electropositive atom *e.g.*, CH_3^-: hybridisation, *sp*^{3}

Q.54 Match the ions given in Column I with their nature given in Column II.

	Column I		Column II
A.	$CH_3-\ddot{\underset{..}{O}}-\overset{\oplus}{C}H-CH_3$	1.	Stable due to resonance
B.	$F_3-C^{\oplus}$	2.	Destabilised due to inductive effect
C.	$CH_3-\underset{CH_3}{\overset{CH_3}{\lvert}}C^{\ominus}$	3.	Stabilised by hyperconjugation
D.	$CH_3-\overset{\oplus}{C}H-CH_3$	4.	A secondary carbocation

Ans. **A.**→ (1, 2, 4) **B.**→ (2) **C.**→ (2) **D.**→ (3, 4)

	Column I	Column II	Explanation
A.	$CH_3-\ddot{\underset{..}{O}}-\overset{+}{C}H-CH_3$	Stable due to resonance secondary carbocation Destabilised due to inductive effect	Stabilised by resonance due to lone pair on O, slightly destabilised by $-I$ effect of O, and is a secondary carbocation.
B.	F_3C^+	Destabilised due to inductive effect	$-I$ effect of F creates electron deficiency at carbon C^+
C.	$CH_3-\underset{CH_3}{\overset{CH_3}{\lvert}}C^{\ominus}$	Destabilised due to inductive effect	$+I$ effect of CH_3 increases electron density at carbon C^-
D.	$CH_3-\overset{\oplus}{C}H-CH_3$	A secondary carbocation stabilised by hyperconjugation	$\overset{+}{C}H$ is attached to two carbon. It can also be stabilised by hyperconjugation.

Assertion and Reason

In the following questions a statement of Assertion (A) followed by a statement of Reason (R) is given. Choose the correct option out of the choices given below in each question.

Q.55 **Assertion** (A) Simple distillation can help in separating a mixture of propan-1–ol (boiling point 97°C) and propanone (boiling point 56°C).

Reason (R) Liquids with a difference of more than 20°C in their boiling points can be separated by simple distillation.

(a) Both A and R are correct and R is the correct explanation of A
(b) Both A and R are correct but R is not the correct explanation of A
(c) Both A and R are not correct
(d) A is not correct but R is correct

Ans. ***(a)*** Both A and R are correct and R is the correct explanation of A.

Simple distillation can be used to separate a mixture of two liquids which do not react and have boiling point difference of more than 20°C. Hence, a mixture of propan-1-ol and propanone can be separated by simple distillation.

Q.56 **Assertion** (A) Energy of resonance hybrid is equal to the average of energies of all canonical forms.

Reason (R) Resonance hybrid cannot be presented by a single structure.

(a) Both A and R are correct and R is the correct explanation of A
(b) Both A and R are correct but R is not the correct explanation of A
(c) Both A and R are not correct
(d) A is not correct but R is correct

Thinking Process The polarity produced in the molecule by the interaction of two π- bonds or between π- bond and lone pair of electrons present on an adjacent atom is resonance.

Ans. ***(d)*** A is not correct but R is correct.

Resonance hybrids are always more stable than any of the canonical structures would be, if they existed. The delocalisation of the electrons lowers the orbital energies, hence increases the stability. The difference between energy of resonance hybrid and most stable canonical form is **resonance energy.** A canonical structure that is lower in energy makes a relating greater contribution to resonance hybrid. Thus, the correct assertion will be energy of resonance hybrid is equal to the sum of energies of all canonical forms in proportion of their contribution towards the resonance hybrid.

Q.57 **Assertion** (A) Pent-1-ene and pent-2-ene are position isomers.

Reason (R) Position isomers differ in the position of functional group or a substituent.

(a) Both A and R are correct and R is the correct explanation of A
(b) Both A and R are correct but R is not the correct explanation of A
(c) Both A and R are not correct
(d) A is not correct but R is correct

Ans. ***(a)*** Both A and R are correct and R is the correct explanation of A.

$$\overset{5}{C}H_3 - \overset{4}{C}H_2 - \overset{3}{C}H_2 - H\overset{2}{C} = \overset{1}{C}H_2$$
Pent-1-ene

$$\overset{5}{C}H_3 - \overset{4}{C}H_2 - H\overset{3}{C} = \overset{2}{C}H - \overset{1}{C}H_3$$
Pent-2-ene

When two or more compounds differ in the position of substituent atom or functional group on the carbon skeleton then, the phenomenan is position isomerism. Double bond is a functional group whose position varies.

Q.58 **Assertion** (A) All the carbon atoms in $H_2C = C = CH_2$ are sp^2- hybridised.

Reason (R) In this molecule all the carbon atoms are attached to each other by double bonds.

(a) Both A and R are correct and R is the correct explanation of A
(b) Both A and R are correct but R is not the correct explanation of A
(c) Both A and R are not correct
(d) A is not correct but R is correct

Ans. ***(d)*** A is not correct but R is correct.

Hybridisation can be determined by counting σ- bond

$$\underset{sp^2}{\overset{3\sigma}{H_2C}} = \underset{sp}{\overset{2\sigma}{C}} = \underset{sp^2}{\overset{3\sigma}{CH_2}}$$

$3\sigma - sp^2$ hybridisation

$2\sigma - sp$ hybridisation

Correct assertion In $H_2C = C = CH_2$, the central carbon is *sp*-hybridised whereas the terminal carbons are sp^2-hybridised.

Q.59 **Assertion** (A) Sulphur present in an organic compound can be estimated quantitatively by Carius method.

Reason (R) Sulphur is separated easily from other atoms in the molecule and gets precipitated as light yellow solid.

(a) Both A and R are correct and R is the correct explanation of A
(b) Both A and R are correct but R is not the correct explanation of A
(c) Both A and R are not correct
(d) A is not correct but R is correct

Ans. ***(c)*** Both A and R are not correct.

Correct Assertion Sulphur present in those organic compound can be estimated by Carius method in which it can be oxidised to H_2SO_4.

Correct Reason Sulphur cannot be seperated from other atoms in a molecule.

Q.60 **Assertion** (A) Components of a mixture of red and blue inks can be separated by distributing the components between stationary and mobile phases in paper chromatography.

Reason (R) The coloured components of inks migrate at different rates because paper selectively retains different components according to the difference in their partition between the two phases.

(a) Both A and R are correct and R is the correct explanation of A
(b) Both A and R are correct but R is not the correct explanation of A
(c) Both A and R are not correct
(d) A is not correct but R is correct

Ans. ***(a)*** Both A and R are correct and R is the correct explanation of A.

In paper chromatography, a chromatography paper is used. It contains water in it,which acts as the stationary phase. A strip of chromatography paper spotted at the base with ink is suspended in a suitable solvent. Solvent acts as the mobile phase.

The solvent rises up the paper by capillary action and flows over the spot. The paper selectively retains different components according to their differing partition in two phases.

Hence, components of ink will migrate at different rates and are separated.

Long Answer Type Questions

Q.61 What is meant by hybridisation? Compound $CH_2=C=CH_2$ contains *sp* or *sp*^{2}-hybridised carbon atoms. Will it be a planar molecule?

Ans. Hybridisation is mixing of atomic orbitals to form new hybrid orbitals. The new orbital have the same total electron capacity as the old ones. The properties and energies of the new hybridised orbitals are an average of the unhybridised orbitals.

$$\overset{1}{C}H_2 = \overset{2}{C} = \overset{3}{C}H_2$$
$$3\sigma \quad 2\sigma \quad 3\sigma$$

Hybridisation can be found by counting number of σ – bonds around the carbon atom.

$$3\sigma = sp^2\text{-hybridisation}$$
$$2\sigma = sp\text{-hybridisation}$$

In allene, carbon atoms 1 and 3 are sp^2-hybridised as each one of them is joined by a double bond. And, carbon atom 2 is sp-hybridised as it has two double bonds at each of its side. Therefore, the two π-bonds are perpendicular to each other, in allene, as shown below.

H_a and H_b lie in the plane of paper while H_c and H_d lie in a plane perpendicular to the plane of the paper. Hence, the allene molecule as a whole is non-planar.

Q.62 Benzoic acid is an organic compound. Its crude sample can be purified by crystallisation from hot water. What characteristic differences in the properties of benzoic acid and the impurity make this process of purification suitable ?

- **Concept Insight** Crystallisation is based on the difference in the solubilities of compound and the impurities in a suitable solvent.

Ans. Benzoic acid is an organic compound that can be purified by crystallisation from hot water due to the differences in solubility properties between benzoic acid and its impurities. This purification method relies on the principle that the pure compound is significantly more soluble in hot water than in cold water, whereas impurities are either highly soluble in both hot and cold water or are insoluble in water altogether. When a crude sample of benzoic acid is dissolved in hot water, both the benzoic acid and water-soluble impurities dissolve. Upon cooling the solution, the solubility of benzoic acid decreases, and it begins to crystallise out due to its low solubility in cold water. However, the impurities either remain dissolved in the cold filtrate (if they are water-soluble) or are filtered out before crystallisation (if they are insoluble). The benzoic acid crystals can then be separated by filtration, washed, and dried.

This method works effectively because

Benzoic acid shows temperature-dependent solubility in water.
Impurities differ in solubility — they are either too soluble or not soluble at all, and hence do not crystallise with benzoic acid.

Q.63 Two liquids (A) and (B) can be separated by the method of fractional distillation. The boiling point of liquid (A) is less than boiling point of liquid (B). Which of the liquids do you expect to come out first in the distillate ? Explain.

Ans. If the difference in boiling points of two liquids is not much, fractional distillation is used to separate them. In this technique, fractionating column is fitted over the mouth of the round bottom flask.

Since liquid A has a lower boiling point than liquid B, it will vaporise first when the mixture is heated. In fractional distillation, the component with the lower boiling point reaches its boiling temperature earlier and gets converted into vapour before the higher boiling point component.

As the mixture is heated, liquid *A* (lower boiling point) vaporises first. Its vapours rise through the fractionating column, undergoing repeated condensation and evaporation, which increases their purity. These vapours then condense and are collected as the first distillate, while liquid *B* remains in the flask until the temperature is raised further.These vapours then pass through the fractionating column, condense, and are collected as the first distillate.

Q.64 You have a mixture of three liquids *A*, *B* and *C*. There is a large difference in the boiling points of *A* and rest of the two liquids, *i.e.*, *B* and *C*. Boiling point of liquids *B* and *C* are quite close. Liquid *A* boils at a higher temperature than *B* and *C* and boiling point of *B* is lower than *C*.

How will you separate the components of the mixture. Draw a diagram showing set up of the apparatus for the process.

Ans. The boiling points are in the order of $A > C > B$.

Liquid *A* can be separated from rest of the mixture of liquid *B* and *C* by simple distillation. *B* and *C* can be separated by **fractional distillation.**

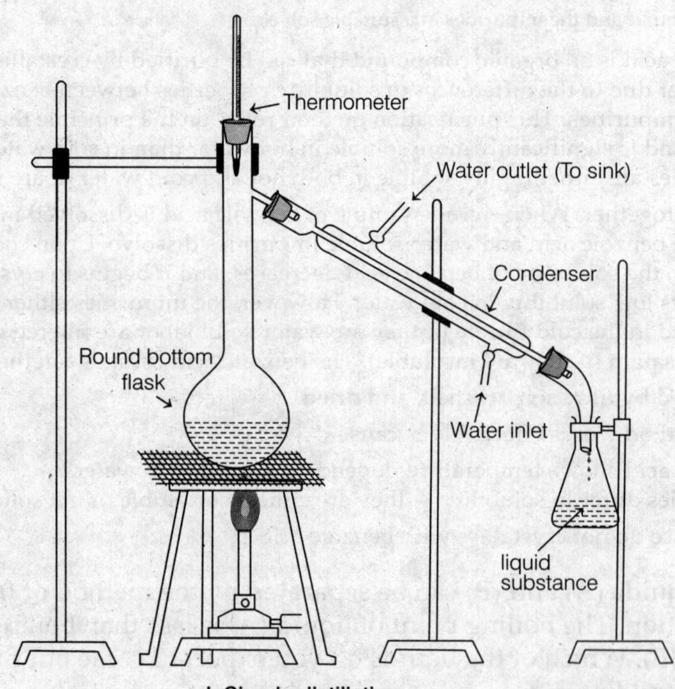

I. Simple distillation

The vapours of a substance formed are condensed and the liquid is collected in conical flask.

Due to the fact that boiling point of *A* is much higher than those of liquids *B* and *C*. This can be done by using apparatus as shown in figure (I).

As the boiling points of liquid (*B*) and (*C*) are quite close but much lower than that of A, hence, mixture of liquids (*B*) and (*C*) will distill together leaving behind liquid (*A*).

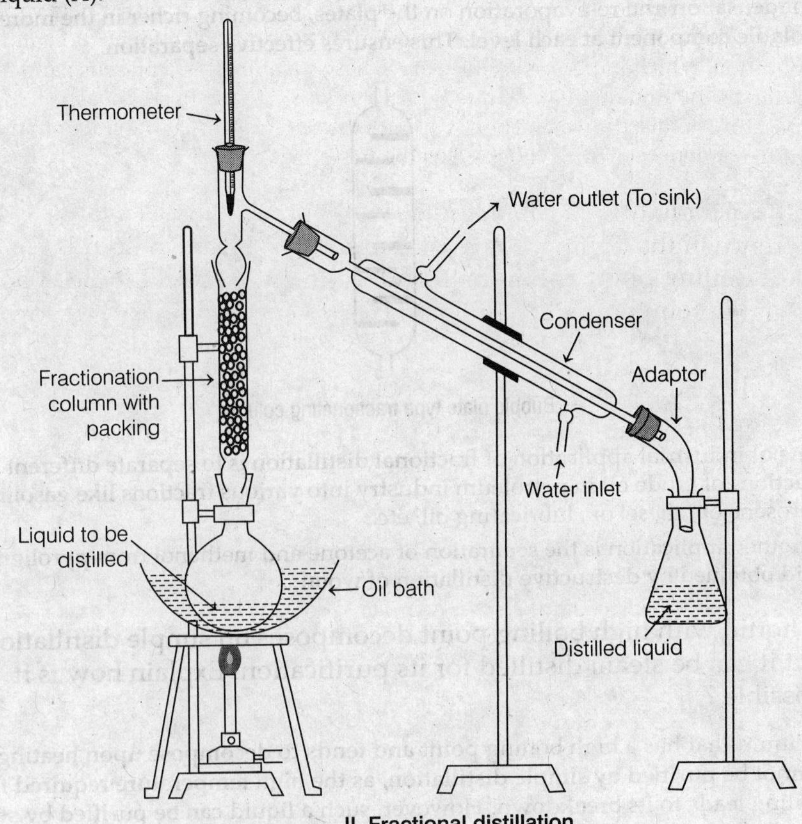

II. Fractional distillation

The vapours of lower boiling fraction reach the top of the column first followed by vapours of higher boiling fractions.

On further heating liquid (*A*) will distill over. Now, place the mixtures of liquid (*B*) and (*C*) in a flask fitted with fractionating column as illustrated in figure (II). On fractional distillation, liquid (*B*) will distill over first and then liquid (*C*) as former possess lower boiling point than that of later.

Q.65 Draw a diagram of bubble plate type fractionating column. When do we require such type of a column for separating two liquids. Explain the principle involved in the separation of components of a mixture of liquids by using fractionating column. What industrial applications does this process have?

Ans. If the difference in boiling points of two liquids is not much, fractional distillation is used to separate them. The technique is that vapour of liquid mixture are passed through a fractionating column before condensation, fitted over the mouth of the round bottom flask.

The process is based on the difference in boiling points of the components. As the mixture is heated, the liquid with the lower boiling point vaporises first. These vapours rise through the fractionating column and undergo multiple cycles of condensation and re-evaporation on the plates, becoming richer in the more volatile component at each level. This ensures effective separation.

Bubble plate type fractionating column

One of industrial application of fractional distillation is to separate different fractions of crude oil in petroleum industry into various fractions like gasoline, kerosene oil, diesel oil, lubricating oil, etc.

Another application is the separation of acetone and methanol from pyroligneous acid obtained by destructive distillation of wood.

Q.66 A liquid with high boiling point decomposes on simple distillation but it can be steam distilled for its purification. Explain how is it possible ?

Ans. A liquid that has a high boiling point and tends to decompose upon heating cannot be purified by simple distillation, as the high temperature required for boiling leads to its breakdown. However, such a liquid can be purified by steam distillation, a technique especially useful for temperature-sensitive compounds like essential oils or organic liquids that are immiscible with water.

Chapter 13

Hydrocarbons

Multiple Choice Questions (MCQs)

Q.1 Arrange the following in decreasing order of their boiling points.

A. n–butane
B. 2-methylbutane
C. n–pentane
D. 2, 2-dimethylpropane

(a) $A > B > C > D$
(b) $B > C > D > A$
(c) $D > C > B > A$
(d) $C > B > D > A$

Ans. *(d)* As the number of carbon in straight chain increases, boiling point increases.
Boiling point decreases with branching

$H_3C—CH_2—CH_2—CH_2—CH_3$ (b. pt = 309.1 K, n-pentane (C)) $> H_3C—H_2C—HC(CH_3)—CH_3$ (b. Pt = 301 K, 2-methylbutane (B)) $> H_3C—C(CH_3)_2—CH_3$ (b. pt = 282.5 K, 2, 2-dimethylpropane (D))

$> H_3C—H_2C—CH_2—CH_3$
(4 carbon atoms with no branching)
b. pt = 273 K
n-butane (A)

Q.2 Arrange the halogens F_2, Cl_2, Br_2, I_2, in order of their increasing reactivity with alkanes.

(a) $I_2 < Br_2 < Cl_2 < F_2$
(b) $Br_2 < Cl_2 < F_2 < I_2$
(c) $F_2 < Cl_2 < Br_2 < I_2$
(d) $Br_2 < I_2 < Cl_2 < F_2$

● **Concept Insight** Reactivity decreases with decrease in electronegativity and electronegativity decreases down the group.

Ans. *(a)* Rate of reaction of alkanes with halogens is $I_2 < Br_2 < Cl_2 < F_2$.
Alkanes react with F_2 is vigorously and with I_2 the reaction is too slow that it requires a catalyst. It is because of high electronegativity of fluorine.

Q.3 The increasing order of reduction of alkyl halides with zinc and dilute HCl is

(a) $R-Cl < R-I < R-Br$ (b) $R—Cl < R-Br < R-I$
(c) $R-I < R-Br < R-Cl$ (d) $R-Br < R-I < R-Cl$

Ans. ***(b)*** As size of halogen atom increases, C—*X* bond strength decreases now. C—I is longest and weakest, so it breaks easily than C—Br and C—Cl. Thus, reactivity order is

$$R—Cl < R—Br < R—I$$

Hence, the reactivity order of reduction of alkyl halides with zinc and dilute HCl increases as the strength of $C-X$ bond decreases.

Q.4 The correct IUPAC name of the following alkane is

$$H_3C-CH_2-\overset{3}{C}H(\overset{2}{C}H(\overset{1}{C}H_3)CH_3)-\overset{4}{C}H_2-\overset{5}{C}H_2-\overset{6}{C}H(\overset{7}{C}H_2-\overset{8}{C}H_3)-CH_2-CH_3$$

(a) 3,6-diethyl-2-methyloctane (b) 5-isopropyl -3-ethyloctane
(c) 3-ethyl-5-isopropyloctane (d) 3-isopropyl-6-ethyloctane

Ans. ***(a)*** The correct IUPAC name is

$$H_3C-CH_2-\overset{3}{C}H(\overset{2}{C}H(\overset{1}{C}H_3)CH_3)-\overset{4}{C}H_2-\overset{5}{C}H_2-\overset{6}{C}H(CH_2-CH_3)-\overset{7}{C}H_2-\overset{8}{C}H_3$$

Longest chain - 8C atom alkane = octane
Branch on 2, 3, 6 follows lowest sum rule.
Branch of 2-C-methyl; 3, 6, C atom-ethyl.
Ethyl comes alphabetically before methyl.
Hence, 3,6-diethyl-2-methyloctane.

Mistake Alert ! *Students may misidentifying the longest carbon chain.*

Q.5 The addition of HBr to 1-butene gives a mixture of products *A*, *B* and *C*.

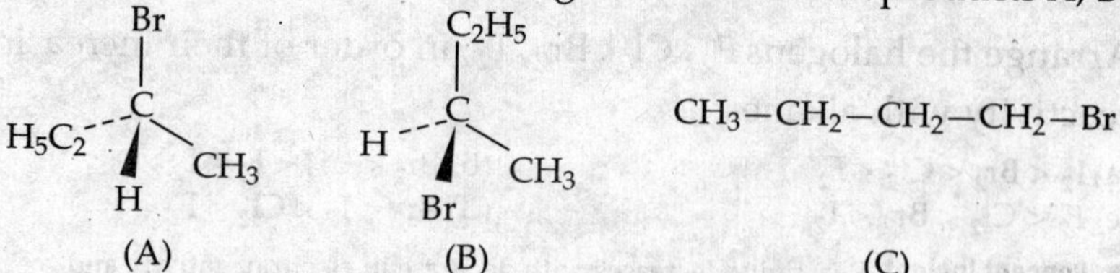

The mixture consists of

(a) *A* and *B* as major and *C* as minor products
(b) *B* as major, *A* and *C* as minor products
(c) *B* as minor, *A* and *C* as major products
(d) *A* and *B* as minor and *C* as major products

Ans. ***(a)*** The alkene is unsymmetrical, hence will follow Markovnikov's rule to give major product.

$$\underset{\text{But-1-ene}}{CH_3-CH_2-CH=CH_2} + H-Br \longrightarrow \underset{(A)\text{ (major product)}}{CH_3-CH_2-CHBr-CH_3} +$$

$$\underset{(B)\text{ (major product)}}{C_2H_5-\overset{*}{C}(Br)(H)-CH_3} + \underset{(C)\text{ (minor product)}}{CH_3-CH_2-CH_2-CH_2Br}$$

Since, *B* contains, a chiral carbon, it exists in two enantiomers (I and II) which are mirror images of each other.

Mirror

(I): Br on C, with H_5C_2, CH_3 and H attached. (II): Br on C, with CH_3, C_2H_5 and H attached.

Q.6 Which of the following will not show geometrical isomerism?

(a) $(F)(Cl)C=C(H)(D)$ (b) $(F)(Cl)C=C(F)(Cl)$

(c) $(H_3C)(H_5C_2)C=C(C_2H_5)(CH_3)$ (d) $(CH_3)(CH_3)C=C(CH_3)(C_2H_5)$

Thinking Process This question is based upon geometrical isomerism. For geomterical isomerism, it is essential that each carbon atom of the double bond must have different substituents.

Ans. ***(d)*** In option (d), a carbon with double bond has two same functional groups (CH_3) attached. The rotation around carbon will not produce a new compound. Hence, geometrical isomerism is not possible.

Q.7 Arrange the following hydrogen halides in order of their decreasing reactivity with propene.

(a) HCl > HBr > HI (b) HBr > HI > HCl

(c) HI > HBr > HCl (d) HCl > HI > HBr

Ans. ***(c)*** As halogen size increases, H—*X* bond strength decreases.

So, HI > HBr > HCl is the order of reactivity with propene.

Q.8 Arrange the following carbanions in order of their decreasing stability.

A. $H_3C-C\equiv C^-$

B. $H-C\equiv C^-$

C. $H_3C-\bar{C}H_2$

(a) A > B > C (b) B > A > C (c) C > B > A (d) C > A > B

Ans. ***(b)*** + *I*-effect decreases the stability of carbanion. Since, $(—CH_3)$ group has + *I*-effect, therefore, it intensifies the negative charge and hence destabilises (*A*) relative to (*B*).

sp hybridised carbanion is more stabilised than sp^3

$$\underset{(B)}{\underset{sp}{CH{\equiv}C^-}} > \underset{(A)}{CH_3—\underset{sp}{C{\equiv}C^-}} > \underset{(C)}{CH_3—\underset{sp^3}{\bar{C}H_2}}$$

Hence, B > A > C

Q.9 Arrange the following alkyl halides in decreasing order of the rate of β – elimination reaction with alcoholic KOH.

A. $CH_3—\overset{\overset{\displaystyle H}{|}}{\underset{\underset{\displaystyle CH_3}{|}}{C}}—CH_2Br$

B. $CH_3—CH_2—Br$

C. $CH_3—CH_2—CH_2—Br$

(a) A > B > C
(b) C > B > A
(c) B > C > A
(d) A > C > B

Ans. ***(d)*** Alkyl halides on heating with alcoholic potash eliminates one molecule of hydrogen halide to form an alkene. Hydrogen is eliminated from β-carbon atom. Nature of alkyl group determines rate of reaction

i.e., 3° > 2° > 1° or A > C > B

$$\underset{(A)}{CH_3-\overset{3°\text{-}\beta\text{-carbon}}{\underset{\underset{\displaystyle CH_3}{|}}{CH}}—CH_2Br} > \underset{(B)}{CH_3-\overset{1°\text{-}\beta\text{-carbon}}{CH_2}-Br} > \underset{(C)}{CH_3—\overset{2°\text{-}\beta\text{-carbon}}{CH_2}—CH_2—Br}$$

Tertiary halides undergo β-elimination faster due to stable carbocation or more substituted alkene.

Q.10 Which of the following reactions of methane is incomplete combustion :

(a) $2CH_4 + O_2 \xrightarrow{Cu/523\,K/100\,atm} 2CH_3OH$
(b) $CH_4 + O_2 \xrightarrow{Mo_2O_3} HCHO + H_2O$
(c) $CH_4 + O_2 \longrightarrow C(s) + 2H_2O\ (l)$
(d) $CH_4 + 2O_2 \longrightarrow CO_2\ (g) + 2H_2O\ (l)$

Ans. ***(c)*** During incomplete combustion of alkanes with insufficient amount of air or dioxygen carbon black is formed which is used in the manufacture of ink, printer ink, black pigments and as filters. Thus,

$$CH_4(g) + O_2(g) \xrightarrow[\text{combustion}]{\text{Incomplete}} \underset{\substack{\text{Carbon}\\\text{black}}}{C(s)} + 2H_2O\ (l)$$

Multiple Choice Questions (More Than One Options)

Q.11 Some oxidation reactions of methane are given below. Which of them is/are controlled oxidation reactions?

(a) $CH_4(g) + 2O_2(g) \longrightarrow CO_2(g) + 2H_2O(l)$

(b) $CH_4(g) + O_2(g) \longrightarrow C(s) + 2H_2O(l)$

(c) $CH_4(g) + O_2(g) \xrightarrow{Mo_2O_3} HCHO + H_2O$

(d) $2CH_4(g) + O_2(g) \xrightarrow{Cu/523/100\ atm} 2CH_3OH$

Ans. ***(c, d)*** Alkanes on heating with a regulated supply of dioxygen or air at high pressure and in the presence of suitable catalysts give a variety of oxidation products.

$$CH_4(g) + O_2(g) \xrightarrow[\Delta]{Mo_2O_3} HCHO + H_2O$$

$$2CH_4(g) + O_2(g) \xrightarrow{Cu/523K/100\ atm} 2CH_3OH$$

Q.12 Which of the following alkenes on ozonolysis give a mixture of ketones only?

(a) $CH_3-CH=CH-CH_3$

(b) $CH_3-\underset{\displaystyle CH_3}{\underset{|}{C}}-CH=CH_3$

(c) cyclopentylidene$=C(CH_3)_2$

(d) $(CH_3)_2C=C(CH_3)_2$

Ans. ***(c, d)*** Alkenes which have two substituents on each carbon atom of the double bond, give mixture of ketones on ozonolysis. Thus, option (c) and (d) give mixture of ketones.

(c) $$\text{cyclopentylidene}=C(CH_3)_2 \xrightarrow[\text{(ii) } Zn/H_2O]{\text{(i) } O_3/CCl_4, 196K} \text{cyclopentanone}(=O) + O=C(CH_3)_2$$

(d) $$(CH_3)_2C=C(CH_3)_2 \xrightarrow[\text{(ii) } Zn/H_2O]{\text{(i) } O_3/CCl_4, 196\ K} (CH_3)_2C=O + O=C(CH_3)_2$$

On the other hand, alkenes (a) and (b) give a mixture of two aldehydes.

(a) $$CH_3CH=CH-CH_3 \xrightarrow[Zn/H_2O]{O_3/CCl_4,\ 196K} CH_3CH=O + O=CHCH_3$$

(b) $$CH_3-\underset{\displaystyle CH_3}{\underset{|}{CH}}-CH=CH_2 \xrightarrow[Zn/H_2O]{O_3/CCl_4,\ 196K} CH_3-\underset{\displaystyle CH_3}{\underset{|}{CH}}-CH=O + O=CH_2$$

Q.13 Which are the correct IUPAC names of the following compound?

$$H_3C-CH_2-CH_2-\underset{\underset{H_3C-CH-CH_2-CH_3}{|}}{\overset{\overset{HC(CH_3)_2}{|}}{CH}}-CH-CH_2-CH_2-CH_2-CH_2-CH_3$$

(a) 5-Butyl-4-isopropyldecane
(b) 5-Ethyl-4-propyldecane
(c) 5-*sec*-Butyl -4- *iso*-propyldecane
(d) 4-(1-methylethyl) - 5 - (1-methylpropyl)-decane

Ans. **(c, d)**

isopropyl or 2- methyl ethyl

$$\overset{1}{H_3C}-\overset{2}{CH_2}-\overset{3}{CH_2}-\overset{\overset{HC(CH_3)_2}{|}}{\underset{4}{CH}}-\underset{\underset{\overset{1}{H_3C-CH}-\overset{2}{CH_2}-\overset{3}{CH_3}}{|}}{\overset{5}{CH}}-\overset{6}{CH_2}-\overset{7}{CH_2}-\overset{8}{CH_2}-\overset{9}{CH_2}-\overset{10}{CH_3}$$

sec. butyl (2°C)

5- sec-Butyl -4 iso -propyldecane

4-(1-methylethyl)-5-(1-methylpropyl)- decane

Although IUPAC name for sec- butyl and isopropyl groups are 1-methyl propyl and 1-methylethyl respectively yet both these names, are also recommended for IUPAC nomenclature.

Q.14 Which are the correct IUPAC names of the following compound?

$$H_3C-CH_2-CH_2-CH_2-\underset{\underset{\underset{\underset{\underset{CH_3}{|}}{H_3C-C-CH_3}}{|}}{CH_2}}{|}}{CH}-CH_2-CH_2-CH_2-CH_2-CH_3$$

(a) 5-(2', 2' - Dimethylpropyl)-decane
(b) 4-Butyl-2,2-dimethylnonane
(c) 2,2- Dimethyl -4- pentyloctane
(d) 5-neo-Pentyldecane

Thinking Process The IUPAC name for neopentyl groups is 2′, 2′ dimethylpropyl.

Ans. **(a, d)**

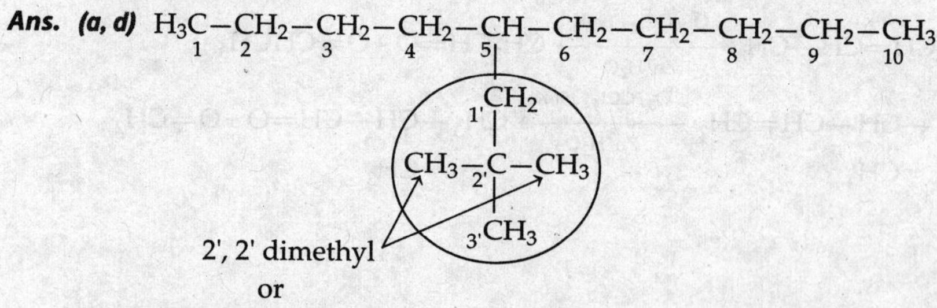

5- (2′,2′- Dimethylpropyl)- decane

5-*neo*- pentyldecane

Q.15 For an electrophilic substitution reaction, the presence of a halogen atom in the benzene ring ....

(a) deactivates the ring by inductive effect (b) deactivates the ring by reasonance

(c) increases the charge density at *ortho* and *para* position relative to *meta* position by resonance.

(d) directs the incoming electrophile to *meta* position by increasing the charge density relative to *ortho* and *para* position.

Ans. ***(a, c)*** For an electrophilic substitution reaction, the presence of halogen atom in the benzene ring deactivates the ring by inductive effect and increases the charge density at *ortho* and *para* position relative to *meta* position by resonance.

When chlorine is attached to benzene ring, chlorine being more electronegative pulls the electron, *i.e.,*–*I*-effect. The electron cloud of benzene is less dense. Chlorine makes aryl halide, moderately deactivating group. But due to resonance the electron density on *ortho* and *para* position is greater than *meta* position.

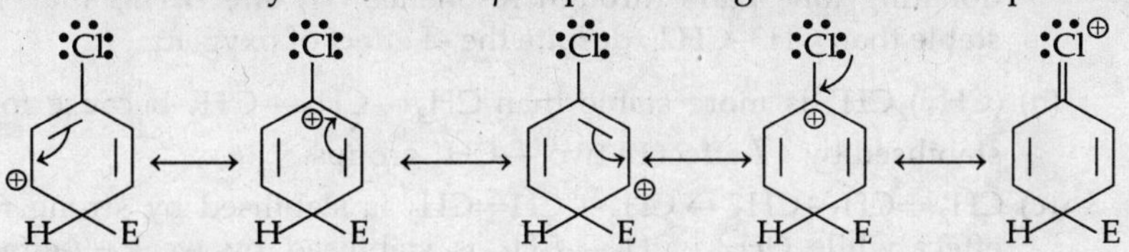

The last structure contributes more to the orientation and hence halogens are *o*-and *p*-directors.

Q.16 In an electrophilic substitution reaction of nitrobenzene, the presence of nitro group..........

(a) deactivates the ring by inductive effect (b) activates the ring by inductive effect

(c) decreases the charge density at *ortho* and *para* position of the ring relative to *meta* position by resonance

(d) increases the charge density at *meta* position relative to the *ortho* and *para* positions of the ring by resonance

Ans. ***(a, c)*** Nitro group by virtue of –*I*-effect withdraws electrons. In an electrophilic substitution reaction of nitrobenzene, the nitro group deactivates the benzene ring by its strong –*I* effect and withdraws electrons through resonance, reducing electron density at the ortho and para positions. As a result, the meta position becomes relatively more reactive toward electrophilic attack.

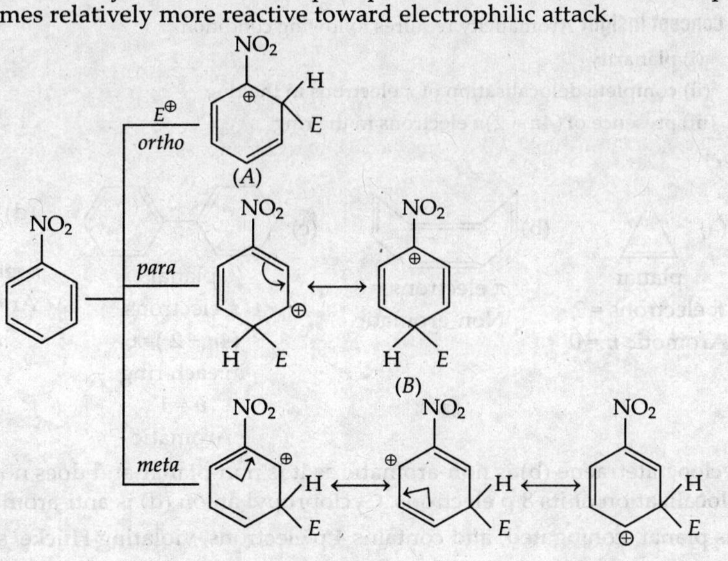

In *ortho*, *para*-attack of electrophile on nitrobenzene, we are getting two structures (*A*) and (*B*) in which positive charge is appearing on the carbon atom directly attached to the nitro group.

As nitro group is electron withdrawing by nature, it decreases the stability of such product and hence meta attack is more feasible when electron withdrawing substituents are attached.

Q.17 Which of the following are correct?

(a) $CH_3—O—CH_2^{\oplus}$ is more stable than $CH_3—CH_2^{\oplus}$

(b) $(CH_3)_2\ CH^{\oplus}$ is less stable than $CH_3—CH_2—CH_2^{\oplus}$

(c) $CH_2 = CH— CH_2^{\oplus}$ is more stable than $CH_3—CH_2—CH_2^{\oplus}$

(d) $CH_2 = CH^{\oplus}$ is more stable than $CH_3—CH_2^{\oplus}$

Ans. ***(a, c)*** (a) In $CH_3—O—\overset{+}{C}H_2$., the oxygen atom stabilizes the carbocation by donating lone pairs through resonance (+R effect).This makes it more stable than CH3–CH2., despite the –I effect of oxygen.

(b) $(CH_3)_2CH^+$ is more stable than $CH_3—CH_2—\overset{+}{C}H_2$ because former has stabilised by + *I*-effect of two $—CH_3$ groups.

(c) $CH_2=CH—\overset{+}{C}H_2 \leftrightarrow \overset{+}{C}H_2—CH=CH_2$ is stabilised by strong resonance effect while $CH_3—CH_2—\overset{+}{C}H_2$ is stabilised by weak +*I*-effect of the CH_3CH_2 group.

(d) In $CH_2=\overset{+}{C}H$, +ve charge is present on the more electronegatiue, *sp*–hybridised carbon while in $CH_3—\overset{+}{C}H_2$, +ve charge is present on the less electronegative sp^2-hybridised carbon therefore, $CH_2=\overset{+}{C}H$ is less stable than $CH_3—\overset{+}{C}H_2$.

Q.18 Four structures are given in options (a) to (d). Examine them and select the aromatic structures.

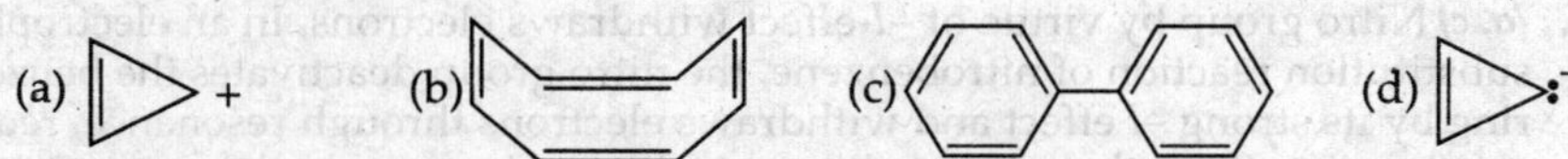

● **Concept Insight** Aromaticity requires following condition

(i) planarity

(ii) complete delocalisation of π electrons in the ring .

(iii) presence of $(4n + 2)\pi$ electrons in the ring.

Ans. ***(a, c)***

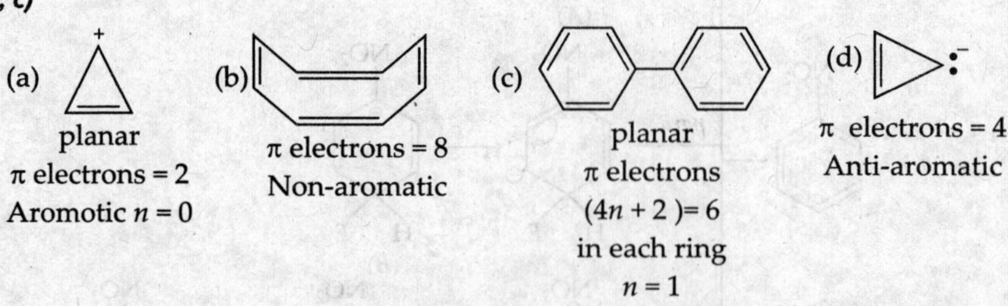

Cyclooctatetraene (b) is non-aromatic as it is non-planar and does not allow delocalization of its 8 p electrons. Cyclopropyl anion (d) is anti-aromatic because it is planar, conjugated, and contains 4 p electrons, violating Hückel's rule.

Q.19 The molecules having dipole moment are ....

(a) 2,2-Dimethylpropane (b) *trans*-Pent-2-ene

(c) *cis*-Hex-3-ene (d) 2, 2, 3, 3 - Tetramethylbutane

Ans. ***(b, c)***

(a) $H_3C-C(CH_3)_2-CH_3$

$\mu = 0$

(b) $CH_3(H)C=C(H)CH_2CH_3$

Different group attached on oposite side $\mu \neq 0$

(c) $CH_3CH_2(H)C=C(H)CH_2CH_3$

$\mu \neq 0$

(d) $H_3C-C(CH_3)_2-C(CH_3)_2-CH_3$

Same group attached

$\mu = 0$

Thus, *trans-pent-2-ene* show net diple moment because different group attached and cis- *Hex* -3- ene show dipole moment because both groups (C_2H_5) are inclined to each other at angle of 60° therefore, have a finite resultant.

Short Answer Type Questions

Q.20 Why do alkenes prefer to undergo electrophilic addition reaction while arenes prefer electrophilic substitution reactions? Explain.

Ans. Alkenes have loosely held pi (π) electrons above and below the molecular plane, so they attract electrophile and show electrophilic addition reactions. Electrophilic addition reaction of alkenes are accompanied by large energy changes so these are energetically favourable than that of electrophilic substitution reactions.

$$>C=C(H)(X) \xleftarrow[-yH]{x^+y^-} >C=C(H)(H) \xrightarrow{x^+y^-} >C(X)-C(Y)(H)(H)$$

Substitution reaction — Addition reaction

Similarly electrophilic addition does not occur in arenes. The π –electrons of double bonds are delocalised due to resonance, so they are stabilised. The electrophilic addition to this double bond changes it into single bond, so there is no resonance and hence, makes the arene less stable due to loss of aromaticity. Arenes take part in electrophilic substitution reaction in which on H is substituted by – *X* from benzene ring so ring remain intact and remain involved in resonance and become stable as before.

Addition reaction $\xleftarrow{x^+y^-}$ Benzene (An arene) $\xrightarrow[-yH]{x^+y^-}$ Substitution reaction

That's why alkenes prefer to undergo electrophilic addition reaction while arenes prefer electrophilic substitution reaction.

Q.21 Alkynes on reduction with sodium in liquid ammonia form *trans* alkenes. Will the butene thus formed on reduction of 2 – butyne show the geometrical isomerism ?

Thinking Process In geometrical isomerism, when same groups are on the same side, it is *cis* and if same groups are on the opposite side, it is *trans* isomer.

Ans. *Trans*-2-butene, so formed by the reduction of 2-butyne is capable of showing geometrical isomerism.

$$\underset{\text{2-butyne}}{\overset{3}{C}H_3-\overset{2}{C}\equiv\overset{1}{C}-CH_3} \xrightarrow[196\text{-}200K]{\text{Na in Liquid } NH_3} \underset{\textit{Trans}\text{-2-butene}}{(CH_3)(H)C=C(H)(CH_3)}$$

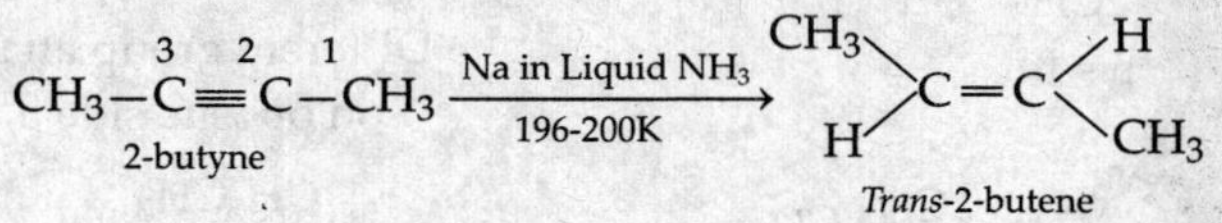

Q.22 Rotation around carbon-carbon single bond of ethane is not completely free. Justify the statement.

- **Concept Insight** The infinite number of momentary arrangements of the atoms in space which result through rotation about a single bond are called **conformations.**
  In ethane, if one carbon atom is kept stationary and other rotated around C – C axis, we have **eclipsed, skew** and **staggered conformation.**

Ans. The rotation around a C— C single bond is hindered by a small energy barrier (1-20 kJ mol⁻) due to weak repulsive interaction between the adjacent bonds. This repulsive interaction is called **torsional strain.** In staggered form of ethane, the electron cloud of carbon hydrogen bonds are far apart. So, repulsion is minimum.

In eclipsed electron cloud of carbon-hydrogen become close resulting in increase in electron cloud repulsion. This repulsion affects stablity of a conformer.

Among all the conformations of ethane, the staggered form has least torsional strain and the eclipsed form has the maximum torsional strain. Hence, rotation around C — C bond in ethtane is not completely free.

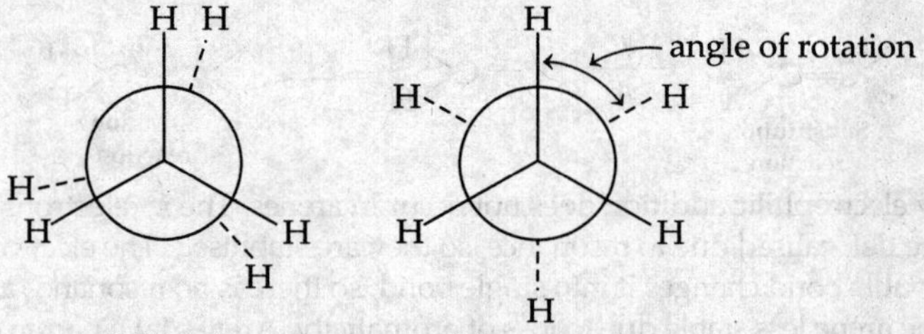

H H
H H H H
Eclipsed

H
angle of rotation
H H
H H
H
Staggered

Newman's projection of ethane

Q.23 Draw Newman and Sawhorse projections for the eclipsed and staggered conformations of ethane. Which of these conformations is more stable and why?

Ans.

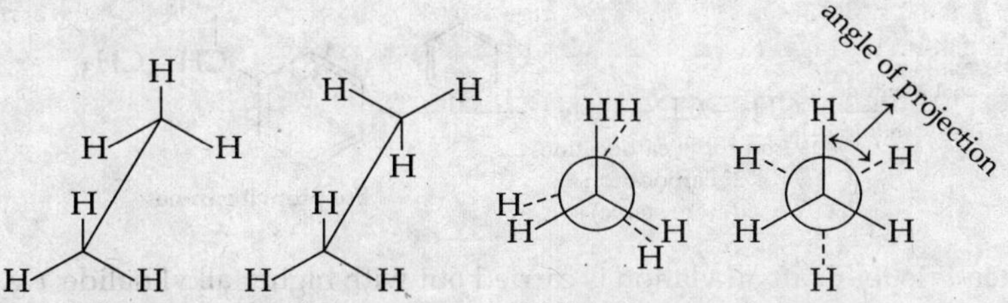

angle of projection

Eclipsed Staggered
Sawhorse projections of ethane

Eclipsed Staggered
Newman projections of ethane

Staggered form of ethane is more stable than the eclipsed conformation, because any two hydrogen atoms on adjacent carbon atoms of staggered conformation are maximum apart while in eclipsed conformation, they cover or eclipse each other in space. Thus, in staggered form, there is minimum repulsive forces, minimum energy and maximum stability of the molecule.

Q.24 The intermediate carbocation formed in the reactions of HI, HBr and HCl with propene is the same and the bond energy of HCl, HBr and HI is 430.5 kJ mol^{-1}, 363.7 kJ mol^{-1} and 296.8 kJ mol^{-1} respectively. What will be the order of reactivity of these halogen acids ?

Ans. Addition of halogen acids to an alkene is an electrophilic addition reaction.

$$CH_3-CH=CH_2 + H^+ \xrightarrow[\text{1st step}]{\text{slow}} CH_3-\overset{+}{C}H-CH_3 \xrightarrow[\text{IInd step}]{X^-,\text{fast}} CH_3-\underset{X}{\underset{|}{C}H}-CH_3$$

First step is slow so, it is rate determining step. The rate of this step depends on the availability of proton. This in turn depends upon the bond dissociation enthalpy of the H – X molecule.

Lower the bond dissociation enthalpy of H – X molecule, greater the reactivity of halogen halide. Since the bond dissociation energy decreases in the order;

$$\text{HI } (296.8 \text{ kJ mol}^{-1}) < \text{HBr } (363.7 \text{ kJ mol}^{-1}) < \text{HCl } (430.5 \text{ kJ mol}^{-1})$$

Therefore, the reactivity of the halogen acids decreases from HI to HCl. *i.e.* HI >HBr >HCI

Q.25 What will be the product obtained as a result of the following reaction and why?

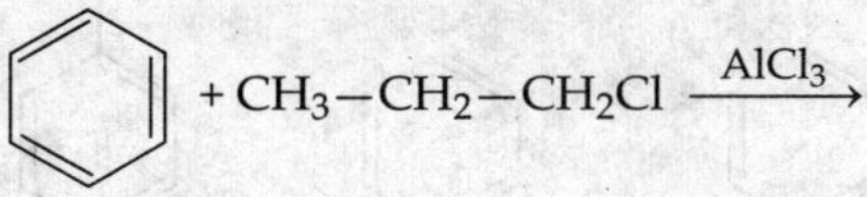

$$C_6H_6 + CH_3-CH_2-CH_2Cl \xrightarrow{AlCl_3}$$

Ans. $CH_3-CH_2-CH_2-Cl + \overset{+}{A}lCl_3 \xrightarrow{-AlCl_4^-} CH_3-\underset{H}{CH}-\overset{+}{C}H_2$

n-propyl chloride

n-propyl carbocation (1°) less stable

$\xrightarrow[\text{shift}]{\text{1,2 hydride}} CH_3-\overset{+}{C}H-CH_3$

Iso-propyl carbocation
2° carbocation
(more stable)

$\xrightarrow[-H^+]{C_6H_6}$ $C_6H_5-CH(CH_3)-CH_3$

Iso-propylbenzene

When Friedel-Craft alkylation is carried out with higher alkyl halide, *e.g.*, *n*–propyl chloride, then *n*-propyl carbocation (1° carbocation) formed which rearranges to form more stable *iso*-propyl carbocation (2° carbocation). Afterward the main product *iso*-propyl benzene will be formed.

Q.26 How will you convert benzene into (a) *p*-nitrobromobenzene? (b) *m*-nitrobromobenzene?

Thinking Process Halogens attached to benzene ring is *ortho and para* directing where as nitro group is *meta* directing.

Ans.

(a) Benzene $\xrightarrow[\text{(Bromination)}]{Br_2, \text{ Anhyd. } FeBr_3}$ Bromobenzene $\xrightarrow[\text{Heat (Nitration)}]{\text{Conc. } HNO_3/\text{Conc. } H_2SO_4}$ *p*-nitro bromo benzene (major product)

(b) Benzene $\xrightarrow[\text{Heat (Nitration)}]{\text{Conc. } HNO_3/\text{Conc. } H_2SO_4}$ Nitrobenzene $\xrightarrow[\text{(Bromination)}]{Br_2, \text{ Anhyd. } FeBr_3}$ *m*-bromo nitrobenzene

Q.27 Arrange the following set of compounds in the order of their decreasing relative reactivity with an electrophile.

Give reason.

$C_6H_5OCH_3$ C_6H_5Cl $C_6H_5NO_2$

Ans. The methoxy group (— OCH_3) is an electron releasing group. It increases the electron density in benzene nucleus due to resonance effect (+ *R*-effect). Hence, it makes anisole more reactive than benzene towards electrophile.

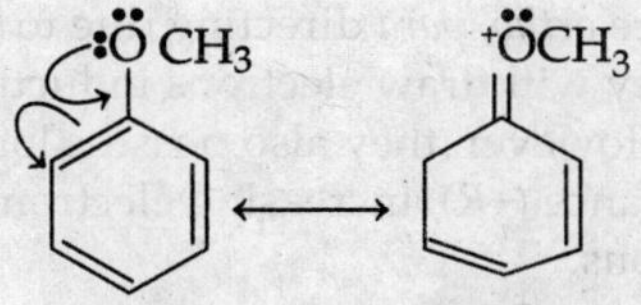

Anisole (+ *R*-effect)

In case of alkyl halides, halogens are moderately deactivating because of their strong – *I* effect. Thus, overall electron density on benzene ring decreases. It makes further substitution difficult.

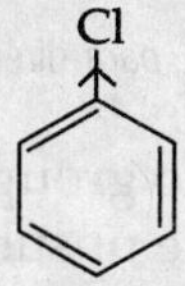

Chlorobenzene

(–*I*-effect)

—NO_2 group is electron withdrawing group. It decreases the electron density in benzene nucleus due to its strong – *R* - effect and strong – *I*-effect. Hence, it makes nitrobenzene less reactive.

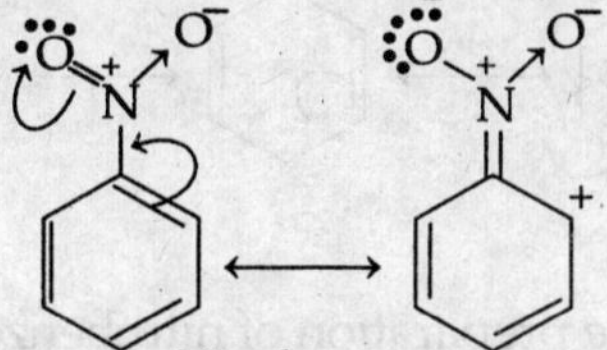

Nitrobenzene

(– *R* and – *I*-effect)

Therefore, overall reactivity of these three compounds towards electrophiles decreases in the following order

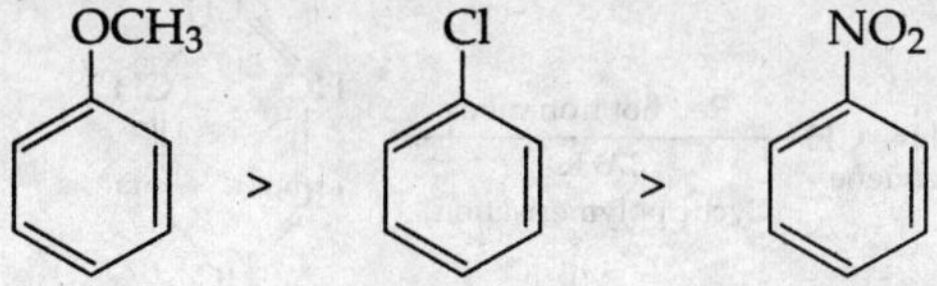

Anisole > Chlorobenzene > Nitrobenzene

Q.28 Despite their $-I$ effect, halogens are o- and p- directing in haloarenes. Explain.

Ans. Halogens have $(-I)$ and $(+R)$ effect, these groups are deactivating due to their $(-I)$ effect and they are *ortho, para* directing due to $(+R)$ effect. Halogens are electronegative, so they withdraw electrons inductively $(-I)$ from the benzene ring, deactivating it. However, they also possess lone pairs which they donate into the ring *via* resonance $(+R)$, increasing electron density particularly at the ortho and para positions.

ortho, *para*-directing influence

Q.29 Why does presence of a nitro group make the benzene ring less reactive in comparison to the unsubstituted benzene ring. Explain.

Ans. The *meta*-directing substituents (like - NO_2 group) withdraw electrons from the benzene ring and thus, deactivate it for further substitution and make the benzene ring less reactive in comparison to the unsubstituted benzene ring.

Nitrobenzene
($-R$ and $-I$ effect)

Q.30 Suggest a route for the preparation of nitrobenzene starting from acetylene?

- **Concept Insight** In nitration of benzene ring conc. H_2SO_4 acts as an catalyst to produce an electrophile NO_2^+. (from HNO_3).

Ans. Acetylene when passed through red hot iron tube at 873 K, undergoes cyclic polymerisation to form benzene which upon subsequent nitration gives nitrobenzene.

$$\underset{\text{acetylene}}{3CH{\equiv}CH} \xrightarrow[\text{(Cyclic polymerisation)}]{\text{Red hot iron tube, 873 K}} \underset{\text{Benzene}}{C_6H_6}$$

$$\text{Benzene} \xrightarrow[\text{Heat (Nitration)}]{\text{Conc. } HNO_3,\ \text{Conc. } H_2SO_4} \underset{\text{Nitrobenzene}}{C_6H_5NO_2}$$

Q.31 Predict the major product(s) of the following reactions and explain their formation.

$$H_3C-CH=CH_2 \xrightarrow[HBr]{(Ph-CO-O)_2}$$

$$H_3C-CH=CH_2 \xrightarrow{HBr}$$

Ans. In presence of organic peroxides, the addition of HBr to propene follows anti Markvonikov's rule (or peroxide effect) to form 1-bromopropane (*n*-propyl bromide)

$$Ph-\overset{O}{\overset{\|}{C}}-O-O-\overset{O}{\overset{\|}{C}}-Ph \xrightarrow[\text{fission}]{\text{Homolytic}} 2Ph-\overset{O}{\overset{\|}{C}}-O^{\bullet} \longrightarrow 2Ph^{\bullet} + 2CO_2$$

$$Ph^{\bullet} + HBr \longrightarrow C_6H_6 + Br^{\bullet}$$

$$H_3C-CH=CH_2 + Br^{\bullet} \xrightarrow{\text{Slow}} \underset{\substack{2^\circ \text{ Free radical} \\ \text{(more stable)}}}{H_3C-\dot{C}H-CH_2Br} \xrightarrow{H-Br} \underset{\text{1-Bromopropane}}{H_3C-CH_2-CH_2Br} + Br^{\bullet}$$

However, in absence of peroxides, addition of HBr to propene follows Markovnikov's rule and gives 2- bromopropane as major product.

$$\underset{\text{Propene}}{CH_3-CH=CH_2} + H^+ \xrightarrow{\text{Slow}} \underset{\substack{\text{More stable} \\ 2^\circ \text{ carbocation}}}{CH_3-\overset{+}{C}H-CH_3} \xrightarrow[\text{Fast}]{Br^-} \underset{\text{2 – bromopropane}}{CH_3-\underset{Br}{\underset{|}{C}H}-CH_3}$$

Q.32 Nucleophiles and electrophiles are reaction intermediates having electron rich and electron deficient centres respectively. Hence, they tend to attack electron deficient and electron rich centres respectively. Classify the following species as electrophiles and nucleophiles.

(i) H_3CO^- (ii) $H_3C-\overset{O}{\overset{\|}{C}}-O^-$ (iii) $\dot{C}l$ (iv) $Cl_2C:$
(v) $(H_3C)_3C^+$ (vi) Br^- (vii) H_3COH
(viii) *R*-NH-*R*

Ans. Electrophiles are electron deficient species. They may be neutral or positively charged, *e.g.*, (iii) $\dot{C}l$, (iv) $Cl_2C:$, (v) $(H_3C)_3C^+$

Nucleophiles are electron rich species. They may be neutral or negatively charged, *e.g.*,

(i) H_3CO^-, (ii) $H_3C-\overset{O}{\overset{\|}{C}}-O^-$,

(vi) Br^-, (vii) $H_3C-\ddot{\underset{..}{O}}-H$,

(viii) $R\ddot{N}HR$

Q.33 The relative reactivity of 1°, 2° and 3° hydrogen's towards chlorination is 1 : 3.8 : 5. Calculate the percentages of all monochlorinated products obtained from 2-methylbutane.

Ans. The given organic compound is

$$CH_3-\underset{}{\overset{\overset{\displaystyle CH_3}{|}}{C}H}-CH_2-CH_3$$

2-methylbutane

This compound has 9 primary hydrogen, 2 secondary and one tertiary hydrogen atoms. Nine possibilities of compound '*A*' because nine methyl hydrogens are present in 2-methylbutane.

$$ClCH_2-\overset{\overset{\displaystyle CH_3}{|}}{C}H-CH_2CH_3$$

A (1°)

Two possibilities for '*B*' compound because two CH hydrogen are present in 2-methylbutane.

$$(H_3C)_2CH-\underset{\underset{\displaystyle Cl}{|}}{C}H-CH_3$$

B (2°)

Only one possibility for '*C*' compound because one CH hydrogen is present in 2-methylbutane.

$$(H_3C)_2\underset{\underset{\displaystyle Cl}{|}}{C}-CH_2-CH_3$$

C (3°)

The relative reactivity of 1°, 2° and 3° hydrogen atoms towards chlorination is 1 : 3.8 : 5. Relative amount of product after chlorination

= Number of hydrogen × relative reactivity

	1° halide	2° halide	3° halide
Relative amount	$9 \times 1 = 9$	$2 \times 3.8 = 7.6$	$1 \times 5 = 5$

Total amount of mono chloro product = 9 + 7.6 + 5 = 21.6

Percentage of 1° mono chloro product $= \dfrac{9}{21.6} \times 100 = 41.7\%$

Percentage of 2° mono chloro product $= \dfrac{7.6}{21.6} \times 100 = 35.2\%$

Percentage of 3° mono chloro product $= \dfrac{5}{21.6} \times 100 = 23.1\%$

Q.34 Write the structures and names of products obtained in the reactions of sodium with a mixture of 1-iodo-2-methylpropane and 2-iodopropane.

Thinking Process This question is based upon Wurtz reaction. Wurtz reaction represents that two alkyl groups can be coupled by reacting alkyl halide with sodium in presence of dry ether.

$$2RX + 2Na \xrightarrow[\text{dry ether}]{\Delta} R-R + 2NaX$$

Ans. (i) $\underset{\substack{|\\CH_3\\ \text{1-iodo-2-methylpropane}}}{CH_3CHCH_2I} + 2Na + 2\underset{\substack{|\\CH_3\\ \text{1-iodo-2-methylpropane}}}{CH_2-CH-CH_3} \xrightarrow{\Delta}$

$$\underset{\substack{|\\CH_3}}{CH_3-CH}-(CH_2)_2-\underset{\substack{|\\CH_3}}{CH}-CH_3 + 2NaI$$
2, 5-dimethylhexane

(ii) $\underset{\substack{|\\CH_3\\ \text{2-iodopropane}}}{CH_3-CH-I} + 2Na + \underset{\substack{|\\CH_3\\ \text{2-iodopropane}}}{I-CH-CH_3} \xrightarrow[\text{dry ether}]{\Delta} \underset{\substack{|\\CH_3}}{CH_3-CH}-\underset{\substack{|\\CH_3}}{CH}-CH_3 + 2NaI$
2, 3-dimethylbutane

(iii) $\underset{\substack{|\\CH_3\\ \text{1-iodo-2-methylpropane}}}{CH_3-CH-CH_2-I} + 2Na + \underset{\substack{|\\CH_3\\ \text{2-iodopropane}}}{I-CH-CH_3} \xrightarrow[\text{dry ether}]{\Delta}$

$$CH_3-\underset{\substack{|\\CH_3}}{CH}-CH_2-\underset{\substack{|\\CH_3}}{CH}-CH_3 + 2NaI$$
2,4-dimethylpnetane

Q.35 Write hydrocarbon radicals that can be formed as intermediates during monochlorination of 2-methylpropane? Which of them is more stable? Give reasons.

- **Concept insight** Hyperconjugation stabilizes free radicals by delocalizing the unpaired electron over adjacent C–H σ bonds of alkyl groups. More the number of α-hydrogens (attached to the carbon next to the radical centre), greater is the hyperconjugation, hence higher the stability of the radical.

Ans. 2-methylpropane gives two types of radicals.

$$\underset{\text{(2-methylpropane)}}{CH_3-\overset{\substack{CH_3\\|}}{CH}-CH_3} \longrightarrow \underset{\text{(I)}}{CH_3-\overset{\substack{CH_3\\|}}{\underset{\bullet}{C}}-CH_3} \text{ and } \underset{\text{(II)}}{CH_3-\overset{\substack{CH_3\\|}}{CH}-\dot{C}H_2}$$

Radical (I) is more stable because it is 3° free radical and stabilised by nine hyperconjugative structures (as it has 9 α-hydrogens)

Radical (II) is less stable because it is 1° free radical and stabilised by only one hyperconjugative structure (as it has only 1 α- hydrogen)

Q.36 An alkane C_8H_{18} is obtained as the only product on subjecting a primary alkyl halide to Wurtz reaction. On monobromination this alkane yields a single isomer of a tertiary bromide. Write the structure of alkane and the tertiary bromide.

Ans. From Wurtz reaction of an alkyl halide gives an alkane with double the number of carbon atoms present in the alkyl halide is obtained. Here, Wurtz reaction of a primary alkyl halide gives an alkane (C_8H_{18}), therefore, the alkyl halide must contain four carbon atoms.Now the two possible primary alkyl halides having four corbon atoms each are I and II.

$$\underset{\text{I}}{CH_3CH_2CH_2CH_2-X} \qquad \underset{\text{II}}{CH_3-\overset{\overset{\displaystyle CH_3}{|}}{CH}-CH_2X}$$

Since, alkane C_8H_{18} on monobromination yields a single isomer of tertiary alkyl halide, therefore, the alkane must contain tertiary hydrogen. This is possible, only if primary alkyl halide (which undergoes Wurtz reaction) has a tertiary hydrogen.

$$\underset{\text{1-halo-2-methylpropane}}{CH_3-\overset{\overset{\displaystyle CH_3}{|}}{CH}-CH_2-X} + 2Na + X-CH_2-\overset{\overset{\displaystyle CH_3}{|}}{CH}-CH_3$$

$$\xrightarrow[\Delta\ -2NaX]{} \underset{\text{2, 5 dimethylhexane (alkane)}}{\overset{6}{C}H_3-\overset{\overset{\displaystyle CH_3}{|}}{\overset{5}{C}H}-\overset{4}{C}H_2-\overset{3}{C}H_2-\overset{\overset{\displaystyle CH_3}{|}}{\overset{2}{C}H}-\overset{1}{C}H_3} \xrightarrow[-HBr]{Br_2\ h\nu} \underset{\text{2-bromo-2, 5 dimethylhexane (3° bromide)}}{\overset{1}{C}H_3-\underset{\underset{\displaystyle Br}{|}}{\overset{\overset{\displaystyle CH_3}{|}}{\overset{2}{C}}}-\overset{3}{C}H_2-\overset{4}{C}H_2-\overset{\overset{\displaystyle CH_3}{|}}{\overset{5}{C}H}-\overset{6}{C}H_3}$$

Q.37 The ring systems having following characteristics are aromatic.

(i) Planar ring containing conjugated π bonds.

(ii) Complete delocalisation of the π-electrons in ring system, *i.e.*, each atom in the ring has unhybridised *p*-orbital, and

(iii) Presence of $(4n+2)$ π- electrons in the ring where n is an integer ($n = 0, 1, 2, \ldots\ldots\ldots$) [Huckel rule].

Using this information classify the following compounds as aromatic/non-aromatic.

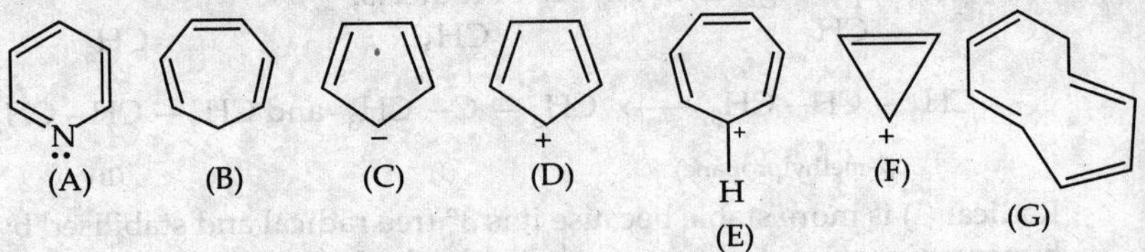

Ans.

	Compound	Planar ring	Complete delocalisation of π-electron	Huckel rule $(4n + 2)\ \pi$ electron	Aromatic or non-aromatic
A.	N	✓	✓	$6\pi\ e^-$ Huckel rule obeyed	Aromatic
B.	sp^3c	×	× Incomplete (sp^3 hybrid carbon)	$6\pi e^-$	Non-aromatic
C.	−	✓	✓	$6\pi e^-$ (4π electrons + 1 l.p.) Huckel rule verified	Aromatic
D.	+	✓	×	$4\pi e^-$	Anti-aromatic
E.	+ H	✓	✓	Huckel rule obeyed	Aromatic
F.	+	✓	✓	$2\pi e^-$, Huckel rule, verified $n = 0$	Aromatic
G.	sp^3c	✓	Incomplete (sp^3 hybrid carbon present)	$8\pi e^-$, Huckel rule, not verified	Non-aromatic

Q.38 Which of the following compounds are aromatic according to Huckel's rule?

(A) 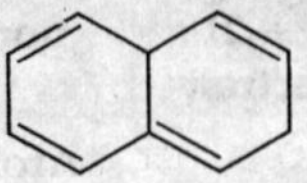 (B) 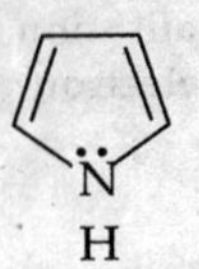 (C)  $H_2C=$ $=CH_2$

(D) 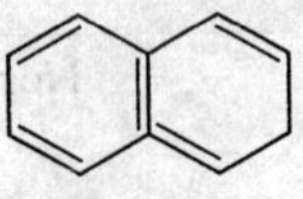 (E) 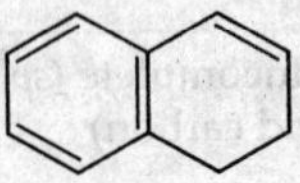 (F)

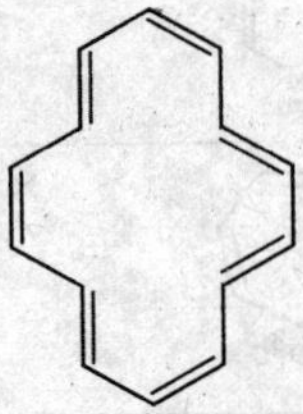

Ans. A. The compound has 8π electrons. It will be non-aromatic. Both rings are non-benzenoid.

B. The compound is aromatic. It has $6\pi e^-$ delocalised electron ($4\pi e^-$ + 2 lone pair electrons), all the four carbon atoms and the N atom are sp^2 hybridised.

C. The compound contains 6π electrons but not in the ring hence, it is non-aromatic.

D. $10\pi e^-$ obeying Huckel rule and the ring is planar. It is aromatic.

E. In this compound one six membered planar ring has $6\pi e^-$ although it has 8π electrons in two rings. It is therefore, aromatic.

F. It has 14π electrons in conjugation and in the planar ring, Huckel rule is verified. It will be aromatic.

Mistake Alert ! *Students may not consider all the conditions for identifying aromatic compounds using Huckel's rule.*

Q.39 Suggest a route to prepare ethyl hydrogensulphate ($CH_3—CH_2—OSO_2—OH$) starting from ethanol (C_2H_5OH).

Ans. Preparation of ethyl hydrogensulphate ($CH_3—CH_2—OSO_2—OH$) starting from ethanol (C_2H_5OH), is the two steps mechanism.

Step I Protonation of alcohol

$$H_2SO_4 \longrightarrow H^+ + {}^-OSO_2OH$$

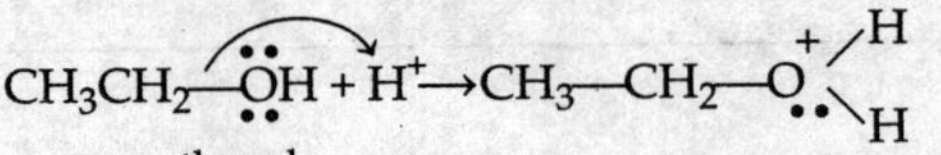

$$\underset{\text{ethanol}}{CH_3CH_2—\ddot{O}H} + H^+ \rightarrow \underset{\text{protonated ethanol}}{CH_3—CH_2—\overset{+}{\ddot{O}}\begin{matrix}H\\H\end{matrix}}$$

protonated ethanol

Step II Attack of nucleophile

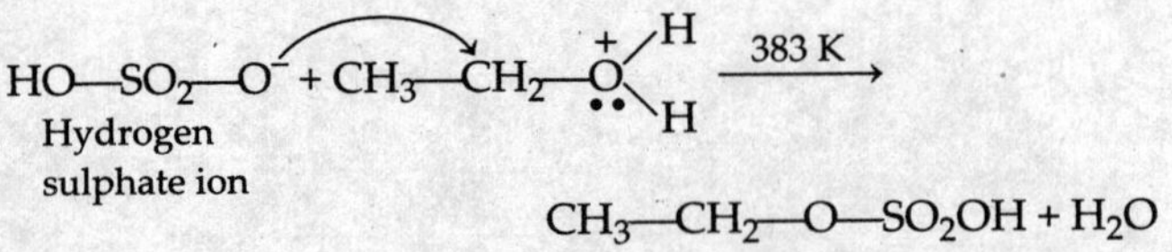

$$\underset{\text{Hydrogen sulphate ion}}{HO—SO_2—O^-} + CH_3—CH_2—\overset{+}{\ddot{O}}\begin{matrix}H\\H\end{matrix} \xrightarrow{383\text{ K}} \underset{\text{ethyl hydrogen sulphate}}{CH_3—CH_2—O—SO_2OH} + H_2O$$

Temperature should not be allowed to rise above 383 K, otherwise diethyl ether will be produced at 413 K or ethene at 433 K.

Matching The Columns

Q.40 Match the reagent from Column I which on reaction with $CH_3—CH=CH_2$ gives some product given in Column II as per the codes given below :

	Column I		Column II
A.	$O_3 / Zn + H_2O$	1.	Acetic acid and CO_2
B.	$KMnO_4 / H^+$	2.	Propan-1-ol
C.	$KMnO_4 / OH^-$	3.	Propan-2-ol
D.	H_2O / H^+	4.	Acetaldehyde and formaldehyde
E.	B_2H_6 / NaOH and H_2O_2	5.	Propane-1, 2-diol

Ans. **A.** → (4) **B.** → (1) **C.** → (5) **D.** → (3) **E.** → (2)

Reagent		Reaction with propene
A. $O_3 / Zn + H_2O$	4.	$CH_3-CH=CH_2$ (ozonide) → HCHO + formaldehyde, CH_3CHO Acetaldehyde
B. $KMnO_4 / H^+$	1.	$CH_3CH=CH_2 \xrightarrow[H^+]{KMnO_4} CH_3COOH + CO_2$ (Acetic acid)
C. $KMnO_4 / OH^-$	5.	$CH_3—CH=CH_2 \xrightarrow[OH^-]{KMnO_4} CH_3—CH(OH)—CH_2(OH)$ Propan-1, 2-diol
D. H_2O / H^+	3.	$CH_3CH=CH_2 \xrightarrow[\text{(Markovikov's addition)}]{H_2O/H^+} CH_3—CH(OH)—CH_3$ Propan–2–ol
E. B_2H_6 / NaOH and H_2O_2	2.	$CH_3CH=CH_2 \xrightarrow[\text{(ii) NaOH}/H_2O_2]{\text{(i) } B_2H_6} CH_3CH_2CH_2OH$ propan–1–ol (Hydroboration oxidation)

Q.41 Match the hydrocarbons in Column I with the boiling points given in Column II.

	Column I		Column II
A.	*n*-pentane	1.	282.5 K
B.	*iso*-pentane	2.	309 K
C.	*neo*-pentane	3.	301 K

Thinking Process To solve this question, keep in mind that branching of hydrocarbons decreases boiling point of the compound.

Ans. A.→ (2) B.→ (3) C.→ (1)

Hydrocarbons		Boiling point	
A.	n-pentane	2. 309 K due to no branch	
B.	*iso*-pentane	3. 301 K due to one branch	$CH_3-CH(CH_3)-CH_2-CH_3$
C.	*neo*-pentane	1. 282.5 K due to two branches	$CH_3-C(CH_3)_2-CH_3$

Q.42 Match the following reactants in Column I with the corresponding reaction products in Column II.

	Column I		Column II
A.	Benzene + $Cl_2 \xrightarrow{AlCl_3}$	1.	Benzoic acid
B.	Benzene + $CH_3Cl \xrightarrow{AlCl_3}$	2.	Methyl phenyl ketone
C.	Benzene + $CH_3COCl \xrightarrow{AlCl_3}$	3.	Toluene
D.	Toluene $\xrightarrow{KMnO_4/NaOH}$	4.	Chlorobenzene
		5.	Benzene hexachloride

Ans. A.→ (4) B. → (3) C.→ (2) D.→ (1)

Reactants		Products
A. Benzene + $Cl_2 \xrightarrow{AlCl_3}$	4.	Friedel Craft's reaction Chlorobenzene (C_6H_5Cl)
B. Benzene + $CH_3Cl \xrightarrow{AlCl_3}$	3.	Friedel Craft's alkylation reaction Toluene ($C_6H_5CH_3$)

C.	Benzene + $CH_3COCl \xrightarrow{AlCl_3}$	2. $C_6H_5-C(=O)-CH_3$ Methyl phenyl ketone (Friedel Craft's acetylation reaction)
D.	Toluene $\xrightarrow{KMnO_4/NaOH}$	1. Oxidation reaction C_6H_5COOH Benzoic acid

Q.43 Match the reactions given in Column I with the reaction types in Column II.

	Column I		Column II
A.	$CH_2=CH_2 + H_2O \xrightarrow{H^+} CH_3CH_2OH$	1.	Hydrogenation
B.	$CH_2=CH_2 + H_2 \xrightarrow{Pd} CH_3-CH_3$	2.	Halogenation
C.	$CH_2=CH_2 + Cl_2 \longrightarrow Cl-CH_2-CH_2-Cl$	3.	Polymerisation
D.	$3\,CH\equiv CH \xrightarrow[Heat]{Cu\ tube} C_6H_6$	4.	Hydration
		5.	Condensation

Ans. **A.** → (4) **B.** → (1) **C.** → (2) **D.** → (3)

	Reactions	Types of reaction	
A.	$CH_2=CH_2 + H_2O \xrightarrow{H^+} CH_3CH_2OH$	4. Hydration	(Addition of water)
B.	$CH_2=CH_2 + H_2 \xrightarrow{Pd} CH_3-CH_3$	1. Hydrogenation	(Addition of hydrogen)
C.	$CH_2=CH_2 + Cl_2 \longrightarrow Cl-CH_2-CH_2-Cl$	2. Halogenation	(Addition of halogen)
D.	$3CH\equiv CH \xrightarrow[Heat]{Cu\ tube} C_6H_6$	3. Polymerisation	Cyclic polymer (CH ring: CH, HC, CH, HC, CH, CH)

Assertion and Reason

In the following questions a statement of assertion (A) followed by a statement of reason (R) is given. Choose the correct option out of the choices given below in each question.

Q.44 **Assertion** (A) The compound cyclooctatetraene has the following structural formula.

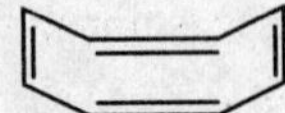

It is cyclic and has conjugated 8π-electron system but it is not an aromatic compound.

Reason (R) $(4n+2)$ π electrons rule does not hold good and ring is not planar.

(a) Both A and R are correct and R is the correct explanation of A

(b) Both A and R are correct but R is not the correct explanation of A

(c) Both A and R are not correct

(d) A is not correct but R is correct

Ans. *(a)* Both A and R are correct and R is the correct explanation of A.

According to Huckel's rule Aromaticity is shown by compounds possessing following characteristics

(i) Compound must be planar and cyclic

(ii) Complete delocalisation of π electrons in the ring

(iii) Presence of conjugated $(4n + 2)$ π electrons in the ring where n is an integer $(n = 0, 1, 2, ...)$ Cyclooctatetraene (C_8H_8) has a cyclic structure with 8 π electrons, which fits the $4n$ rule ($n = 2$) for anti-aromaticity. To avoid being anti-aromatic, it adopts a non-planar (tub-shaped) conformation that prevents full conjugation, making it non-aromatic. Since the ring is not planar, the $(4n + 2)$ rule cannot apply, and the molecule remains non-aromatic.

Q.45 **Assertion** (A) Toluene on Friedel Crafts methylation gives *o*- and *p*- xylene.

Reason (R) CH_3-group bonded to benzene ring increases electron density at *o*- and *p*- position.

(a) Both A and R are correct and R is the correct explanation of A

(b) Both A and R are correct but R is not the correct explanation of A

(c) Both A and R are not correct

(d) A is not correct but R is correct

Ans. *(a)* Both A and R are correct and R is the correct explanation of A.

Toluene has $-CH_3$ group attached to benzene. $-CH_3$ group activates the benzene ring for the attack of an electrophile.

In resonating structure of toluene, electronic density is more on *ortho* and *para* position. Hence, substitution takes place mainly at these positions.

Q.46 **Assertion** (A) Nitration of benzene with nitric acid requires the use of concentrated sulphuric acid.

Reason (R) The mixture of concentrated sulphuric acid and concentrated nitric acid produces the electrophile, NO_2^+.

(a) Both A and R are correct and R is the correct explanation of A
(b) Both A and R are correct but R is not the correct explanation of A
(c) Both A and R are not correct
(d) A is not correct but R is correct

Ans. *(a)* Both A and R are correct and R is the correct explanation of A. In nitration of benzene with nitric acid, sulphuric acid acts as a calatyst. It helps in the formation of electrophile, *i.e.*, nitronium ion, NO_2^+.

$$HNO_3 + H_2SO_4 \longrightarrow NO_2^+ + 2HSO_4^- + H_3O^+$$

$$C_6H_6 \xrightarrow[H_2SO_4]{HNO_3} C_6H_5NO_2 + H_2O$$

Q.47 **Assertion** (A) Among isomeric pentanes, 2, 2-dimethylpentane has highest boiling point.

Reason (R) Branching does not affect the boiling point.

(a) Both A and R are correct and R is the correct explanation of A
(b) Both A and R are correct but R is not the correct explanation of A
(c) Both A and R are not correct
(d) A is not correct but R is correct

Ans. *(c)* Both A and R are not correct

Correct assertion Among isomeric pentanes, 2, 2- dimethylpentane has the lowest boiling point.

Correct reason Branching decrease the boiling point.

Long Answer Type Questions

Q.48 An alkyl halide C_5H_{11} *(A)* reacts with ethanolic KOH to give an alkene *'B'*, which reacts with Br_2 to give a compound *'C'*, which on dehydrobromination gives an alkyne *'D'*. On treatment with sodium metal in liquid ammonia, one mole of *'D'* gives one mole of the sodium salt of *'D'* and half a mole of hydrogen gas. Complete hydrogenation of *'D'* yields a straight chain alkane. Identify *A, B, C* and *D*. Give the reactions involved.

Ans. The reaction scheme involved in the problem is

$$\underset{\text{Alkyl halide}}{\underset{(A)}{C_5H_{11}Br}} \xrightarrow{\text{Alc. KOH}} \underset{\text{Alkene}}{\underset{(B)}{C_5H_{10}}} \xrightarrow{Br_2/CS_2} \underset{\text{Dibromo alkane}}{\underset{(C)}{C_5H_{10}\,Br_2}} \xrightarrow[-2HBr]{\text{Alc. KOH}} \underset{\text{Alkyne}}{\underset{(D)}{C_5H_8}} \xrightarrow{H_2} \text{Straight chain alkane}$$

$$\underset{\text{Sodiuma alkylide}}{C_5H_7^- Na^+} + \frac{1}{2}H_2, \text{Na, Liq. } NH_3$$

Hydrogenation of alkyne (*D*) gives straight chain alkane hence all the compounds (*A*), (*B*), (*C*) and (*D*) must be straight chain compounds. Alkyne (*D*) form sodium salt which proves that it is terminal alkyne. Involved reactions are as follows

$$\underset{\substack{\text{1-Bronopentane}\\(A)}}{CH_3—CH_2—CH_2—CH_2—CH_2—Br} \xrightarrow{\text{Alc. KOH}} \underset{\substack{\text{Pent-1-ene}\\(B)}}{CH_3CH_2CH_2CH{=}CH_2} \xrightarrow[CS_2]{Br_2}$$

$$\underset{\substack{\text{1, 2-Dibromopentane}\\(C)}}{CH_3—CH_2—CH_2—\overset{\overset{Br}{|}}{C}H—\overset{\overset{Br}{|}}{C}H_3} \xrightarrow{\text{KOH (Alc.)}} \underset{\substack{\text{pent-1-yne}\\(D)}}{CH_3CH_2CH_2C{\equiv}CH} \xrightarrow{H_2/Pt}$$

$$\underset{n\text{-pentane}}{CH_3CH_2CH_2CH_2CH_3} \xrightarrow[\text{Liq. } NH_3]{Na} \underset{\substack{\text{sod. salt of pent-1-yne}\\(E)}}{CH_3CH_3CH_3C{\equiv}C^-Na^+} + \frac{1}{2}H_2$$

Mistake Alert! *Students may get confused that alkyl halide (A) can be bromopent-2-ane. But it can't be bromopent-2-ane because dehydrobromination of (A) would have given pent-2-ene as the major product in accordance with Markovnikov's rule.*

Q.49 896 mL vapour of a hydrocarbon '*A*' having carbon 87.80% and hydrogen 12.19% weighs 3.28 g at STP. Hydrogenation of '*A*' gives 2-methylpentane. Also '*A*' on hydration in the presence of H_2SO_4 and $HgSO_4$ gives a ketone '*B*' having molecular formula $C_6H_{12}O$. The ketone '*B*' gives a positive iodoform test. Find the structure of '*A*' and give the reactions involved.

Ans. To determine the molecular mass of hydrocarbon (A) 896 mL vapour of $C_xH_y(A)$ weighs 3.28 g at STP

22400 mL vapour of C_xH_y (*A*) weighs $\frac{3.28 \times 22400}{896}$ g/mol at STP

$$= 82 \text{ g/mol}$$

Hence, molecular mass of $C_xH_y(A) = 82 \text{ g mol}^{-1}$.

Calculation of Empirical formula of '*A*'.

Element	%	Atomic mass	Relative ratio	Relative no. of atoms	Simplest ratio
C	87.8	12	$\frac{87.8}{12} = 7.31$	$\frac{7.31}{7.31} = 1$	3
H	12.19	1	$\frac{12.19}{1} = 12.91$	$\frac{12.91}{7.31} = 1.66$	$4.98 \approx 5$

Thus, Empirical formula of *A* is C_3H_5.

$\therefore$ Empirical formula mass = 36 + 5 = 41

$$n = \frac{\text{Molecular mass}}{\text{Empirical formula mass}} = \frac{82}{41} = 2$$

Molecular mass is double of empirical formula mass.

$\therefore$ Molecular formula is C_6H_{10}.

To determine the structure of compounds (*A*) and (*B*)

$$\underset{(A)}{C_6H_{10}} \longrightarrow \text{2-methyl pentane} \quad \left(\begin{matrix} CH_3 \\ CH_3 \end{matrix}\!\!>\!CH-CH_2-CH_2-CH_3\right)$$

Hence, hydrogenation of hydrocarbon (*A*) requires 2 moles of hydrogen to form 2-methylpentane. Therefore, hydrocarbon(A) is an alkyne having five carbon atoms in a staight chain and a methyl substituent at position 2. Thus, the possible structures for the alkyne (*A*) are I and II.

$$\underset{\text{I}}{CH_3-\underset{\large CH_3}{\underset{|}{CH}}-CH_2-C\equiv CH} \qquad \underset{\text{II}}{\begin{matrix} CH_3 \\ CH_3 \end{matrix}\!\!>\!CH-C\equiv C-CH_3}$$

Since, addition of H_2O to alkyne (*A*) in presence of Hg^{2+}, give a ketone which gives positive iodoform test, therefore, ketone (*B*) must be a methyl ketone, *i.e.*, it must contain a $COCH_3$ group.

Now, addition of H_2O to alkyne (II) should give a mixture of two ketones in which 2- methylpentan-3-one (minor) and 4-methylpentan -2-one ketone (B) (which shows +ve iodoform test) predominates.

$$\underset{(A)}{\begin{matrix} CH_3 \\ CH_3 \end{matrix}\!\!>\!CH-C\equiv C-CH_3} \xrightarrow[Hg^{2+}]{H_2O/H^+} \underset{\text{2-Methylpentan-3-one (minor)}}{\begin{matrix} CH_3 \\ CH_3 \end{matrix}\!\!>\!CH-CH_2\ COCH_3}$$

$$+ \underset{(B)\ \text{4–Methylpentan 2-one}}{\begin{matrix} CH_3 \\ CH_3 \end{matrix}\!\!>\!CH-CO-CH_2CH_3}$$

In contrast, addition of H_2O to alkyne (I) will give only one ketone, *i.e.*, 4- methylpentan-2- one which gives iodoform test.

$$\begin{matrix} H_3C \\ H_3C \end{matrix}\!\!>\!CH-CH_2-C\equiv CH \xrightarrow[Hg^{2+}]{H_2O/H^+} \begin{matrix} CH_3 \\ CH_3 \end{matrix}\!\!>\!CH-CH_2-\overset{\overset{\large O}{\|}}{C}-CH_3$$

Thus, hydrocabon C_xH_y (*A*) is 4-methylpent –1–yne, 4-methylpentan-2-one gives +ve iodoform test.

Q.50 An unsaturated hydrocarbon '*A*' adds two molecules of H_2 and on reductive ozonolysis gives butane-1, 4-dial, ethanal and propanone. Give the structure of '*A*', write its IUPAC name and explain the reactions involved.

Ans. The scheme of reaction is

$$\text{Compound}(A) \xrightarrow[\text{Ozonolysis}]{\text{Reductive}} \underset{\text{ethanal}}{CH_3-\overset{\overset{\large H}{|}}{C}=O} +$$

$$\underset{\text{Butane-1, 4 dial}}{O=\overset{\overset{\large H}{|}}{C}-CH_2-CH_2-\overset{\overset{\large H}{|}}{C}=O} + \underset{\text{Propanone}}{O=\overset{\overset{\large CH_3}{|}}{C}-CH_3}$$

Thus, structure of *A* may be given as

$$\underset{\text{2-methylocta-2, 6-diene}}{CH_3-\overset{\overset{\large H}{|}}{C}=\overset{\overset{\large H}{|}}{C}-CH_2-CH_2-CH=\overset{\overset{\large CH_3}{|}}{C}-CH} \longrightarrow$$

The reactions involved in the question

$$CH_3CH=CH-CH_2-CH_2-HC=C\begin{matrix}CH_3\\CH_3\end{matrix} \xrightarrow[196\text{-}200\ K]{O_3/CCl_4}$$

$$CH_3\underset{O-O}{CH \overset{O}{\;}\; CH}-CH_2CH_2-\underset{O-O}{CH\overset{O}{\;}\;C}\begin{matrix}CH_3\\CH_3\end{matrix} \xrightarrow{Zn/H_2O}$$

$$\underset{\text{Ethanal}}{O=CHCH_3} + \underset{\text{Butane-1, 4-dial}}{O=CH-CH_2-CH_2-CH=O} + \underset{\text{Propanone}}{\begin{matrix}CH_3\\CH_3\end{matrix}C=O}$$

Q. 51 In the presence of peroxide addition of HBr to propene takes place according to anti Markovnikov's rule but peroxide effect is not seen in the case of HCl and HI. Explain.

Ans. $$\underset{\text{propene}}{CH_3-CH=CH_2} + HBr \xrightarrow{\text{Peroxide}} \underset{n\text{-propyl bromide}}{CH_3-CH_2CH_2Br}$$

The mechanism of the reaction is

$$\underset{\text{Peroxide}}{R-O-O-R} \xrightarrow[\text{Homolytic}]{\Delta} 2R\dot{O}$$

$$R\dot{O} + H-Br \xrightarrow{\text{Fission}} ROH + Br$$

Step I $CH_3—CH=CH_2 + \dot{Br} \xrightarrow{\text{\&low}} CH_3—\dot{C}H—CH_2Br$

Propene

Step II $CH_3 - \dot{C}H - CH_2Br + H - Br \xrightarrow{\text{Fast}} CH_3 - CH_2 - CH_2Br + \dot{Br}$

Propene

1-Bromopropane

or

n-propyl bromide

Peroxide effect is effective only in the case of HBr and not seen in the case of HCl and HI. This is due to the following reasons.

(i) H — Cl bond (103 kcal/mol) is stronger than H — Br bond (87 kcal/mol) Cl is more electronegative than Br, so H—Cl bond is highly polar and will not give —Cl free radical.

(ii) H — I bond has less polarity and gives iodine free radical ($I^\cdot$) but iodine free radicals readily combine with each other to form iodine molecules rather attacking the double bond.

Chapter

14

Environmental Chemistry*

Multiple Choice Questions (MCQs)

Q.1 Which of the following gases is not a green house gas?

(a) CO (b) O_3 (c) CH_4 (d) H_2O vapour

Thinking Process Greenhouse gases are atmospheric gases like CO_2, CH_4, and H_2O vapour that trap infrared radiation emitted from Earth's surface. They absorb this heat and re-radiate it back, preventing it from escaping into space. This causes the greenhouse effect and leads to global warming.

Ans. *(a)* Carbon dioxide, water vapour, methane, ozone, oxides of nitrogen, chlorofluoro carbons etc; are green house gases. CO is not a green house gas.

Q.2 Photochemical smog occurs in warm, dry and sunny climate. One of the following is **not** amongst the components of photochemical smog, identify it.

(a) NO_2 (b) O_3

(c) SO_2 (d) Unsaturated hydrocarbon

Ans. *(c)* The components of photochemcal smog are O_3, PAN, nitrogen oxide , acrolein an formaldehyde. SO_2 is not responsible for photochemical smog.

- **Concept Insight** The smog which is formed in presence of sunlight is called **photochemical smog.** This occurs in summer when NO_2 and hydrocarbons are present in large amounts in atmosphere.

Q.3 Which of the following statements is **not** true about classical smog?

(a) Its main components are produced by the action of sunlight on emissions of automobiles and factories.

(b) Produced in cold and humid climate.

(c) It contains compounds of reducing nature.

(d) It contains smoke, fog and sulphur dioxide.

- **Concept Insight** Gases released by automobiles and factories are not responsible for classical smog.

Ans. *(a)* Smog are of two types-**classical smog and photochemical smog.**
Classical smog occurs in cold humid climate. It is a mixture of smoke, fog and sulphur dioxide. Chemically it is a reducing mixture thats why, it is also called as **reducing smog.**

Note (*) *This chapter has been deleted from latest NCERT.*

Q.4 Biochemical Oxygen Demand, (BOD) is a measure of organic material present in water. BOD value less than 5 ppm indicates a water sample to be.

(a) rich in dissolved oxygen. (b) poor in dissolved oxygen.
(c) highly polluted. (d) not suitable for aquatic life.

Thinking Process The total amount of oxygen consumed by microorganisms (bacteria) in decomposing organic matter present in certain volume of a sample of water is called Biochemical Oxygen Demand (BOD) of the water.

Ans. *(a)* Water is considered to be pure if it has BOD less than 5 ppm whereas highly polluted water has BOD more than 17ppm.

Thus, water having BOD less than 5 ppm is rich in dissolved oxygen.

Q.5 Which of the following statement(s) is/are wrong?

(a) Ozone is not responsible for green house effect.
(b) Ozone can oxidise sulphur dioxide present in the atmosphere to sulphur trioxide.
(c) Ozone hole is thinnig of ozone layer present in stratosphere.
(d) Ozone is produced in upper stratosphere by the action of UV rays on oxygen.

Concept Insight The warming of earth's due to re-emission of sun's energy absorbed by the earth followed by its absorption by CO_2 and H_2O vapour present near the earth surface and then its radiation back to earth is called green house effect.

Ans. *(a)* O_3 (Ozone) is responsible for greenhouse effect. Its contribution is about 8%.

Q.6 Sewage containing organic waste should not be disposed in water bodies because it causes major water pollution. Fishes in such a polluted water die because of

(a) large number of mosquitoes
(b) increase in the amount of dissolved oxygen
(c) decrease in the amount of dissolved oxygen in water
(d) clogging of gills by mud

Ans. *(c)* Dissolved oxygen is essential for aquatic life. Organic waste is oxidised by microorganisms using dissolved oxygen. Hence, oxygen from water decreases. It is harmful for aquatic life.

Q.7 Which of the following statements about photochemical smog is wrong?

(a) It has high concentration of oxidising agents.
(b) It has low concentration of oxidising agent.
(c) It can be controlled by controlling the release of NO_2, hydrocarbons, ozone etc.
(d) Plantation of some plants like pinus helps in controlling photochemical smog.

Ans. *(b)* Photochemical smog or Los Angles smog was first observed in Los Angles in 1950. It is formed due to photochemical reactions taking place when air contain NO_2 and hydrocarbons.

The concentrations of O_3, PAN, *R*CHO and R_2CO builds up in the atmosphere. These compounds produce irritation in the eyes. Photochemical smog has high concentration of oxidants such as O_3, organic oxidant etc.

Q.8 The gaseous envelope around the earth is known as atmosphere. The lowest layer of this is extended upto 10 km from sea level, this layer is

(a) stratosphere (b) troposphere (c) mesosphere (d) hydrosphere

● **Concept Insight** The atmosphere is divided into four major regions

(i) Troposphere (ii) Stratosphere
(iii) Mesosphere (iv) Thermosphere

Ans. *(b)* Troposphere is the lowest region of the atmosphere. It extends upto the height of ~ 10 km from sea level. Troposphere is a turbulent, dusty zone containing air, much water vapour and clouds.

Q.9 Dinitrogen and dioxygen are main constituents of air but these do not react with each other to form oxides of nitrogen because ....

(a) the reaction is endothermic and requires very high temperature.
(b) the reaction can be initiated only in presence of a catalyst.
(c) oxides of nitrogen are unstable.
(d) N_2 and O_2 are unreactive.

Ans. *(a)* Major components of atmosphere are dinitrogen, dioxygen and water vapour

$N_2 = 78.08\%$, $O_2 = 20.95\%$.

Both do not react with each other as nitrogen is an unreactive gas. The triple bond in N_2 is very stable and its dissociation energy is very high. Both react with each other at very high temperature.

$$N_2(g) + O_2(g) \xrightarrow{3000^\circ C} 2NO(g)$$

Q.10 The pollutants which come directly in the air from sources are called primary pollutants. Primary pollutants are sometimes converted into secondary pollutants. Which of the following belongs to secondary air pollutants?

(a) CO (b) Hydrocarbon
(c) Peroxyacetyl nitrate (d) NO

Ans. *(c)* Hydrocarbons present in atmosphere combine with oxygen atom produced by the photolysis of NO_2 to form highly reactive intermediate called free radical. Free radical initiates a series of reaction.

Peroxyacetyl nitrates are formed, which can be said as secondary pollutants.

$$\text{Hydrocarbon} + O \longrightarrow RCO^\bullet \text{ (free radicals)}$$

$$RCO^\bullet + O_2 \longrightarrow RCO_3^\bullet$$

$$RCO_3^\bullet + NO_2 \longrightarrow \underset{\text{Peroxyacetyl nitrate}}{RCO_3NO_2}$$

Q.11 Which of the following statements is correct?

(a) Ozone hole is a hole formed in stratosphere from which ozone oozes out.
(b) Ozone hole is a hole formed in troposphere from which ozone oozes out.
(c) Ozone hole is thinning of ozone layer of stratosphere at some places.
(d) Ozone hole means vanishing of ozone layer around the earth completely.

Ans. *(c)* Ozone hole is thinning of ozone layer of stratosphere at some place.

Two types of compounds have been found to be the most responsible for depleting the ozone layer are (i) NO (ii) chlorofluoro carbon

$$NO + O_3 \longrightarrow NO_2 + O_2$$
$$CF_2Cl_2 \xrightarrow{hv} {}^{\bullet}CF_2Cl + Cl^{\bullet}$$
$$Cl^{\bullet} + O_3 \longrightarrow ClO^{\bullet} + O_2$$
$$ClO^{\bullet} + O \longrightarrow Cl^{\bullet} + O_2$$

These reactions occur in stratosphere.

Hence, statement (c) is correct.

Q.12 Which of the following practices will not come under green chemistry?

(a) If possible, making use of soap made of vegetable oils instead of using synthetic detergents.

(b) Using H_2O_2 for bleaching purpose instead of using chlorine based bleaching agents.

(c) Using bicycle for travelling small distances instead of using petrol/ diesel based vehicles.

(d) Using plastic cans for neatly storing substances.

Ans. *(d)* Using plastic cans for neatly storing substances will not come under green chemistry. Water in lakes and rivers have been polluted by the use of plastic materials. As it is non-biodegradable.

Multiple Choice Questions (More Than One Options)

Q.13 Which of the following conditions shows the polluted environment ?

(a) pH of rain water is 5.6.

(b) Amount of carbon dioxide in the atmosphere is 0.03%.

(c) Biochemical oxygen demand 10 ppm.

(d) Eutrophication.

Ans. *(c, d)* Polluted water may contain nutrients for the growth of algae, which covers the water surface and reduces the oxygen concentration in water. This leads to anaerobic condition, accumulation of abnoxious decay and animal death. This is process of eutrophication.

The amount of oxygen required by becteria to break down the organic matter present in a certain volume of sample of water, is called Biochemical Oxygen Demand. Clean water would have BOD value of 5 ppm whereas highly polluted could have BOD value of 17ppm or more.

Normally rain water has pH of 6 due to H^+ ion formed by reaction of rain water with carbon dioxide in the atmosphere. When the pH of the rain water drops below 5.6, it is called acid rain.

Thus, options (c) and (d) indicate a polluted environment.

Q.14 Phosphate containing fertilisers cause water pollution. Addition of such compounds in water bodies causes ....

(a) enhanced growth of algae
(b) decrease in amount of dissolved oxygen in water
(c) deposition of calcium phosphate
(d) increase in fish population

● **Concept Insight** The process in which nutrient enriched water bodies support a dense plant population which kills animal life by depriving it of oxygen and results in subsequent loss of biodiversity is known as **eutrophication.**

Ans. *(a, b)* Fertilisers contain phosphates as additives. The addition of phosphates in water enhances, algae growth. Such profuse growth of algae covers the water surface and reduces the oxygen concentration in water.

This leads to anaerobic condition, commonly with accumulation of abnoxious decay and animal death. Thus, bloom infested water inhibits the growth of other living organisms in the water body.

Q.15 The acids present in acid rain are ....

(a) Peroxyacetylnitrate
(b) H_2CO_3
(c) HNO_3
(d) H_2SO_4

Ans. *(b, c, d)* CO_2 is slightly soluble in water forming carbonic acid.

$$CO_2 + H_2O \longrightarrow H_2CO_3$$

The oxides of nitrogen undergo oxidation reaction followed by reaction with water vapours to form nitric acid.

$$NO + O_2 \longrightarrow 2NO_2$$
$$2NO_2 + H_2O \longrightarrow HNO_3 + HNO_2$$

The oxidation of SO_2 into SO_3 in presence of dust particles or metal ions. SO_3, then react with water vapours to form H_2SO_4.

$$2SO_2 + O_2 \xrightarrow[\text{or metal ions}]{\text{Dust particles}} 2SO_3$$
$$SO_3 + H_2O \longrightarrow H_2SO_4$$

Q.16 The consequences of global warming may be ....

(a) increase in average temperature of the earth
(b) melting of Himalayan Glaciers
(c) increased biochemical oxygen demand
(d) eutrophication

Ans. *(a, b)*

If the rate at which solar radiation arrives the earth remains constant but the amount of CO_2 in the air increases, then the heat radiated back to the earth will increase consequently and the temperature of the earth's surface will increase.

This increase in temperature will disturb the thermal balance on the earth and could cause glaciers and ice caps to melt.

Short Answer Type Questions

Q.17 Green house effect leads to global warming. Which substances are responsible for green house effect?

Ans. The various gases which bring green house effect responsible for global warming are the following with relative contributions

Various gases	Relative contribution
Carbon dioxide	50%
Water vapour	2%
Nitrous oxide	4%
Ozone	8%
Chlorofluorocarbons	17%
Methane	19%

Q.18 Acid rain is known to contain some acids. Name these acids and where from they come in rain?

Ans. Acid rain contains H_2CO_3, HNO_3 and H_2SO_4. H_2CO_3 is formed by the dissolution of CO_2 of the air in which the water vapour present.

$$CO_2 + H_2O \longrightarrow H_2CO_3$$

Forest fires and lightning are the natural sources of nitric oxide (NO). Nitrogen oxides are also produced by combustion engines, aircraft, furnaces, incinerators, industrial plants.

Nitric oxide slowly reacts with atmospheric air and produce NO_2. NO_2 dissolves in water to form HNO_3.

$$3NO_2 + H_2O \rightleftharpoons 2HNO_3 + NO$$

Sulphur oxides are produced by the burning of fossil fuels and in extraction of metals from their sulphide ores etc. Sulphur dioxide also produces sulphuric acid in the similar way.

$$SO_2 + O_2 + H_2O \xrightarrow[\text{Metal oxide}]{\text{Soot particles}} H_2SO_4 + [O]$$

Q.19 Ozone is a toxic gas and is a strong oxidising agent even then its presence in the stratosphere is very important. Explain what would happen if ozone from this region is completely removed?

Ans. The ozone layer is a natural protective layer found in the stratosphere, approximately 20 to 35 km above the Earth's surface. This layer protects the earth from the harmful effects of the ultraviolet radiation of the sun.

A depletion of ozone layer is a serious threat to life on the earth. A mere 5% decrease in ozone concentration may lead to a rise of up to 20% in skin cancer cases. Ultraviolet radiation is also the factor for disease of eyes, including cataract formation.

It can cause genetic mutations and destroy crops and other forms of vegetation. Aquatic animals and aquatic plants are also generally affected by UV-radiation.

Q.20 Dissolved oxygen in water is very important for aquatic life. What processes are responsible for the reduction of dissolved oxygen in water?

Ans. The processes which are responsible for the reduction of dissolved oxygen in water are-use of phosphatic and nitrate fertilisers, detergents, the discharge of human sewage and organic waste from food, paper and pulp industries.

The microorganisms which oxidise organic matter also utilise oxygen dissolved in water. Moreover during night, photosynthesis stops but the aquatic plants continue to respire, resulting in reduction of dissolved oxygen.

Q.21 On the basis of chemical reactions involved, explain how do chlorofluorocarbons cause thinning of ozone layer in stratosphere?

Ans. Chlorofluorocarbons are introduced into the atmosphere from aerosol sprays in which they function as propellants and from refrigerating equipments in which they act as coolants. It is also used as solvents.

It has very long life and stay in atmosphere for years and ultimately reach the upper layer of atmosphere (stratosphere) where it decompose in presence of UV-radiation of the sun. On account of decomposition, it forms chlorine atom or free radicals.

$$CF_2Cl_2 \xrightarrow{h\nu} {}^{\bullet}CF_2Cl + Cl^{\bullet}$$

The highly reactive chlorine radical then reacts with ozone (O_3) and converts it into oxygen and destroys the ozone layer.

$$Cl^{\bullet} + O_3 \longrightarrow ClO^{\bullet} + O_2$$

$$ClO^{\bullet} + O \longrightarrow Cl^{\bullet} + O_2$$

It has been found that one molecule of chlorofluorocarbon can destroy one thousand ozone molecules in the stratosphere, leading to its depletion.

Q.22 What could be the harmful effects of improper management of industrial and domestic solid waste in a city?

Ans. *All the solid wastes either domestic or industrial are of two types*

(i) biodegradable and

(ii) non-biodegradable

If the disposal of these wastes is not properly done, these wastes may find their way into sewers and some may be eaten up by the cattle. The non-biodegradable waste like polythene bags, if swallowed by cattle, can result into their death.

Q. 23 During an educational trip, a student of botany saw a beautiful lake in a village. She collected many plants from that area. She noticed that villagers were washing clothes around the lake and at some places waste material from houses was destroying its beauty.

After few years, she visited the same lake again. She was surprised to find that the lake was covered with algae, stinking smell was coming out and its water had become unusable. Can you explain the reason for this condition of the lake?

Thinking Process This phenomenon shows the process of eutrophication. Eutrophication is the process in which the waste materials are enters into water. As a result, formation of algae is accelerated and concentration of dissolved oxygen decreases.

Ans. The process of eutrophication is responsible for this condition of lake. The domestic waste and organic compounds such as detergents can provide plant nutrients which can enhance the growth of algae and aquatic plants.

These are decomposed by the bacterial population giving disagreeable odour and spoiling the beauty of the lake.

Q.24 What are biodegradable and non-biodegradable pollutants?

Ans. Biodegradable pollutants are those which are decomposed by bacteria *e.g.*, sewage, cow dung, fruit, vegetable etc.

Non-biodegradable pollutants are those which cannot be decomposed by bacteria e.g., mercury, aluminium, lead, copper, DDT etc.

Q.25 What are the sources of dissolved oxygen in water?

Ans. *The following are the sources of dissolved oxygen in water*

(i) Photosynthesis by aquatic plants

(ii) Due to direct contact of the water surface with air, *i.e.*, natural aeration

(iii) Mechanical aeration

Q.26 What is the importance of measuring BOD of a water body?

Ans. Biological Oxygen Demand (BOD) is the measure of level of pollution caused by organic biodegradable material. These biodegradable materials are decomposed by microorganism (bacteria) consuming dissolved oxygen.

Low value of BOD indicates that water contains less biodegradable material.

Q.27 Why does water covered with excessive algae growth become polluted?

Ans. Presence of excessive algae growth shows that water contains a lot of phosphate due to inflow of fertilizers, etc., from the surroundings.

The decomposition of algae growth produces bad smell and unattractive appearance making it unfit for recreational use like swimming, boating etc. Further, decrease in dissolved oxygen may be harmful for aquatic species like fishes etc.

Q.28 A factory was started near a village. Suddenly villagers started feeling the presence of irritating vapours in the village and cases of headache, chest pain, cough, dryness of throat and breathing problems increased. Villagers blamed the emissions from the chimney of the factory for such problems. Explain what could have happened. Give chemical reactions for the support of your explanation.

Ans. The symptoms observed in a village indicate that nitrogen oxide and sulphur oxide are released from the chimney of the factory. These are produced by the burning of fossil fuels such as gasoline, coal, natural gas etc. In an automobile engine, at high temperature when fossil fuel is burnt, dinitrogen and dioxygen combine to yield NO is, *i.e.*, nitric oxide.

$$N_2 + O_2 \xrightarrow{1200-1500°C} 2NO$$

$$2NO + O_2 \xrightarrow{1100°C} 2NO_2$$

SO_2 is produced by burning of sulphur containing fossil fuel or by roasting of sulphide ores such as iron pyrites, copper pyrites etc.

$$Cu_2S + O_2 \longrightarrow 2Cu + SO_2$$

Q.29 Oxidation of sulphur dioxide into sulphur trioxide in the absence of a catalyst is a slow process but this oxidation occurs easily in the atmosphere. Explain how does this happen? Give chemical reactions for the conversion of SO_2 into SO_3.

Ans. The oxidation of sulphur dioxide into sulphur trioxide can occur both photochemically or non-photochemically. In the near ultraviolet region, the SO_2 molecules react with ozone photochemically.

$$SO_2 + O_3 \xrightarrow{hv} SO_3 + O_2$$

$$2SO_2 + O_2 \xrightarrow{hv} 2SO_3$$

Non-photochemically, SO_2 may be oxidised by molecular oxygen in presence of dust and soot particles.

$$2SO_2 + O_2 \xrightarrow{\text{Particulates}} 2SO_3$$

Q.30 From where does ozone come in the photochemical smog?

Ans. Sunlight cause photochemical decomposition of NO_2 into NO and O.

$$NO_2 \xrightarrow{hv} NO + [O]$$

Atomic oxygen is highly reactive and combines with diatomic oxygen and forms ozone.

$$O_2 + O + M \longrightarrow O_3 + M$$

where, M is inert gas such as nitrogen. This, O_3 is formed during the formation of smog.

Q.31 How is ozone produced in stratosphere?

- **Concept Insight** In stratosphere, a photon with a wavelength between 180 nm and 240 nm breaks the O_2 molecule into atomic oxygen.

Ans. Ozone in stratosphere is a product of action of UV-radiations on dioxygen (O_2) molecules. The UV radiation split apart molecular oxygen into free oxygen atoms. These oxygen atoms combine with the molecular oxygen to form ozone.

$$O_2(g) \xrightarrow[\text{UV-radiation}]{hv} O + O$$

$$O_2(g) + O(g) \underset{\text{radiations}}{\overset{\text{UV}}{\rightleftharpoons}} O_3$$

Q.32 **Ozone is a gas heavier than air. Why does ozone layer not settle down near the earth?**

Ans. In stratosphere, the formation of O_3 goes on continuously but O_3 is also decomposed by UV- radiation between 240 nm to 360 nm.

$$O_3 \xrightarrow{(240\text{-}360\text{ nm})} O_2 + O$$

The O-atom reacts with second O_3 molecule

$$O_3 + O \longrightarrow 2O_2$$

Net reaction $$2O_3 \longrightarrow 3\,O_2$$

Thus, the reaction form a delicate balance in which the rate of O_3 decomposition match the rate of O_3 formation and dynamic equilibrium exists and maintains a constant concentration of O_3.

Q.33 **Some time ago formation of polar stratospheric clouds was reported over Antarctica. Why were these formed? What happens when such clouds break up by warmth of sunlight?**

Ans. In summer season, nitrogen dioxide and methane react with chlorine monoxide and chlorine atoms forming chlorine sinks, preventing much ozone depletion, whereas in winter, special type of clouds called polar stratospheric clouds are formed over Antarctica.

These polar stratospheric clouds provide surface on which chlorine nitrate gets hydrolysed to form hypochlorous acid. It also reacts with hydrogen chloride to give molecular chlorine.

$$ClO^{\bullet}(g) + NO_2(g) \longrightarrow \underset{\text{Chlorine nitrate}}{ClONO_2(g)}$$

$$Cl^{\bullet}(g) + CH_4(g) \longrightarrow {}^{\bullet}CH_3(g) + HCl(g)$$

$$ClONO_2(g) + H_2O(g) \xrightarrow{\text{Hydrolysis}} HOCl(g) + HNO_3(g)$$

$$ClONO_2(g) + HCl(g) \longrightarrow Cl_2(g) + HNO_3(g)$$

When sunlight returns to the Antarctica in the spring, the sun's warmth breaks up the clouds and HOCl, Cl_2 are photolysed by sunlight.

$$HOCl(g) \xrightarrow{h\nu} HO^{\bullet}(g) + Cl^{\bullet}(g)$$

$$Cl_2(g) \xrightarrow{h\nu} 2Cl^{\bullet}(g)$$

The chlorine radicals thus formed, initiate the chain reaction for ozone depletion.

Q.34 **A person was using water supplied by Municipality. Due to shortage of water he started using underground water. He felt laxative effect. What could be the cause?**

Ans. The laxative effect is observed only when the sulphates present in water have concentration greater than 500 ppm. Otherwise, at moderate levels it is harmless.

Matching The Columns

Q.35 Match the terms given in Column I with the compounds given in Column II.

Column I		Column II	
A.	Acid rain	1.	$CHCl_2$-CHF_2
B.	Photochemical smog	2.	CO
C.	Combination with haemoglobin	3.	CO_2
D.	Depletion of ozone layer	4.	SO_2
		5.	Unsaturated hydrocarbons

Ans. **A.** → (3, 4) **B.** → (4, 5) **C.** → (2) **D.** → (1)

A. **Acid rain is due to oxides of carbon, sulphur (unsaturated hydrocarbon) and nitrogen.**

B. **Photochemical smog is formed by unburnt fuel (unsaturated hydrocarbon and SO_2).**

C. **Carbon monoxide with haemoglobin is poisonous.**

D. **Chlorofluorocarbon ($CHCl_2$-CHF_2) cause ozone depletion.**

Q.36 Match the pollutant(s) in Column I with the effect(s) in Column II.

Column I		Column II	
A.	Oxides of sulphur	1.	Global warming
B.	Nitrogen dioxide	2.	Damage to kidney
C.	Carbon dioxide	3.	'Blue baby' syndrome
D.	Nitrate in drinking water	4.	Respiratory diseases
E.	Lead	5.	Red haze in traffic and congested areas

Ans. **A.** → (4) **B.** → (5) **C.** → (1) **D.** → (3) **E.** → (2)

A. **Low concentration of sulphur dioxide causes respiratory disease *e.g.*, asthma, bronchitis etc.**

B. **The irritant red haze in the traffic and congested places is due to oxides of nitrogen.**

C. **The increased amount of CO_2 in air is mainly responsible for global warming.**

D. **Excess nitrate in drinking water cause methemoglobinemia (blue baby syndrome).**

E. **Lead can damage kidney, liver, reproductive system etc.**

Q.37 Match the activity given in Column I with the type of pollution created by it given in Column II.

	Column I (Activity)		Column II (Effect)
A.	Releasing gases to the atmosphere after burning waste material containing sulphur	1.	Water pollution
B.	Using carbamates as pesticides	2.	Photochemical smog, damage to plant life, corrosion to building material, induce breathing problems, water pollution
C.	Using synthetic detergents for washing clothes	3.	Damaging ozone layer
D.	Releasing gases produced by automobiles and factories in the atmosphere	4.	May cause nerve diseases in human
E.	Using chlorofluorocarbon compounds for cleaning computer parts	5.	Classical smog, acid rain, water pollution, induce breathing problems, damage to buildings, corrosion of metals

Ans. **A.** → (5) **B.** → (4) **C.** → (1) **D.** → (2) **E.** → (3)

A. Classical smog, acid rain, water pollution, induce breathing problems, damage to buildings, corrosion of metals.

B. May cause nerve disease in human.

C. Water pollution.

D. Photochemical smog, damage to plant life, corrosion to building material, induce breathing problems, water pollution.

E. Damaging ozone layer.

Q.38 Match the pollutants given in Column I with their effects given in Column II.

	Column I		Column II
A.	Phosphate fertilisers in water	1.	BOD level of water increases
B.	Methane in air	2.	Acid rain
C.	Synthetic detergents in water	3.	Global warming
D.	Nitrogen oxides in air	4.	Eutrophication

Ans. **A.** → (1, 4) **B.** → (3) **C.** → (1) **D.** → (2)

A. Phosphate fertilisers increase growth of algae increasing BOD level, causing eutrophication.

B. Methane oxidises to CO_2 which causes, global warming.

C. Synthetic detergents increases BOD level.

D. Nitrogen oxide mix with water forming nitric acid (acid rain).

Assertion and Reason

In the following questions a statement of Assertion (A) followed by a statement of Reason (R) is given. Choose the corrcet option out of the choices given below in each question.

Q.39 **Assertion** (A) Green house effect was observed in houses that used to grow plants and these are made of green glass.
Reason (R) Green house name has been given because glass houses are made of green glass.

(a) Both A and R are correct and R is the correct explanation of A.
(b) Both A and R are correct but R is not the correct explanation of A.
(c) Both A and R are not correct.
(d) A is not correct but R is correct.

Ans. *(c)* Both A and R are not correct.

In cold countries, sunlight required to grow plants is less. Hence, plants are kept in a house made of glass, placed in such a manner, so that sunlight enters the green house, heat up the soil and plants.

The warm soil and plants emit infrared radiations. Since, glass is opaque to infrared radiations, it partly reflects and partly absorbs these radiations.

Q.40 **Assertion** (A) The pH of acid rain is less than 5.6.
Reason (R) Carbon dioxide present in the atmosphere dissolves in rain water and forms carbonic acid.

(a) Both A and R are correct and R is the correct explanation of A
(b) Both A and R are correct but R is not the correct explanation of A
(c) Both A and R are not correct
(d) A is not correct but R is correct

Ans. *(b)* Both A and R are correct but R is not the correct explanation of A.

Normally rain water has a pH of 5.6 due to the presence of H^+ ions formed by the reaction of rain water with carbon dioxide present in the atmosphere.

$$H_2O\,(l) + CO_2(g) \longrightarrow H_2CO_3(aq)$$
$$H_2CO_3(aq) \rightleftharpoons H^+(aq) + HCO_3^-(aq)$$

When the pH of rain water drops below 5.6, it is called **acid rain.**

Q. 41 **Assertion** (A) Photochemical smog is oxidising in nature.
Reason (R) Photochemical smog contains NO_2 and O_3, which are formed during the sequence of reactions.

(a) Both A and R are correct and R is the correct explanation of A.
(b) Both A and R are correct but R is not the correct explanation of A.
(c) Both A and R are not correct.
(d) A is not correct but R is correct.

Ans. *(a)* Both A and R are correct and R is the correct explanation of A.

When fossil fuel are burnt, a variety of pollutants are emitted into the earth's troposphere. Two of the pollutants that are emitted hydrocarbons (unburnt fuels) and nitric oxide (NO).

When these pollutants build up to sufficiently high levels, a chain reaction occurs from their interaction with sunlight in which NO oxidises to NO_2. This NO_2 in turns absorbs energy from sunlight and breaks up into nitric oxide and free oxygen atom.

$$NO_2(g) \xrightarrow{h\nu} NO(g) + O(g)$$

Oxygen atoms are very reactive and combine with O_2 in air to produce ozone.

$$O(g) + O_2(g) \rightleftharpoons O_3(g)$$

Q.42 **Assertion** (A) Carbon dioxide is one of the important green house gases.

Reason (R) It is largely produced by respiratory function of animals and plants.

(a) Both A and R are correct and R is the correct explanation of A.
(b) Both A and R are correct but R is not the correct explanation of A.
(c) Both A and R are not correct.
(d) A is not correct but R is correct.

Ans. *(b)* Both A and R are correct but R is not the correct explanation of A.

Carbon dioxide is one of the important green house gases. It is largely produced by the combustion of fossil fuels like coal, natural gas, petroleum, etc.

Q.43 **Assertion** (A) Ozone is destroyed by solar radiation in upper stratosphere.

Reason (R) Thinning of the ozone layer allows excessive UV radiations to reach the surface of earth.

(a) Both A and R are correct and R is the correct explanation of A.
(b) Both A and R are correct but R is not the correct explanation of A.
(c) Both A and R are not correct.
(d) A is not correct but R is correct.

Ans. *(d)* A is not correct but R is correct.

Ozone layer is found in the stratosphere. The depletion of ozone layer (creation of ozone hole) is taking place due to reaction with NO (produced from natural sources or human activity or in the exhaust gases of engines of supersonic planes) or by reaction with **chlorofluorocarbons** (CFC's) called **freons** (produced from aerosol sprays used in propellents or from refrigerators where they are used as coolants).

The ozone hole allows the UV radiations to pass through and reach us, increasing chances of skin cancer.

Q.44 **Assertion** (A) Excessive use of chlorinated synthetic pesticides causes soil and water pollution.

Reason (R) Such pesticides are non-biodegradable.

(a) Both A and R are correct and R is the correct explanation of A
(b) Both A and R are correct but R is not the correct explanation of A
(c) Both A and R are not correct
(d) A is not correct but R is correct

Ans. *(a)* Both A and R are correct and R is the correct explanation of assertion.
Insecticides, pesticides and herbicides cause soil and water pollution. They are non-biodegradable.

Q.45 **Assertion** (A) If BOD level of water in a reservoir is less than 5 ppm it is highly polluted.

Reason (R) High biological oxygen demand means low activity of bacteria in water.

(a) Both A and R are correct and R is the correct explanation of A.
(b) Both A and R are correct but R is not the correct explanation of A.
(c) Both A and R are not correct.
(d) A is not correct but R is correct.

Ans. *(c)* Both A and R are not correct.

Amount of oxygen required by bacteria to breakdown the organic matter present in a certain volume of a sample of water is called Biochemical Oxygen Demand (BOD).

If BOD level is less than 5 ppm, water is almost pure. High biological oxygen demand means high activity of bacteria in water.

Long Answer Type Questions

Q.46 How can you apply green chemistry for the following?

(a) To control photochemical smog.
(b) To avoid use of halogenated solvents in drycleaning and that of chlorine in bleaching.
(c) To reduce use of synthetic detergents.
(d) To reduce the consumption of petrol and diesel.

Ans. (a) The most straight forward way to reduce photochemical smog is to minimise the release of oxides of nitrogen and hydrocarbons to the atmosphere. The following methods can be applied to minimise the oxides of nitrogen and hydrocarbons.

(i) By fitting efficient catalytic converters in automobiles, the harmful gases are converted catalytically into harmless gases.

(ii) By spraying certain compound into the atmosphere which generate free radicals that readily combine with the free radicals that initiate the reactions forming toxic compounds of the photochemical smog.

The compound diethyl hydroxylamine has been found to posses smog inhibiting property.

(iii) Certain plants such as pinus, juniparus, pyrus, irtis etc., can metabolise oxides of nitrogen.

(b) Solvents used to dryclean clothes are usually chlorinated compounds which are carcinogen. Suitable detergents which work in liquid carbon dioxide have been discovered to replace the chlorinated compounds.

For bleaching of clothes in laundry, H_2O_2 and not Cl_2 is used which gives better results and is not harmful. Earlier, Cl_2 gas was used for bleaching paper. Chlorine is highly toxic in nature. It's use has been replaced by H_2O_2 in presence of a suitable catalyst.

(c) To reduce the use of synthetic detergents as cleaning agent, emphasis should be made on the use of soaps prepared of vegetable oils. The vegetable oils are biodegradable while detergents do not undergo biodegradation.

(d) Instead of petrol and diesel, the use of **CNG** (Condensed Natural Gas) and **LNG** (Liquified Natural Gas) has been preferred as they are pollution free fuels.

The other sources such as hydrogen, ethyl alcohol, etc., can be tried in place of petrol and diesel.

Q.47 Green plants use carbon dioxide for photosynthesis and return oxygen to the atmosphere, even then carbon dioxide is considered to be responsible for green house effect. Explain why?

Ans. Carbon dioxide is a natural constituent of atmosphere and is vital for all forms of plant life. It forms about **0.033%** by volume of atmosphere. It helps to maintain the temperature of the earth required for living organisms.

A balance of CO_2 is maintained in air because CO_2 is produced from respiration, burning of fossil fuels and decomposition of lime stone but at the same time, it is consumed in photosynthesis by plants.

However, human activities have disturbed this balance and CO_2 level in atmosphere is in increasing order. This has happened due to deforestation, burning of more fossil fuel and industrialisation. It has been estimated that CO_2 concentration has risen about 25% in the past century.

During the past nearly 120 years, the average temperature of the planet has increased by somewhere between 0.4°C to 0.8°C. Current estimated are that doubling the CO_2 concentration will result in a temperature increase in between 1.0°C and 3.5°C. In green house effect, contribution of CO_2 is 50% and of other trace gases is also about 50%.

Q.48 Explain how does green house effect cause global warming?

Ans. Visible light from the sun reaches the earth and heats it up. However, when the earth cools, the energy is re-emitted from the earth's surface in the form of infrared radiation which have **longer wavelength** and **heating effect**.

These infrared radiation can be absorbed by CO_2 and H_2O vapours. The heat thus absorbed is radiated back to the surface of the earth. In this way, warming of the earth occurs.

If the rate at which solar energy is arriving the earth remains constant but the amount of CO_2 in the air increases, the heat radiated back to the earth will increase. Consequently, the temperature of the earth's surface will increase.

Hence, **global warming** depends on the concentration of those gases which are responsible for green house effect.

Q.49 A farmer was using pesticides on his farm. He used the produce of his farm as food for rearing fishes. He was told that fishes were not fit for human consumption because large amount of pesticides had accumulated in the tissues of fishes. Explain how did this happen?

Ans. **Pesticides** from soil are transferred into the crops and from the crops these are transferred into rearing fish food. Pesticides entered [into water through rearing fish food and finally entered into the bodies of the fishes.

Therefore, pesticides are transferred from lower trophic level to higher trophic level through food chain. Over the time, the concentration of pesticides in fishes reach a level which causes serious metabolic and physiological disorders.

Q.50 For dry cleaning, in the place of tetrachloroethane, liquified carbon dioxide with suitable detergent is an alternative solvent. What type of harm to the environment will be prevented by stopping use of tetrachloroethane? Will use of liquified carbon dioxide with detergent be completely safe from the point of view of pollution? Explain.

Ans. Tetrachloroethane, $Cl_2CH—CHCl_2$ is suspected to be carcinogenic and also contaminates the ground water. The harmful effect will be prevented by using liquified CO_2 along with suitable detergent.

Use of liquified CO_2 along with detergent will not be completely safe because most of the detergents are non-biodegradable and they cause water pollution. Moreover, liquified CO_2 will ultimately enter into the atmosphere and contributed to the green house effect.